BRAZIL SINCE 1964:
MODERNISATION UNDER
A MILITARY RÉGIME

BRAZIL SINCE 1964: MODERNISATION UNDER A MILITARY RÉGIME

A Study of the Interactions of
Politics and Economics in a Contemporary
Military Régime

GEORGES-ANDRÉ FIECHTER

With a foreword by
PROFESSOR JACQUES FREYMOND

Translated from the French by
ALAN BRALEY

A HALSTED PRESS BOOK

JOHN WILEY & SONS
New York – Toronto

© Institut Universitaire de Hautes Etudes Internationales 1972
This translation © The Macmillan Press Ltd 1975

All rights reserved. No part of this publication
may be reproduced or transmitted, in any
form or by any means, without permission.

This translation first published in the United Kingdom 1975 by
THE MACMILLAN PRESS LTD
London and Basingstoke

*Published in the U.S.A. and
Canada by Halsted Press, a
Division of John Wiley & Sons, Inc.,
New York*

Library of Congress Cataloging in Publication Data

Fiechter, Georges André.
　Brazil since 1964 – modernisation under a military régime.

　Translation of Le régime modernisateur du Brésil, 1964–1972.
　Originally presented as the author's thesis, Geneva, 1972.
　"A Halsted Press book."
　Bibliography: p.
　Includes index.
　　1. Brazil—Politics and government—1954–
　2. Brazil—Economic conditions—1945–　　　　I. Title.

F2538.2.F4813　1972　　　320.9'81'06　　　75–16325
ISBN 0–470–26332–6

Printed in Great Britain

To Françoise

Contents

Foreword ix
Author's Note xii
Introduction xiv

PART ONE   BRAZILIAN RETROSPECT   1
    1   Political Development   3
    2   Sociological Development   10
    3   Economic Development   17
    4   The Military Phenomenon   23

PART TWO   THE STERN CALL TO ORDER   35
    5   Institutional Act No. 1   37
    6   Castello Branco and the 'Sorbonne' in Search of a Basis of Government   39
    7   The Four Black Months   44
    8   Castello Branco's Tactics   47
    9   Links with the Outside World   49
    10   Campos' Economic Plan (P.A.E.G.)   51
    11   The P.A.E.G. in Action   58
    12   The AMFORP Affair   61
    13   Rational Exploitation of the Land and of Minerals   64
    14   An Appeal for Dialogue   68
    15   Discussion about the P.A.E.G.   70
    16   The Disunity of the Industrialists   72
    17   'Castellism' between the Anvil and the Hammer   75
    18   The Political System Takes its Revenge, and is Dismantled   78

PART THREE   AUTHORITARIAN CONSOLIDATION   85
    19   Castello Branco again Takes the Initiative   87
    20   Costa e Silva: the Price of Saving the Economic Policy   89
    21   Castello Branco Provides Continuity   92
    22   The Nationalist Counter-attack   95
    23   Repercussions of the Fiscal Reform   98
    24   The New Image of Labour   102

Contents

25	The Elections in the Autumn of 1966	108
26	A Way of Securing the Future: Constitutional Reforms	112
27	The Political Reforms which Flowed from the Plan	118
28	The Attempt at Humanisation	123
29	The New Economic Objectives	127
30	Failure of the Enlarged Front	130
31	Humanisation Comes to a Dead End	133
32	The 'Unauthorised' Opposition	136
33	Costa e Silva between Two Fires	155

PART FOUR AN APPRAISAL OF MODERNISING AUTHORITARIANISM 163

34	Nationalist Inflexibility	165
35	The End of Costa e Silva	169
36	The Military Triumvirate	170
37	The Succession	174
38	The Path Chosen by President Médici	178
39	The Opinion of the Silent Majority	182
40	Towards Political Normalisation?	184
41	The Distortions still to be Overcome	192

CONCLUSION INTEGRATION THROUGH PRACTICAL ACHIEVEMENTS 207

Notes 213

Bibliography 287

Index 307

Foreword

During the eight years which he spent in Brazil, first as a student and then as a manager in industry, Monsieur Georges Fiechter not only faced problems, he also learnt to know a country and its people. Not for him the big-city round from São Paulo to Rio to Belo Horizonte or the well-trodden tourist routes. Without making himself out to be an explorer, he left the highways in order to see what went on in the by-ways, and journeyed away from the main roads to wander in the countryside and the forest. His view of Brazil includes peasants and Indians as well as workers, students and all types of middle-class city dwellers.

These remarks are designed only to show how the author approaches his subject, and to emphasise that Georges Fiechter is not a mere writer of political essays, but a practical man. When, therefore, after fifteen years he once more embarked upon research, he was able to base his thinking on facts directly observed over a long period, on practical experience, on daily contact with ordinary people and with a social environment reflecting a nation in all its variety. At the same time his perception of the basic problems was sharpened and his feel for the correct way of tackling them became surer. During his time in Brazil, Georges Fiechter got under the Brazilian skin without ceasing to be Swiss. He took his stand both within and without the object of his critical attention – and that is no mean advantage.

The subject he has chosen is both important and topical. Events in Brazil have given rise to controversy. Not only the legitimacy of the régime which came into power in 1964 has been questioned, but also its aims, its methods of government, its political capacity and its effectiveness. There have been unceasing arguments and struggles, in Parliament, in the press, in the streets, in the universities and within the Church and the Army. The generals in power have seen ranged against them, united in opposition though divided in action, the ambitious and redoubtable orator Carlos Lacerda, Dom Helder Câmara, archbishop of the poor, and Marighela, the Che Guevara of Brazil. Through the clash of parties, factions and men, beyond the arguments about revolution and counter-revolution, violence and counter-violence, guerilla warfare and anti-guerilla measures, all the basic problems affecting developing societies have been argued, and all the fundamental choices placed under review – the compatibility of democratic control with economic development, the political, economic and social content of development models, inflation, growth and its distortions, the system of ownership, private investment, imperialism and militarism, the changeover from a subsistence economy to a market economy, the agricultural proletariat, the urban proletariat, the ecological results of exploiting the resources of the Amazon basin, freedom of opinion and the part universities should play.

It must have required courage and even daring to attempt to describe developments in Brazil during a period so hectic and revolutionary as this. In an atmosphere so fraught with passion, and dealing with unresolved problems, with arguments between men who had staked their convictions and their lives on one side or the other, 'scientific' research presents unusual difficulties. However hard one may try to be objective, one is open to criticism from all sides.

Georges Fiechter has refused to be daunted by the obvious risks involved in choosing such a vast subject. But he has a good defence against any charge of superficiality. His on-the-spot observations have been supplemented and verified by systematic scrutiny of the available sources, and by wide reading in the abundant literature on Brazil. Thus his observations and conclusions are well documented.

Yet the numerous sources quoted, and the careful attention to detail, have not been allowed to blur the overall picture. Readers will appreciate the way in which the author has succeeded in combining a sense of the sweep of history and the movement of events with an analysis of social structures. The protagonists are delineated in their social and political setting. Beyond their confrontations, the play of deeper forces is perceived, the influence of collective emotion and of the national character. And the most interesting aspect of this work is its analysis of the way in which political and economic factors were interacting. This undertaking has been attempted many times, and with varied success. Monsieur Fiechter's reconstruction carries conviction – and that is not the least of the merits of this book.

There will doubtless be continuing argument about the economic and political choices made by the men who have succeeded one another in power since 1964. The results they achieved and the methods they used will be disputed. Mention will be made of the great question mark hanging over the development of the Brazilian nation, represented by the fate of that part of the population whose life is lived outside the play of political forces and economic calculations.

But whichever side of the argument one favours, whichever solution one recommends, one cannot escape the basic problem posed by this study of the modernisation of a developing country – how should it be governed? Monsieur Fiechter's book gives conclusive confirmation to something we knew all along from many examples – that development cannot take place without some form of constraint. The only matter for argument is what sort of constraint, and who should exert it?

Geneva
November 1972

JACQUES FREYMOND

Author's Note

The Revolution[1] of 1 April 1964 marks a fresh chapter in the life of Brazil, both politically and economically. The Army, tired of the incoherence of the political successors of Getúlio Vargas, the father of 'populism'[2] in Brazil, seized power and, departing from the traditional role of guarantor[3] given to it by the Constitution, decided to assume the responsibilities of power. The object of the present work is to analyse the development of this military power in its new guise as an actor on the political stage, seeking to win the approval of an audience of civilians.

The eight years covered by this book are but a tiny span compared with Brazil's five hundred years of history or even her 150 years as an independent State; but they have witnessed a spectacular population explosion. Numbering only $3\frac{1}{2}$ million in 1819, the population increased to 17·4 million by 1900 and 76 million by 1963. Yet in the mere eight years from 1964 to 1972, a further 20 million were added to this total, an increase of more than 25 per cent. So one out of every four Brazilians now alive was not even born when the Military seized power – a fact which presents the modernising régime both with a tremendous potential and a permanent challenge.

We have chosen the typology of Dankwart A. Rustow[4] as a methodological frame of reference in preference to that of Gabriel Almond[5] or Samuel Huntington[6] as it appears to be better adapted to the Brazilian scene than the two last-named, even though Huntington's is an essential aid to the discussion of certain aspects of the situation.

We shall, then, use the concept of modernisation in the sense given to it by Rustow. It 'denotes rapidly widening control over nature through closer co-operation among men'.[7] It is an 'ethically neutral'[8] concept which should 'transform both man and society, but most of all man's mind.'[9] 'Human history conceived as a history of progress', it implies 'an intellectual, a technological and a social revolution'.[10]

Although much has already been published concerning present-day Brazil, there is not, as far as the author is aware, any systematic non-American work about the ruling military régime, and the few recent American works deal with other aspects. We shall try to fill this gap by reconstituting the facts as objectively as our powers of perception permit. To this end we shall accept the risk of historical pointillism which is involved in going, where necessary, into some detail. The alternative would be to invite the defects of many publications which are often one-sided because they present too general a picture.

For it is impossible to recapture the cut and thrust of the opposing forces which clashed from 1964 onwards, without placing them in the historical perspective of Brazil. Therefore the first part of this book, after a summary of the political development of the country, consists of an analysis of the evolution of Brazilian society and a brief glance at the economic transformations which have influenced it. The emergence of the military phenomenon will also be retraced.

Next we shall follow the course of the various political and economic choices made by the modernising régime.

We shall distinguish the three following phases:[11]

the first, which can be described as a 'stern call to order' within a formal democratic framework, lasted until Institutional Act No. 2 was promulgated on 27 October 1965;

the second, that of 'authoritarian consolidation', ended with Institutional Act No. 5 on 13 December 1968, which set the seal on the installation of a *de facto* dictatorship with virtually unlimited powers;

the third, which has not yet ended, is the stage at which the alliance between the Military and the technocrats has brought about accelerated economic growth, a reaffirmation of the national identity and the restoration of authority, thus facing the modernising régime with the further task of preparing to meet the problems of political and social equality.[12]

Finally, without claiming to have reached generally valid conclusions, we shall endeavour, on the basis of the achievements we have studied, to decide whether the modernising régime in Brazil is still free to evolve towards 'a military revolution that, producing fundamental changes in the political institutions and the social structure of a people, erects on those bases a new civilian order',[13] or whether this road has already been closed by certain irreversible actions.

Note: The term 'billion' is used in the French and American sense, meaning one thousand million.

Introduction

Brazil is first and foremost a nation whose people display a deep-seated national pride, human warmth, a spirit of enterprise, tolerance, a certain nonconformism tinged with humour, charmingly attentive manners, a happy knack of extricating themselves from difficulties and a love of women, rhythm and football. I have to begin by mentioning these commonplaces; for they have created one of the most attractive civilisations it has been my good fortune to know.

It is also a country of continental dimensions,[1] in which uncontrolled population growth[2] aggravates the problems, and in which advanced methods of production exist alongside archaic ones, and ostentatious riches coexist with sordid poverty.

Lastly, it is a nation[3] endeavouring, by the adoption since April 1964 of a co-ordinated development policy, to find practical ways round the pitfalls along the road which leads from the possession of an abundance of potential resources to the satisfaction of the real needs of its population.

My object in undertaking this work, though I myself am a foreigner in Brazil, was twofold: to present a coherent picture of contemporary Brazil in its struggle towards a better economic future; and, as regards the problems attending this development, to complement the studies published by Brazilian sociologists and structural economists[4] by depicting the causal chain of events. For however interesting the schematic interpretations of such writers may be, they do less than justice to the complexities of a situation which is not really reducible to the simplicities of ready-made ideological concepts.

At the risk of over-simplifying their point of view, which to my mind only partially illuminates the total reality, one might describe it as follows:[5] starting from a bipolar model containing a dominant (or central) capitalist system and peripheral satellite (or dominated) systems, the evolution is presented as the struggle of the former to keep the latter within its orbit. It implies both the systematic exploitation of the country dominated and the inevitable pauperisation of its proletariat. As the structuralists see it, dependence operates at three levels: that of quantifiable observation, monopolisation of the decision-making function, and the disequilibrium caused in the balance of payments by this situation.

When it comes to demonstration, the analysis assumes that all the industrialisation in Brazil has taken place through the adoption by a wealthy élite of types of consumption appropriate to the dominant system, leading to the production of goods unsuited to the primary needs of the country.

The process, they claim, occurred in three phases: the first, called the traditional industries phase, witnessed the rise of still rudimentary manufactures utilising the abundant labour available. With the wages they earned, the labourers were able partially to enter the economy.

The demand so created enabled somewhat more advanced industries to be set up and to grow under the shelter of protective tariffs. This was the phase of import substitutes. Brazil shut out imports and, to counteract this check to lucrative trade, the dominant country transplanted its production methods into the dominated country by setting up branches of its own industrial undertakings. But the newer technologies absorbed more and more capital while requiring less and less labour. This phenomenon, together with the disturbance of the traditional country/city balance, resulted in a squeeze on wages which ultimately led to a contraction of the home market (one way of beating this being to export).

During the third stage a modern production system was established, providing the higher income-groups with durable or semi-durable consumer goods having a high unit price. This new dynamic sector, of which the automobile industry is characteristic, injects into the dominated country masses of capital coming from the dominating system, attracted both by the favourable conditions it finds there and by the internal logic of large capitalist industrial firms. It stimulates the demand for skilled or semi-skilled labour, to the detriment of the unskilled labourers who form the majority of the nation. This creates a division between industrial workers and the mass of the people, and through this vicious circle of wealth the market becomes organised around the classes which have money incomes, thrusting the rest of the population increasingly aside.

If we accept this analysis, it follows that the change from a primary-products exporting economy to an industrialised one has simply reinforced the foreign domination which has succeeded in imposing on the subject country its own technology and habits of consumption. However, for a time the new classes which benefit from industrial development may find an artificial equilibrium with the alienated masses by the application of compensatory mechanisms, such as wage inflation under Brazilian populism. But as soon as the rate of growth of the dependent capitalism is affected by these palliatives, the only means of preventing a break between the 'haves' and the alienated masses is to resort to force. This is what is said to have happened in April 1964.

Clearly, this structuralist explanation of the 1964 Revolution leaves out too many facets of reality to stand up to a detailed analysis of the facts. Dealing with dependence through monopolisation of decisions, the analysis notes that by the introduction of modern techniques, Brazilian industry has become internationalised. As investment by the dominant system was channelled first and foremost into the dynamic sectors (unlike the sequence of events in other countries, where is was concentrated on the extraction of primary materials), it possesses a strategic advantage enabling it to control the flow of goods coming on to the market. It is no longer simply a question of profits being transferred abroad, but of the role of foreign enterprises which, working to plans made by decision centres of centralised capitalism outside the country,[6] no longer consider the dominated country in which they operate as a sovereign nation, but as a market. This idea is then contrasted with the social function of industrialisation (as an instrument of the indigenous power of the nation) in so far as it is thought to lead the foreign enterprise to play a political role by virtue of the network of interests and patronage which it can bring into play.

On the third aspect of dependence, that of the balance of payments situation, the analysis simply assumes that disequilibrium is the inevitable consequence of capitalist domination. It is, says the theory, the result of the inability of agriculture (in the absence of structural changes) to meet the demand created by the growth of the towns, and to counter the dependence of exports on a few products, for which demand is inelastic, and the need to import increasing amounts of capital (and foodstuffs) which leads to a deterioration of the terms of trade. Reference is also made to the outflow of foreign exchange due to technical assistance agreements and royalty payments, the export of profits and the servicing of foreign debt, swollen to excess by infrastructure costs and other State deficits.

According to those who favour this approach to Brazil's problems, these three aspects of dependence also explain the establishment of the military régime. For just when the populist model of government became bankrupt in 1964, the middle classes had got used to following the cycle of the dominant capitalism which imposed its own momentum upon them. Consequently, they were unable to offer the country a real national alternative, and inevitably the Army stepped in to fill the vacuum. This change was all the easier to effect because the military bureaucracy, linked by training and by the technology which it used to the dominant capitalism, was acceptable to the latter from an ideological point of view and was also quite well prepared to play this part; moreover, as the disappearance of its traditional function, that of fighting wars, had deprived it of a principal *raison d'être*, it was in search of a fresh mission in life. And since in a period of coexistence the distant Communist enemy who had replaced the traditional South American enemy no longer appeared to pose a real threat, the Army set up in his stead an internal enemy, namely those citizens who wanted to interfere with the existing national structures. Thus, it is argued, the interests of the Military ran parallel to those of the dominant capitalism and of the local sub-systems for which internal order was a prime necessity. According to the structuralists, the doctrines of international interdependence and national security, which were to be the keynotes of action for the governments which owed their advent to the 1964 Revolution, came about because of this compatibility of interests.

We shall see in the course of this study that this view is based on too one-sided a selection of facts to give a true historical account; nevertheless it does have the merit of highlighting the decisive part which was played by the modern technology which Brazil has adopted.

For this process must henceforth be considered as irreversible. Unless we take the view that the sacrifices which the people of Brazil have already made are simply expendable for the sake of a scorched-earth type of self-sufficiency policy, favoured by certain extremists, interdependence has come to stay. There is moreover no cause to regret this, since 'interdependence postulates independence. Division of labour internationally presupposes the existence of national units willing to play their part.'[7]

We are dealing here with human realities, not theoretical ideas – with a political choice which, leaving aside semantic problems and replacing the pejorative connotations of committed sociologists by saying 'leader economy' and 'associated economy', can enable Brazil to grapple with the problems posed by the rapid modernisation of a country of continental dimensions in which 'success depends on thinking larger than life'.[8]

If opting for technology results in distorting the economy at certain points, so be it. But these distortions must be alleviated by setting in motion a more equitable distribution of incomes, so that by the end of the century the living standard of the rural masses in Brazil may be raised to the point at which, freed from the chains of poverty, they may aspire to a concern with human values and what lies behind them. Such is the objective of plans for development in Brazil; they endeavour to extend interdependence to the four corners of the earth, becoming increasingly impatient of ideological frontiers and choosing with complete impartiality, in each specific case, the solution most favourable to the interests of the nation.

This institutionalised pragmatism of modernising Brazil has

borrowed from foreign ways of life whatever is calculated to enable her to achieve with the least delay the economic growth which necessity dictates, and hence it is not caught in the straitjacket of a preconceived plan.

The mixture of policies and plans has changed during the lifetime of the three governments which have successively ruled since 1 April 1964 as, one by one, the first objectives were attained. But through them all has run the central theme of determination to adapt the instruments of government to the essential needs of accelerated development. This was the endeavour that fostered the birth of the technostructure.[9]

It was born of the need for rational control over an erratic economic system which had led to the weakening of the legislature on which a Constitution adopted after the ending of a dictatorship had conferred, by overcompensation, paralysing powers in this respect. The same urgency lay beneath the adoption of measures for the maintenance of public order, without which no growth is possible.

Despite the mistakes, abuses and some injustices that could have been avoided, it is thanks to the material results of this development that Brazil has regained hope, that basic human need, without which there is no fortitude to wait for the better days to come. In Tibor Mende's words, this hope is capable 'of transforming useless suffering into useful suffering'.[10] And in the light of what has already been achieved, this hope could persuade the masses who are still outside the mainstream of the economy to accept for yet another generation[11] the heavy sacrifices laid upon them by economic development.

PART ONE
Brazilian Retrospect

Compared with neighbouring countries in South America, Brazil has been blessed with exceptionally favourable circumstances, many of them fortuitous. Thanks to them, her colonial period was a time of stability and progress, of unification and comparative freedom from bloody conflicts.

For example, Brazil's geographical unity was largely predetermined by nature even before the country was discovered. The Treaty of Tordessillas, concluded in 1494, divided the future colonies between Spain and Portugal, giving the latter country suzerainty over the land extending to some 940 miles to the west of Cape Verde and the Azores. Ever since 'the Island of Vera Cruz' was discovered in 1500,[1] and despite the many attempts to wrest it from their grasp,[2] the Portuguese have held it and conferred on it a cohesion lacking in neighbouring territories, thus giving birth to the first tropical civilisation of modern times.[3]

By a similarly favourable accident of history, events in Europe[4] compelled the Portuguese Royal Family to make Rio de Janeiro its capital in 1808. The presence of the Royal Family gave rise to an unprecedented economic and cultural advance leading to the establishment of an extremely effective administrative structure, modelled on that of Portugal. Thanks to this administration, Brazil, which had become a kingdom in 1815 and a constitutional empire in 1822, was able peacefully to end its allegiance to the mother country without bloodshed.

Brazil has also found ready to hand a hitherto inexhaustible succession of exploitable raw materials, one taking over as another was nearing exhaustion. Such were dyewoods, sugar, gold, diamonds, minerals, rubber and coffee. This has enabled Brazil to avoid the hazards of cyclic development associated with economies dependent upon a single product. In proverbial wisdom this exceptional good fortune has of course come to be regarded as a natural right – a feeling expressed in the popular saying, 'God is a Brazilian'.[5]

Nevertheless, Brazil cannot be accounted for simply by a

combination of favourable circumstances. A brief review of the country's political, sociological and economic development will give us a better insight into the present phase of development and an appreciation of the accelerating pace of events in every sphere.

1 Political Development

Ever since it was discovered, Brazil has been ruled by a minority. This minority has indeed grown in numbers and diversity over the centuries, especially since 1889 when the country became a republic. Whereas in 1908 the proportion of the population entitled to vote was only 5 per cent, it had risen to about 16 per cent by 1945 when the *Estado Novo* ended. By 1962 the electorate comprised 25 per cent of the population, and in 1970, under the military régime, this had risen to 32 per cent.[1]

This trend towards participation in political life, albeit noticeable, may be considered by some to be insufficient; but it should be remembered that nearly half (48 per cent) of the population is below the age of 18 at which, under the Constitution, citizens are entitled to exercise their civic rights. In reality, only about 20 per cent of the population, consisting of illiterates and soldiers, is at present without the means of political expression.[2] It is also worthy of note that in Switzerland until 1971 the proportion of electors in national elections was only 26.4 per cent of the total population, as women did not have the vote.[3]

To see how this élite is made up we must take a look at Brazil's sociological development. For the first three centuries of her history, Brazil was under the direct rule of the Portuguese crown. Under this aristocratic régime in which all appointments and investitures were made by the King or on his behalf[4] an authoritarian, centralised structure was established. Brazil received institutions based on those of Portugal[5] and the 'Order of government of 15 September 1548', defining the powers of the first representatives of Lisbon, may be regarded as Brazil's first constitution. Up to 1714 Brazil had forty-one governor-generals. These were followed by fourteen viceroys, and in 1808 King John VI, exiled from Portugal, came to rule.

The arrival of the sovereign, accompanied by his far-seeing counsellors and part of the Portuguese nobility, was an important landmark in the development of the power structure. The large provincial landowners came to take up residence at Rio de Janeiro, as did also the members of the new mercantile classes, the very stuff of a capitalist upper-middle class; and these people, moving on the fringes of royalty, sought to become integrated into the system. The political and cultural activity engendered by the Court favoured the formation of a veritable Brazilian ruling class, which soon developed a sense of national identity.

In 1815 John VI under the title of 'King of Portugal, the Algarve and Brazil', transformed the colony into a kingdom which he governed until his return to Lisbon in 1821. A year later his son, the Prince Regent, yielding to the demands of the Brazilian ruling class around which even then the institutions of government revolved, proclaimed the independence of Brazil. In the presence of the Court, the heads of government departments, the Army and the populace, Pedro I accepted the title of 'Emperor and defender in perpetuity of Brazil'. Constitutionalism had triumphed, changing the very essence of power, without violence – and without any participation by the people.

Under the Constitution of 25 March 1824, which owed much to Benjamin Constant's theories, executive authority passed to a ministry. However, a fourth power was created, the moderating power. 'This keystone of the entire political organisation is delegated solely to the Emperor, so that he may unceasingly watch over the maintenance of the independence, balance and harmony of the other centres of governmental power.'[6] This moderating power, the principle of which was later to be taken up by the Army, was to fashion all the modern history of Brazil.

After the defeat at Ituzaingo in 1827, the Government was compelled to recognise part of what is now Uruguay as independent. The Emperor, censured by the Army, abdicated in 1831 in favour of his son, not yet of age. Pedro II ascended the throne in 1840. He was then fifteen, and his reign lasted until the Republic was proclaimed in 1889. Thanks to him, the new political institutions gained strength and the country once more knew peace, despite the ruinous Paraguayan war (1865–70) which witnessed the birth of a new military mystique.

It was during those years that, under the influence of the young intellectuals who had come back from Europe, groups of leading politicians joined together to form political parties. By 1870 there were three such parties generally recognised, the Liberal party which was formed in 1831, the Conservative party, formed in 1837, and the Progressive party, composed of moderates who had left the two first-named parties. There were also two more recently formed advanced parties, the Liberal–Radical party which favoured reforms, and the Republican party.

These parties were essentially clubs for the well-to-do, many of whom were erudite as well. The middle class, which was developing as industrialisation took shape and the traditional order of colonialism weakened,[7] did not as yet play a significant part in institutional life.

So it was that the destinies of the Republic, which was proclaimed on 15 November 1899, nineteen months after the abolition of slavery, were in the hands of an oligarchy which, though divided in its political views, was united in the defence of its interests.

In the absence of any principle of authority to replace the Emperor after the landed aristocracy, with the support of the Army, had dethroned him, they set up a federalist form of government which has lasted right up to the present time. In this way the tradition of dependence on the large landowners of the old provinces received a new lease of life and the country lived under an order of things dominated by 'the policy of Governors'.[8]

Thenceforward the outcome of federal elections was to depend on the governors of the principal states, since the candidates put forward after they had made their choice were automatically elected by an electorate made up of dependants of the landed oligarchy. This hold upon the electoral system was the more secure because the overwhelming majority of the population lived on the land, not in cities. In 1872 Brazil's three principal cities, namely Rio de Janeiro, Bahia and Recife, had a combined population of 570,752 or 5·2 per cent of the national total. By 1900 they accounted for 7·2 per cent but São Paulo, which in 1872 was eighth in order of size, had moved up to second place with 239,820 inhabitants; Bahia came third, and Recife had dropped out of the first three.

During this period Rio de Janeiro became the undisputed political centre. From 274,972 inhabitants in 1872 the capital's population increased to 811,443 in 1900. And although that represented only 4·66 per cent of the total population, with 693 inhabitants to the square kilometre the city boasted cultural and administrative facilities far superior to those found elsewhere in Brazil, whose average population density was only 2·06 to the square kilometre.[9]

The 'Old Republic' had a stormy history, marked by political abuses. The *'tenentes'*[10] movement in 1922 marks the first step of importance taken by the bourgeoisie towards gaining political power. The failure of the rising had a polarising effect on the opposing factions and the régime came to an end when Getúlio Vargas, carried to power by the 'Liberal Alliance', became temporary President in 1930 and remained as Head of State until 1945.

The system of government which he introduced marked the end of the exclusive hegemony of the landed proprietors. Nonetheless there was no real participation by the people, and to facilitate the task of government Vargas assumed dictatorial powers from 1937 to 1945. Nevertheless the *Estado Novo* witnessed considerable growth in the Brazilian economy, and when Vargas was removed from power by the Military, about 12·7 per cent of the total population were employed in industry and the service sector.[11]

In the economic sphere Vargas[12] favoured direct state participation in industry, and this provided an admirable training ground for top-grade technical and administrative[13] managers. It was these people who in 1964, in alliance with the Army, were to form the base of the technocratic pyramid which took over the running of the country. Another result of Vargas' policies was the formation of an urban working class, organised on a corporative basis and enjoying considerable social advantages.

This heterogeneous urban population in time upset the traditional play of electoral forces, which had been reintroduced by the Constitution of 1946. This was the 'populist' phase – the election through universal suffrage of leaders who prevailed by their personal magnetism,[14] such as Vargas, who was re-elected as President in 1950, Kubitschek or Quadros at federal level, or Adhémar de Barros or Carlos Lacerda at provincial state level.[15]

The populist régime, which lasted until the Revolution of 1964, was still numerically formed by an élite,[16] for in 1946 the electorate represented only 16 per cent of the population. It was populist only in so far as it drew its strength from a direct appeal to the electors (who were an unorganised mass), without the interposition of an electoral college. This situation imposed its own special rules and stratagems upon the conduct of politics; in order to succeed it was essential for a politician to establish his 'brand image'. He had to become recognisable to those who – he hoped – would vote for him. In a country as large and as complex as Brazil this calls for time and money, which is why there were so few leading contenders. This constant reappearance of the same leaders running on up-dated tickets was one of the factors which set the Military, accustomed as they were to a faster rotation of men and appointments, against the professional politicians.

Strictly speaking, there were no national parties. It was the local sections which determined their objectives and elected their candidates, or had them elected, on what were basically regional programmes. Under the prevailing electoral procedures, the politicians when once elected formed groupings under a nation-wide title, but this implied neither ideological agreement nor the obligation to vote in the same way.

Three large parties stood out from the rest. Two of them had been founded by Vargas to serve as a political base at the time when the Military had compelled him to abandon the dictatorship of the *Estado Novo* in 1945. One of these parties, the P.T.B. or Partido Trabalhista Brasileiro, known as a workers party, which was led by João Goulart after Vargas' suicide in 1954, looked to the urban population for its electoral base.[17] In the Parliament which was elected in 1962 this party had 114 deputies out of 409, and 17 senators out of 66. The other party, the P.S.D. or Partido Social Democrático was the situationist party of Juscelino Kubitschek, which drew its electoral strength from the country and the small towns. It fielded 117 deputies and 22 senators. The distinguishing mark of the third party was its opposition to the system established by Vargas. This was the U.D.N. or União Democrática Nacional, and there was competition for its leadership among holders of differing views. Just before the 1964 Revolution it nominated the Governor of Guanabara, Carlos Lacerda, as its candidate for President of the Republic. It drew its support from the same classes as the P.S.D. but was stronger in the larger towns where it could count upon the votes of the new middle classes. It had 93 deputies and 16 senators.

There were also ten other recognised parties, including the P.S.P., Partido Social Progressista, the party of Adhémar de Barros, Governor of the State of São Paulo, with 25 deputies and two senators, and the P.D.C. or Partido Democrático Cristão with 19 deputies and one senator. The P.C.B. or Partido Comunista Brasileiro, which followed the Moscow line was led by Luis Carlos Prestes and after a breakaway in 1962 the P.C.D.B. or Partido Comunista do Brasil, followed the Peking line. Neither party has had a legal existence since 1947.

Nevertheless, these two parties were tolerated by the Goulart Government; they had their own newspapers[18] and were supported by a political coalition, the Frente Parlamentar Nacionalista. Together with a party drawn from the student movement[19] and workers organisations[20] they constituted what was usually called the radical or negative left as distinct from the positive left which gravitated around a sort of nationalist élite of which the ex-Finance Minister, San Thiago Dantas, or the economist, Celso Furtado, are excellent examples.

In the absence of doctrinal bonds, the strangest combinations could occur in the course of political manoeuvring. Since the object of the exercise was to be elected, some unlikely alliances were apt to occur.[21] Hence it is not surprising that electors, ill-informed and ill-prepared, were often tempted to sell their votes and sometimes succumbed to the temptation. Nor is it surprising that the rural tradition whereby agricultural workers vote in accordance with the wishes of the owner of their land is still very much alive, which means that the political machine of the rural states operates at the federal level in a way which does not reflect their structure locally.

> The federal system, by conferring wide powers upon the Senate – in which the small agricultural states in the most backward regions exercise a decisive influence – places legislative power under the control of a minority of the population living in areas where the interests of large landowners are extremely powerful. As the representation of each state in the chamber is proportional to its population, illiterate persons are represented by those who can

read and write in their respective states. Consequently the vote of a citizen living in a state with an 80 per cent illiteracy rate has five times the weight of that of another person living in a state where everybody can read and write. Since the traditionalist oligarchy is strongest in the most backward states, the electoral system helps to perpetuate its preponderance of power.[22]

Once they had entered Parliament politicians were not obliged to abide by a programme. They would, of course, endeavour to further the interests of their own 'clients',[23] but not necessarily those of their constituency, and this led to a widening gulf between Congress and the will of the electors. Yet the politicians were powerful, thanks to the powers conferred on them by the Constitution of 1946. For without them no reform could be undertaken. They feared change as soon as it looked as if vested interests would be affected and in this respect they followed an old local saying: 'Leave things as they are and see what will happen'.

Yet they themselves could compel the executive to incur unprogrammed expenses, which enabled them to torpedo any coordinated plan for stabilisation or development. As they owed much to many people and did not hesitate to use their powers to fulfil these obligations, they helped to worsen the deficit in state finances.

The president was therefore obliged to be constantly manoeuvring, and since he had to keep on the right side not of a few political groupings but in fact of the 475 individuals who made up the parliament, his freedom of action was extremely limited. Celso Furtado, whose Three-Year Development Plan succumbed to this situation, wrote of it:

> To remain legitimate, a government had to act in accordance with the principles of the Constitution while at the same time broadly fulfilling the hopes of the masses who had elected it. But in trying to carry out the substance of the mandate received from the masses to whom it had given pledges during the elections, the chief executive was bound to come into conflict with the Congress over which the traditional governing class exercised firm control.[24]

Consequently the President was caught in between two incompatible principles, that of the legitimacy of authority which involved fidelity to the rules of the Constitution, and that of keeping the promises made to the electoral base which elected him by direct suffrage. Only his personal skill could put off for a time the inevitable conflict, as happened with Vargas and with Kubitschek.

It is these involved wheels within wheels that Brazilians call 'the system'; it includes all those who directly or indirectly have benefited from the populist régime. It is a tangible reality with its own rules and boundaries, never explicit but always there. Everybody who is active in public life, including the Military, knows these rules and follows them instinctively in normal times.

The system cannot be defined in cut-and-dried terms. The political scientist Oliveiro S. Ferreira has said that although it has no clear-cut constituents, it is comparable to an organism which reacts as a whole, as though by reflex, when one of its vital organs is threatened.[25]

Philippe C. Schmitter takes the view that:

> despite obvious differences in interest and attitude, the *sistema* was formed by sedimentation, not by metamorphosis. Intersectorial flows of capital and entrepreneurial talent, inter-élitist family contacts, generalised fear of the enormous latent potential for conflict of such a weakly integrated society, heterogeneity within the rural, commercial, industrial, and proletarian classes – all have helped seal the compromise. The success of this non-antagonistic pattern in turn ensured a continuity in the political culture and a reinforcement of those attitudes stressing the avoidance of conflict, dialogue, ideological flexibility, tolerance and compromise.[26]

Hélio Jaguaribe, who prefers a dialectical definition, believes that the 'system' reflects a situation in which

> an unstable equilibrium between the dominant groups and basically the inability of any of them to assume control of the political functions in the name of the dominating class as a whole, is one of the main features... This compromise situation means that those who carry out the functions of government no longer directly represent the groups which exercise hegemony over certain basic sectors of the economy and of society. The new political structure... no longer constitutes the immediate expression of the social and economic hierarchy, nor yet the immediate expression of the interests of a single social class. The Head of State is beginning to act as an arbiter in a compromise situation which... from now on will have to reckon with another partner – the urban masses of the people – and the representation of the masses in the play of politics will be controlled by the Head of State himself.[27]

In March 1964, President Goulart violated the rules of this game and ceased to 'act as an arbiter in a compromise situation'; he became identified with the *avant-garde* of a single section of the population and the remainder of the social body, 'feeling itself to be threatened', took the initiative to break the vicious circle.

2 Sociological Development

Under the colonial régime, social relations were bi-polar. On the one hand were the Portuguese aristocracy, landed noblemen and owners of the sugar mills, and on the other hand the slaves, at first Indians and then from 1538 onwards, negroes. Around the masters there gravitated a society composed of their relatives, allies and economic dependants, soldiers, craftsmen and workers. This bi-polar grouping formed patriarchal, patrician, and paternalist communities, flanked by a caste of rich merchants, priests (mostly Jesuits) and clerks.

It was a hybrid régime in which feudal elements coexisted with slave-owners and capitalists. According to a recent estimate, Brazil had about 100,000 inhabitants around the year 1600. The large landowners represented some 2 per cent of the total, and coloured slaves 60 per cent. Between these two, the trading class connected with the export sector accounted for 4·8 per cent of the population, whites living in towns 7 per cent and whites not concerned with the export business 26·2 per cent.[1] These figures underline the importance which the course taken by the racial question, so closely linked with the problem of slavery, was to have in the social history of Brazil.

In 1819 the population of Brazil was 3,598,312.[2] According to this estimate, 35 per cent of this population lived in the north (Amazonas and Pará) and the north-east (Maranhão, Piauí, Ceará, Rio Grande do Norte, Paraíba, Pernambuco and Alagoas) and 50·2 per cent in the east (Sergipe, Bahia, Espirito Santo, the State of Rio de Janeiro and the city of Rio, seat of the Court). The southern states (São Paulo, Paraná, Santa Catarina and Rio Grande do Sul) contained only 12 per cent of the population, and the middle-west (Goiás and Mato Grosso), 2·8 per cent. Coloured slaves numbered 1,081,174 and represented 30 per cent of the total population. Contrary to general belief, this proportion was about the same throughout the country,[3] and the southern states had 28·9 per cent of slaves.

The first official census of Brazil, taken in 1872, or sixteen years before slavery was abolished, showed a total population of 9,930,478.[4] Since 1819 the number of slaves had increased by 50 per cent to 1,510,806 but now represented only 15·2 per cent of the population. The most pronounced drop in the slave population took place in the north and the north-east, where their numbers fell from 406,560 in 1819 to 318,399 in 1872, representing only 9·3 per cent of the population compared with 32·3 per cent in 1819. There were 4,246,428 free coloured persons, about 96 per cent of them being of mixed parentage.[5]

If we add these two sections of the non-white population together we find that they represented 59 per cent of the Brazilians. Thus in 1872 the proportion of coloured people was practically the same as in 1600, but their status had undergone a radical change. Not only were 74 per cent of them free, but some of them occupied enviable situations in life, and this well before the formal abolition of slavery in 1888, which was all the easier because of this situation.

This pluralist and evolving system of inter-personal relations on which the pattern of racial relations in Brazil was formed was probably due to the fact that the Portuguese colonists, most of whom were of humble origins, were without white women and hence did not obey sexual taboos or practise endogamy. Motivated both by these traditions and by the European ideal, Brazilian society recognised and accepted as white a whole range of colour mixtures, a circumstance which saved it from the dualism in racial matters which grew up in the United States. For in Brazil human traits are not defined in terms of racial origin but in terms either of physical characteristics such as colour of skin or shape of face, etc., or material characteristics such as wealth or costume, or again by cultural characteristics. This principle of differentiation has made possible a considerable degree of social mobility, thanks to the tacit 'whitening' which is a permanent feature of Brazilian society.

The 1950 census confirmed this trend. Out of a population of 52 million only 27 per cent declared themselves as half-breeds and 11 per cent as blacks, whereas in 1872 the corresponding figures were 41 per cent and 18 per cent.[6] Obviously, even in this 'multi-racial system of social classification'[7] there is still a hiatus between the idyllic image and the practical reality; the whiter the skin, the easier is social ascent. Nevertheless it is a fact that integration has proceeded so far that the question of race has never been susceptible of exploitation as a political weapon in its own right, even after the populist régime was installed.[8]

One other factor was to play a decisive role in the social evolution of Brazil; industrialisation and its consequences for the employment market, which caused urbanisation to proceed faster and depopulated the countryside. Encouragement was still given to such migration both by the relative stagnation in rural, badly paid employment[9] and by the social legislation introduced by Getúlio Vargas, which was extremely favourable to wage earners.[10]

It is impossible to exaggerate the impact of this phenomenon on the traditional social structures (in 1920, 23 per cent of the population lived in cities; by 1970 this proportion had increased to 56 per cent).[11] For the concentration of the peasant masses in cities, where they can more easily be educated and where they are no longer under the traditional sway of landed proprietors, brought about a shift in the centre of gravity of political power towards the urban centres, whose inhabitants became the major voting force in the electoral procedure re-established by the 1946 Constitution.

As regards the modification of social structures, it is worth noting that the speed with which the industrial revolution took place prevented the formation of class-consciousness among the urban masses, themselves divided into workers in regular employment and the pool of labour, either out of work or only in occasional full employment.

Unlike the classic European pattern of the nineteenth century, industrialisation in Brazil, as Celso Furtado noted,

> did not pass through the phase of disorganisation of semi-urban craft activities. Thus the first generation workman was not conscious of having suffered a process of social demotion; on the contrary, since most of them had come from conditions tantamount to those of a rural serf, as was true of the mass of immigrants from Minas Gerais and the north-east towards São Paulo, *workers felt themselves from the outset to have been integrated into a movement towards a higher social status.*[12]

This special circumstance may help to explain why it has never been possible to interpret the Brazilian reality in terms of 'the inexorable logic of the class struggle'.[13] It also explains why attempts to put into practice the theory of a struggle of the working class (whether armed or not) for socialism have failed, becoming in fact suicide operations for the *avant-garde* of the proletariat, led by men who lacked real contact with the social base by which they believed they were supported.[14]

Admittedly, it is not easy to define the social stratification of modern Brazil. This is shown, for example, by the difficulties met by the Brazilian sociologist Vinhas[15] who attempted an analysis using Marxist typology as a starting point, defining the concept of class by reference to its connection with the ownership of the means of production.

First of all he describes the proletariat in Brazil by isolating ten parameters, three of which are universal and seven typically local. According to the first three, the proletariat is defined as a social category which is:

i. made up of various groups who are deprived of the means of production (including land);
ii. exploited by the owners of these means, to whom they sell their labouring power in order to live;
iii. imbued with a view of the world opposite to that of the classes which exploit them.

The seven national characteristics of this proletariat are:

  i. they are of rural origin and consist of descendants of Indians, black slaves and immigrants;
 ii. they consist of various wage earners employed in all the sectors of an economy in which growth is unbalanced and exhibits regional distortions;
iii. they are being joined by a growing number of skilled wage earners (technicians, scientific workers and similar groups) as well as the large rural and urban masses, poverty stricken and under-developed, whose incomes scarcely suffice for existence;
 iv. they constitute a heterogeneous class, constantly changing and from certain points of view still lacking defined social frontiers;
  v. they include factory workers, white-collar workers and workers in the towns and the countryside in service industries, transport and the primary sector;
 vi. they are developing into a self-conscious class though still as yet mainly an identifiable class;
vii. they enjoy increasing regard and power in society.[16]

After proposing these definitions, he attributes to the proletariat a specific weight of 50 per cent of the active population, i.e. approximately 14 million persons. The basic core of the proletariat is taken to be on average 30 per cent of the active population, and to be as high as 60 per cent in São Paulo and the city of Rio de Janeiro.

Over against the proletariat stands the exploiting bourgeoisie; at the top of the ladder is the class of rich landowners, entrepreneurs and bankers. This great bourgeoisie, whether capitalists, landowners, merchants or industrialists, is characterised by ownership of land, the means of production and capital, by exploitation of the surplus value of labour, by economic power, by political strength and by the prestige surrounding it.

Between these two poles comes the petty bourgeoisie including those who also have land, means of production or unearned income, and those who are self-employed in the liberal professions. It has advantages over the rest of the population, though it has neither the prestige nor the economic and political power of the oligarchy.

One of Vinhas' merits is that he was able to show the need to employ a typically Brazilian typology. He was also able to demonstrate that in Brazil the proletariat is an emergent class, still in the stage of formation and settling down. He remarks pertinently that in practice, a number of different strata of the proletariat are to be found, both from a philosophic and organic point of view, and he notes that only a very small proportion of the potential trade unionists among the proletariat are so organised. He also confirms an observation we have made about political reality there, namely the lack of rapport between the 'enlightened minorities', the *avant-garde* of the proletariat as it were, and their followers.

On the other hand, the criteria he has selected make it difficult for him to define the petty bourgeoisie. He cannot find the right place for the new middle class, largely composed of non-property owning wage-earners who nevertheless cannot be considered as part of the proletariat. The dilemma is not a new one, but it is particularly important in Brazil because of the size of this stratum which 'from the point of view of class structure is not entirely separate from the social strata which make up the petty bourgeoisie',[17] but which nevertheless 'tends to be proletarian in its thinking'.[18]

He therefore has to supplement the dialectic of the Marxist theory of classes by assigning to this group, as did Lenin before him, 'a special position between the other classes, belonging to the bourgeoisie as regards its relations, its opinions, etc. . . . but associating itself in some measure with the workers'.[19]

In fact the realities of Brazil fit in better with a typology based upon observation and income statistics. This typology is used by L. C. Bresser Pereira, who shows the genesis and rise of the middle class, which grew from 1·5 per cent of the population in 1877 to 26 per cent in 1950.[20]

While emphasising the dangers inherent in generalisation, Professor Bresser Pereira goes by the following pattern, which he quantifies on the basis of the 1950 census figures.[21]

At the top of the pyramid there is an upper class representing about 1 per cent of the population, having as its common denominator the possession of financial wealth. This is the former oligarchy of the large landowners, the exporters of primary products and the large-scale bankers, who have been joined by industrialists and businessmen who have succeeded financially. As regards the latter, it is interesting to note that a survey carried out in 1963–4 shows that only 16 per cent of the industrialists in São Paulo are the sons or grandsons of Brazilians. Generally speaking they are either recent immigrants (50 per cent) or children of immigrants (34 per cent). In order of numerical importance their countries of origin were Italy, Germany, Portugal and the Lebanon. The majority (57·8 per cent) is of middle-class origin; 16·7 per cent came from poor families, 21·6 per cent from wealthy families and only 3·9 per cent from families which are members of the local oligarchy.[22]

This sociological origin of heads of businesses in the most highly industrialised state in Brazil – immigrants of middle-class origin – throws some light on the reactions of some of them when faced with the problems posed by development under the aegis of international capitalism and, in particular, their receptive attitude towards foreign capital and know-how.

Beneath this class, Professor Pereira distinguishes three middle classes. First come the upper-middle class, containing the liberal professions and university staffs, high-ranking civil servants and military men, directors of businesses, professional managers and similar grades. This is the old bourgeoisie, enlarged by new additions. Typically it is a class which imitates the consumption profile of the upper class, though it does not have the same amount of wealth. It accounts for some 2 per cent of the population.

Next comes what is called the middle-middle class, made up of middle- and lower-ranking officers, white-collar workers, middle managers, master craftsmen, foremen and artisans. It comprises about 6 per cent of the population.

The third class, called the lower-middle class, consists of military other-ranks, lower-grade employees in service occupations and industry, petty officials, skilled workers, etc. This petty bourgeoisie – whose fate is linked to industrialisation and which is drawn directly from the least privileged class, from which it has managed to rise thanks to the opportunities provided by growth – forms approximately 18 per cent of the population.

Lastly there are the rural and urban poor, comprising the vast majority of the population, about 73 per cent. Although these percentages must of course be considered as orders of size, nevertheless they are confirmed in substance by a recent study based on the preliminary results of the 1970 census.[23]

On the basis of this study, taking as a bench mark the declared income of the active population expressed as a multiple of the highest minimum wage in the country,[24] 1 per cent of respondents, corresponding to the upper class, earned each month more than 10·8 minimum wages; 9·1 per cent of the respondents, corresponding to the upper-middle and middle-middle classes earned between 2·7 and 10·8 minimum salaries monthly; 21·5 per cent of the respondents; corresponding to the lower-middle class earned between 1·08 and 2·7 minimum salaries monthly, and 68·4 per cent of the respondents, corresponding to the poor class, earned less than 1·08 minimum wages per month.[25]

The increase in the percentage represented by the middle classes, which rose from 26 per cent of the population in 1950 to 30·6 per cent in 1970, and the corresponding decline of the lower class, reflect the development which has taken place in Brazil during those twenty years.

The following table, of American origin,[26] also confirms the growth of the middle classes though its definitions are not sufficiently specific to facilitate comparison with the data given above.

DISTRIBUTION OF THE SOCIAL CLASSES IN BRAZIL

Percentage of population in:	1920	1950	1955
	%	%	%
Upper and upper-middle classes	3.5	5.0	6.0
Lower-middle and upper-lower classes	26.5	45.0	52.0
Lower-lower class	70.0	50.0	42.0
	100.0	100.0	100.0

Thus the available statistics show clearly that the outstanding sociological phenomenon of industrialisation in Brazil is the growth of the middle class.

Whereas under the colonial régime the middle class consisted mainly of passive elements (relations and allies of the oligarchies) who were provided with administrative sinecures, most members of the new middle class have direct links with the process of production, of which they form as it were the backbone. Thus there has occurred not simply a quantitative break but also a qualitative transformation.

It was against this background that industrialisation brought into being a mass society which made possible the advent of populism, yet without the crystallisation of class-consciousness, and without the necessary conditions for a coherent dialogue of the parliamentary type between the various actors. Political action remained at the psychological level and was drowned in a sea of rhetoric of ill-defined aspirations, grievances and sectional interests.

It is also worth noting that although this capitalist-type economic growth provided an avenue whereby ever broadening sectors of the population could achieve somewhat better living standards, the middle class is by no means homogeneous. The strategic position which it occupies, both in the private sector of the economy and in the political, administrative, and economic machinery of the state, has enabled it to acquire a privileged status in Brazilian society. But the extent of these privileges varies enormously, and this must inevitably give rise to latent tensions between the extreme poles of the middle class.

When the Revolution came, these tensions were aggravated by the consequences of inflation which ate into the private incomes of the traditional middle class, caused fundamental changes in its habits, lowered its material standard of living and damaged its prestige. It shrank the wages of the lower-middle classes like dried skins, and they, feeling that they were falling back into the proletarian condition from which they had emerged, began to question the efficacy of industrialisation as a means of achieving social mobility. It led the young who had enjoyed subsidised higher education to question both the future and the society in which they were growing up.

The realisation that the populist régime had not delivered the goods, together with fear caused by political instability and by the rousing of the popular masses by incitement to pursue unrealistic aims, spurred the middle class to recover at least temporarily a semblance of cohesion and to join forces on a common programme steered by the armed forces. But once order was restored, the disagreements within the middle classes reappeared and the tensions intensified. This study will trace the conflagration which followed when they reached flash-point.

3 Economic Development

Brazilian economic history is composed of point and counter-point, of periods of prosperity and decline. The 'Paubrasil' which gave the country its name and which was used as a dye, was the first article to be exported. Next, the culture of the sugar-cane, which was imported by the Portuguese and is admirably suited to the *massapés*, the fertile land by the north-east seaboard, brought wealth to the colony throughout the whole of the seventeenth century. To the sugar-cane Brazil owes its colonial, paternalist and slave-owning aspect. When the Antilles in their turn broke Brazil's near-monopoly, diamonds stepped into the breach, with the addition of gold which was discovered about 1696 in Minas Gerais, and of which Brazil was the largest exporter in the world. Then Ouro Prêto completed with Salvador and in 1763 the port from which gold was exported, Rio de Janeiro, replaced Salvador as the capital.

Once finished, this cycle left behind it centres of settled population inland, and these centres facilitated the exploitation of the reserves of mineral ore, one of the best developed national assets since that time.

From 1860 and for the next half century, it was the turn of rubber to vitalise the state of Amazonas, where the population increased from 57,000 inhabitants in 1872 to 250,000 in 1900.[1] At that time Manaus was amazingly prosperous. But the rubber plants strewn about the virgin forests were exploited uneconomically and the plantations in Java, which had been created from illegally exported Brazilian stock, soon overtook them with higher productivity, and the market collapsed.

But now coffee, fraudulently imported from French Guyana and first introduced in Pará and at Rio de Janeiro, had found its preferred climate in the red earth of São Paulo by 1830.[2] Notwithstanding a number of crises, the fruit of these plants is even today Brazil's main export product. These new sources of wealth brought into the economic circuit a hitherto rare social stratum, the paid rural workers, and led to the creation of a manufacturing sector from 1850 onwards. Indeed, between 1901 and 1912 the country passed through an extraordinary phase of industrialisation.[3] But this first burst of development came to a halt, undermined by speculation and by the absence of an infrastructure.

Paradoxically, it was the dramatic fall in the prices obtainable for coffee (both the supply and demand of which are inelastic in the short term) caused by the world economic slump of the thirties which led to the economic take-off[4] of Brazil. This process, which was described by Celso Furtado as 'a textbook example of industrialisation by import substitution'[5] may be summarised as follows.[6]

From 1927 to 1929 the high prices obtainable for coffee led to excessive development of the plantations. These came into production from 1930 onwards and caused a surplus which coincided with the world economic crisis. On the international market the price of coffee fell by two-thirds, from 23 American cents a pound in 1928 to 7 or 9 cents a pound. This fall was not counterbalanced by a sufficient increase in demand, which remained about the same. In spite of an alteration to the exchange rate, the price obtainable fell to below the cost of production. To prevent planters who were facing ruin from leaving the coffee to rot on the plants, thus causing a crisis through the multiplier effect of unemployment which the cessation of coffee cultivation would cause, the Government decided to buy the coffee at a price higher than the world price. But this defence of the coffee exporters, which also necessitated storing enormous quantities of unsaleable coffee,[7] placed a heavy burden on the country, reaching 'up to 10 per cent of the national product'.[8]

In order to reduce the cost of storing it, part of this reserve of coffee was destroyed. Thus the country accepted a non-productive investment which enabled the level of employment to be maintained and hence supported overall demand during the depression.[9]

Finance was provided by expanding credit, in other words by increasing the amount of money in circulation and hence constantly depreciating the cruzeiro. This meant of course that the prices of foreign products rose, and as Brazil's capacity to import decreased, so the cost of imported goods rose. Thus the policy of defending coffee resulted indirectly in stimulating local production of goods as substitute for foreign imports the prices of which had become prohibitive. These new opportunities for investment at a high marginal earnings/capital rate[10] induced the capitalists from the traditional sectors of coffee production and export to channel some of their resources into the production of manufactured goods which offered a more immediate profit.[11] They invested mainly in relatively simple productive technologies such as the foodstuffs industry, toilet and perfumery goods, pharmaceuticals and light engineering – all these activities offering the fastest returns on investment.

Two pointers will show the effectiveness of this induced industrialisation: between 1930 and 1940 12,232 manufacturing establishments were started whereas during the preceding decade only 4697 were started;[12] furthermore, 'between 1929 and 1937, whereas the volume of imports fell by 23 per cent, industrial production increased by 50 per cent'.[13]

During the Second World War, Brazil's growth slowed down,[14] owing to the difficulty of importing capital equipment which was due no longer to lack of foreign exchange but to the absence of suppliers, since the developed countries were wholly taken up with their war efforts. To bring some relief to this situation, local industry then began to produce some equipment involving simple technology which could not be imported. When peace returned, the Brazilian Government renewed its policy of supporting the price of coffee, and it held the cruzeiro at the same parity as it had for the Second World War, notwithstanding the rise in the cost of living.[15]

This external over-valuation of the currency, by stimulating the import of foreign products some of which were unnecessary, rapidly drained away the monetary reserves that had been accumulated during the war.[16] Between 1945 and 1947 imports increased by 40 per cent in quantity and by 80 per cent in value.[17] But this overvaluation also enabled industry to purchase equipment on unusually favourable terms, because in effect the import of capital equipment was being subsidised by the nation as a whole.

When the reserves were nearing exhaustion the authorities, who still refused to devalue the currency, had to abandon their liberal trading policy and in 1947 they introduced selective control of imports involving import licences and, from 1953 onwards, multiple exchange rates, and these measures naturally tended towards the protection of industrial interests.

The policy of defence of coffee resulted in prices rising strongly once more. In 1946 the average price per sack was U.S. $22·41 whereas by 1955 it had reached U.S. $61·62. During the same period the terms-of-trade index jumped from 100 to 251.[18] Nevertheless the Government did not allow the coffee producers and dealers to keep all the gains from their transactions. By withholding some of the foreign exchange[19] earned on coffee exports it gathered some financial reserves. This exchange it transferred to the industrial sector, in so far as industrialists were thereby helped to continue to buy equipment at favourable prices. This sector also enjoyed effective protection, so much so that it was almost impossible to import consumer goods[20] or even manufactured goods if locally produced 'similar' goods (in the widest sense of the term) were on sale.[21] Once again this situation provided numerous opportunities for very profitable investment, and between 1946 and 1955 industrial production increased by 122 per cent.

In addition to the traditional light industry, a modern industrial sector was developing. For instance between 1948 and 1955 the metallurgical industry and the chemical sector increased their production by 172 per cent and 608 per cent respectively. Between 1947 and 1955, production of capital equipment increased by 147 per cent, while at the same time the share of such goods in total imports fell from 39·3 per cent to 27·2 per cent.[22]

But industrialisation was not undertaken on a planned basis and bottlenecks became more and more noticeable. In 1953 a fresh round of devaluation began. The Government frequently changed the rate of exchange of the currency, and dollars for use in importing essential products (under the multiple exchange-rate system) had risen from 18·72 cruzeiros to 1293 cruzeiros[23] when the Military came to power in 1964. This represented a fall of 7000 per cent!

Inflation assumed almost unmanageable proportions. Between 1951 and 1960 the overall price index increased on average by 23·9 per cent per annum.[24] But for 1963 the rate was 81·3 per cent[25] and it looked like increasing to 144 per cent in 1964[26] unless draconian measures were taken. After 1955, the terms of trade began to deteriorate as a result of the fall in the price of coffee, thus reducing Brazil's capacity to import. The rate of growth of real product, which showed an average of 6·8 per cent per annum between 1947 and 1955, fell to 3·2 per cent in 1956. And now the effects of failure to invest in basic industries during the preceding period of industrialisation began to be felt. As Professor Bresser Pereira observed, it was during that period that many businessmen and industrialists acquired a taste for quick profits made with relative ease, and this explains the small interest shown by the private sector in Brazil in investment of the slowly maturing type.

The Economic Action Plan of the Government (P.A.E.G.) presented by the minister Roberto Campos after the 1964 Revolution, was to confirm this observation. After stating that between 1947 and 1961 the marginal earnings/capital ratio was 0·5 per cent,[27] the author of the P.A.E.G. emphasised that this very favourable ratio could be attributed to the extensive nature of agricultural production, to the concentration of investment in the manufacturing sector, mainly in the industrial branches where the capital/earnings ratio is small (and hence where the earnings/capital ratio is high), to the comparatively very small proportion of investment in dwellings and in certain public utility services, and lastly to the fact that imported equipment was brought into company accounts at its subsidised rate of exchange.[28]

In 1956, to save the situation, President Kubitschek decided not to put a check on consumption by deflationary measures. He chose to go for expansion under the twin banners of setting up an automobile industry, symbol of technological growth, and of creating Brasilia, the symbol of the continental dimensions of the country.

His calculated risk paid off. The new capital, which was to cost something like a thousand million dollars,[29] came into being in the heart of Brazil and the automobile industry, financed by foreign capital attracted by various concessions,[30] was producing 134,371 vehicles by 1960;[31] 97 per cent of their components were also manufactured in Brazil. Eleven years later, in 1971, the country was producing 516,067 vehicles, more than Argentina, Mexico, Chile, Peru and Uruguay combined.[32] The direct and indirect effects of this policy breathed new life into industrialisation. Between 1956 and 1961, industrial production grew at the rate of 11 per cent annually.[33] The leading sectors gave the impetus to this expansion.

Although not all the objectives set out in the 'Programme of Aims'[34] of the Kubitschek Government were attained, his policy has undoubtedly been a growth factor, even though it was based on exploiting the short-term opportunities without regard to the consequences which were to follow during the sixties.

One of the liabilities of this phase, described by Professor Mario Henrique Simonsen as 'industrialisation at any price'[35] was the transfer of a considerable part of the national savings into the modern sectors of industrialisation either by direct association with foreign capital or in the form of investment in activities arising from its employment. This phenomenon helped to distort the industrial structures by directing production towards satisfying the demand for durable consumer goods, which arose from the privileged groups of the population.

However, with Kubitschek there was born in Brazil a veritable mystique of economic development. But a high price was paid for it. In 1962 the real product rose by only 5·3 per cent and in the following year this growth rate fell to 1·5 per cent, giving a negative per capita product of minus 1·1 per cent.[36]

No more palliatives were available and the main distortions of the system had to be faced. Some of them were as follows:

aggravation of the disparities between the various regions of Brazil due to the concentration of the industries in the centre-south of the country, when there was no infrastructure capable of providing mobility of labour and circulation of goods (per capita income in São Paulo, for example, was double the national average);

distortion of industrial structures mentioned above resulting in the existence of large amounts of under-utilised capacity in some sectors, not necessarily those which were essential to national development, whereas the infrastructure, for which the state was responsible, was inadequate;

a trend towards the over-mechanisation of factories and plant resulting from the policy of indirect subsidies for imports of equipment. This stimulated the use of advanced productive technologies which often were ill-adapted to the actual size of the internal market, and which required skilled labour which is scarce in Brazil, but did not give any jobs to the unskilled workers who abound in the country;

resort to inflation in order to raise the level of overall expenditure (consumption + investment) beyond the level of incomes (consumption + savings).[37] In the short term this option enables under-utilisation of the factors of production to be avoided, but in the medium and long term it has uncontrollable after-effects;

relative stagnation in the agricultural sector, left to itself by the mystique of development. In this area hardly any further investment was undertaken because, as the price of the inputs had increased as a result of the policy of import substitution, and as internal prices had not followed the same curve as industrial prices, profit margins had been severely trimmed;

lack of administrative staffs of sufficient calibre to enable the State to monitor the application of its economic programmes. This problem falls under the general heading of insufficient investment in human factors.

At the beginning of 1964, the political and social repercussions of these distortions had reached such proportions that the country was becoming ungovernable within the existing constitutional framework. A way out had to be found . . .

4 The Military Phenomenon

The intervention of the Brazilian Military[1] in the political life of the country carries on a long tradition. It was the Army that precipitated the abdication of Pedro I in 1831 and which in 1889 brought to birth the Republic, the first two presidents of which were marshals.

From that time onwards the Army has inherited the 'moderating power' of the Emperor, which has been conferred upon it in the successive constitutions. These constitutions, while defining the Army as a permanent national institution entrusted with the defence of the country, the maintenance of law and order and the task of guaranteeing the working of the constitutional organs of government, also authorise the Army to obey only within the limits set by the law.[2] This clause has conferred on the Military a right of arbitrage with respect to the legitimacy of the Government, a right of which they make both frequent and discreet use.

To cite some recent examples, between 1930 and 1961 the Army intervened in this manner five times, yet without installing itself in power.[3] Each time, having more or less successfully accomplished the mission it had assumed as the defender of constitutional legitimacy, the Army retired from the scene. Only in April 1964 was its action the prelude to a military régime. It is therefore pertinent to ask what it was that caused the Army to abandon this tradition of active but discreet vigilance, and why this qualitative mutation in its role appeared.

Probably there is no single answer to this question, but the starting point for the transformation is without doubt the fact that officers in the Brazilian armed forces became military professionals, a fact which was all the more significant in that a similar development did not take place in the civilian area of politics and administration, in spite of the progress that has been made in this direction since Vargas.

We shall see how, in the circumstances prevailing in Brazil, the professionalism of the Military led the officers on to structural militarism, and finally to a military régime; but before we begin our studies of these three aspects of developments it is not without interest to recall the definition of militarism given in the 1949 edition of Larousse: 'Describes, *usually pejoratively*, the exaggerated preponderance of the military elements in the nation';[4] whereas the 1971 edition gives a very different interpretation: 'The feeling and doctrine of those who favour the preponderance of the military element in the nation.'[5] Similarly, if we wish to look at the problem dispassionately it is as well to leave aside the affective potential, the element of instinctive suspicion, with which the concept of militarism is often loaded.

Now let us take up the three analytical tools that we have made to assist our study of this phenomenon. 'Military professionalism' is a social status which implies a permanent responsibility (as distinct from that of the citizen-soldier) *vis-à-vis* the nation. Ideally, it is characterised by an *esprit de corps* which puts unity of the Army above personal interests or differences of opinion. It is conditioned by a common training, of increasing length and complexity,[6] by discipline based upon freely accepted hierarchical values, and by the shared vision of a future for the nation which it is possible to forge.[7] Although very much aware of the problems in the world surrounding them, 'professional' officers nevertheless do not take action, as an organised body, on the political stage, except within the framework of the laws of the constitution.

In short, military professionalism is to armed forces what management is to a business. In the mental flow-chart of these two types of managers, political and social problems are outside their line of authority, and it is left to other specialists located in another 'box', namely the politicians, to carry responsibility for dealing with such matters.

But when the professional officers become aware that their education and technical training are better than those of the rest of the nation, and that the 'line management' of the politicians is not yielding the required results, and when in consequence they try to transpose their experience from the field of military to that of civil affairs, military professionalism is being transformed into structural militarism.[8]

This drift is all the more pronounced where most of the civilian officials exhibit a very low degree of training or administrative efficiency, as in many developing countries, and Brazil in particular. There is of course nothing surprising about this disparity of education and training if one considers the large sums allocated to training in military budgets, and the small sums allocated to this item in the budgets of civilian ministries.

There is no doubt that in practice military professionalism and structural militarism are permanently interwoven in varying degrees. It is also plain that among the officers there are always groups who are more or less committed to the pursuit of objectives which lead from one to the other. But the important fact is that if one distinguishes between these two strands, it becomes clear that only in the wake of a number of external events, such as a severe crisis in the structure of the civil power which threatens the very being of military professionalism, will all the officers turn towards structural militarism.

This is what happened in 1964: for then Goulart attacked the hierarchical principle by supporting the rebellion of the sergeants against their officers; he assailed their social status by granting to workers wage increases above those of the Military; he acted as though he wished to challenge the Brazilian system of alliance by making way for Communism and as a result of his incoherent policies the national economy was made bankrupt and the way to the future for Brazil seemed to be blocked.

Finally, when 'structural militarism' is favourably regarded by civilians, grown tired of a crisis situation which goes on and on, it tends to develop into a military régime which may have some very different side to it. Rustow, whose classification we have adopted for this purpose, shows that a régime of this kind may evolve along five principal lines:

1. At one extreme, the soldiers may retain power for a minimum of time, quickly returning to their barracks and restoring the Government to civilian hands.
2. At the opposite extreme, the soldiers may stay in power permanently inaugurating a stable military oligarchy.

Among the intermediate possibilities are:

3. A series of military coups leading to a condition best characterised as praetorianism.
4. A prolonged twilight situation between civilian and military rule.
5. A social and political revolution under military aegis which, by removing the conditions that led to the coup, establishes civil government on a new and more secure basis.[9]

It follows that a somewhat lengthy period of gestation is needed before a military régime appears, because three factors have to be present for this to happen: first the creation of a 'military professionalism', secondly the emergence of a political will which induces 'structural militarism' and thirdly the support of civilians who will not look for intervention by the Military until they have exhausted all the less hazardous possibilities.

In 1964 these three conditions were fulfilled in Brazil, and that is why the Revolution took place. Hence it is important to know what it was that enabled the Revolution to be conceived by the Military and to study the currents which brought the Brazilian Army to that point. From the psychological point of view, the military question which goes back to the Paraguay war of 1865 to 1870 is the starting point of the whole sequence of development.[10] The Army lost 40,000 men during this campaign and felt itself to have been betrayed by a civilian ministry which refused to provide it with the material tools it required, and abandoned by an Emperor who it thought was unmoved by the sacrifices which it had cost the 'defenders of the nation's honour' to gain the victory. The Army turned in upon itself and for the first time became conscious of its unity and of its responsibility as an organised body. As a Brazilian historian has written, this feeling in due course engendered 'a vague messianic attitude and a feeling that the Army, which was pure and uncorrupted, had a moral mission to fulfil, in regenerating the public life of the country... slowly the officers became possessed by a kind of mystique, a feeling that they were destined to be the saviours of Brazil from the ignoble acts of partisans'.[11]

This realisation did not immediately result in the formation of a military professionalism, but it compelled the officers to ask themselves what part they had to play. In fact they took an active part in political life. Dominated by the positivist trend, they were to bring about the abdication of the Emperor and the proclamation of the Republic under the sign of 'Order and Progress' which is still inscribed on the national flag.

The 'Canudos' campaign of 1896-7, during which some hundreds of '*jagunços*'[12] held at bay units of the Army, symbolised a new stage. The officers, hitherto obsessed by external enemies, found themselves face to face with the problems of maintaining order inside their own country. This concern was to become a constant factor in the thinking of the Military, and as a result the Army both developed a network of ways and means of communication[13] criss-crossing the country and also established garrisons at various points inland. But on the eve of the First World War the national Army consisting of 29,752 officers and men[14] was still more of a hope than a reality. For effective military power was held by the state governors who maintained armed militias. And between 1894 and 1930 these militias outnumbered the federal contingent stationed in each state by an average of about ten to one.[15]

Nevertheless, professionalism triumphed thanks to the core of officers (lieutenants and captains) who had been trained by the Prussian Army to which they had been detached for periods of two years. The ideas which this group brought back from Germany spread rapidly along the military network through the instrumentality of their publication *A Defeza Nacional*, first published on 13 October 1913. This journal emphasised the modernising role which it was the Army's duty to play among the archaic institutions of the country.

Under the influence of their experience in Prussia, the group of Germanophiles did all they could to promote the development of a strong national army under the control of a federalist central government, at a time when the individual states were gaining power at the expense of the central Government. These ideas were in open conflict for half a century and not until the military régime of 1964 came to power was the process of centralisation speeded up, a fact which was exemplified when the state militias were brought under the control of the national Army.

Just after the Treaty of Versailles, Brazil called in a French military mission to modernise its Army.[16] The twenty-six officers, led by General Gamelin, who went to Brazil in 1920, gave absolute priority to the professional training of officers. They endeavoured to train officers to be forward looking, adaptable, capable of political reasoning and of original thinking, and their style was a hallmark of the Brazilian Army up to the Second World War. This influence helped to give officers the feeling of belonging to an intellectual and technical élite, but it also brought them into increasingly open opposition against the politically corrupt and economically retarded circles from which the higher echelons of the civilian ministries were drawn.

Their revolt took the form of *tenentismo*, a movement of young lieutenants, a handful of whom on 5 July 1922 staged a rising at the Fort of Copacabana. The insurrection was not successful but the demands for reforms which they made were not forgotten. In 1930 the 'Old Republic' was overthrown by pressure from the Military and Getúlio Vargas was appointed Head of State.

This civilian leader, who had spent a short period in the Army, fulfilled some of the aspirations of military professionalism. He laid the foundations for centralising the institutions and made a start with economic and social development. The Army, to which an authoritarian and nationalist president was by no means unwelcome, was also happy about the leading positions given to certain officers in the economic and political administration. The axiom of military thinking in Brazil – that economic growth goes hand in hand with professionalism among officers – dates from this period.

The combat experience gained by the expeditionary force which took part in the Italian campaign alongside the American troops during the Second World War initiated a new military dimension for Brazil. The officers involved learnt to work in a war machine administered according to the usages of Western democracy. There they learnt the cult of efficiency, planning and mastery of the technical means. Under the influence of American instructors, the Brazilian Army became imbued with the signs of military professionalism. From then onwards promotion was to depend on qualifications as shown by the results obtained in the officers' schools[17] which all officers of the new generation had to attend at intervals throughout their careers.[18]

These developments were consummated on 20 August 1949 when the Superior War College (Escola Superior de Guerra, E.S.G.) was opened, and thenceforward it was to be the framework within which officers would affirm the share they intended to take in determining the national objectives; it was also the platform from which they would expound and explain their doctrine: in it military professionalism had reached full maturity.

The E.S.G. was modelled on the National War College in America, but its curriculum goes far beyond that of the College. After an introductory period, instruction in the E.S.G. was divided into six parts – public affairs, psychological and social affairs, economic affairs, military affairs, logistics and mobilisation, intelligence and counter-espionage, doctrine and co-ordination. At least as much emphasis is placed on the development of the country as on security itself. This institution, known generally as the 'Sorbonne', was to play a decisive part in formulating the objectives of the high priests of military professionalism during the first phase of the military régime of 1964, and we must now examine it rather more closely.

The E.S.G. rapidly became more than an institution for military education, and developed into a laboratory of advanced studies in which civilian and military aspirations were examined and debated. In fact, about 50 per cent of the participants were civilians representing a cross-section of the country's life[19] – civil servants, industrialists, businessmen, bankers, members of parliament, federal judges, professors, economists, doctors, journalists, men of letters and members of the Catholic clergy.[20] The course lasted for one academic year and full-time attendance was required. In addition to courses, seminars, conferences and practical work, study tours and visits were among the teaching methods used.[21] The object was to discover and formulate a doctrine for the future of Brazil, to set out the basic objectives for the country and to initiate specific programmes of action to achieve them, taking account of any obstacles known to exist. An active and powerful old boys' association ensured that those who had passed through the school remained in touch. It published a magazine, organised discussion lunches, seminars, refresher courses and conferences, and had a liaison officer in each of the key ministries.

Furthermore, through the medium of the Social Research and Studies Institute (I.P.E.S.) which was a private body financed by businessmen[22] in which many leading figures of the E.S.G.[23] were active, certain subjects were studied in depth and detailed schemes for reforms were worked out from the viewpoint of an enlightened and progressive capitalism, on the eve of the Revolution.

This virtually permanent dialogue between leading figures in civilian and military life threw up two concepts which subsequently became key elements in the policy of Castello Branco. The first stressed the fact that national security and economic development were inter-dependent, and that since the fighting of a modern war required the active consent of the whole nation, means must be found of mobilising its will, its unity and its productive capacity. Thus in addition to its traditional requirements, national security implied planning of the national life so as to optimise production and the economy while minimising internal tensions. To this end, while retaining a framework of democracy and reform, it became necessary to centralise and strengthen the executive and to provide it with a structured, competent planning organ.

According to the second concept, part of the economic backwardness found in under-developed countries was due to internal pressures resulting from the world-wide ideological struggle and these pressures represented a serious threat to the internal security of the nation. The world ideological struggle itself was defined uncompromisingly as taking place between the Communist bloc and the non-Communist bloc. In this conflict Brazil, the world's leading Catholic country, was bound to take a resolutely non-Communist stance and therefore its natural ally should have been the United States which was the champion of anti-Communism. The logical concomitant was to seek to achieve national security by a total anti-subversion strategy penetrating all activities throughout the country, and this in turn would lead back to the need for a strong centralised authority with planning capability.

Relatively little detail was given as to the political means by which the needed reforms could be achieved within the framework of democracy, but the profound structural modifications which would be required were set out. These objectives included weakening the power of the traditional oligarchy,[24] reducing the number of political parties, preventing the formation of local electoral alliances for the sole purpose of winning this or that seat, overhauling the electoral system, transport and education, eliminating inflation, promoting agricultural reform and creating a financial market. Another aim was to strengthen the nationalised sector and eliminate state enterprises which were making losses, while still calling upon capital and the private sector, whether Brazilian or foreign, where they could be of use.

Hence, thanks to E.S.G., Castello Branco was able to base his action as soon as he came to power on a doctrine which had been adopted by a core of military men and civilians, the 'old boys' of the Sorbonne. They had acquired a certain harmony of view concerning Brazil's problems and the solutions to them, and some of them were technically prepared to take on governmental duties.

In order to study in greater depth the military phenomenon of which we have examined the historical development, we must take a close look at the socio-economic profile of the officer corps and at the method of recruiting for the Army.[25] Alfred Stepan, the American political scientist, who published in 1971 a detailed study of the Brazilian military men,[26] had access to sources not normally available to civilians. We shall utilise the statistical data which he was able to gather, to highlight six parameters which are characteristic.

1. *More than four-fifths of the young officers belong to the middle-middle and lower-middle classes.*
An analysis of the dossiers of the 1031 cadets who entered the military academy between 1941 and 1943 and of the 1173 cadets of the 1962–3 classes bears out this statement, going by the father's occupation. On this criterion (which is far from perfect, but sufficient for a first approximation) in the first group 19.8 per cent still belonged to the upper class or the upper-middle class, but in the second group this proportion had fallen to 6 per cent. Of these the sons of landowners who at the beginning of the war accounted for 3.8 per cent, were only 0.5 per cent twenty years later.

The middle-middle and lower-middle classes supplied 77.9 per cent of the cadets during the first period. In the second the proportion had noticeably increased to 86.9 per cent.[27] Those coming from the poor classes accounted for 2.3 per cent between 1941 and 1943 but only 0.4 per cent in 1962–6.[28] Nearly half of the cadets (43 per cent) came from families having six or more children, and for most of them free access to the military academy both in respect of tuition and maintenance constituted their only chance of social mobility.

Cross-checking this sub-division by what the cadets of the 1962–6 classes said about the financial situation of their families, we note that not many of them said they had rich parents: 24 per cent said that their family environment was 'above average', 67 per cent 'average' and 9 per cent 'below average'.

This social stratification has an economic explanation. The poorest strata of the population very seldom receive secondary education[29] and consequently they do not have access to careers as officers. The lower-middle and middle-middle classes, whose incomes are limited but who in the urban centres have publicly maintained schools available, have the requisite qualifications to take the entrance examination to the A.M.A.N. As this academy is non-paying it attracts candidates who otherwise would not have the necessary finance to receive a full education. The well-to-do class – the upper-middle and upper classes – are free to choose either the military channel which is relatively slow but costs nothing, or public or private higher education which is costly but fast, and which brings in immediate returns, since educated youths with management potential are immediately snapped up by the business world.

The difference between military pay and salaries in the private sector accentuates still further the comparative advantages of going into civilian life[30] for young people who wish to be earning without delay an income well above the national average. This situation undoubtedly causes some concern to the Military, for they regard it as threatening the prestige of their profession and as a danger to the development of Brazil. Looking at it from their own point of view, namely that of service to the nation, they wonder where the engineers, doctors, economists, administrators and teachers who are so badly needed in the backwoods, and who hitherto have been largely supplied by the Army, will come from if everybody tries to turn his education into money in terms of a market economy.

2. *The young cadets do not come either from the most industrialised states or from the poorest rural ones.*
The majority comes either from the capital or from rural states of average development. The files of the cadets of the 1964–6 classes show that only 14 per cent of them came from the north-east,[31] whereas the population of these nine states represents 35 per cent of the population of Brazil.[32] São Paulo, the industrial capital of the country, supplied only 8.3 per cent of the cadets, whereas its population represents 18.3 per cent of the total. On the other hand, the city of Rio de Janeiro and the state of Rio Grande do Sul sent the strongest contingents, namely 42 per cent and 14 per cent from populations representing respectively 4.6 per cent and 7.7 per cent of the total.

The reasons for this imbalance are the defective school system in the north-east, the many other job opportunities offered by São Paulo, the presence of a large body of civil servants in Rio de Janeiro, and the military tradition of Rio Grande do Sul. It should not be overlooked that the small number coming from São Paulo might have far-reaching consequences, in as much as the opinions of the most powerful state in Brazil are hardly heard in the structural militarism which is in a state of formation. (In 1935 for example, not a single general on active service came from the state of São Paulo and in 1964 there were only three, and those were one-star generals.)[33]

It is also noteworthy that since nearly half of the cadets are the sons of civil servants or military families (48 per cent), the officers of the future will probably be inclined towards adopting solutions involving the state rather than turning to private initiative.

3. *Until 1966 the education and training of officers tended to be carried out in a closed circuit.*
For one thing, the proportion of cadets who were officers' sons rose from 21·2 per cent in 1941–3 to 34·9 per cent in 1962–6. Moreover whereas in 1939 61·6 per cent of all cadets came from civilian secondary schools, between 1962 and 1966 this percentage had fallen to 7·6. The other 92·4 per cent had attended secondary schools financed and managed by the Army (where teaching and maintenance are free for the sons of career soldiers).

There is no doubt that this closed-circuit education hastens the development of *esprit de corps* and of military professionalism; but it runs the risk of lacking external stimuli in a situation where, as Stepan notes, 'up to 90 per cent of the present post-war generation of army officers in Brazil entered the military academic system around the age of twelve'.[34]

In 1966 the Military took a number of steps in an endeavour to reverse this trend. For instance, the top three male scholars leaving a recognised secondary school were enabled to enter the A.M.A.N. without an examination. These officers did have some success since between 1967 and 1969 the percentage of cadets coming from civilian schools rose to nearly 50 per cent.[35]

4. *Contrary to the traditional idea, the Army does not play a decisive part either in human integration or national integration.*
This is due to its geographical organisation and the method of recruitment. One of the most important tasks of the Army is 'the integration of the territory', which has become essential owing to the imbalance between the relatively thickly populated Brazilian littoral and the enormous tracts of hinterland that have been untouched by the currents of colonisation.[36]

This idea, together with the need for an effective defensive coverage, has determined the way in which the troops are organised. There are in fact four armies, with headquarters at Rio de Janeiro (First Army), São Paulo (Second Army), Porto Alegre (Third Army) and Recife (Fourth Army),[37] and their divisions are broken down into regiments and battalions sometimes separated by hundreds of kilometres.

For reasons of economy, there is no federal or central recruitment. To avoid travel and subsistence costs, each unit recruits locally the men it needs.[38] As most of the garrisons are in urban centres, 'most of the draftees are urban and serve in a unit less than ten miles from their homes and families'.[39] This is partly true also of the career soldiers, except during the periods when they are sent on training courses or when they are attached to the ministry.[40]

There are two other factors which militate in favour of a preponderance of city dwellers in the Army. These are the care taken by the responsible officers to avoid causing depopulation of the countryside, and their preference for recruiting conscripts who can read and write, owing to the difficulties experienced by those who cannot do so in handling the equipment of a modern army, and the fact that the former are more numerous in the cities. In fact, the officers do indeed engage some illiterates, to fulfil what they call their 'quota of sacrifice', but even so these would represent on average no more than 5–8 per cent of recruits, the proportion varying inversely with the degree of technicality of the armament.[41]

Thus it is clear that, contrary to common belief, hardly any mixture of types takes place either regionally between cities and the country or nationally between different regions. This latter circumstance makes of the Army in some sense a number of regional militias, which might conceivably reduce its effectiveness as an instrument of the central government in the event of an internal conflict.

5. *The officers in charge of operational units (regiments and battalions) enjoy more authority and freedom of action than in a compact army.*
This is a result of the geographical dispersion which we have just mentioned. The top brass must take into account the views of the lieutenant-colonels and colonels in order to make sure that the Army retains its cohesion. This consultative procedure is an essential factor in the formation of the military consensus which is necessary if structural militarism is to flourish.

6. *The Army is a very small minority of the total population, and this minority is tending to diminish still further.*
In 1960 with 263,100 men, the Army formed 0·37 per cent of the total population and of these effectives the 20,000-odd officers represented about 0·022 per cent of the population. In 1969 there were only 194,350 men, or 0·20 per cent of the total population, in the Army. (Of these effectives, 120,000 were in the ground forces, 44,350 in the Navy and 30,000 in the Air Force.) Between 1966 and 1969 the military budget averaged 2·2 per cent of the gross national product, or six dollars per inhabitant.[42]

To sum up, the available statistics pinpoint the characteristics of the corps of officers who, free to stand at arm's length from vested interests and the *status quo*, described itself as 'the people in uniform... acting as an instrument of transformation'.[43]

Coming, as 90 per cent of them did, from the middle-middle and lower-middle classes, most of them from administrative states like Guarabara, or semi-developed ones like Rio Grande do Sul, the officers did not identify with the extremes of riches or poverty which were characteristic of the country in its state of economic development. Their education and training lined them up with the modernising élite and they were all in favour of industrial development, conceived as the necessary economic basis for the establishment of social justice, and the only means of guaranteeing the security of the nation threatened by Communism and subversion. The way in which the Army was organised enabled them to preserve strong regional links while at the same time encouraging them to give close study to the problems posed by the integration of Brazil as an essential factor in the defence of the territory. Lastly, since they formed only a minute minority of the population, necessity and discipline alike led them to place the cohesion of their group above their personal differences.

Nevertheless, since the majority of them came from cities, were they not in danger of relegating the rural question into the background of their concern? And as the entrance qualifications were raised, might this not exclude the weaker members of the social body from a military career? And again, might not the preponderance of petty bourgeois in 'the best structured institution of the middle classes'[44] limit the vision of the officers in matters concerning the problems of the least favoured strata of the population? However, in the preamble to Institutional Act No. 1, these questions appear to be answered in the negative. The Revolution, it says, has to interpret 'not only the interests and the will of a single group, but the interests and will of the whole nation'.[45] Could this declaration of intent stand up to the practical realities of power? That is the question to which we shall now seek an answer.

PART TWO

The Stern Call to Order

On 1 April 1964, the armed forces seized power in Brazil. The movement was supported by large sectors of the population and there was no resistance by the people. The populist President, João Goulart, fled to the south of the country.[1] Auro de Moura Andrade, President of the Senate, then declared the presidency vacant and in accordance with the provisions of Article 79 of the Constitution swore in the President of the Chamber of Deputies, Ranieri Mazzili, in the small hours of 2 April. Two days later Goulart, having given up all hope of a return, took refuge in Uruguay.

Events moved so swiftly, the victory was so complete and the absence of reaction so total that nobody yet knew what form the new régime would take. For their part, the civilian politicians who had supported the rising of the Military were still sufficiently convinced that the soldiers would return to their barracks as they had done in 1954, 1955 and 1961, to submit to them on 8 April a draft 'emergency law' which they thought would settle the matter.

On the ninth the die was cast, and in a unilateral action the commanders in chief of the Army, Navy and Air Force published Institutional Act No. 1 based on the constitutive power of revolutions,[2] and thereby inaugurated a modernising military régime. Democracy in its populist form had had its day in Brazil.

PART TWO

The Stern Call to Order

5 Institutional Act No. 1

Institutional Act No. 1 was the cornerstone of the revolutionary edifice in Brazil during its initial phase. It still breathed democratic ideas, even though it placed on record the failure of the constitutional procedures which 'did not come into play to remove power from the Government which, of set purpose, was preparing to bolshevise the country'.[1] If the habitual bargaining between Congress and the President, introduced by Getúlio Vargas, was rejected, the Constitution of 1946 was still the framework of reference:

> to make quite clear that we are not seeking to radicalise the revolutionary process, we decide to maintain the 1946 Constitution, and shall confine ourselves to modifying it in those sections dealing with the powers of the presidents of the Republic... we have also decided to retain the National Congress subject to the reservations made concerning its powers by the present Institutional Act.[2]

The purpose of these modifications was

> to provide the new government which will be sworn in with the indispensable means for the task of the economic, financial, political and moral reconstruction of Brazil, to enable it to grapple directly and immediately with the serious and urgent problems on which the restoration of internal order and of the international prestige of our country depend.[3]

The eleven articles of Institutional Act No. 1, which was to remain in force until 31 January 1966, set up a relatively authoritarian framework for the Government; they made the following provisions.

Regarding the election of the president:

(a) that the president and the vice-president should be elected within forty-eight hours by an absolute majority of members of Congress;
(b) that their mandate should expire on 31 January 1966 (the date on which the constitutional mandate of ex-President Goulart was to expire);
(c) that reasons for ineligibility were modified so as to enable an officer on the active list to be elected, thus enabling the victorious army effectively to manage the country.

Regarding the powers of the president:

(a) the right of initiative concerning constitutional amendments and bills. A time limit was fixed for the discussion of these texts in the Congress. Once the period was ended, if no vote had been taken the bills were to be considered as approved;

(b) the right of exclusive initiative for laws creating or increasing public expenditure. The Chambers were no longer authorised to introduce amendments with the object of increasing the proposed commitments;

(c) the right to decree martial law or to prolong it for thirty days in those cases foreseen in the Constitution subject to submission to Congress within ten days.

Regarding sanctions:
(a) a suspension for six months of constitutional or legal guarantees of irremovability and security of office if prejudice had been caused to 'the security of the State or the democratic régime and the moral integrity of the public administration';[4]

(b) the suspension for two months of the limitations enshrined in the Constitution as regards abrogation of civil rights for a period of ten years and the setting aside of legislative mandates at all levels 'in the interests of national peace and honour'.[5]

Concerning the future:
Fixing the date of 3 October 1965 for the election of the president and vice-president of the Republic, and their investiture on 31 January 1966.

The authors of this Act had designed it to put an end to the crisis of power which had been present in Brazil since Jânio Quadros resigned as President in 1961, having failed to impose a Gaullist-type solution to the problem of his relations with Parliament. Henceforth the Executive was to have the necessary powers to carry out a co-ordinated economic policy which would not be constantly threatened by the demagogic and irrational interventions of certain politicians of the traditional type.

The elected representatives of the people, although suspected of corruption and sometimes of subversion, were firmly fenced in by the Military, who nevertheless seemed ready to allow them to play a real part in the life of the country in so far as they agreed to accept the new *de facto* situation.

On 11 April Congress ratified the choice of the High Command by appointing General Humberto de Alencar Castello Branco,[6] Chief of General Staff of the Army and operational co-ordinator of the Revolution, as President of the Republic. The vice-presidency however was given to a civilian, a traditional politician belonging to the main party in the former régime, José Maria Alkimin.

The choice of a soldier fulfilled a widely expressed wish. Sources as diverse as for example the Governor of Guanabara, Carlos Lacerda;[7]

the Federation of Industries of the State of São Paulo;[8] the Brazilian Rural Society;[9] the Rio de Janeiro Women's Union,[10] and the influential newspaper *O Estado de São Paulo*,[11] inspired by different and sometimes conflicting motives, were unanimous on the subject. Paradoxically, they were all demanding an officer without any political affiliations to resolve an eminently political crisis.

6 Castello Branco and the 'Sorbonne' in Search of a Basis of Government

The new President, who left active service with the rank of marshal to assume his new functions on 15 April, was a man of stern temperament and became more so after he was widowed.[1] His keen feeling for authority did not prevent him from having deep democratic convictions. There was no doubt as to his personal disinterestedness and integrity. He will undoubtedly leave an indelible mark on the period we are studying, though it is likely that historians of Brazil will attribute to him an even more important role than is at present the case. Born in 1900 in the State of Ceará right in the middle of the 'polygon of drought', this north-easterner was an officer's son. He received his military training in the south of the country, at Porto Alegre, and had a brilliant career. For he combined practical experience with an amazing grasp of theory. He was Chief of the Third Section of the General Staff (Operations) of the Brazilian Expeditionary Force, the only Latin-American ground force to have fought side by side with the Allies in Italy; Commander of the Fourth Army in Brazil; he twice passed out top of his class; he was a graduate of the French Ecole Supérieure de Guerre (E.S.G.) and of the US Staff and Command School;[2] Director of the Department of Studies of the E.S.G. and Director-General of military education in Brazil. Thus he was one of the Brazilian officers who had actual combat experience. His contact with the American Army left him not only with an understanding of the vital role of logistics but also the conviction that only relentless work and a rigorously realistic analysis of one's own weaknesses could justify any hope of victory.

Castello Branco's thought was also deeply influenced by the theories of the E.S.G., through which the élite of the Army pass and of which thereafter he became the figurehead. He was to make the great minds of this institution the nerve-centre of power.[3] (It should be noted however, as Professor Stepan's study had shown,[4] that the experience of this group of generals is not typical of Brazilian military men.)

Hence Castello Branco inaugurated a régime founded on the doctrine of the Superior War College. He hoped to be able to complete his task before his mandate ended on 31 January 1966; he made it clear that this was his aim, and it is said that he nourished the hope of having by that time made sufficient progress to hand over power to a civilian successor.[5]

This feeling of urgency, his conviction that the time available was short, was a characteristic trait of the President; perhaps he owed it to that military discipline which in Brazil calls for constant renewal of the officer corps. The compulsory retiring age for a colonel is 59, for a brigadier-general 62; for a major-general 64 and for a full general 66. And if age itself does not each year bring about changes in two appointments of generals, seven of major-generals and twelve of brigadier-generals, the High Command orders any early retirements that may be needed to ensure this mobility.

However, realities within the nation cannot be remodelled at breakneck speed, therefore the military régime had to find a basis for governing, in view of the well-known fact that 'tanks and machine guns... are an excellent instrument for ousting the old rulers: they are quite useless for the task of governing a society'.[6]

And so Castello Branco had to change his tune before very long. Barely three months after his investiture, he had to prolong his own mandate until 15 March 1967 and to have the elections put back to October 1966, by means of Constitutional Amendment No. 9 of 22 July. By so doing he assured himself of three years as President, which was considered the minimum period essential for carrying out his programme of reforms.[7]

The resistance which the President encountered came mainly from two sources. On the one hand there were the civilians who had played a part in the Revolution and who, not yet having grasped the extent of the changes which the régime intended to bring about, wanted to revert at once to their former political habits; on the other hand there were certain officers who did not share the legalist and internationalist views of the leaders of the Sorbonne.

Just after the Revolution, there was confusion in the civilian camp. Apart from the many who, as of old, were anxious to defend their vested interests, four candidates (three governors who were allies of the revolutionaries, and one ex-President) were candidates for the presidency in the elections which were to have taken place in October 1965 under Institutional Act No. 1. They were Adhémar de Barros, the powerful Governor of São Paulo, Brazil's most vigorous state; José de Magalhães Pinto, Governor of Minas Gerais whence the first troops of the Revolution set out; Carlos Lacerda, the popular Governor of Guanabara who controlled the city of Rio de Janeiro, and finally the father of Brasilia, former-President Juscelino Kubitschek, who was a senator and the nominated candidate of the largest party in parliament. Using different means to pursue their aims, each of them sought to turn the new circumstances to account in bending the institutions in their favour. But their electoral ambitions were sharply curbed by the relentless call for austerity in the economic and social policy of Castello Branco, and in seeking means of circumventing it they precipitated a break between the civilians and the Military.

It is very surprising that, knowing the various currents of opinion which threatened him, Castello Branco made no effort whatsoever to win public opinion over to his side. His administration furnished hardly any examples of systematic effort at propaganda, public relations, indoctrination or even efforts to make himself understood, let alone approved, by the Army or by the people. The régime was characterised by a consistency and an intellectual rigour which looked like pride or disdain to a people for whom the heart was more important than the head, and the thrilling personality-cult which was the legacy of populism the only political reality which they knew and understood.

In this respect Castello Branco, possibly reacting against such attitudes, would not listen to other people's advice or accept any compromise. When he said that the Revolution would be judged by its fruits and not by its promises, the President was talking like one of the engineering manufacturers of the old school who thought that a product would sell because it was good, whereas the consumer society also requires it to be sold to them by marketing, to convince them of the advantages of the goods offered.

The climate of disharmony in which Brazil lived through the first four months of the régime was increased by the difficult period of adjustment through which the Army was passing. For although the tiller had been seized by leaders trained by the Sorbonne, other voices were raised by those who wanted to impose their structural militarism on the nation.

Of the latter, the main trend, which soon came to be known as the 'hard line' was followed by many of the younger officers, those who wanted to see more radical solutions applied. Mostly line commanders, these officers had virtually no staff experience and had not learned that politics is the art of the possible. Hence their analysis of the problems of Brazil was more doctrinaire than that of their elders. They considered that the crisis was in the main caused by two basic factors, corruption and Communist subversion. Being nationalists in the strict sense of the term, they also regarded the power of foreign capital as an external disturbing influence, in so far as it strengthened the private sector over against State enterprises which, these officers considered, were in a better position to exploit the country's wealth.

However, it can be said that at least to begin with, this was more a difference of degree than a head-on clash. Those in favour of the hard line wanted to strike while the iron was hot, to root out the evil, to punish and make examples of 'the subversive agents of international Communism' and the 'men corrupted by the system' so that the Military, who by definition were 'clean, stern and efficient', could thereafter rebuild a more just, authentically Brazilian country, whatever price had to be paid in social or economic terms during an intermediate phase.

The Sorbonne people recognised that changes must be made, but they also saw the importance of taking into account the complexity of Brazil, of things as they were in the nation and of international constraints, and of employing wise tactics by relying on the people least identified with the civilian political system in order to reach as quickly as possible the primary objectives – to get the economy once more on the move and to reform the institutions.

In fact this divergence of views had existed for a long time. Although, for example, the older ones among the 200-odd generals of the three arms still serving in 1964 were deeply influenced by the liberal heritage of *tenentismo*,[8] this attachment was not universally shared either by all the generals or by those up-and-coming officers who were likely to replace them during the next ten years.

This is demonstrated by the demands made in the manifesto of the Civilian–Military Patriotic Front (Frente Patriotica Civil–Militar),[9] published in December 1963 under the title of 'The Ten Commandments of the Law of the People'.[10]

1. Dissolution of the Congress in order to restructure the popular democratic base of the country by a new constituent assembly.

2. Confiscation of all fortunes acquired by shady business deals, embezzlement, administrative frauds or any other illicit means, with the cancelling of the political rights of all involved.

3. Distribution to the peasants of all uncultivated lands with the obligation of immediate cultivation and with direct financial and technical assistance guaranteed.

4. Energetic combating of the high cost of living and inflation by

the intervention of the state in the means of production and distribution and the suppression of taxes on basic necessities of life.

5. Elimination of excessive bureaucracy and unification of the social welfare system, and the guarantee of medical and hospital care to all workers including rural workers.

6. Abolition of all forms of government intervention in the trade unions.

7. Preferential concern for the solution to the problems of the north and the north-east and other under-developed regions of the country in all national development plans.

8. Defence and development of Petrobrás[11] and of the great State industries. Control of the remission of profits abroad and the requirement that profits be reinvested in the development of the country.

9. Extension of free primary, secondary, technical and higher education by the state for the training of poor students.

10. The pursuit of an independent foreign policy, opposed to all forms of totalitarianism and imperialism, respect for the rights of self-determination and condemnation of the monstrous arms-race in accordance with the democratic and Christian principles of Brazil.

The text will be seen to contain some of the ideas of the Sorbonne, more or less radicalised. It does however show a marked preference for a nationalistic authoritarianism of which the interdependence policy of Castello Branco, soon to be branded as *entreguista* (sell-out) could easily fall foul.

It should however be stressed that beyond any doctrinal differences the officers were united by one overpowering conviction, namely that the armed forces as an organised body could not govern the country unless the officers[12] formed a common front. Did not an alert observer answer a questioner during a crisis with the words: 'Don't worry, the Army disciplinary code will win!'?[13]

7 The Four Black Months

Even before Castello Branco came to power the revolutionary High Command had published the first list of demotions on 10 April. This purge affected those who had been most closely identified with the former régime. Persons whose civil rights were suspended in this way included the ex-President Jânio Quadros; President João Goulart and his brother-in-law Leonel Brizola, a leader of the 'negative' left and Governor of Rio Grande do Sul; Miguel Arraes, Governor of Pernambuco; the economist Celso Furtado; and Ambassador Josué de Castro.[1] In addition to the civilian leaders, on 11 April for the first time in the recent history of the country,[2] 122 officers were also deprived of their appointments.

The left and the trade unions were hard hit and soon thrown into confusion. The pilot university of Brasilia was purged with the utmost severity. Simultaneously, hundreds of military police inquiries, or I.P.M. (Inqueritos Policial Militar) were started. The 'hard-line' colonels who made themselves responsible for this went to work with frightening zeal. In view of the flood of excesses, Castello Branco appointed a general commission of inquiry, C.G.I. (Comissão Geral de Investigação)[3] on 27 April under Marshal Estevão Taurino de Rezende, with whom he had had occasion to work in the past and whose anti-Communist sentiments were well known. In May Marshal de Rezende authorised the I.P.M. to keep in custody all witnesses for a maximum of fifty days before taking their statements. This aberrant measure says much about the practices of the I.P.M., but it was taken in order to put an end to even more flagrant abuses.

These inquiries were supposed to bring to light Communist subversion and corruption, but in fact they produced little that was new in the way of information.[4] None the less they went on for years, and often degenerated into a veritable witch-hunt based on the wildest definitions of Communism. Without going into details, which have already been published in writings exhibiting varying degrees of impartiality,[5] it must be emphasised that, taken as a whole, the repression was less violent than was feared in view of the conditions ruling at the time. It was violent enough partially to satisfy the hard-line officers and must have brought at least some of them to the notice of Brazilians throughout the country. But since, as Marshal Taurino de Rezende, the Head of the C.G.I. himself said, 'compared to corruption the problem of Communism in Brazil is insignificant',[6] some of the inquisitors unfortunately did not withstand the financial temptations to which they were subjected and their malversations sullied the image of austere purity which the hard line likes to project concerning itself in business and financial circles.

On 8 June, Castello Branco set aside the senatorial mandate of former-President Kubitschek and withdrew his civic rights for a period of ten years. This step had become unavoidable both because the former President was a focus for the opposition and also because the hard liners, supported by the War Minister, General Costa e Silva, who was possibly preparing to offer himself as a candidate for the presidency, were demanding Kubitschek's head.

In their view he epitomised all the excesses of populism, and the symbol had to be struck down; he was sent into exile accused of many things including acts of administrative corruption and illegal self-enrichment, though such acts had never been held against him by the people. However, there appears to be every indication that Castello Branco would have preferred to avoid taking this step against a man whose popularity was indisputable.

So he had to throw out some ballast. But he obtained in exchange observance of the provisions of Article 10 of Institutional Act No. 1, which abolished with effect from 15 June the power conferred on the President of annulling any elective mandate, notwithstanding pressure by the hard liners who publicly demanded its prolongation, Marshal Taurino de Rezende being their spokesman.

When 15 June finally arrived, Castello Branco could feel comparatively satisfied. He had managed to set limits to the inevitable repression and thanks to him fewer than 8 per cent of the 5000 persons on whom the military extremists had set their sights, lost their political rights. But the main thing was that during this time his technocrat colleagues were able to draw up their plans for economic recovery and prepare their reforms in peace, and meanwhile to take a certain number of immediate steps, such as abolishing the subsidies paid on imports of wheat, petrol and newsprint, which had been achieved by means of a preferential rate of exchange.

As for Parliament, it came under a running fire of bills which had to be debated within the time-limits allowed by Institutional Act No. 1. The bills which were approved included the law relating to legislation and regulation of the right to strike,[7] various fiscal measures including one which abolished the freedom from income tax of writers, professors, judges and journalists, the code standardising the budgetary and accounting procedures of the Federation, of the states, of the Federal District and of the municipalities,[8] and also the new rules liberalising transfers of profits abroad.[9]

This latter law has been described as 'undoubtedly the most important single measure designed to restore the confidence of foreign investors'.[10] And yet all it did was to put into practice the recommendations made by the National Economic Council as long ago as

1962. The limit imposed on transfers of profits abroad was abolished, but a progressive tax was instituted in the event of more than 12 per cent of the initial capital plus reinvested profits on average over a period of three years being exported.

By the end of June it was evident that the economic recovery measures could not be put into operation within the period allowed to the Government by Institutional Act No. 1. On 17 July Parliament prolonged Castello Branco's mandate by an overwhelming majority[11] and he consequently remained as President until March 1967.

However, this was far from being a victory, as this extract from a handwritten note which he sent on 30 July to his son and his grandchildren shows with devastating clarity:

> This is not a letter, scarcely a word ... I am in fact the guardian of a bankruptcy in which the estate is in an unbelievable mess. It is a Herculean task. I am relying upon many people, on the patience of the nation and on the aspirations of a vast number of Brazilians. I do not allow myself to be deceived by misleading popularity. Always I endeavour to see things simply, even humbly. It appears that the Military place their trust in me, but there is no militarist policy.[12]

The election of the new president, which should have taken place in November 1965 was, *ipso facto,* adjourned for a year. At the same time the voting procedure was modified so that in October 1966 the successful candidate could be a serving soldier, and had to obtain an absolute majority of votes, not the simple majority which sufficed in elections before that time.

Carlos Lacerda, the only nationally known candidate after his rival Kubitschek had been eliminated, already saw himself in his mind's eye as the country's leader, and he reacted violently. He issued numerous ill-judged statements, as insulting as those that he let fall concerning General de Gaulle while touring Europe and the United States, whence he returned in haste as soon as he learnt of the bill submitted to Parliament.

And so in less than five months the Army had finally over-stepped the bounds of its traditional role as moderator and become fully involved in the political life of the country, not only at the level of the generals but also by the active participation of the whole of the officer corps.

8 Castello Branco's Tactics

From then onwards, Castello Branco took a definite tactical line. Whenever he considered it absolutely necessary he yielded to the demands of the hard liners but he immediately riposted by going in for reforms in other areas, especially in the economic or social field. In this way he sought to induce the survivors of the old political system to support his government willy-nilly, since it alone could save them from the completely frustrating régime which was the aim of the hard liners.

Hence the next few months witnessed a series of revealing incidents, of which the case of the Governor of Goiás, Mauro Borges Texeira, was typical. Borges, a reserve colonel, sided with the Revolution and supported Castello Branco's candidature during the consultations which took place at Rio between the most influential governors just after the Revolution on 3 and 5 April.[1] But he was the son of Senator Pedro Ludovico Texeira, one of the pillars of the 'feather-bed' party, the P.S.D. (Partido Social Democrático), the largest party in the former Parliament. Not only that, but he had left-wing sympathies which he did not trouble to hide. He had supported the elevation of Goulart after the resignation of President Quadros,[2] he had visited the Soviet Union and he introduced reforms in governing the State of Gioás. This was more than enough to cause the hard-line officers to accuse him of Communism or even subversion.

There had already been an opening skirmish in May 1964 when Borges had been compelled to accept the forced resignation of three of his colleagues, whose political rights were suspended to boot. Nevertheless, Borges was still in charge of his State which is of considerable strategic importance since the Federal District of Brasilia forms an enclave within it. Those who favoured the hard line could not stomach such a situation and, with the help of the political machine of the U.D.N. (União Democrática Nacional) which was seeking to enlarge its territory, they stepped up the pace of the I.P.M. which was currently being carried out.

General Kruel from Rio Grande do Sul, later to become Head of the Federal Public Security Department, took charge of the inquiries and in November he summoned Borges to appear as a witness. The press, which was still completely free, took up Borges' cause wholeheartedly. They criticised the accusations that were levelled and questioned the value of the admissions made by Pawel Gutko, a mentally unstable person, from whom they had probably been extorted by torture.[3] Borges appealed to the Supreme Court to give him the benefit of the Habeas Corpus Law and the Court, displaying their independence, granted the request[4] on 23 November, notwithstanding the hints dropped by Castello Branco who knew that the Military would not tolerate a source of active opposition.

Three days later on 26 November, the President stripped Borges of his powers and issued a decree notifying the intervention of the Federal Government in the matter. He placed one of his most capable assistants, Colonel Carlos de Meira Mattos, in charge of the State of Goiás.

The Chamber of Deputies approved Castello Branco's decision by 192 votes to 140, contrary to the recommendation of the *rapporteur* of the competent committee. This vote showed that since Kubitschek had been ousted, the leaders of the P.S.D. had understood that the executive would not allow itself to be diverted from its aims, and they therefore sacrificed Borges.

Under the Constitution, Meira Mattos had sixty days in which to resolve the crisis. This former lecturer on tactics then gave a brilliant demonstration of his skill. He countered the majority P.S.D.–P.T.B. candidate for the Legislative Assembly of Goiás, which, like the leaders of the coalition, had resigned itself to dropping Borges, by nominating as a candidate a hard-line colonel whom he knew would be unacceptable. Then when, as he expected, the other side in consequence took up the cudgels, he called in the President who made a concession by proposing the name of a trusted friend, Marshal Emílio Rodrigues Ribas Junior. The Legislative Assembly thought it had gained a major victory and although it refused to ratify the accusations of the I.P.M. against Borges, it declared the governorship vacant for reasons of necessity and on 8 January 1965 elected Castello Branco's candidate.

This typically Brazilian solution had something in it for everyone. Borges had lost his governorship but he had kept his civil rights. Moreover, he came out of the affair as a national hero of the people thus gaining political capital which could be useful to him in the future. The P.S.D.–P.T.B. coalition had not lost face, for it had given up the struggle only because the national rulers were implacable and to avoid permanent intervention by the Federal Government. As for the U.D.N. it had succeeded in breaking the hold of the Goiás P.S.D.–P.T.B. coalition machine several months before the gubernatorial elections, which were due to take place in October. And whereas Castello Branco had not pulled in his horns in face of the left, none the less this gesture of ideological firmness approved by the hard liners had not prevented him from having the candidate of his choice appointed.[5]

After having at least partially satisfied the demands of the hardline officers in this way, and knowing that for the moment at any rate he could bank on the rediscovered unity of the armed forces, the President took advantage of the favourable chance to settle an apparently insoluble problem, that of the Fleet Air Arm, which had been a bone of contention between the Navy and the Air Force ever since the time of President Kubitschek.

At that time Brazil possessed an aircraft carrier, the *Minas-Gerais*, so named in honour of the state from which the President came, and there was a dispute as to whether the aircraft and their pilots should come under the Navy or the Air Force. The dispute had reached such proportions that the expensive ship, immobilised in the roadstead of Rio de Janeiro, had been nicknamed by the *carioca* urchins:[6] 'Le Bel Antonio', meaning the powerless one.

In the new government two air ministers in succession had resigned rather than accept a compromise solution, and to replace them Castello Branco called in Marshal Eduardo Gomes, a former *tenente* and an unsuccessful candidate in the presidential elections of 1945 and 1950,[7] whose prestige and authority were unassailable. On 26 January, eighteen hours after re-establishing order in Goiás, the President imposed his decision by decree: the Navy was to give up its aircraft to the Air Force and would receive in exchange the Air Force's anti-submarine helicopters. At last the *Minas-Gerais* could become operational, but considerable sections of both arms were dissatisfied and went to swell the ranks of those opposed to Castello Branco.

9 Links with the Outside World

While these confrontations were taking place, the new government had to address itself to the problems which awaited it in the international field. Fortunately the diplomatic front was comparatively quiet, as the United States had decided to recognise the new régime with an alacrity which is rare in diplomatic usage. As early as 2 April, President Johnson had cabled his 'warmest good wishes'. This rapid recognition, which was due to the efforts of the American Ambassador in Rio, Professor Lincoln Gordon, started the rumour that the march of the soldiers in Brazil 'had been organised and directed by North American imperialism, and that it had been carried out with the support of President Johnson, the managers of the International Monetary Fund, the authors of the programme of the Alliance for Progress, the leaders in the Pentagon, the F.B.I. and C.I.A.'[1] No credible support has ever been adduced for this interpretation, and it would now appear to be demonstrated by serious studies that no direct intervention by the United States occurred.[2]

It was in fact entirely in accordance with the line of conduct marked out by the Superior War College that the régime altered the foreign policy of the country and brought it firmly into the Western camp, as was shown by the breaking off of diplomatic relations with Cuba on 13 May 1964, the campaign for the creation of an Inter-American Peace Force,[3] and international intervention in the Dominican Republic in 1965, for which Brazil furnished the strongest South American contingent.[4] In the words of President Castello Branco, yesterday's neutralism, which was due to 'emotional immaturity' and 'running away from the realities of international life' was replaced by a 'fundamental choice issuing from cultural and political fidelity to the Western democratic system'. Put positively, 'the maintenance of independence presupposes acceptance of some degree of interdependence in the military, economic or political spheres' because 'in very many instances Brazil's interests run parallel to those of Latin America, the American continent and the Western community'.[5] But financially the situation was critical. Brazil owed more than $4000 million[6] covering loans and the financing of the State deficit. Repayments and interest due in 1964 and 1965 amounted to $1800 million,[7] which represented between 46·4 per cent and 54·1 per cent of all receipts from exports likely to come in during those two years.[8]

Unable to service its debt, the country was compelled either to obtain foreign aid or to declare a unilateral moratorium, and this was discussed many times during the last months of the Goulart Government. This being so, it is not surprising that high priority was given to returning to a measure of financial orthodoxy which was called for by the country's foreign creditors. Both the Finance Minister, who had been a vice-governor of the International Monetary Fund, and Roberto Campos, who, as Ambassador to Washington, had taken part in March 1963 in the desperate negotiations of Goulart's Chief of the Treasury, Francisco Clementino San Thiago Dantas, knew very well the specific conditions that would be laid down by the American Government, the I.M.F. and the World Bank in this respect.[9]

The serious way in which the new régime tackled this task paid off, and servicing of the foreign debt was rephased. Following the visit by a mission of twenty experts sent by the World Bank at the end of 1964 to study the basis for integrated development on the spot, international aid picked up again.[10] More and more private investment was coming in, since the guarantee agreement between Brazil and the United States was signed in February 1965, increasing from $28 million in 1964 to $70 million in 1965.[11]

10 Campos' Economic Plan (P.A.E.G.)

Castello Branco entrusted two distinguished experts with the formulation and execution of the economic policy which he proposed to adopt. These were Professor Octavio Gouvêa de Bulhões,[1] whom he appointed Minister of Finance, and Professor Roberto de Oliveira Campos, former Ambassador to Washington, whom he placed in charge of an extraordinary new ministry known as the Ministry of Economic Planning and Coordination.[2]

Campos, who had been educated by the Jesuits and thereafter trained in the United States, later summed up the framework for his action as he saw it, in these lapidary words: 'The Revolution of 1964 was a harsh call to reality, an attempt to replace passion by reason in the management of economic affairs.'[3]

He considered that those events had delivered a mortal blow 'to three cherished myths of the populist illusion':

(a) sustained development can be reconciled with galloping inflation;
(b) real wages can be increased at will by the Government independently of any increase in productivity;
(c) a nationalist policy can be followed, irrespective of the economic and social constraints of the country.

These mistakes of the old order had created several fundamental distortions, which had caused the 'stagflation' prevalent in Brazil when the Revolution took place. Some of the distortions are as follows.

With regard to 'conjunctural distortions', inflation was raging at the rate of 25 per cent for the first quarter of 1964, a rate which by geometrical progression would have given 144 per cent for the year; some prices were artificially frozen for reasons of social policy (corn, milk, petrol, rents, newsprint, public utility services, etc.); paternalism in the field of wages had created a privileged group among trade unionists.

Structurally, agriculture was neglected and the system for distributing agricultural products inadequate; industrialisation was unbalanced, concentrating on import substitution, neglecting exports and relying on advanced techniques but requiring but little labour; there was under-investment in the material and human infrastructure (education, dwellings, etc.).

Institutionally, there was a lack of bodies capable of formulating and executing a financial policy (it was not until 1965 that the Central Bank of Brazil was set up) and the absence of an organised financial market.

Starting from these premises – which are almost the same as the diagnosis made by Celso Furtado in 1962[4] – Campos, after three months of work, submitted to Congress on 14 August a recovery plan which was published in November 1964 under the title 'Economic Action Plan of the Government, 1964–1966, P.A.E.G.'.

It should be noted that notwithstanding its name, the P.A.E.G. had more to do with diagnosis and statements of general policy than with the detailed plan of action. Roberto Campos defined it as follows:

> Simply a programme of co-ordinated government activity in the economic sphere. The overall quantitative data are used purely indicatively. The object of this effort is to formulate a strategy of development and an action programme for the next two years during which the foundations of a better articulated and longer term planning system will be laid.[5]

Bearing in mind that the ship was leaking, and in view of the exiguity of the available data base, Campos could not do more. Faced with the pressing problems of the country's life, he took action even as he drew up plans. In any event he could not allow himself to become the prisoner of an excessively rigid framework.

When the P.A.E.G. was published the Government, which had been in power for eight months, had already taken a large number of tactical steps, some of which were termed emergency and others long-term measures, which had been made known to the public and were presumed to be justifiable as fitting in with the principles that had been announced.

Roberto Campos' strategy was to give absolute priority to the fight against inflation, while endeavouring to stimulate economic growth.[6] With this in view, he opted for a 'gradual-rapid' approach and not for a radical programme.[7] This stand was courageous in so far as it ran counter not only to the views of many economists in Latin America who regarded inflation as the necessary stimulus for the development of their continent, but also to those experts of the International Monetary Organisations (and of the representatives of the governments who were Brazil's creditors) who saw an almost mystic virtue in an immediate return to monetary stability.

The P.A.E.G., which had in the main a traditional approach, isolated inflation as the main cause of the economic stagnation which prevailed, and interpreted this phenomenon as the result of an unbalanced budget, caused by the fact that the Government was injecting into the economy a volume of financial instruments greater than the volume it was withdrawing, thus causing the budget to be constantly in deficit. This perpetual inflation of the volume of money caused permanent tension between employers and wage-earners who were fighting to get high nominal wages. So both prices and wages escalated, and this gave an upward thrust to monetary demand.

In as much as the authorities covered their budgetary deficit almost exclusively by the issue of liquidities, an imbalance between the existing global supply and demand was set up. In the short term, as global supply did not have the necessary elasticity to follow monetary demand, equilibrium could be restored only by a general rise in the level of prices. However, once the fresh balance is achieved, the purchasing power of that part of the population living on fixed wages appears to fall, and those affected therefore campaign for compensating increases. In so far as they are successful, which is always likely given the sentiments of populist régimes, production costs rise and businesses need more working capital. Consequently the productive sector of the economy begins to exert pressure on the financial system. Generally speaking the requested credits are granted on the assumption that the economy must not be allowed to run down, and this inflates the means of payment and the price level still further.

Since the mechanism is cumulative, as soon as the general level of prices rises, whether under his own steam or for outside reasons, the means of payment begin to expand faster, and these are the monetary bearers of inflation.

The five main objectives set forth by the P.A.E.G. are the corollaries of this diagnosis.

1. Gradually to reduce the rate of inflation so as to arrive at a tolerable situation, of the order of 10 per cent annually in 1966.
2. To increase the rate of growth of the economy up to the 6 or 7 per cent per annum achieved during previous years.

3. To smooth out the disparities between sectors of the economy and regions of the country[8] and also tensions due to social disequilibria, by improving living conditions.
4. To create through an intensive investment policy viable conditions of productive employment sufficient to absorb the increasing inflow of labour (1·1 million new jobs a year were needed).
5. To correct the tendency to balance of payment deficits.

At first sight these immediate objectives may appear modest, but it should not be forgotten that during the first quarter of 1964 inflation reached a staggering 25 per cent, that a number of corrective measures would have to be taken to eliminate the distortions due to the freezing of certain prices, and also that the population was growing at something like 3 per cent per annum!

But Campos and Bulhões had an ace that no minister in the recent past had held – the unconditional support of a completely disinterested president, uninterested in personal popularity almost to the point of masochism. Freed from the problems of power, for which Castello Branco would provide them with *ad hoc* solutions, authoritarian in the main, they could concentrate on their task without worrying about the moans of the various pressure groups which in Brazil as elsewhere have always known how to be very vocal, on the principle of the local proverb which says that 'if the baby doesn't cry he won't be fed'. Having determined their strategy, Campos and Bulhões tried to attain their goals by calling in a few well-chosen technocrats, acting in spite of an administrative machine of proven inefficacy.[9]

In general Campos followed a strategy of so proportioning his monetary and budgetary policy as to achieve internal and external equilibrium in a situation of demand–pull inflation. Certainly the plan recognised the existence of certain tensions which were due to costs (especially consequent upon the raising of nominal wages) but the therapy selected was basically monetary and budgetary in character.

A contraction in demand had to be induced in an endeavour to stabilise it at the level of the maximum capacity of supply, so as to maintain the system in equilibrium while securing full employment of the factors of production. In order to achieve this result, three policies had to be regulated and 'dosed' in a mutually compatible way, namely:

i. government credit policy;
ii. the policy of private sector credit;
iii. wages policy, piloted by the State with its compulsory minimum wage requirement.

The government credit policy was formulated in such a way as to minimise the inflationary impact of the budgetary deficit. Since it was impossible to reduce current expenses in the short term (in particular the salaries of civil servants and military personnel and of nationalised sector employees),[10] and since it was taken for granted that public investment could not be reduced without putting at risk economic growth, emphasis was placed on increasing receipts.

This was attempted in two ways: the fiscal system was rationalised and adjustable treasury bonds were floated to encourage savings despite the residual inflation, while at the same time efforts were made to curb state expenditure and to reduce the budgetary deficit by restoring the ability of government monopolies and nationalised or mixed-capital enterprises to become profitable, both by raising prices and by internal reorganisation.

Since it would take some time for these initiatives to bear fruit in the public sector, the budget would in fact be balanced at the expense of the private sector, which would transfer part of its income to the State, thus increasing to that extent its costs of production. The policy of private sector credit would be managed in such a way as to maintain the real liquidity level of the productive system without allowing the growth of the loans granted by the banking system to result in an unplanned increase of means of payment. A formula which took into account both the increase of prices and costs and of the growth of the physical volume of production, was perfected. However, given the random character of the available statistics in Brazil, instead of basing their calculation on the growth of gross national product at current prices, called for by the theory, the economic technocrats used as a standard the fluctuations in the total of the means of payment. But this method does not give results comparable with those of the first-mentioned unless it be assumed that the speed of circulation of money remains constant, which was not in fact the case. This gave rise to insurmountable problems in certain branches of industry.

Wages policy postulated maintenance of the workers' share in the net internal product (at factor cost).[11] For this purpose an annual readjustment formula was worked out, taking account both of the average increase in the cost of living during the preceding twenty-four months, of the expected inflationary residue for the following twelve months, and of the estimated increase in productivity[12] during the period. But in practice the last two parameters were systematically underestimated and until 1967 the workers' share in the net internal product was on a diminishing trend.

According to the P.A.E.G., the outcome of the concerted action of the Government on the three basic elements of its strategy should have been to give it control of the volume of money in circulation. The object was to hold the increase to ceilings of 70 per cent in 1964, 30 per cent in 1965 and 15 per cent in 1966. This objective was compatible with the hoped-for decrease in the rate of inflation which was supposed to fall to 25 per cent in 1965 and to 10 per cent in 1966, this being considered an acceptable level.[13]

Other measures were also drafted to accelerate economic growth:

intensification of public and private investment, bringing in foreign capital;

a systematic export policy;

a top-priority housing programme;

reform of the agricultural sector both in production and marketing;

concerted action on wages, rate of exchange and credits, with the object of discouraging the substitution of labour by automation (elimination of artificial distortions in factor costs).

Although the P.A.E.G. was optimistic to a fault as regards its main objectives, namely the fight against inflation and the rate of growth, nevertheless it did enable Brazil to make progress along the road of modernisation.

Roberto Campos himself implicitly endorses this observation when he writes:

Perhaps the major accomplishment of the P.A.E.G. lies not so much in the attainment of specific goals as in the major concentrated effort that was made in the direction of institutional reforms and modernisation. Those reforms were to be economic and social (fiscal, agrarian and housing) and instrumental (banking and administrative).[14]

The partial failure of the P.A.E.G. was due partly to its intrinsic weaknesses which stemmed from its lack of adaptation to Brazilian realities, and partly to unforeseen events.

First it is important to note that the success of the plan adopted by the P.A.E.G. to combat inflation entailed the rapid application of monitoring indicators, which were theoretically possible but nonexistent in practice. Since the sources of inflation were defined as the propensity of government to live beyond its means and the tendency for the total income of the workers to exceed the contribution made by this factor in the formation of the national product, corrective action had to be directed to these two areas. The latter was particularly important because apart from the social repercussions of any interference with wages, the marginal propensity of wage earners to consume – especially in the lower strata – is a form of unity. Consequently any fluctuation in this area is reflected almost one to one on the market and errors of the order of a few per cent have effects of some magnitude. This is what happened in Brazil where, between 1964 and 1967, global demand was contracted beyond the point of equilibrium.

In order to eliminate its budgetary deficit, the State appropriated part of the income of the private sector by rationalising its control over rates and taxes, by increasing the tax burden, by readjusting the prices for the goods and services it supplied, and by modifying the parity of the cruzeiro.[15] These fresh burdens should have been held to a total within the capacity of the private sector to transfer. However, since they were arrived at by reference to the size of the budgetary deficit that had to be met, this limit was passed too quickly, causing costs to increase with immediate effect on prices.

The increase in prices accentuated the imbalance between supply and demand, which itself had been contracted too suddenly. Thus in 1965, for want of accurate and rapidly available indicators, the economic recession took hold before the authorities had time to act and without causing any substantial decrease in the rate of inflation.

Three causes for this latter phenomenon can be discerned. First there was the excessive increase in the monetary circulation. The P.A.E.G. foresaw a quantified progression of bond issues and credit, but this was greatly exceeded. For one thing, this objective was based on the hypothesis that the speed of circulation of money would remain constant whereas in fact it increased between 1964 and 1966, and inflation could not be held in check. Faced with a private sector threatened with financial strangulation, the authorities found themselves compelled to put the brake on the process of restoring equilibrium, by supporting internal demand with a liberal credit policy. Furthermore, the policy of encouraging exports, the contraction of imports due to the crisis and the inflow of foreign money resulted in the accumulation of large credit balances in the balance of payments, which in turn compelled the Government to make issues beyond the planned level.

Secondly, the trend towards increasing costs mentioned earlier was aggravated still further by the increasing rates of interest charged in the financial system, brought about by the favourable terms on which new government issues were launched.

Thirdly, as the market had contracted, propensity to invest in the private sector diminished. In fact in 1965-6 most industries had some unused productive capacity, and in view of the Government's wages policy, prospects of increased demand in the short term were not good.

The internal contradictions between the strategy adopted and the means available to monitor its progress, as we have shown, do not detract from the basic characteristic of P.A.E.G. which was 'a change in the view of the authorities as regards the problem of inflation. For the first time, this was attacked in a co-ordinated and incisive way'.[16] Nevertheless, this thumbnail analysis of the main lines of the theoretical foundations upon which the economic policy of the first revolutionary government was based will give some idea of the difficulties and the opposition which it was to encounter at all levels.

11 The P.A.E.G. in Action

The arguments about the P.A.E.G. began even before August, and numerous criticisms were voiced. The attitude of the nationalist and left-of-centre groups who were opposed to this endeavour to streamline Brazilian capitalism and make it internationally outward looking, is understandable. Less so is that of the industrialists and coffee producers and merchants, who were frightened off by the fresh taxes and the restrictions on credit. By the end of 1964, the economic crisis which was appearing on the horizon perturbed some leaders in the business world, and their complaints were added to the political and military tension.

Imperturbable and convinced that the measures he had taken were right, Castello Branco did nothing to justify or explain the reasons for the choices he had made, and the gap between his government and the people grew wider and wider.

Roberto Campos,[1] who was virtually Prime Minister, later defined his strategy as 'the gradual transition from the objective of warding off catastrophe to the objective of growth by applying a "creative orthodoxy" '.[2] As regards the fight against inflation which for him was the most important thing, in addition to a number of subsidiary actions, he had a vote taken on the law[3] which revived the concept of monetary correction on the basis of coefficients established quarterly by the National Economic Council[4] in accordance with predetermined criteria. This was done on 17 July 1964, the day on which Castello Branco's mandate was prolonged. With this law, savings, 'the foundation of current production and the sine qua non of new investments'[5] once more became worth while! The law, which initially applied to the capital market, to taxation and to measures designed to stimulate production, was the keystone of the technique designed to eliminate the distortions caused by inflation, which were paralysing the industrial sector.

Those who lived through the period would agree that the introduction of monetary correction represented a complete revolution in thought and action after years of galloping inflation, during which those in business had learnt one basic rule about money that is steadily losing its value: get into debt at once, because tomorrow when you have to repay, your debt will cost you less than it does today.[6] The provisions of the law were as follows:

(a) The State would issue national treasury readjustable bonds, Obrigações Reajustaveis do Tesouro Nacional (O.R.T.N.). Whereas inflation had practically snuffed out the demand for government securities (which found no takers except by way of compulsory tax supplements or by the mandatory investment of bank funds with the monetary authority), the issue of O.R.T.N.s was a definite success with the public, and enabled the Government's deficit to be financed without resort to the printing of bank-notes.[7]

(b) The automatic correction of fiscal debts. This put an end to one of the paradoxes of Brazilian tax law. For up to that time bad payers who used every legal means to put off paying their taxes made a profit even if in the end they lost their case in the courts; because when at last they paid the nominal amount due, they paid it in money that had depreciated very considerably!

(c) The monetary correction of fixed business assets, which became mandatory whereas under the previous law it had only been optional. The accounting gain thus shown was subject to a tax of 5 per cent.[8] Nevertheless the authorities, knowing that they were in fact not taxing a real profit but a piece of book-keeping (which does not produce any new wealth) abolished this tax in January 1967 by Law 4506 which was passed in November 1964 (in the intervening period, no choice was left to industry but to consider payment of this unfair tax as a contribution to the national recovery effort).

(d) Depreciation rates, which until then had been based on historic cost, were thenceforth calculated on current values (in stages until 1966 and wholly from 1967 onwards).

(e) A new adjustment was inaugurated, that of circulating capital (*manutenção do capital de giro proprio*) which enabled monetary correction to be applied to the circulating assets of businesses.[9] Thus was a vicious circle broken: for the tax collector, raising taxes on notional profits arising from monetary depreciation[10] had become a principal means by which businesses were losing their capital. And in order to protect their financial substance, they had worked out a whole battery of more or less ingenious self-defence measures, aimed at evading the tax by fraudulently swelling their overheads. This may have resulted in equilibrium being more or less maintained, but the procedure was unhealthy from the point of view of both productivity and ethics.

(f) Monetary correction could also be applied to the value of buildings. In the event of a sale, the gains tax (*lucro-imobiliario*) was no longer levied on the difference between historic cost and the price paid, but on the actual gain after up-dating the cost. This measure helped to reduce the number of sales contracts signed at doctored prices to avoid arbitrary imposition of the tax.

The introduction of monetary correction was further developed during the next few years, but even in 1964 two other important laws made significant use of this instrument. The first[11] set up a 'building bank' by founding the National Housing Bank (Banco Nacional de Habitação, B.N.H.) which was to play an essential part in the building industry; it also authorised the setting up of building credit societies which could issue building letters of credit subject to monetary correction (as were all loans under the system).

The second of these laws[12] instituted the indexing of rents while at the same time laying down differential correction criteria so as to enable the lag in the prices of old rental agreements to be gradually made up. For reasons of social equity, no readjustment could be made earlier than sixty days after each increase in the compulsory minimum wage.

Thanks to these measures, savings were once more channelled into civil construction, thereby making a start on solving the problem of housing and of giving work to unskilled labourers. But legislative activity in matters affecting the economy did not stop there. A law for reforming the banking system[13] was passed and it served as the basis for a law which was passed the following year[14] laying down the structure for the capital market, and also for the decree-laws[15] whereby fiscal advantages were given to taxpayers who agreed to invest in the under-developed parts of the country.

Another problem which Roberto Campos had to tackle was the inadequacy of public utility services, which did not have the financial means to meet the growing needs. Indeed, their prices were ridiculously low, and the companies carrying out these tasks as concessionnaires were unable to finance the new investment that would have been necessary. However, the law of 1958 gave them the right to calculate their earnings, which were limited to 10 per cent of invested capital, on the basis of an up-to-date valuation of their fixed assets. But past governments, in order to gain cheap popularity with the masses, had refused to apply these provisions and compelled them to work on the basis of historic costs.[16] This *de facto* situation, together with the fear of expropriation under the Goulart régime, amply explains why much of the equipment was so ancient.

In November, Decrees No. 54936-8 reaffirmed the provisions of the law of 1958 and provided a way out of the impasse, because they were applied both to concessions let by the Federal Government and also to those let by individual states.

The combined effect of these so-called corrective inflation measures coming into effect simultaneously was a sharp increase in the cost of living. And now that the cost of living had increased, what would happen to wages? Would they too be readjusted in accordance with monetary correction indices? On this matter Roberto Campos made a delicate choice, which was needed if the various elements of his anti-inflation strategy were to remain compatible. Bearing in mind that the compulsory minimum wage had been doubled by the former Government in February 1964 and that he had had to agree to raise military pay in April and then the pay of civil servants in June (which cost the Treasury something like 600 million new cruzeiros) he decided to let things stay as they were.[17] He also laid down the procedure for future adjustments. They were to be calculated by reference to the average real purchasing power during the preceding twenty-four months, and no longer in relation to the peak rate.

In practice, from 1964 to 1967 at all events, wages, except those of specialists in demand by industry, rose more slowly than the cost of living. Unskilled workers earning the minimum wage were the most affected and they found little comfort in knowing that a law was passed slapping an additional 7 per cent tax on dividends distributed to shareholders.[18] Although they had no means of expressing it, their disenchantment was added to the disgruntlement of other sectors mentioned above.

12 The AMFORP Affair

It was against this background that the announcement that the Government was going to buy back the largest public utility company under foreign ownership, AMFORP (American and Foreign Power

Utility Company), set political controversy going again. This was no new departure. The project had been the subject of heated discussions since 1962, and in fact in April 1963 an agreement had been signed and announced by Goulart's Finance Minister, San Thiago Dantas. According to this agreement, the ten subsidiaries of AMFORP were to be handed over to the Brazilian authorities against a payment of $135 million, a quarter of which was to be paid in cash and the balance invested locally in enterprises other than public utilities.

The radical left, led by the President's brother-in-law, Leonel Brizola, and the nationalist right wing under the banner of Carlos Lacerda, had united to attack the proposed repurchase even at the time because they said that the price proposed for this 'heap of junk' was exorbitant, and the contract had not been ratified. This sudden turnabout had aroused undisguised irritation in the United States, and AMFORP was one of the main bones of contention between the United States and Brazil.

In October 1964 Parliament passed a motion for carrying through the purchase on procedures based on those contained in the 1963 agreement. In the prevailing circumstances, this had a considerable psychological impact and was taken to be 'another important step indicating Brazil's serious intent to re-establish good international economic relations'.[1]

But Carlos Lacerda, still embittered by the events of July, did not take it that way. He considered that the purchase should not have been subject to negotiation between governments but decided simply by a judicial procedure in Brazil, and he started a campaign against the 'ideological neo-colonialism' of this 'scandalous' measure taken by a government which in his opinion was too ready to follow the directives of international technocrats – 'these doctors who give their treatment by correspondence'.

Either for reasons of friendship or of prudence (both hypotheses have been advanced) Castello Branco did not react at once. Lacerda was in fact supported by many officers, especially the younger hard liners who, fired with enthusiasm for what he had done as Governor of Guanabara, saw in this 'president-eater' a man of action, an authentic nationalist and a crusader for anti-Communism; moreover he had a firm electoral base among the civilian population. Lacerda toured the country, putting his case with intensified vigour[2] and campaigning to obtain the official nomination of his party, the U.D.N. (which had become the fulcrum of the revolution in Parliament), at the national convention which was due to take place on 8 November at São Paulo in preparation for the presidential elections of 1966.

His efforts were crowned with success and he was nominated by

309 votes out of 318. In his speech of thanks he said to the delegates: 'The Revolution has a government which needs us and we will not refuse them our aid. It will have a candidate for the presidency and this candidate will be the one whom you have just chosen.' Castello Branco did not share this view but, anxious to avoid a break, he confined himself to saying that it was premature for anyone to throw his hat into the ring twenty months before the elections. He added that his Government had no intention of endorsing the nomination of the successor, and he concluded on a revealing note by emphasising that he was by no means certain that parties and candidates would withstand 'the sun and the dew of 1965'. Lacerda's oratorical effects were beginning to influence people, and in view of the magnitude of the repercussions of the Goiás affair, the President summoned the Governor on 3 December to define his position clearly vis-à-vis the régime. From then onwards Lacerda avoided direct attacks, but he continued to oppose Minister Roberto Campos through the writings of the journalists of the *Tribuna da Imprensa*, his old daily newspaper, as an 'agent of colonialism and the trusts'. His intemperate language and the violence of his attacks, which often bordered on mental instability, as well as his inordinate ambition, soon led to a decline in his popularity.

Writing about the AMFORP episode some years later in 1972 the aged Marshal Cordeiro de Farias, who was the founder of the Superior War College and Minister of the Interior[3] just after the Revolution, confirms our opinion in an article concerning the 150th anniversary of Brazilian independence:[4]

> The mass of the people, always influenced by newspapers which are entirely free, does not have the background to judge certain decisions taken by the government.
>
> I recall for example what President Castello Branco had to put up with when he repurchased the main part of this organisation of the electrical energy sector for a price which many people thought was excessive and damaging to Brazil. In terms of his philosophy of government, Castello had decided to find a solution to a problem that had become a political one, being convinced that this was necessary to safeguard the future. The result is that eight years after the Revolution our energy potential, if my memory is correct, has more than tripled.[5] Further developments are planned and finance for them is assured.

13 Rational Exploitation of the Land and of Minerals

Having dealt with the problem of AMFORP which then became the nucleus of a new nationalised company, Eletrobrás, Castello Branco attacked the very foundations of the Brazilian oligarchy by getting to grips with another taboo, the agrarian problem. On 30 November, a few days after Mauro Borges had been stripped of his powers, he had the Statute of the Land[1] passed by Parliament.

This text defines agrarian reform as 'the complex of methods whose aim is to ensure better distribution of land – by modifying the organisation of its ownership and use – with the aim of fulfilling the requirements of social justice and of increasing productivity'.[2] This law went beyond the demagogic slogans that had been constantly rehashed during the preceding years, and contained a set of co-ordinated measures calculated gradually to integrate the rural masses into the money economy. This involved in 1964 about 40 million people, nearly 54 per cent of the whole population.

The fundamental obstacle in the way of any previous attempt at reform on a large scale was paragraph 16 of Article 141 of the Constitution of 1946, which required that in the event of expropriation, compensation must be paid beforehand in cash. This encumbrance was removed by Constitutional Amendment No. 10 which was voted on 9 November 1964, stipulating that compensation would be paid by means of readjustable state bonds.

Paradoxically, in March 1963 under a so-called left-wing régime a coalition of U.D.N. and P.S.D. members of parliament known as 'Ação Democrática Parlamentar', most of whom were still members in November 1964, had torpedoed a similar project. The text, which was unambiguous, satisfied neither the liberals, who thought it didn't go far enough, nor the conservatives, who thought it was too far-reaching and authoritarian. There may indeed be differences of opinion as to its doctrine, but undeniably it abolishes the main institutional obstacles and creates the necessary instruments for its application provided it is supported by a political will, which a legislator cannot of himself create.

The expropriation 'for reasons of social interest' foreseen by the law in priority regions took into account the dual nature of the agrarian structure of the country. For the distribution curve of land ownership in country areas was strongly asymmetrical. At one extreme, 2·8 per cent of the holdings registered in the cadastre covered 50 per cent of the area in private ownership whereas at the other extreme 35·9 per cent of the total number of properties make up only 1·81 per cent of the area recorded.[3]

Thus ultra-small holdings, of which there were 1,200,000, were just as real a phenomenon as the 60,000 or so large-scale holdings,[4] 27 of which measure over 247,000 acres each. Because of this disparity, the Statute of the Land approached reform as an integrated long-term process, with a very flexible concept of the 'family holding' as starting point. The area of such a holding was calculated by reference to the variable rural module, a concept which was defined by six parameters which change according to the type of agriculture, its geographical situation in relation to the nearest urban centre, the type of soil and the agricultural use to which the ground was put.

The spearhead of the system was a new rural land tax which might be progressive or regressive in its effects. It was calculated according to coefficients which took into account the area of the property, its location, its degree of exploitation with respect to the modular norm, and enabled production on holdings where the land was worked efficiently to be stimulated while not penalising those which were located a long way from marketing areas, though speculation was penalised.

The Federal State collected the tax (though this would normally be done by the municipalities) and this largely eliminated local political influences. Two *ad hoc* bodies were set up for applying the law, the Brazilian Institute of Agrarian Reform (Instituto Brasiliero de Reforma Agraria, I.B.R.A.) and the National Agricultural Development Institute (Instituto Nacional do Desenvolvimento Agrario, I.N.D.A.). The legislators wanted to create a geographical division of work between the two bodies, I.B.R.A. being responsible for the reform of land holdings in what are known as the priority zones, while I.N.D.A. was to deal with 'colonisation' and agricultural development in the rest of the country. But this duality led to operational problems, because within an overall concept it is impossible in practice to separate land redistribution from questions concerning development. Furthermore, the demographic pressure which is experienced on the sub-divided holdings in the priority zones may require both some local amalgamation and the channelling of migratory currents towards the colonisation of non-priority regions.

The Statute of the Land, which resulted from the work of experts, was introduced more with long-term economic developments in view than as a means of bringing about social changes and immediate results, however desirable these might be. The nub of the analysis was the inefficiency that was found in the man/land relationship both in the *latifundia* and on the minuscule holdings. In the latter, there was an excess of men over land whereas in the former there was an excess of land over workers.

Emphasis was placed on increasing the agricultural resources of the country and on developing distribution networks suitable for the products involved. Existing bottlenecks had to be overcome by a better distribution of the factors of production. These measures entailed the modification of archaic patterns of land ownership, wherever changes were essential. Hence land redistribution was no longer just a panacea; ideology had given way to the economic choice. In practice, the Statute of the Land, although it has been still further developed by succeeding governments, will hardly show any visible results for many years to come.[5]

Profiting from other examples, I.B.R.A. and I.N.D.A. wished to avoid at all costs disturbing agricultural production, which in 1964 represented about 20 per cent of the gross domestic product in Brazil, so as to avoid the risk of being unable to satisfy the food needs of the towns. Before taking action, these agencies undertook studies in depth which included the creation in December 1965 of a rural cadastral survey containing detailed information on 3,400,000 holdings covering over 758 million acres.[6] This apparent absence of tangible action has left the impression that the agricultural sector, which is traditionally a source of discouragement to planners because effort expended on it does not show quick results, has remained the 'least popular child'[7] of the Revolution.

The objections of the structuralists to the Statute of the Land did not however make much impression on Castello Branco, since the solution of the case of the Governor of Goiás had resulted in his having the practically unanimous support of the Army. He took advantage of this circumstance to deflate an old populist myth, that of the control of mineral wealth.

On 23 December 1964, relying on a judgment given by the Supreme Court and with the help of the Senate, which now gave a literal interpretation to Article 6 of the Mining Code of 1940 which had been contested by the previous government, he issued a call to the private sector, inviting it to take an interest in the intensive exploitation of Brazil's subterranean riches. He also gave foreigners the right to acquire shares in Brazilian companies operating in this sector with the exception of the reserves of hydraulic power, the extraction of petroleum, coal and fissile material.

These fresh directives reversed a trend which went back as far as Vargas. After having explicitly declared that the Federal State would become responsible for new mining enterprises only if the private sector refused to do so, the Government declared the five following objectives to be basic and to have priority in national development.

1. The immediate and systematic exploitation of known reserves.
2. Intensified prospecting throughout the national territory.
3. Revision of the Mining Code.
4. Promotion of mineral production both for local processing and for export.
5. Aid to projects the execution of which would reduce or eliminate imports of mineral products.

This was a courageous decision in as much as for Brazilians the fear of foreigners getting a stranglehold on these raw materials might be described as a 'gut reaction' not susceptible to argument.[8]

It was useless to point out that Brazil covers more than half its requirements by imports, that nature has endowed the country very generously,[9] that this potential source of foreign exchange would not be transformed into wealth unless it could be exploited, or that by so doing development could be accelerated; nothing doing there. The picture of President Vargas, with crude oil dripping from his hand outstretched to the people, saying 'O petroleo é nosso' (The oil belongs to us) precluded reasoned argument and these primary products continued to be imported to the value of about $450 million per annum.

But although Castello Branco's decision went against the grain of popular feeling, it was soon taken up by industry. The fiscal conditions designed to get the process going and the techniques subsequently established as part of an overall ten-year plan, bore fruit. Prospecting was intensified under the aegis of a mixed economy company, the Mineral Resources Research Company (Companhia de Pesquisa de Recursos Minerais, C.P.R.M.). In 1970 28 million tons of iron ore were exported compared with 9.7 million in 1964, and exports of manganese grew to 1.6 million tons compared with 832,000 tons in 1964, and these exports resulted in earnings approximating $250 million.[10] The largest iron-ore producer, the Companhia Vale do Rio Doce, a State-controlled company, signed medium- and long-term contracts with its customers in Europe, Japan and the United States in 1970 for delivery of 324 million tons of crude ore and 'pellets' to a value of $2600 million. In order to maintain this programme, Brazil was due to double its exports of ore in 1973 and for this purpose investments of the order of $500 million were planned.[11] Thus was developed an important source of foreign exchange which helped to release Brazil from its dependence on coffee.

This contribution to the country's economy was carried out without the fears of the hard-line nationalists being realised.

Compared with the total investment, of the order of $1200 million made in this sector in 1969, only 100 million or 8 per cent was owned by foreigners.[12]

14 An Appeal for Dialogue

Right at the beginning of 1965, Castello Branco was in a relatively strong position. Nevertheless, in spite of the apathy of public opinion, there was unrest in some sectors. And indeed the rate at which the Government was issuing laws and decrees was certainly bewildering. Some 250 laws came into force in 239 days, to say nothing of the decrees and other decisions. Criticism arose against 'the disorderly proliferation of bills which both by their number and by the intrinsic errors which they contain leave the national economy in a state of constant uncertainty'.[1]

The President was able to rally the hard liners to him, but in view of the fundamental reform of the political system which he planned to bring about, he felt a need to reinforce his fulcrum in Parliament. He chose the party of Carlos Lacerda, 'the main pillar of the Revolution' and contrived to have a good 'parliamentary revolutionary bloc'[2] created around this formation, which was also joined by part of the P.S.D.–P.T.B.[3] opposition, and which thus had control of the legislature. This manoeuvre ensured that Octavio Bilac Pinto, a guardian of the anti-Vargas tradition and President of the U.D.N. would be elected President, and made sure that the populist candidate M. Ranieri Mazzili,[4] who had occupied this high office for the last seven parliaments, would be defeated. With his majority assured, Castello Branco could then venture to take two steps along the road of democratisation. As a first step, he allowed the election of the mayor of São Paulo, the centre of the country's economy and 'the city which never stops'[5] to take place. This was the first time the people had voted since the Revolution, and those favoured the hard line made no secret of their disquiet at this decision by the President.

Paradoxically, the trial of strength went awry because the results, which were announced on 21 March, could be interpreted as a victory either for one side or the other. For Air Force general José Vicente de Faria Lima was one of the men who had supported the

Revolution, but he was also one of the old faithfuls of ex-President Jânio Quadros, whose civil rights had been suspended by the régime, and his whole campaign was waged under the sign of the broom which was the electoral emblem of the deposed President. Notwithstanding this ambiguous situation, Castello Branco put his trust in Faria Lima and was not disappointed. Thanks to his talent for work and his overflowing energy, the new mayor seemed to be everywhere at once in his city, and under his administration the infrastructure of São Paulo underwent the development of which it was greatly in need. The growing popularity of the 'Brigadier' was such that he could later be regarded as a potential candidate of the Castellist wing of the Army for the presidential elections of 1971, but his death on 4 September 1969 prevented this scheme from coming to fruition.

In the second place, Castello Branco set up the Consultative Planning Council or CONSPLAN (Conselho Consultivo do Planejamento), which reported directly to him, with Roberto Campos as executive secretary. This was the first official endeavour to obtain a wider exchange of views on the Government's economic policy, as the Council was authorised both to consider these matters and to make suggestions concerning them.

When the first meeting took place in March, Castello Branco took the trouble to introduce his policy personally, saying that his object was to win on five fronts consisting of the following.

The fatalism of consumers who, thinking that prices were bound to go on rising, no longer tried to haggle with their suppliers.

The indifference of producers towards problems of quality and price, because owing to the insatiable inflationary demands they were used to selling any old thing at any price, and therefore simply passed on any increased costs to the consumer.

The illusion of wage-earners who, led astray by promises of high wages, more than the economy could justify, gave fresh twists to the tragic prices spiral.

The frustration of savers who seeing their savings whittled away chose to spend their money immediately or tried to smuggle it abroad, whereas the country needed productive investments.

The irresponsibility of users of luxury products who by their conspicuous waste and frivolity increased the despair of the needy and displayed a degree of wealth incompatible with the feeling of social cohesion and the urgent necessity to concentrate available resources on development.

Strictly speaking the CONSPLAN was not a representative body.

All its members were appointed by the President either on his own initiative or from lists submitted by sectors concerned. Nevertheless, by its very composition it inevitably brought together divergent points of view, for there were four representatives from industry, four delegates from the trade unions, one member of the National Economic Council, four experts (two economists, a sociologist and an engineer) of whom two had to be university professors, three officials from economic planning bodies in the provincial states, regions and communes and one spokesman for the mass media.

The President's readiness to have free discussion was proved by his appointment of Professor Antonio Dias Leite, who was known both for his intellectual stature and for his opposition to the P.A.E.G.; this pillar of the positive left in search of a Brazilian project for development was to become Minister of Energy and Mines in 1969 in the Costa e Silva Government. A militant Catholic, he looked at events in Brazil in the perspective of the social doctrine of the church and wanted constructive discussion in which the largest possible number of trends and standpoints would be represented. The only ones he did not want were those who 'uncompromisingly maintained extreme points of view . . . and groups subject to external influence'.[6]

In his first speech to CONSPLAN Dias Leite himself said: 'Having been invited . . . I repeatedly told the President of the Republic and the Planning Minister that in line with my previously known views, I shall continue to differ from them concerning the very basis of the economic policy at present being followed.'[7]

15 Discussion about the P.A.E.G.

The first working session, held in April 1965, opened at a time when the depression which could be seen to be coming was worrying the ruling classes and when military order had just been disturbed for 48 hours by a mini guerilla uprising launched in the State of Rio Grande do Sul, incited by ex-President Goulart's brother-in-law, Leonel Brizola.[1]

And although the complete failure of this uprising reassured for the time being, the hard liners, haunted by subversion, the industrial crisis in São Paulo where unemployment had increased from 1 per cent in January to 9 per cent in March (and was to reach 13·5 per cent in June) led to the publication by the National Confederation of Industry, just before the meeting, of a document in which the P.A.E.G. was said to be responsible for the situation.

On the platform, Dias Leite did not mince his words. He considered that the course that had been chosen did not meet Brazil's real needs and might well lead the country into a situation of political, economic, and social stalemate. The P.A.E.G., which could not gain the support of the majority of the population, was inconsistent and its objectives were mutually incompatible, he said. Furthermore, it was imprudent because it relied on aid from outside which was largely dependent on political decisions outside the Government's control. He said that a substitute should be found for contributions from abroad by a forced increase in the propensity to save, an increase in the share of G.N.P. levied by the State, and an increase in the efficiency of the economic system. The keystone of the national development he favoured would be a 'nucleus of economic expansion' (transport, oil, electric energy, the steel and iron-ore industries) which, placed under State control, would inject dynamism into the economy. Conversely all the other sectors would be either given back or left to private initiative. Recalling the 'large and justified credit of confidence which was opened to the revolutionary government' Dias Leite gave voice to one fear – that of seeing the strategy of the P.A.E.G., which 'breaks with tradition by courageously repudiating very many ideas which are mistaken and not calculated to further the progress of the national economy, but which unfortunately also throws away some of the useful fruits of previous experience', become the policy of lost opportunities.[2] This discussion, of which a summary was published,[3] was favourably received by part of the middle classes. Taking the torch from the hands of Dias Leite from May onwards, in the National Economic Council (C.N.E.) the industrialist Fernando Gasparian called for a systematic re-evaluation of the objectives of the P.A.E.G.:

> Our council, he said, is nowadays regarded by the country as the body which sets the indices and the monetary correction tables... whereas the main task which was given to us by the federal Constitution is constantly to study the economic life of the nation with the object of suggesting to the competent authorities adequate standards of conduct... the C.N.E. should be the sounding-box of expert opinion in Brazil. I therefore propose that the Council declares itself to be in permanent session...[4]

Gasparian, who described himself as a 'nationalist in the true sense of the word',[5] and who thought that 'the Brazilian reality is more complex than one would imagine from reading the textbooks',[6] took up the preceding arguments and particularly emphasised the lack of statistical control data available to the Government for evaluating the results of its actions. However he backed up his own statements by using an avalanche of statistical data, which had as shaky a basis as those of Roberto Campos.

Public opinion was kept informed of these discussions by the press and television. In May, Carlos Lacerda joined the opposition in an inflammatory speech which was broadcast on television. Roberto Campos replied through the same medium and much was heard of 'demand–pull inflation' or 'cost–push inflation'.

Finally in July the National Economic Council approved the P.A.E.G., but the Government, aware that some of the remarks about it were well founded, changed the direction of its economic policy on several points. Some immediate measures, such as the reduction of indirect taxes on certain industrial products, were taken 'with the aim of accelerating growth', in the words of Roberto Campos. 'Anti-cycle action made necessary by your failure' replied Gasparian.[7] Whatever the truth, they helped to re-establish the psychological climate needed for an upswing, and thanks to the lift given by an excellent harvest, the crisis came to an end.

16 The Disunity of the Industrialists

The discussions about the P.A.E.G. showed the lack of cohesion among industrialists, who were deeply divided, and most of whom were content to leave things to the technocrats. This is one of the paradoxes of the Castello Branco régime; he wanted to provide for the development of the country within the capitalist framework, but yet did not take into account the interests of the owners of capital and heads of businesses.

The mixture of admiration, fear and unconscious envy of business heads which characterised the rulers of the country is partly explained by their provenance: soldiers and technocrats drawn from the middle-middle class. They admired the economic results that were achieved in unstable and often difficult conditions, but they were fearful of the possibilities open to some people with unreasonably large fortunes.

The unspoken reserve of the Government, not towards the private sector itself but towards some of its leaders, was well illustrated during the discussions about the P.A.E.G. The nationalist wing directed its attack against the financial policy of the Government, which they said would have the effect of allowing foreign firms, making use of their subsidiaries in Brazil, to buy up at rock-bottom prices Brazilian businesses strangled by the credit restrictions. From 1966 onwards this phenomenon, which was known as denationalisation, become the theme song of certain industrialists who considered that the aid facilities[1] introduced by the authorities were totally inadequate.

Roberto Campos protested vigorously and what he said is very revealing concerning the state of mind which prevailed in the technostructure:

> The present Government does not intend to set out to please everybody ... the problem facing us is not that of the immediate convenience of a few persons who may draw profits from inflation. The great challenge facing the Government, business leaders and wage earners is not to shore up this or that isolated firm but to recreate conditions in which free initiative can be economically and socially justifiable in our country.[2]

The Minister of Industry and Commerce, Paulo Egídio Martins, later confirmed the clinical approach of his colleague when he said: 'Some businesses have closed their doors, and others will soon be forced to cease trading. However, a case-by-case examination shows that most of these closures were due either to poor management or to the fact that they were not in line with the economic conditions which the country requires.'[3]

Roberto Campos was trying to effect the transition in Brazil from the stage of pioneer capitalism to that of mature capitalism, conscious of its obligations to society. This for instance was the spirit in which he launched the idea of a voluntary price-freeze, the procedure for which he felt would be likely to have a good psychological effect on public opinion. Known as Interministerial Instruction No. 71, this text gives credit and tax advantages to firms who agree to freeze their prices on their own initiative. Firms were free to join this movement or not; nevertheless there was a certain pressure from the Government in that State contracts would in future only be given to those who agreed to the new rule.[4]

The project was an interesting one, but it had at least two faults. First, consumers and wholesalers, under the illusion that stability had returned, immediately lost one of their motivations for making purchases. The stocks that had been warehoused for speculative purposes flooded on to the market, and the traders who had been hoarding them did not replace them, which led to underproduction in industry. Furthermore, the completely inadequate administrative apparatus was soon swamped by the justified requests for price increases which piled up on, over, under and around the desks of the unfortunate officials whose task it was to keep a check on the documentation. This led to tragi-comic shortages and gluts, and it was years before the system had been sufficiently run-in and simplified to be tolerable.

Instruction 71 is a typical example of the main drawback of planning 'from above'. It is conceived on a theoretical basis, without sufficient account being taken of the incredible drag of inertia which time-honoured habit gives to all bureaucracies whether government or private, and which seems to increase in inverse proportion to the skill of the bureaucrats. It is the everlasting hiatus between the ideal and its realisation.

In his criticisms of the P.A.E.G., Antonio Dias Leite gave considerable weight to this factor as exhibited in Brazilian private enterprises. He attacked the faulty appraisal by the authors of the P.A.E.G. 'both of the nature of the private sector and of its motivation and its real capabilities'.[5]

His analysis is worth repeating here:

> In Brazil, the dynamism characteristic of private initiative is still indissolubly linked to the spirit of adventure and the burning desire to make large profits which are the accompaniment of capitalism in its formative stage. It is completely unrealistic to try to dissociate at a stroke the good qualities and the faults of these businesses by means of laws and regulations which cannot be applied by the administrative machine of the country... any attempt to change this structure by force will defeat itself, as we have already seen in several instances.
>
> This does not mean that we have anything against the disciplinary measures taken by the Government against tax frauds or the favouritism of the official banks... but only that we do not believe in a policy of trying to modernise businesses by coercion with the two weapons of taxes and credits... we believe in the national private initiative sufficiently to favour an endeavour to employ to the full its potential energy by a policy guaranteeing it wide freedom of action, even at the cost of overcoming comparatively slowly the waste, inefficiency and abuses which we know it to exhibit. In our opinion, the task of rejuvenating the system, indispensable though it is, cannot be properly carried out unless it has the support of the employers and unless procedures are

instituted which facilitate modernisation. The disadvantages of this way of doing things will undoubtedly be fewer than those involved in an attempt to manage and monitor the private sector by a bureaucracy which is neither large enough nor good enough for the job.[6]

The prevailing attitude in some sectors of industry revealed by this controversy was to play a significant psychological role in the results of the P.A.E.G. and in the differences that were to arise between those who favoured industrialisation 'Brazilian style' and those who saw a value to society in applying the methods of management practised by foreign companies that were 'rich and experienced'[7] and who consequently were prepared to see those Brazilian companies that were generally patriarchal and incapable of withstanding competition, go to the wall.

This division among the employers ensured freedom of action for the technocrats and saved the Government from having to face a united front which might have been able to counterbalance the Government's military supporters.

17 'Castellism' between the Anvil and the Hammer

While Castello Branco was making it clear that he favoured democracy, the hard liners were harnessing a new war horse, by playing up the case of the former governor of Pernambuco, Miguel Arraes, whose powers had been taken from him at the time of the Revolution. This leftist leader, whose popularity had even been sufficient to disturb Goulart, had been in prison for more than a year and had been subject to many military police interrogations on the assumption that he had carried out 'subversive intrigues in collaboration with Communist elements from the north-east'.

On 20 April 1965 the Supreme Court decided to release him, a decision which was opposed by the responsible officers of the I.P.M. who had the Governor in custody. Determined to vindicate the authority of the law, Ribeiro da Costa, President of the Court, at once sent a scathing telegram to one of the leading hard liners,

General Edson de Figueiredo. On receiving it, Figueiredo protested that the Army had been insulted and Castello Branco had to enter the lists. He had Arraes freed but obtained a soothing letter from the federal judge to pour oil on the troubled waters.

But in view of the reactions, the President found it necessary to make the following declaration of faith:

> ... the home front of democracy should not be endangered by those who, instead of trying to fulfil their task whether extraordinary or ordinary, really want to transform themselves into a self-appointed power; this is quite unacceptable and would also hinder the fulfilment of the objectives of the Revolution. It matters little that their intentions may be patriotic for in reality, instead of helping to strengthen and consolidate the régime, they are helping to breach those sectors which should be the pillars of our democracy... all this happens because they have forgotten that the justice or the improvements they wish to see are indissolubly linked to a system, and never the result of isolated impulses which divide when they should unite. I am therefore bound to affirm that the Government conceives its duty to be never to agree to any short-circuiting of authority. Public opinion does not want agitation whether in the Government or on the part of those who cannot resign themselves to not holding the reins of power. The people want order based on law, they want elections, they want the Government to exercise its legitimate authority, they want to feel the support of the armed forces, united among themselves, for putting the country on its feet again... this is the path which the Government intends to tread inexorably in the fulfilment of its duty and the exercise of its prerogatives.[1]

Happily, the decision to take part in military action in the Dominican Republic as part of the Inter-American Peace Force which was placed under Brazilian command, provided a temporary safety valve for the aggressive mood of the hard liners and on 8 June 1965 Miguel Arraes was given a safe conduct to enable him to travel to exile in Algeria.[2] The President also decided to fire a warning shot across the bows by relieving two of the more outspoken colonels of their functions of I.P.M. and punishing them for indiscipline. These were Gerson de Pina, a professor at the Military College, and Osnelli Martinelli, one of the founders of the extreme right military movement LIDER (Radical Democratic League).[3] Having thus secured his rear, Castello Branco was able to direct his attention to Parliament and on 22 April he submitted the draft of a new electoral code which was intended to replace the one then in force, which had been on the statute book since 1950.

This was accompanied by an 'organic statute of the political parties'. The proposed electoral code[4] did not contain any startling novelties. Its 383 articles embodied improvements, supplements and clarifications and tried to leave nothing to chance. It contained two important changes. Parties were forbidden to make alliances in any election carried out by proportional representation, although these were permitted in case of an election by majority vote, and there were to be single lists of candidates for president and vice-president (as well as for the positions of governors and vice-governors, mayors and deputy-mayors). Hence the election of one candidate to office automatically entailed the election of his co-runner.

The 'statute of political parties' sought to limit the number of parties on the scene, in order to simplify the choice for the electors. It was also an endeavour to clean up political life by forbidding the parties to accept funds or assistance from public bodies and from any business trading for private profit. To counterbalance this, a 'special assistance fund for political parties' under the control of the electoral tribunal, was set up. A further provision was that candidates once elected were forbidden thenceforth to change their political allegiance during the lifetime of the parliament.

The conditions which were laid down for the existence of a party[5] in fact only allowed two parties to continue in being (the P.S.D. and U.D.N.) while it left three of them with the hope of surviving (P.T.B., P.S.P. and P.D.C.).

In June 1965 a bill setting out the conditions on which candidates for future elections would be eligible was also submitted to Parliament.[6] There was lively discussion and in all 819 amendments were proposed. The announcement of elections in October was taken as a sign that normalisation would soon return, and as a decisive step towards the *controlled* assimilation by the Revolution of such parts of the former political system as could be salvaged.

The reforms which were imposed were an essential element in Castello Branco's strategy, for it was unthinkable, in terms of the internal logic of the régime, to leave the field free to demagogues of the past in a confrontation which would affect half the country (including the city of Rio de Janeiro, capital of the State of Guanabara, and Minas Gerais) when the electors had not yet seen anything but the negative aspects of deflation. The President hoped by means of these new laws to be able to increase the participation of the people in the life of the nation while not incurring an excessive risk, because henceforth selection would be made at candidate level. He appears to have aimed at neutralising the old political system from the inside.

But as we have seen, the circumstances were scarcely favourable to a calculated risk which was both delicate and dangerous. Castello

Branco could not ignore this; but he was probably afraid of being rushed by those who saw no other way out but ideological 'hardening'. A few months later when inaugurating a course at the Superior War College he criticised such ideas in these terms:

> ... the so-called movements of national salvation lower the political government of the nation ... they nearly always talk about a 'symbolic man', a 'providential man', a 'strong man' ... who does nothing but weaken the institutions and even the country, using fear to transform the government of the nation into an instrument of oppression and violence.[7]

But this time the situation got beyond his control and his endeavour to establish a democratic middle term was destined to be crushed between the anvil of the political system and the hammer of the hard line.

18 The Political System Takes its Revenge, and is Dismantled

Under the provisions of the electoral law, governors were not allowed to canvass for a renewal of their mandate, and consequently the attention of observers was directed chiefly towards the three key centres of Guanabara (Carlos Lacerda), Minas Gerais (Magalhães Pinto) and Goiás.[1]

The campaign got into top gear at once. After various skirmishes, Carlos Lacerda had the candidature of his Education Secretary, Carlos Flexa Ribeiro, endorsed by his party, the U.D.N. He felt fairly sure that his protégé would win, even though he did not make much impression on the common people in Rio de Janeiro. The opposition, by contrast, was looking for a figure-head capable of attracting the electors to him. And so the P.T.B., the party of ex-President Goulart, named their former presidential candidate, Marshal Henrique Baptista Duffles Texeira Lott, who was 70 years old, as their first choice. Hélio de Almeida had been disqualified by the provisions of the new code, as he had been a minister in 1963.

But on 6 September 1965 the Superior Electoral Tribunal refused to register the candidate under the recently issued rules which required candidates to have lived in the district for a certain period, whereas Lott was domiciled some kilometres outside the city of Rio, in the neighbouring state.

The P.T.B. then agreed to join forces[2] with the P.S.D., Kubitschek's party, in supporting Ambassador Francisco Negrão de Lima, a pillar of the old régime whose debonair good looks concealed a remarkable strength and who had the advantage of being on friendly terms with Castello Branco.

In Minas Gerais, Magalhães Pinto persuaded the U.D.N. to adopt a man who was hardly known in politics, Roberto Resende. The P.S.D., whose first favourite, the extremely rich banker Sebastião Paes de Almeida, was declared unacceptable under the terms of the laws in force because of the 'bounties' distributed during his previous electoral campaigns, opted for another of Kubitschek's protégés, Israel Pinheiro.

In Goiás, where the elections bore the aspect of a settling of accounts through intermediaries between the supporters of the deposed Governor, Mauro Borges and the Federal Government, the U.D.N. chose Otávio Laje de Siqueiros, while the P.S.D. supported José Peixoto da Silveira.

On 3 October nearly 7 million people out of about 10 million registered electors, went to vote. When the votes were counted, five states[3] out of eleven had been won by the opposition. Of the three test locations only one, Goiás, chalked up a victory for the U.D.N.

Negrão de Lima won Guanabara in the first round by 582,000 votes, which was about 52 per cent of the total against 442,300 for Lacerda's candidate. In Minas Gerais, Israël Pinheiro pulled off the same success by 855,000 votes against 690,000 to his U.D.N. opponent, thus administering a severe blow to the position of Magalhães Pinto within the party. The next day Juscelino Kubitschek disembarked at Rio, having come from Paris where he had been living in exile for sixteen months. This sudden arrival roused the anger of the Military, who summoned him without delay to appear before the I.P.M. responsible for investigating subversive activities.

Public opinion interpreted the results as a comeback by the populist system, even though the President's immediate circle did not appear to regret the lesson that had been given to Carlos Lacerda and Magalhães Pinto for, as was to be demonstrated later, Negrão de Lima and Israel Pinheiro co-operated loyally with Castello Branco. But this finesse was lost on the officers, who saw their 'revolution' reeling under the blows of the myrmidons of the old system. This time, it was not only the hard liners who were outraged; there was a veritable groundswell of protest. Voices were raised loud and clear, and the whole Army demanded, if not federal intervention in the states which had gone over to the opposition then at least a firm refusal to swear in the elected candidates in December. The agitation which followed during the next twenty days sounded the death knell of any hopes for a return to civilian rule; the former political leaders had overshot the mark.

After 5 October a group was organised to overthrow the President, led by General Affonso Augusto de Albuquerque Lima, Chief of Staff of the First (Rio de Janeiro) Army.[4] Besides the hard-line colonels, including the spokesman for the extreme right LIDER organisation, Osnelli Martinelli, who had not forgiven the measures taken against him, some members of the Navy joined in the plot.[5]

It became necessary for the Minister of War himself to take the situation in hand. So he went to the Vila Militar, the headquarters of the First Infantry Division at Rio, where nearly all the officers of the First Army had met. There were discussions in which Costa e Silva took the part of the Government. After having contacted Castello Branco again he said, among other things: 'The army is not a political body but an organ of support and it will accept the decisions of the President concerning the investiture of the new governors.' But this instruction did not prevent him from solemnly affirming: 'Your leaders are as revolutionary as you and the President of the Republic has authorised me to confirm to you that any return to the old order is barred for ever.'[6] The net result was that a compromise had been reached which represented a distinct hardening of the régime.

The crisis was as short as it was serious, but it was to have a decisive effect on the future of Brazil. For it showed that Costa e Silva was not only the intermediary between Castellism and the hard line but, more importantly, that he was the only candidate for the succession to Castello Branco whom the Army would accept.

On 6 October, after a long meeting with his military ministers and his Minister of Justice, the President submitted a number of bills for approval by Parliament. They were designed to extend the powers of the executive, to strengthen the power of the Federal Government over the State governors, to extend the competence of the Military in cases of subversion and of national security, to lay down strict rules concerning freedom of speech and of action for persons who had been deprived of their civil rights, to abolish the privilege of special courts for persons who had occupied executive office in the State (such as the ex-Presidents Quadros and Kubitschek) and to ensure that the Government would control the Supreme Court by increasing the number of judges.[7]

A further fundamental alteration to the presidential election procedure was put forward whereby the President would be nominated by Parliament and no longer elected by universal direct suffrage. This was too much for the Minister of Justice, the liberal Milton Campos,[8] who handed in his resignation the same day.

On 8 October Carlos Lacerda, still under the influence of certain hard liners who had not agreed to the Vila Militar compromise, broke with Castello Branco, and said so over a televised programme. He said that the President 'this individual who is ugly outside and horrible inside', had 'betrayed the Revolution' by taking steps to ensure that Kubitschek candidates were elected and by 'allowing a restoration of the "system" and of a dynasty to take place'. He called upon the Army which he said should 'place itself at the service of the nation'.[9]

Castello Branco, who was touring in southern Brazil, saw that he would have to clarify matters once more. He emphasised that there could be no question of the restoration of men or the system which had been cast aside by the Revolution, but he also said that 'the nation should democratically abide by the verdict of the ballot box' and that his action had been taken in order to ensure 'the survival of democratic institutions'.

In spite of these promises, on 15 October a group of captains signed a proclamation calling upon their superiors to overthrow the President, and were duly arrested for so doing. On 19 October the key post of the Ministry of Justice, which had been unoccupied since the resignation of Milton Campos, was filled by Juracy Magalhães, recalled by Castello Branco from his post as Ambassador in Washington. This skilled politician, an old-stager in the U.D.N., a reserve general who had been one of the *tenentes* in 1922, was entrusted with the task of piloting the constitutional amendment bills through the parties' political labyrinth.

But the pill was too bitter to be easily swallowed, and notwithstanding the warnings given by the Minister, who made it clear to the deputies and senators that 'the Government has other means of achieving its aims', agreement could not be reached. On 24 October Juracy Magalhães made one last effort. Appealing on television, he begged members of parliament to vote for 'these instruments which the Revolution needs in order to pursue its task within a framework of law'.

Meanwhile the President of the Supreme Court, Ribeiro da Costa, once more fed the flames. He published an article in which officers were recommended to 'leave politics and go back to their barracks'. On 22 October, Costa e Silva made a public rejoinder in which he said that 'the Army ... will know no rest until the house has been put in order again', whatever may be thought by 'a man who is a bad judge, even if he is a minister'.[10]

On the twenty-sixth the civilian dissidents stood up to be

counted. The Supreme Court unanimously re-elected Ribeiro da Costa as its President, and soundings in Parliament showed that there were not enough deputies in favour of the government bills to ensure that they would be passed when voting took place next day, though it looked as if they would be accepted by the senators.

That evening, the military ministers were called to Brasilia and as of midnight the serving soldiers in the three armed forces were placed on alert in the areas of São Paulo, Guanabara and Minas Gerais.

Parliament never got a chance to give its verdict, for on the morning of 27 October 1965, Castello Branco made a moving speech to the nation, beginning with the following words which expressed his inmost thoughts: 'The Revolution in Brazil, like any national movement, is subject to different contingencies and circumstances.' At the end of the speech he indicated his decision to enact Institutional Act No. 2.

He gave two reasons why this was necessary. First, that the country needed peace in order to work at its economic development and the well-being of its people, and that there could be no peace without authority which was an essential prerequisite of order; secondly that the object of the constitutive power of the Revolution which inheres in the Government is not only to institutionalise it but to ensure the continuity of the task which it intends to carry out. The bill, which partially amended the 1946 Constitution, dissolved the political parties in their existing form and gave exceptional powers to the President *vis-à-vis* Parliament, the State and the judiciary, until his term of office expired on 15 March 1967.

Notwithstanding the declaration by Juracy Magalhães that 'the Head of State will be at pains to use the exceptional powers which have been conferred upon him with prudence and moderation', the about-turn was now seemingly complete. Paradoxically, although Castello Branco had lost a battle, he was more than ever prepared to continue the struggle. Freed from the hindrances of the parliamentary system which he had tried to keep at arm's length he went on with his task until the end of his term of office with more vigour and success in reforming the institutions than during the eighteen months which had just come to a close. For Brazilians the stern call to order now gave way to authoritarian consolidation.

Thus the first stage of the Revolution did not end with a 'reform coup', which as Samuel Huntington has suggested 'should be viewed as a healthy mechanism of gradual change, the non-constitutional equivalent of periodic changes in party control through the electoral process'.

Yet the crisis, which had been set off by a military faction, did not turn into Rustow's 'Praetorian' model, for the professionalism of the officer corps enabled the tradition of obedience to superiors to overcome any seditious urges. Although Castello Branco had strengthened the authority of the military term in the theorem, the régime none the less remained a 'military–civilian twilight'.

So although the first essential condition for development towards a military revolution, namely 'preserving or re-establishing discipline within the Army'[12] had been fulfilled, the second, namely to force the retreat of the rival group from the political scene, had not been totally achieved. In this regard, Castello Branco had succeeded in gaining the remainder of his term of office, i.e. the further seventeen months during which he would still be in power, even though henceforth he must know that his successor would be more likely to follow the hard nationalist line of the officers than that of the Sorbonne.

Having then satisfied, at least in part, the negative requirements on the critical path of a military revolution in Rustow's schema,[13] the 'twilight' régime had yet to bring about the two positive conditions required, namely a programme capable of dealing with the main political, social and economic problems facing Brazil and also a civil structure which could form a suitable supporting base for such a programme. Consequently Castello Branco again took the initiative and hastened the introduction of reforms which were essential to the fulfilment of the plans that had been drawn up to achieve the above-mentioned objects.

PART THREE

Authoritarian Consolidation

Institutional Act No. 2, which was signed by the President and all the members of his government on 27 October 1965, set up a truly authoritarian régime.

This instrument, like the preceding one, was based on the constitutive power of revolutions, but it went much further and its 33 articles contained two kinds of provisions. There were those which made permanent changes in the 1946 Constitution and there were clauses of a temporary nature with a validity expiring, as did the act itself, on 15 March 1967.

In the main the former simplified the procedure for revising the Constitution, confirmed the presidential initiative both in this area and also in financial matters and kept in being the accelerated procedure that had been in force since April for passing bills introduced by the Government. They established a far-reaching form of the judicial organisation, by the creation of federal courts of first instance for all proceedings in which the Federal State was directly or indirectly involved, and by increasing the number of judges – in the Supreme Court from eleven to sixteen,[1] in the Federal Appeal Tribunal from nine to thirteen and in the Supreme Military Tribunal from eleven to fifteen,[2] as well as by giving the latter powers to judge civilians whenever they were accused of crimes against the security of the State or against military institutions. They also set limits to the grant of indemnities to members of legislative bodies and provided that the president and vice-president of Brazil would thenceforth be elected by Parliament.

A limit was set to the individual liberties guaranteed by the Constitution in that 'notwithstanding, no propaganda for war or subverting the established order, or inciting to race or class prejudice, shall be tolerated'.[3] The object of the latter measures was to increase the powers of the president by renewing the period of emergency which had ended.

The powers given to the head of state included that of decreeing a state of siege without reference to Parliament for 180 days; of deciding upon federal intervention in provincial states to deal with internal unrest or to ensure respect for the laws; of dismissing parliament at will and legislating by decree; of demoting civilian or military officials declared to be 'incompatible with the aims of the Revolution'; of voiding the mandate and suspending for ten years the civil rights of individuals; of imposing a number of specified sanctions on persons affected by these measures;[4] and of enacting supplementary acts and decree-laws in matters affecting national security.

In addition to the temporary clauses there were a number of practical revisions. These included the establishment of pay parity between civil servants in the three levels of government; the clean-up of misappropriation of funds controlled by the municipalities; the empowering of judges carrying out any initial investigations into offences by the press of judging such cases, extension of the time limits for proscription of such offences and the extension of certain presidential powers at the level of State governments. Lastly, all registered political parties were dissolved and organisation of new parties was to be undertaken in accordance with the law of 15 July 1965.[5]

The act stated that the next head of state must be elected before 3 October 1966 (the implication being that the present parliament would do the electing, not the next one, which would elect the president and the vice-president) and it specified that Castello Branco was not eligible.

Three supplementary acts completed the work. The first, also dated 27 October, set out the measures and sanctions that could be taken against persons deprived of their civil rights. The second, dated 1 November, laid down the temporary provisions that would be in force pending the establishment of the federal courts of first instance; and the third, also dated 1 November, set out the ways in which the articles dealing with the suspension of constitutional guarantees and civil rights would be applied.[6]

19 Castello Branco again Takes the Initiative

Castello Branco did not however change his line of action. Firmly resolved to consolidate an authority which he intended to maintain unchallenged until the end of his mandate,[1] he again took up the initiative after having lost it for a brief while. With his indefatigable perseverance he set about building a supporting infrastructure on which his policy could be firmly built for the future.

Tackling the most urgent questions first, he took a step that was intended to strengthen his grip on the Army. In November, a trusty member of the 'Sorbonne', General Jurandir de Bizarria Mamede, was recalled from Amazonia and appointed to head the élite units of the prestigious Vila Militar. General Albuquerque Lima, who had been too enthusiastic in his opposition to Castello Branco, was sent away from Rio to the south, to command the second cavalry division. On 21 November 1965 the extreme right radical–democratic league (LIDER) was dissolved and those officers who protested most loudly were silenced at the first opportunity. On 23 November the President considered himself to be strong enough to give his 'hard' wing this warning in a speech which he made in Salvador: 'We do not recognise any autonomous force among the military'.[2] Having thus brought them to heel, Castello Branco could once more concentrate his efforts on reforming the institutions. He undertook this operation at two levels, that of public opinion and that of the parliamentary deputies.

With regard to opinion, the President tried to show that although he held all the aces, he nevertheless wanted a dialogue to begin. With this in view, he made no use of his prerogatives against civilians.[3] He allowed all the governors who had been elected on 3 October 1965 to be invested and between November and January he undertook a considerable rearrangement of his cabinet in which a number of technocrats were replaced by men with a political following, most of them being reserve officers.

For example, Arnaldo Sussekind, the Minister of Labour, formerly an official in the ministry, was replaced by the deputy Walter Peracchi Barcelos; the outgoing Governor of Paraná, Ney Braga, was given the agriculture portfolio; and Juracy Magalhães was given that of foreign affairs, giving up his post of Minister of Justice to Senator Mem de Sá, while the Navy portfolio was given to Admiral Zilmar Campos de Araripe Macedo.

To satisfy the business fraternity a young São Paulo industrialist,

Paulo Egidio Martins, was appointed Minister of Commerce and Industry. But the most significant change from the point of view of the intellectuals was the replacement of the Minister of Education and Culture, Flavio Suplicy de Lacerda, who had become their *bête noire* because of his harshness, by the leader of the majority in the Chamber of Deputies, Pedro Aleixo, formerly a professor of penal law. This pillar of the U.D.N., who first became a federal deputy in 1934, was on the list with Costa e Silva and was to become Vice-President of the republic.

Castello Branco acted with considerable skill in dealing with the parliamentary deputies. Far from dismissing them he promulgated on 20 November Supplementary Act No. 4 which laid out the temporary procedures for setting up new political formations which were to replace the dissolved parties within a period of forty-five days. This act was needed if elections were to be held in the last quarter of 1966 as planned, since it would have been impossible by that time to apply all the provisions of the electoral law. The principal clause imposed a minimum of 120 deputies and 20 senators before a party could be provisionally constituted while awaiting final acceptance, which would be effected once the results of the voting were known.

In arithmetical terms, there were three possible formations, since Parliament contained 409 deputies and 66 senators. But in political terms it was certain that only two organisations would be viable since 250 deputies and 40 senators had already in November indicated that they would join the governmental group ARENA (the National Renewal Alliance) whose allegiance Castello Branco was determined to have for himself. Therefore the opposition members were obliged to unite their forces under a single banner, the M.D.B. (Brazilian Democratic Movement); indeed, they had some difficulty in fielding a sufficient number of senators to enable them to be registered.[5]

On 5 February 1966, Institutional Act No. 3, enacted by Castello Branco in his capacity as President of the Republic and Commander in Chief of the Armed Forces, completed the edifice. The elections of the State governors were fixed for 3 September, the presidential election for 3 October 1966 and elections for the new parliament for 15 November.

Henceforth, the governors and vice-governors would no longer be elected by universal direct suffrage but indirectly, by the majority of members of the State legislative assemblies. The mayors of the State capitals and of the communes affecting national security were to be nominated by the governors, while the mayors of other communes would continue to be elected by direct voting. Lastly, any person putting himself up for election was obliged to resign from any government office that he might occupy three months before the election, whereas the former law required six months of incompatibility.[6]

It was Castello Branco's hope that these provisions, which were promulgated because it was 'urgently necessary to take steps to avoid the frustration of the main aims of the Revolution' and to 'preserve political and social peace and harmony in the country', would enable him to establish at State and key-municipality level a network of men ready to serve with single-mindedness a certain conception of the democratic ideal, before his mandate came to an end. But this very instrument accentuated even more the intensity of the dilemma in which the régime found itself, for in order to ensure the continuance of its modernising policy it was driven to reduce still further the participation of the people in working out the destiny of the nation.

20 Costa e Silva: the Price of Saving the Economic Policy

Costa e Silva could not remain unmoved by the President's action. He knew that although the President respected his military qualities, he did not regard him as an ideal successor. Although the links between the two men were of long standing, their careers had followed different paths. Arthur da Costa e Silva was a born soldier popular with the officers, who had climbed to his high rank without showing any special brilliance. He did not claim to be an intellectual, had never been admitted to the Superior War College, and frankly preferred horse races to textbooks. Nor had this former *tenente* of 1922 been a member of the expeditionary force sent to Italy. He owed his advancement to a fortunate combination of circumstances. For when the Revolution took place he was the senior army general on active service at Rio since his only possible ranking competitor, General Oswaldo Cordeiro de Farias, one of the 'Sorbonne' people, was in Curitiba at the time. And so on 1 April 1964 he simply occupied the main office at the War Ministry with which he was familiar because he was a departmental head there, and took over without further formality the functions of Commander in Chief of the national army.[1] It was in this capacity that he signed the First Institutional Act of the Revolution.

In the crisis of 25 October 1965 he became the candidate of the Army, whose views he had always tried to put forward to Castello Branco while endeavouring not to take sides in politics. But the President would have liked to see the continuity of the régime in the hands of a 'thinking' officer more in touch with the civilian world and capable of dominating the will of the military men rather than in the hands of an 'interpreter', even if he had been a commanding officer of the tank force.

Knowing these hesitations, Costa e Silva put his spoke in first. Early in January 1966 he announced officially that he would be a candidate. He thus repeated his manoeuvre of 1964 by forestalling any other military candidature, since any such announcement would imperil the unity of the Army.

Castello Branco was angered, and he let it be known that the initiative taken by his War Minister was 'inopportune'. For a time he tried to find a viable alternative, but he then realised that the situation was irreversible. For already the M.D.B., perceiving an unexpected chance of dividing the armed forces, was making advances to the general whose candidature, to be admissible, had to be endorsed by a political party. This was a curious state of affairs in which the hard line, the left-wing opposition, Carlos Lacerda and Adhémar de Barros, joined forces to counteract Castello Branco.

Resigning himself to the inevitable, the President thenceforward directed his efforts to bringing Costa e Silva within the Castellan fold, the consolidation of which he did everything possible to hasten.

The son of the President has in his files a document dated 1966 which illuminates Castello Branco's thoughts at the time when the campaign aimed at separating him from Costa e Silva was in full spate. In this text of limited circulation, sent to the main leading figures in the Government under the title 'Aspects of the Presidential Succession', he wrote:

> The Government, with its serious political responsibilities, must have a share in preparing for the presidential succession. As he has said since 1964, the President will not stand for re-election, nor does he wish to determine the choice of his successor. However, it is still permissible for him to take part in the selection and he will do this with a large group of men who will of necessity include the three military ministers... It is regrettable that lies, abuse and any other weapon have been used to weaken the President and strengthen the candidate [Costa e Silva] by representing him as the mainstay of the country. Nevertheless as far as I am concerned these facts do not cause any resentment nor do

they separate me from the War Minister. But they do rouse in me the determination not to give way or be discouraged, but on the contrary to become more worthy of my office. I shall do my utmost not to be a president who gives way to ultimatums, from whichever side they come.[2]

On 1 February an agreement was reached whereby the candidate would receive the investiture at ARENA but that in consideration of this he would undertake to preserve at least the 'revolutionary security apparatus' (meaning to keep the officers designated by Castello Branco at their posts), and also to guarantee continuity of the economic and financial policy of the Government, this being an absolute condition for receiving support from Castello Branco.

A few days later, Costa e Silva left to undertake a tour abroad during which at the President's request, he was to endeavour both to sound out international reactions with regard to Brazil and also to explain the meaning of the Institutional Acts, those 'vigorous instruments of democracy' which had enabled the country to preserve at least its two main expressions, Parliament and freedom of the press.

On 26 May ARENA held a session in which General Arthur da Costa e Silva was officially nominated as its candidate for the presidency. Seeing his ambitions frustrated, Oswaldo Cordeiro de Farias, who was the first commandant of the Superior War College and who was undoubtedly the intellectual superior of the chosen candidate, resigned from his position as Minister of the Interior. Negotiations designed to obtain the support of the M.D.B. for him were unsuccessful, and early in June this provisional party abandoned the idea of submitting a candidate.

An incident was also provoked in May by another of the most senior four-star generals, a supporter of the Revolution from its outset and an ultra hard liner, General Justino Alves Bastos, Commander of the Third Army (Rio Grande do Sul). He exerted pressure to obtain exemption from the required residence qualification so that he could submit his candidature for the post of governor of Rio Grande do Sul. When the President refused he denounced the new Electoral Code as a 'monstrosity' and declared that under the present régime 'the poor are poorer than ever'.[3] He was immediately relieved of his command and replaced by a staunch supporter of Castello Branco, General Orlando Geisel, brother of the head of his military establishment.

There were other verbal skirmishes, such as the sharp criticisms of the Government uttered by two generals who were judges of the Supreme Military Tribunal, Pery Constant Bevilacqua and Olympio Mourão Filho.[4]

21 Castello Branco Provides Continuity

Castello Branco refused to be halted in his course by these warning signs of latent discontent. Although he was accused in consequence of preparing forcible measures to maintain himself in power as Vargas had done in 1937, he nevertheless hardened his position to the extent that he judged necessary for the consolidation of the two pillars of his régime, the economic policy and institutional reform.

Hence, paradoxical though it may seem, the way the country was bludgeoned during the final months of the President's term of office was intended only to hasten acceptance of the sacrifices which all would be required to make in order that Costa e Silva in his turn would be able to inaugurate a more humane government without any surrenders.

At the end of April 1966 the setting aside of the mandates of elected persons began. True, only local worthies were affected, but these events broke the relative calm of the preceding months and shook public opinion. On 5 June, to the astonishment of all, the blow fell on one of the civil leaders of the Revolution, the powerful Governor of São Paulo, Adhémar de Barros whose party, the P.S.P., had obtained in 1950 the largest number of votes ever cast in the State.

In fact, it was entirely in line with the 'purifying' creed of the Revolution to eliminate this former – and potential – candidate for the presidency of the Republic, the archetype of populism, whose electoral agents had launched the slogan 'he steals, but he gets things done'.[1]

Until then the Government had perforce had to bear with the Governor, nuisance though he was, because he was supported both by the Commandant of the Second Army, his friend General Amaury Kruel, and by a very numerous State militia, but always with an ill grace (even though Castello Branco had considered it preferable to stamp out the I.P.M., led by General Dalisio Mena Barreto, who had revealed some flagrant cases of corruption in the administration of São Paulo).

It was only since March that Adhémar de Barros had been openly at odds with Castello Branco, and endeavoured to hinder his designs. For he both gave active support to the presidential ambitions of General Amaury Kruel, who was flirting with the M.D.B., and also tried to gain control of the legislative assembly of São

Paulo, going so far as to try to prevent its president, the ARENA deputy Roberto de Abreu Sodré, a patrician whom Castello Branco had selected as 'his' candidate for the post of governor in the September elections, from being re-elected. But even these excesses could have been pardoned if Adhémar, as he was popularly called, had not tried to do something which would have endangered the anti-inflationary struggle, the keystone of the President's economic policy; he decided to issue some public debt bonds for the State of São Paulo, as he had done before when they became known as 'Adhémaretas'. He did not reckon with the iron will with which Castello Branco was pursuing his objectives, aimed at recreating a healthy currency. Consequently, faced with this threat, Castello Branco threw political prudence to the wind, decided he had had enough and forthwith set aside the mandate of the opposing governor and suspended his civil rights. He replaced him at once with the Vice-Governor Laudo Natel, a banker in his prime, whose popularity was based on the fact that he was President of São Paulo's main football club.[2]

And so the last representative of populism in Brazil who was still in office, fell because he tried to take a financial initiative which ran counter to the views of the central Government. In former years no notice at all would have been taken; this was indeed the end of an epoch.

The next few weeks were not easy ones for the President. He had to devote most of his time to the political scene and leave Roberto Campos to promote his economic projects. For all was not going according to plan in preparations for the new governors. In Rio Grande do Sul, for example, one faction of ARENA refused to endorse the choice of Peracchi Barcelos, Minister of Labour, as presidential candidate, and joined forces with the M.D.B. in supporting an extremely able lawyer who was tipped as a future judge of the Supreme Court, Rui Cirne Lima.

The Government reacted violently. On 14 July the powers of four deputies in the State legislative assembly were set aside notwithstanding the opposition of the Minister of Justice, Mem de Sá, a gaucho himself, who refused to comply and instead resigned. To ensure that the warning did not pass unnoticed, more than twenty local deputies had their mandates set aside in the twelve states in which voting was to take place. As time was getting short and dangerous surprises had to be avoided at all costs, on 18 July Supplementary Act No. 16, dealing with loyalty to the party, imposed voting discipline at State and federal level. It was thenceforth mandatory for deputies and senators to vote for the candidate presented by their party. There was however nothing to stop them from abstaining if they wished to do so. Since these provisions applied both to the election of governors and to the election of the president of the Republic, they avoided candidatures proposed by a single party from being transformed spontaneously into a 'national union' election, the political interpretation of which public opinion would find it difficult to decipher.[3]

The M.D.B. then decided to boycott the gubernatorial elections and also the presidential ones. Faced with this agitation, and with the threat of the collective resignation of all M.D.B. members of parliament (which would deal a blow at the form of democracy which Castello Branco was desperately trying to preserve) the Government let it be known that it would punish with automatic suspension of civil rights for ten years any politician who resigned as a sign of protest. At the same time the President was obliged to reshuffle his cabinet which had been decimated by the electoral fever.

Costa e Silva resigned on 1 July.[4] He was replaced by Marshal Adhémar de Queiroz, Chairman of Petrobrás, an outstanding representative of the 'Sorbonne', a veteran of the Italian campaign and personal friend of Castello Branco. Carlos Medeiros da Silva replaced Luiz Vianna Filho, who gave up the Ministry of Justice and presented himself as a candidate for the post of governor of Bahia; the eminent lawyer and industrialist Luiz Gonzaga do Nascimentoe Silva took over the Ministry of Labour vacated by Peracchi Barcelos who thenceforth could rely on being elected governor of Rio Grande do Sul;[5] Severo Fagundes Gomes was appointed Minister of Agriculture, as Ney Braga had decided to canvass election as a senator to represent his state, Paraná, in the Upper Chamber.

Carlos Lacerda himself renewed his attacks, which were increasingly aimed at the results of the economic policies followed by Roberto Campos, whilst at the same time trying to spare Costa e Silva whom he hoped to win over as an ally. Paradoxically, this right-wing figure, a persecutor of Communists, was now on a leftist platform and, of all things, was even making advances to his sworn enemies João Goulart, Juscelino Kubitschek and Jânio Quadros.

On 3 September 1966 the legislative assemblies of the twelve states[6] each elected their governor.[7] Careful preparations had been made for the elections and they produced no disagreeable surprises for the Government, which thenceforth had seventeen governors who supported the régime. Of the five remaining ones, two, Israël Pinheiro of Minas Gerais who had rejoined the ranks of ARENA, and Negrão de Lima of Guanabara, left it to the President to decide. The three others[8] were guided by their sense of what was politically right.

Thus the first objective had been achieved. Castello Branco could leave his successor a disciplined group of governors, easier to manage, who would be more amenable to the centralising requirements of the national economic planning, than the 'kinglets' whom he had inherited from the previous government, namely Magalhães Pinto, Adhémar de Barros, Mauro Borges and Carlos Lacerda.

22 The Nationalist Counter-attack

Meanwhile the arguments about economic policy suddenly flared up again. The measures taken by the Government to contain the crisis of 1965 had lost something of their efficacy,[1] and during the second half of 1966 business leaders were becoming more and more critical.

However, since it would be hardly helpful (and possibly dangerous) to shout too loud during a period of 'revolutionary stabilisation', the so-called nationalist industrialists emphasised the ideological aspects of the P.A.E.G. Their spokesmen in the CONSPLAN and in the National Economic Council therefore concentrated their attack on the denationalisation[2] of Brazilian undertakings. They based their arguments on an extremely wide definition of the phenomenon caused by 'the massive entry into Brazil of foreign firms which either take over their Brazilian competitors or drive them to bankruptcy or just consign them to semi-stagnation'.[3] According to these spokesmen the Government was to blame for having authorised two methods of financial transfer, the 'swap' and Instruction 289. These methods, they said, 'place Brazilian investors in a shocking situation of inferiority vis-à-vis their foreign competitors who are located in Brazil'.[4] Their protests were loud enough to cause a parliamentary Committee of Inquiry to be appointed in 1967, and to influence somewhat the decisions taken by Castello Branco's successors. Their arguments sensitised public opinion to a considerable degree and therefore merit further consideration. The private swap had been introduced in 1953 to promote the inflow of hard currency at a time when the balance of payments was unfavourable. Hence the new régime had inherited a debit balance amounting to $364·2 million on 21 December 1963.[5]

The term 'private swap' carried an unusual connotation in Brazil. In reality it was a fixed-term loan (generally for three years) in foreign currency guaranteed by the Bank of Brazil into which the foreign currency was paid. In consideration the bank passed on, on payment of interest, part of these funds (about 50–60 per cent) converted into cruzeiros, to the transferee in Brazil. On the due date the cruzeiros were returned to the Bank of Brazil which in its turn repaid the original sum with interest in foreign currency to the foreign lender, who thus had the benefit of an exchange guarantee. But the local borrower had received for use a smaller quantity of cruzeiros than would have resulted from an exchange operation at the official rate.[6]

In theory anybody could undertake a private swap operation, but in practice it was predominantly used by companies whose head offices were abroad. In this way they were able to finance the operations of their subsidiaries in Brazil without increasing their fixed investments. However, swaps did not provide the foreign lender with undiluted advantages, because in order to guarantee his loan against devaluation he generally had to set aside twice as much hard currency as would have been necessary if the foreign exchange market had been utilised in the normal way. However, since in this procedure the expenses were known in advance and could therefore be budgeted for, the financial managers of the lending businesses could look upon the cost of setting aside the additional capital required and during the period in question as a kind of 'devaluation insurance premium'.

As early as 15 January 1965, after an initial examination of the situation, the new Government had limited swap facilities.[7] Instruction 289 of the SUMOC (Superintendência da Moeda e do Crédito),[8] which was adopted at that time, introduced a rather similar procedure except that the exchange risk was no longer borne by the Treasury but by the transferee of the funds. The only guarantee that was given – admittedly an important one – was a guarantee that the foreign exchange could be repatriated on expiry of the contract, but at the rate of exchange ruling on the day of repatriation.

Roberto Campos intended this measure to 'decompress the home credit market . . . and to set up a permanent source for injecting foreign money, a kind of "working capital fund", which would be extremely useful, especially when the balance of payments was passing through a difficult phase'.[9] He defended it as follows: 'As it was necessary to limit the expansion of credit in the fight against inflation, if no way had been open to foreign businesses giving them access to foreign savings, they would have had to meet their needs from Brazilian capital and thus compete with Brazilian companies for the scarce resources available . . .'[10]

For the uninitiated, these '289' loans appeared to be an incredibly good thing since their nominal rate of interest was approximately that of the country of origin, i.e. 6 or 7 per cent per annum, whereas in Brazil it was virtually impossible to find money at less than 36 per cent. But since various taxes and fees had to be borne by the operation both coming and going in addition to these nominal interest rates, and since when the contract matured the borrower also had to reimburse the equivalent to the interim devaluation of Brazilian currency, the real cost in cruzeiros was not very different from the local market rate (although in most cases it was not quite so high).[11]

Although, like swaps, 289s were in theory available to anybody, the so-called foreign companies[12] in practice were almost the only ones to use them.[13] From this point of view, the difference between the real cost and the nominal rate appeared as an 'excuse of internationalist technocrats' to a public opinion conditioned by the harangues of the nationalists supported both by the Federation of Industries of São Paulo and by a large part of the Army, including the hard-line colonels.

It cut no ice that the economic policy turned in good results faster than had been anticipated, and after the end of 1965 for the first time for several years brought about a favourable balance of payments; its opponents, far from applauding, looked on this as one more proof of their case. They claimed that the hard currency inflows served to strengthen the hold of foreigners over Brazil, and they accused the régime in scarcely veiled terms of selling the country down the river. 'Even if the Government were to do nothing, that in itself would be extremely serious. But unfortunately that is not all that has happened'[14] ... 'denationalisation has received a strong impetus from measures which unjustifiably favour the interests of the powerful foreign organisations ... while Brazilian enterprises were stagnating, foreign companies had no reason to refrain from expanding. On the contrary, the weakness of their local competitors was a standing invitation to capture fresh positions.'[15]

What the nationalists did not take into account was the climate of affairs outside Brazil in 1965–6.

Far from having expansionary ideas, the treasurers of the multinational companies which had plenty of money were extremely reluctant to touch the melting money of this 'country of the future',[16] and were prone to accuse the managers of their local companies of being starry-eyed when they suggested that more money be invested. It was this lack of confidence which largely explains the success of the 289s which were used principally as a source of circulating capital, to be renewed as often and for as long as the need was felt.

The deeper reasons for the choice of this method of financing are not connected with its cost, which was in fact quite high, but were partly to be found in the guaranteed repatriation of the funds in foreign currency and also in the fact that, although transfers of interest were taxable at the same rate as transfers of dividends, they were considered as overhead expenses, which dividends were not. None the less those who mounted this counter-attack, again with the aid of statistics that were not examination-proof, nevertheless did something to create the image of a government which thought more about future horizons than immediate realities.

In truth they were not entirely wrong, and Roberto Campos betrayed a certain technocratic bias when he said to the parliamentary Committee of Inquiry: 'Some people complain about a so-called denationalisation of the economy, citing specific industries that have been taken over by foreigners in the pharmaceutical, textile or precision engineering sectors. They forget that in a dynamic capitalist economy internationalisation and renationalisation are taking place side by side... taking the overall view, since the 1964 Revolution more nationalisation than denationalisation has taken place. There has been unfortunately too much State control, but that is another story.'[17]

In the absence of data supported by proper statistics,[18] the argument remained open, but the planners of the Costa e Silva Government took good note of the conclusions in the report of the parliamentary Committee of Inquiry which was published in September 1968. The facts it revealed were as follows: overall, the share owned by foreign companies in the economy oscillated between $7\frac{1}{2}$ and $8\frac{1}{2}$ per cent. But in the processing industry this rose to 31 per cent of the total capital, and even around 100 per cent in the automobile industry. Of the thousand largest firms in Brazil, 40 per cent were state managed, 29 per cent were in Brazilian private hands and 31 per cent belonged to foreign groups.[19]

23 Repercussions of the Fiscal Reform

In fact the argument about denationalisation went too far for the immediate comfort of either side; it revealed the disorientation of many Brazilian heads of business, their ideas and habits deeply disturbed by the coalition of the military and the civilian technocrats in the government, and feeling as if their foreign colleagues were more in favour with the Government than they were.

One of the nationalist leaders expressed in a nutshell this frustration. In a speech to students at São Paulo he said in March 1966:

> Development necessarily implies that those who are ready to participate in the process while fully accepting its risks and toils should have first place...
>
> Conversely, those who do not adapt to this new state of affairs are condemned to increasing mediocrity... In the case of Brazil, this reaction takes the form of a systematic distrust of success in business. The idea of enrichment is linked with that of corruption or illegal subterfuge... In the Brazil of today, simply to mention that a person who was born poor has become rich is already looked upon as a veiled accusation. Members of the élite of entrepreneurs are considered to be a 'new class' and seldom is it admitted that that any of them has made any contribution whatsoever to the progress of the country. Industrialists are labelled monopolists, managing production units of low productivity which survive, at the expense of the masses, thanks to all kinds of favours obtained by heaven knows what means.[1]

The cause of these complaints is to be sought in the fiscal measures that were enacted by the Government, which suddenly took a stranglehold on industrialists and businessmen who were not usually inclined to worry about the tax laws.

As early as 22 May 1964, Constitutional Amendment No. 7 had given the authorities the right to change the level of taxes as they wished, during the tax year and even retrospectively. Then came a series of measures: Law No. 4357 of 16 July which brought in monetary correction on amounts owing to the tax man, as mentioned earlier; a 30 per cent rise in indirect taxes[2] which accounted for about two-thirds of the Federal State's tax receipts; an increase of direct taxation,[3] taxation of dividends,[4] and above all, on 14 July 1965 a new definition of the crime of tax fraud, which became punishable by imprisonment.[5]

At once it was popularly said that if this 'Prussian' measure were to be applied, the whole country would have to be transformed into one vast gaol. But the final blow was given by the sudden alteration of the system of indirect taxes (the tax on consumption imposed by the Federal State and the tax on 'sales and consignment' which went to the provincial states) which was replaced by a modern tax system. The former was replaced by a tax on manufactured products (I.P.I.) and the latter by a tax on the circulation of goods (similar to the European value added tax). All of these measures, hitherto enacted singly, were consolidated on 1 December 1965 by Constitutional Amendment No. 18.[6]

As there were not enough competent civil servants to make these measures work properly, the new laws were applied with an unsurpassed degree of arbitrariness. Furthermore, since tax inspectors receive a high percentage of the fines which they inflict (and are not subject to any penalty if the accused after a long and costly lawsuit proves his innocence) there was a run of alleged offences, often without foundation.[7]

Taxes, which nobody had talked about before, became overnight the hot drawing-room topic. The walls of São Paulo were covered with giant posters representing an eye with a computer for its iris, and bearing the warning 'Look out, the computer is watching you!' The result was electrifying. Federal State gross tax receipts increased from 18·1 per cent of the gross national product in 1963 to 24·4 per cent in 1966, rising to 26·3 per cent in 1968. Net receipts jumped from 11·8 to 17 per cent.[8] Direct taxes, which bore hardest, rose from 5·2 to 8·9 per cent during the same period, whilst indirect taxes rose from 12·9 to 17·4 per cent. In real terms, the Federal State collected 34·4 per cent more in 1966 than in 1963.

Tax collection became part of the Brazilian way of life; the number of persons who had to complete a tax declaration as their income exceeded the maximum for P.A.Y.E. rose from 580,000 in 1968 to 7 millions in 1971. The number of taxable corporate bodies on the other hand remained relatively stable, oscillating around 380,000, but the direct taxes they paid jumped from 121 million cruzeiros in 1963 to 1812 billion in 1970, an increase of about 55 per cent in real terms, taking account of inflation.[9] During the next few years, every taxable person received a numbered card which he had to produce whenever he bought anything costing a fair amount of money. *Time*, having told of a wealthy Brazilian businessman who said 'we are all running scared,' went on to write 'The days of easy evasion are numbered.'[10]

A surprisingly candid confession, but one which shows how acute the problem was, occurs in the report of the parliamentary Committee of Inquiry. Referring to the assistance granted by the Government to companies in Brazil by means of the various funds mentioned above, the author of the report states:

> The appearance of these funds coincided with a phase of weakness of the Brazilian businesses, some of them being in serious financial difficulties, so much so that they were not in a position to meet certain of the conditions required for obtaining these subsidies. One such condition, for example, was the obligation to submit a certificate of payment of dues or a clearance receipt from the

Social Security.[11] But in very many instances the firms were in debt to the Social Security...[12]

The committee also emphasised the extent to which the burden of taxation weakened the private sector: 'In fact, the inefficiency of the tax authorities results in a disproportionate share of taxes being paid by a small group of enterprises which owing to their size and level of organisation, *cannot employ the usual methods of fraud.*'[13]

The author of the report omitted to add that one of the reasons why the Brazilian technocrats were relatively lenient towards foreign companies was precisely the fact that most of these companies were bound to keep strictly within the law, even if only to satisfy the internal auditors who were sent from time to time unannounced by their head offices.

But life went on. The Government decided to give assistance to the textile industry which was the worst hit by the crisis, and in October 1966 it afforded it some taxation relief. The two Brazilian shipping companies merged in November to find a way out of their difficulties;[14] massive investments were injected into the national infrastructure and working parties consisting of industrialists and technocrats were set up in March to prepare the Ten-Year Development Plan.

In actual fact, notwithstanding the weeping and gnashing of teeth, heads of business had so much to do and looked after their jobs with so much zeal that the Governor-elect of São Paulo, Roberto de Abreu Sodré, had to remind them of their civic responsibility during a business dinner given in his honour:

> If civilians become immersed in their special concerns and forget their duty to their country, how can you wonder if military men take their place even to the extent of organising civilian society as well?... Either the heads of private business must be resolutely committed to help in building a civilian order, taking a personal part in the political struggle and accepting its risks... or they will have the chagrin of seeing others do it... and they have no option but to look on passively while the State intervenes with increasing emphasis in economic life, pressing on to complete State control.[15]

24 The New Image of Labour

The new policy subjected the workers in Brazil to severe pressures. When the Revolution took place, several trade union leaders had been arrested and the unofficial workers' organisations such as the C.G.T., 'remotely controlled by the Communist Party',[1] were proscribed. Those trade unions most closely identified with the former régime were placed under 'federal management' and some of them were dissolved after inquiries had been completed.[2]

It should however be noted that in Brazil trade unionism was a key element in the 'system' set up by Getúlio Vargas to win for himself the control and support of the working class. Hence the trade unions were not free, spontaneously created bodies but creatures of the Government. In structure they resembled the corporations under Mussolini and they depended for their existence on subsidies and the goodwill of the Ministry of Labour.[3] Their leaders, nicknamed 'Pelegos',[4] were more like federal mercenaries than sincere militants. They lived within the legal paternalist framework which expressed the ambiguity of populism. Situated between the élite and the masses 'they are constantly wavering between urging the claims of the people and maintaining a *status quo* which is characterised by the fact that the dominant interests have the deciding voice'.[5]

Hence it is not surprising that, alongside this official trade union movement, more revolutionary leaders had set up their own networks, such as the Comando Geral dos Trabalhadores (C.G.T. in Brazil) led by certain former members of the Brazilian Communist Party,[6] the Comando Geral de Greve (C.G.G.) or the Pacto Sindical de Unidade e Ação (P.U.A.) in which the railwaymen and dockers were represented. As the law also allowed trade unions to be set up in rural areas, such unions began to be formed from 1963 onwards following the initial impetus given by the peasant leagues of Francisco Julião and by the clergy in the north-east.

As well as these organisations mention should also be made of student organisations such as the A.P. (Ação Popular), a progressive Catholic group[7] which was formed by university youth movements and was deeply committed to the literacy campaign, and U.N.E. (União Nacional dos Estudantes), the official student union, financed by the Ministry of Education and strongly infiltrated by Communist elements. These together formed the 'Jacobin' wing of the united front on which Brazilian left-wing politicians and intellectuals relied for support.

When the Goulart régime came to an end this wing predominated and, if Government propaganda is to be believed, its influence on the working class appeared to be so strong that it had helped to bring about the alienation of the middle class which was frightened by 'the massive infiltration of Communism'.[8] But when it came to the crunch, the few leaders found they had no followers, and the Army had no difficulty in purging their ranks of those who were considered to be subversives; they were in fact punished all the more heavily for having misled public opinion by their intemperate rhetoric.

But Government, aware that no economic development could take place without the participation of the workers, gave priority in its concerns to reconstructing the trade unions. As early as August 1964 Roberto Campos stated as follows the reasons why it was necessary to create a new image of labour:

> There is no more urgent task than to rethink the part which labour has to play in the life of the nation, both because of the tremendous contribution it can make and because of the way it has been misled in the past. Ever since the time of Vargas the labour movement has been paternalist and has therefore lost its authenticity; for lack of realism it became a prey to demagogy ...[9]

Ever since 1943 the organisation of labour in Brazil[10] had been based on social legislation among the most advanced in the world, resting mainly on two pillars, assistance and the concept of 'stability' of employment.[11]

This latter standard implied that if a worker's contract was broken, he had a right to compensation equal to the amount of his highest monthly wage multiplied by the number of years in the job.[12] After ten years he could no longer be dismissed except for serious misdemeanours (which were enumerated in the law) duly proved before an *ad hoc* tribunal.[13] If in the court's opinion the case had not been proven, but in the light of all the circumstances it was not desirable for the worker to return to his job, the court could (though it was not obliged to) 'authorise the firm to dismiss him for incompatibility' on payment of compensation equal to double the amount that would have been payable if he had remained for less than ten years.[14] The same rules applied in case of *force majeure*, liquidation of the company, closure of a branch, etc.[15]

Although these measures were well intended, in practice they became distorting factors. Thus, for example, since under the populist régime the labour courts were by definition on the side of the wage earners, some companies preferred systematically to dismiss their employees after seven or eight years of service to avoid the risk of finding themselves landed with a 'stable' labour force from which it became difficult if not impossible to obtain a sufficient average profitability since lack of enthusiasm for work was not one of the acceptable reasons for dismissal. The social cost of this rotation of labour, which would be disastrous even in an advanced economy, was obviously even greater in a country lacking in skilled labour. Furthermore, since enterprises were not obliged to set up reserves to meet the cost of compensation, these amounts constituted a hidden liability in the balance sheets which in certain cases might exceed the intrinsic value of the company.

In the end wage earners had become veritable prisoners of the system. For though after ten years the enterprise could no longer get rid of its employee, neither could the employee leave his employer without losing the advantages of 'stability'. Furthermore, his chances of promotion or of receiving a voluntary rise were very slim, for any advantage granted to him would automatically become potentially a heavy burden on the employer since, as we have seen, the separation payment was equal to two months of the highest remuneration multiplied by the number of years of service. And when an employee who started working for a firm when he was twenty years old for example reached the age of sixty, this would entail a fresh obligation amounting to 80 times the rise that had been granted. So the employer was tempted to leave him forgotten in his corner until he reached retiring age, since the pension was then paid by the Social Security Department of the State and the employer would not be liable to pay any indemnity. When the Revolution took place, 'stability' had been on the statute book for more than twenty years and nobody dared openly challenge the validity of this conquest by labour.

Castello Branco's policy was directed towards the creation of a representative form of trade unionism,[16] without however abandoning the positive aspects of previous legislation, and it could not simply duck the problem. Nevertheless, it took the new régime more than two years, during which it had enacted some important measures dealing with labour,[17] to put forward an alternative, and not until 13 September 1966 was Law No. 5107 (Decree Law No. 20) instituting the Service Time Guarantee Fund[18] adopted.

The creation of this fund represented a decisive step in rationalising the relations between employers and workers. From that time onwards, each employer had to pay in monthly 8 per cent of the total wage bill of his business[19] to individual accounts in the name of each member of his staff, and these accounts were blocked. The funds, which were managed by the National Housing Bank (B.N.H.), produced interest and also had the benefit of monetary correction.

In this way workers, instead of having only a hypothetical right, had savings in their own names that they could draw upon in certain specified circumstances such as on marriage, on purchasing a house, in sickness or unemployment, or when dismissed. If a worker left his firm voluntarily he kept his book and did not lose any of his rights. If he was dismissed without 'valid reason' proven, the employer was obliged to pay an additional amount into the account for registration in the book.

This meant that businesses were subject to a fresh financial burden because they had to pay an additional monthly 8 per cent of the pay slip into their workers' accounts; but in return they could operate a proper personnel policy, undertake training, make career plans, etc., without being worried about the coming of 'stability'.

The country was the gainer too, since the money collected in this way enabled the B.N.H. to build dwellings, thus helping to resolve one of the most basic problems. By 31 December 1971 some 767,000 houses had been financed in contrast to the mere 4000 a year that had been started under State auspices throughout the previous thirty years.[20]

The law provided for a transitional period and allowed workers already in employment the free choice between the old formula and the new one. Their existing rights were preserved and they also had the option of transforming them immediately into money.[21]

It goes without saying that such a noteworthy change gave rise to argument. Cries of scandal came from both left and right. The left spoke of 'an attack on the rights of the workers' while the right spoke of 'intolerable burdens for business', for social security payments could in fact total up to 82·3 per cent of wages.[22]

It should be noted that these various attacks launched against the Government were often the fruit of ideological conceptions rather than of the facts themselves.[23] Sometimes they were orchestrated abroad as well. For example, as late as 1971 a 'Cahier libre' published in Paris reproduced in the following words the interpretations which had been put forward at the time:

> The economic motivation of the 1964 *coup d'état* was twofold – to secure the profits of foreign capital and to halt inflation. A way was found that was convenient for the employers but disastrous for the working class, a wages freeze ... In the absence of repressive laws against the labour movement ... a law was needed to act directly on wages and concretely on employees as a group ... The solution was found in 1965,[24] when the ex-Ambassador of Brazil to Washington ... produced the law known as the Service Time Guarantee Fund which enabled employees to be dismissed at any time by paying them a ridiculously small sum taken from a fund maintained for this purpose by the boss.[25]

In the end, under pressure from the Government and from some industrialists, it became generally recognised that the new formula did have its good points and the majority of companies and workers became members of the scheme. By the end of 1971 more than 6 million individual accounts had already been opened and the B.N.H. which in that year was converted into a public enterprise with a capital of a thousand million cruzeiros and a network of 900 agents throughout the country, was managing about Crz. 99 billion (about $177 billion) coming from the Service Time Guarantee Fund. In 1971 the monetary correction credited amounted to Crz. 15 billion and the interest thereon to Crz. 413 million; and in the same year payments made by businesses represented Crz. 37 billion and workers were able to withdraw Crz. 16 billion from their accounts under the laws in force.[26]

However, in 1966 the workers had no immediate cause for rejoicing because the cost of living was increasing more rapidly than their incomes. Decree Laws No. 15 and 17 of 1 August put a tighter clamp on the wage freeze, which the Labour Courts had slightly alleviated by interpreting somewhat broadly the official indices of average real purchasing power for the preceding twenty-four months, calculated by the National Economic Council.[27] In the statement giving the reasons for the first of these measures, it is indicated that the Government had to take this action to end the 'grant of wages increases which were running counter to the general direction of economic and financial policy'.[28]

The minimum wage, which was doubled in February 1964, was increased by only 57 per cent on 1 March 1965 and by 27 per cent on 13 March 1966, whereas the cost of living in Rio de Janeiro rose by 91·4 per cent in 1964, by 65·9 per cent in 1965 and by 41·3 per cent in 1966.[29]

This disparity was immediately recognised, and even APEC (Análise e Perspectiva Econômica), a private body but one that was very close to the Government, had the following comments in its annual publication:

> We do not yet have adequate statistics to gauge ... what the share of workers in the national product amounts to. But the partial figures we have indicate a reduction of real wages in 1966. This drop is evident at least as regards the minimum wage. The cause is to be found in an under-estimation of the residual inflation, which was estimated at 10 per cent for the year whereas the overall increase in prices was nearly 40 per cent. In a large number of collective agreements, the Labour Court has granted a little more than would have been permissible under a strict application of the formula on wages policy and this went some of the way towards limiting the effects of the error in calculating residual inflation. Nevertheless, these measures were not enough to avoid a reduction in real wages for various classes of people.[30]

An important specialised banking international agency, in an internal document on Brazil dated January 1971, stated that 'in the 1964–7 period the minimum wage rate fell by about 18 per cent in real terms; other workers did not fare as badly as those whose incomes were tied to the minimum wage, but most still suffered significant decline in real wages'.[31]

Even the elements seemed to cold-shoulder the recovery policy, and the harvests were affected by bad weather. Agricultural production, which in 1965 had shown a year-by-year rise of 13.8 per cent, fell back to 3.1 per cent in 1966, and this caused a rise in home prices which partly explains the sudden increase in the cost of living.

To crown it all, 1966 was marked by a psychological catastrophe for the people of Brazil the impact of which it is hard to appreciate: Brazil was eliminated from the World Cup in London after being defeated both by Hungary and by Portugal.

Now in the country of the Southern Cross football is the national honour, the reason for being and the joy of living rolled into one. Surprising though it may be to a European to see football mentioned here as an important element in the political climate at the end of Castello Branco's régime, it has to be accepted that for Brazilians the sport is a veritable passion which transcends the barriers of class, race or fortune. The four largest stadia in the country will hold 583,000 people[32] and in 1967 for example over 2347 football teams were officially counted in the State of São Paulo alone.

One can speak without exaggeration of a cult of football of which all are adherents some fanatics and others moderates, and that is why the World Cup, which takes place every four years, is a sporting event of the highest importance. As the Brazilian team had won it in 1958 and 1962, if they carried off the Jules Rimet cup for the third time, this prestige trophy would remain permanently in Brazil. All hopes were raised, and great popular rallies had already been organised. As ill luck would have it, the team, very ill-prepared, lost ignominiously and although those in the know were not really surprised, the people transformed the defeat into an orgy of national mourning.

It was in this atmosphere that the election of Costa e Silva, who was expected to introduce a more human régime, rekindled the hope of better days to come.

25 The Elections in the Autumn of 1966

During the three months preceding the election, Costa e Silva campaigned as if he had to be elected by the people. Accompanied by his wife, Dona Yolanda, he criss-crossed the country, shook hands, attended inaugurations, took part in innumerable banquets. Always affable and smiling, talking a lot but never giving away his future policy, playing with his enormous dark glasses, he did a public relations job which paid off all the better because it contrasted strongly with the 'clinical' style of Castello Branco.

The broadest of jokes about the future President passed from mouth to mouth – a kind of humour of which Brazilians are very fond which had completely disappeared since 1964. It is even said that Costa e Silva put them about himself to aid his popularity and to further the non-intellectual image which he affects. Politically he promised to 'humanise' the régime, to hasten re-democratisation, to concern himself with social problems and to champion a kind of economic nationalism. Yet he avoided firm undertakings and when detailed questions were pressed home, he replied more often than not that his 'experts would study the matter'. The press gave considerable support to the campaign and, as radio and television did the same just before his election, Costa e Silva succeeded in projecting a popular image of himself that was fully acceptable.[1]

On 3 October 1966 Parliament elected Marshal Arthur da Costa e Silva President of Brazil by 295 votes and 41 abstentions (out of the 472 deputies and senators forming the two Chambers).[2] Part of the opposition which had not submitted a candidate boycotted the session, but before voting took place the leaders of the M.D.B. set out the attitude of their party which was opposed to 'the system of indirect election and not to the candidate himself'. Deputy João Herculino of Minas Gerais mounted the speaker's rostrum dressed all in black to warn of the 'death of democracy' and Senator João Abraão of Goiás denounced the election as a 'shameful farce' because, he said, the only choice recognised by the people was that of Juscelino Kubitschek.[3] The uproar which ensued compelled the President to suspend discussion for several minutes before votes were counted.

No sooner had the results been announced than Costa e Silva, who celebrated his sixty-fourth birthday that day, was presented to Congress with his companion on the list Pedro Aleixo, who became Vice-President. In his speech he took up the main themes of his campaign and declared: 'I do not admit that anybody has the right to doubt that my intentions are democratic... I now have to accomplish what is the supreme aim of the Revolution of March 1964, and that is to establish a true democracy in Brazil'.[4] Until his term of office began on the following 15 March, Costa e Silva while preparing himself for his new tasks played a relatively inconspicuous part in public life.[5]

Political interest was centred on the parliamentary elections which were due to take place on 15 November 1966; 22,387,251 electors[6] had to vote by direct suffrage to renew one-third of the Senate, the whole Chamber of Deputies and all of the Provincial State Legislatures.

It was the first time the people had voted since the Revolution and Castello Branco was determined that the people should be able to make a free choice. Although he was willing to see a new opposition appear, he nevertheless would not agree to its being represented in Parliament by certain survivors of the former régime. For this purpose he took action at the stage when parliamentary candidates were registering as such, which had to be done before 15 October. On 12 October he gave orders that the mandates of six federal deputies suspected of corruption or subversion and accused of having made contact with ex-Presidents Goulart and Kubitschek in order to promote an anti-Government alliance should be annulled. They included the very rich Sébastião Paes de Almeida, who had been Goulart's Finance Minister.

The President of the Chamber, Audoto Lucio Cardoso,[7] a personal friend of Castello Branco, opposed this act and put the six deputies under his protection in Brasilia. Eight days later on 20 October by Supplementary Act No. 23 Parliament was put into recess until the week after the elections. To ensure that this decision was immediately carried out, Colonel Carlos de Meira Mattos occupied the parliament building at the head of a detachment in combat uniform. Audoto Cardoso resigned in view of this 'scandalous attack on the dignity of the civil power'.[8]

But the deputies had understood the warning, and in the event certain potential candidates did not stand. For as the leaders of the two parties knew that refusal to accept nominations would in principle be based on allegations of Communism (the report of the Commission of Inquiry having been made public in October),[9] of subversion or of corruption, they preferred to submit the names of candidates unofficially to the security authorities before presenting them to the election officers in order to avoid unwelcome surprises. Even so, not all those who were nominated passed through the net, since the criteria of the electoral code of July 1965 had been modified again,[10] to reduce possibilities of abuse to a minimum. For example, before being accepted candidates now had to state how much wealth they possessed, and this had to agree with their income tax declaration; they also had to submit a certificate of good character.

The election campaign could not begin until the nominations had been received and agreed, and responsibility for this was entrusted to the parties, which had to set up financial committees for the purpose of monitoring receipts and expenses in each constituency. Any candidate who contravened these rules or incurred election campaign expenses for his own account, would be immediately suspended. There was also stricter surveillance of the election procedure and inter-party committees of inspection were created. The campaign itself passed off relatively quietly and did not arouse much interest. Candidates were forbidden to mention certain subjects; for instance, neither individuals nor the Government were to be defamed; there were to be no calls to violent action likely to disturb the peace: nor was public opinion to be inflamed or 'urban property negatively affected'.[11]

There was no shortage of attacks, but they centred on rather well-worn themes such as the 'arbitrary dictatorship' set up by Castello Branco who had 'betrayed the Revolution'. Apart from some groups of students, the populace was hardly roused from its apathy and the candidates' speeches did not excite much comment, except in the press and on the radio and television where the opposition had the same facilities as the Government party.

Even if the elections of 15 November 1966 were slightly manipulated at the stage of candidate selection, they went off peacefully and formally at least as freely as under the preceding régime if not more so. The invigilation system and the power of dissuasion which the electoral officials had was sufficient to prevent certain time-honoured faults from being perpetrated.[12]

The number of citizens who voted was 17,285,556, and if they wished to demonstrate their dissatisfaction with the régime they could either vote for the opposition, or send in unmarked voting papers as the students recommended.[13] When the votes were counted, ARENA had won 277 seats in the Lower House (with 8,731,635 votes) and the M.D.B. 132 (4,195,470 votes). Nevertheless the large urban states of Guanabara, Rio de Janeiro and Rio Grande do Sul had majorities in favour of the M.D.B. and at São Paulo the ARENA candidates only just got in.[14]

It is interesting to note that it was the rural states which brought victory to the Government, and also that of the 409 deputies, 186 were elected for the first time. This proportion of 45·5 per cent is indicative of a good deal of fresh blood coming in to the Brazilian parliament, which was one of Castello Branco's aims.[15] As regards the

State Legislative Assemblies, ARENA won 731 seats (with more than 9 million votes) and the M.D.B. 345 (with more than 5 million votes).

In the three states that were bastions of the opposition, namely Guanabara, Rio de Janeiro and Rio Grande do Sul, the assemblies were controlled by the M.D.B.[16] The latter party won forty-eight more seats countrywide than it had in the previous parliament. In the Federal Senate, ARENA was easily the winner since the M.D.B. had only four senators elected out of the twenty-three places to be filled,[17] including João Abraão.

These elections could not be interpreted as reflecting either the popularity or the unpopularity of the régime but they could be considered as a 'snapshot' of the division of the country's political forces at the end of 1966. In short, the Brazilian electors had once more adapted to the situation prevailing in the country and had supported the Government.

In a careful analysis of the reasoning of those who abstained, the political scientist Cândido Mendes de Almeida, himself an opponent of the government, observed that

> the incidence of protest showed little slackening of the social will and met with small response. They were confined to the intelligentsia with a little overlap from some sectors of the liberal professions and student groups, and could not easily be given a class connotation. They certainly did not affect the proletariat groups. These more than any others showed by their behaviour at the elections their attachment to the electoral process. The ceremony of voting viewed as a symbol of acquired social status, itself linked to the necessity of playing one's part in the elections, made non-participation unthinkable.[18]

He emphasises that it 'is not possible to establish any relationship of growing intensity in terms of identification of the social strata enabling a gradation to be perceived between left-wing radicalism still voting in the M.D.B. and the result of the voting, based on unmarked or spoilt voting papers'.[19] He notes that the electors showed a clear tendency to vote as they had voted previously and that 'those opposition candidates who were able to use the "mass media" were better off in the final result'.[20]

This dominant reflex of the electorate 'prevented the M.D.B. group of elected deputies and senators from expressing either sociologically or politically a response from the people as a whole able to meet the challenge thrown down by the technocrats'.[21] He supports this interpretation by noting that out of the thirty-six candidates from the M.D.B. list in Guanabara, a third came forward with electoral platforms 'full of opposition and ideological emphasis.

Only three of them were elected and not one came in the top third of the successful candidates'.[22]

This traditional inclination to a certain political conformity, stimulated by Castello Branco's perseverance and unwillingness to compromise, explains why the Government party ARENA which had been unknown a few months before had a comfortable majority, sealed by the elections, in the new Parliament which began its work at the same time as the President-elect in March 1967. Costa e Silva, who thought that he could rely on its support, therefore went ahead with his 'humanising' programme.

26 A Way of Securing the Future: Constitutional Reforms

The President wanted to leave his successor a renewed political structure and a new legal framework in which he would be constrained to follow the main lines of Castellian policies. Castello Branco pursued this aim with all his energy during the last months of his Government which, as if seized by a veritable 'regulations fever' promulgated some 191 decrees and laws, one institutional act and 17 supplementary acts before 15 March 1967. In order to underpin Costa e Silva's freedom of action still further, or to constrain him more effectively, he cleared the way in advance by annulling the civil rights of 90 persons.[1]

Institutionally, the most important measure was undoubtedly the promulgation of the new Constitution which was to come into force on 15 March 1967. From April 1966 onwards the Minister of Justice, the liberal Mem de Sá, had entrusted a committee of four lawyers[2] with the task of producing a new charter incorporating the permanent elements of the Institutional Acts that had been enacted since 1964 together with their supplements.

The work of these lawyers had been published on 25 August,[3] but did not meet Castello Branco's wishes. He had then instructed his new Minister of Justice[4] to produce a text that was more in line with the aims of the Revolution. This draft, when published on 6 December, aroused lively protests both from the opposition and from the members of ARENA. By means of Institutional Act No. 4 which was published next day in the official gazette, an extraordinary session of Parliament was convened from 12 December 1966 to 24 January 1967 to debate, reject, modify or promulgate the new draft Constitution following an accelerated procedure.[5] In the meantime and until the new Constitution came into force, the executive could legislate by decrees on matters touching national security, administration and finance.

Thereupon the opposition broke up. It was partly egged on by Carlos Lacerda who had just concluded the Pact of Lisbon with Juscelino Kubitschek[6] in order to strengthen his 'enlarged front'[7] and to create a centre-left party[8] named in theory the People's Democratic Reform Party ready for the 1971 elections. For the benefit of public opinion he directed his attack at the new official appellation of the country which was henceforth to be known as the Federative Republic of Brazil instead of the United States of Brazil, a change which, not without reason, contained hints of increasingly centralised government. Although the time allowed for discussion was limited, the debate was extremely animated, as Castello Branco had let it be known that nobody's civil rights would be suspended while the extraordinary session lasted. More than 1500 amendments were proposed, but most of them were not accepted.

At the same time a law aimed at the press and entitled Rules for Freedom of Expression and Information was submitted to Parliament on 21 December. The journalists concentrated their fire on this bill, which threatened them directly, and thus attention was diverted from the debates about the Constitution. Castello Branco must have been the first to congratulate himself about the diversion – indeed perhaps it was he who engineered it.

This passage is surprising in as much as until then the régime had been careful to avoid any interference with freedom of expression, barring some limited and well-defined cases.[9] But the new bill, without directly conflicting with the clauses in the draft Constitution submitted by the Government concerning the freedom of expression which was fully guaranteed,[10] and concerning the ownership of journalistic undertakings,[11] had very strict provisions regarding offences committed by the press, and also applied to all the media.[12] This stiffening of the law was not mentioned in the speech made by the Minister of Justice on the reasons for the bill; these referred to purely technical matters: 'whereas the present law No. 2083 of 12 November 1953 urgently requires reformulation in view of the gaps that have become apparent in its application after more than 13 years of existence...'

The press and the media were unanimous in considering that the definitions in the bill were too vague, though they recognised the need for a new code, and they protested against the extremely severe increases in the penalties to which offenders were liable.

At the First National Meeting of the Press, Radio and Television which was held in the Federal Capital on 11 and 12 January 1967 a motion known as the Declaration of Brasilia was passed and was signed by nineteen professional unions. This document states: 'At the time when Brazil is endeavouring to break the barrier of underdevelopment and when the complex problems of this stage have to be overcome in a democratic manner, the existence of this régime depends upon freedom of thought, of discussion and of information.[13]

This challenge resulted in 363 amendments which were discussed between 16 and 19 January by an *ad hoc* committee of Congress. The text as finally issued[14] provided for severe penalties. In certain cases, such as press offences whereby the President of the Republic was accused or attacked, they could amount to as much as thirteen years and four months' imprisonment accompanied by fines up to 66 times the minimum monthly wage.[15]

In principle arrests had to be based on a legal warrant, but in an emergency they could be effected by administrative procedure. In the latter event the file had to be sent at once to the Ministry of Justice which had the duty of submitting the case within five days to the Federal Appeal Court. If the Court's judgment was contrary to the administrative decision, the Government was liable to reimburse any losses suffered by the wrongly accused organ of information.

Notwithstanding its severity, the new code was decidedly more acceptable to journalists than the original draft. However, the bill had been too much sweetened to be fully acceptable to the régime, and (to change the metaphor) a few of its lost teeth were given back to it by the new decree concerning national security which was enacted by the President only two days before Costa e Silva took up his office, and which also included the information media.[16]

Even so, on the whole most commentators finally agreed with the opinion expressed by Freitas Nobre: 'Although the present law contains some negative and contradictory aspects, it is technically better adapted to the present state of information.'[17] They also agreed that, taken together with the provisions of the Constitution in force, the new rules would still enable the written and spoken media to carry out their task.[18]

The new Constitution of the Federative Republic of Brazil was then promulgated on 24 January 1967.[19]

It was a centralising Constitution which incorporated the main features of the Institutional Acts and thus confirmed the very decided reinforcement of the powers of the President over against those of Parliament and the provincial states. This Constitution was not introduced simply for tactical reasons; on the contrary it expressed the very essence of Castello Branco's thought at the end of some thirty months of political life, as the documents filed in his personal archives show. The written *aide-mémoire* dated 30 August 1966, composed for the meeting of the National Security Council held on that date to discuss the constitutional problem, makes this clear: 'To sum up, it is worth repeating that the Constitution in force [that of 1946] is also one of the causes of the crisis in Brazil and that at this stage of our development present circumstances offer us an excellent opportunity of remedying it ... [for] there are two distinct phases to the Revolution and there is no doubt that the first one will end on 15 March 1967 when [Costa e Silva becoming President] the second stage will commence.'[20]

The most interesting innovations were the economic ones. For the first time they gave the Federal Government the powers to apply, and have the provincial states apply, a national policy for growth and development, thus confirming the importance that the President attached to this matter. Thus the Federal Government was empowered to intervene in a provincial state should action have been taken contrary to governmental directives on economic or financial matters, and this gave the central Government a means of controlling the not infrequently hare-brained initiatives of the State governors.[21] The twenty-two states were also given four years in which to reduce their staffing expenses by one half.

Planning was built into the system, it became compulsory to budget programmes, and for their execution only the President of the Republic could introduce laws apportioning money or those which would have the effect of increasing public expenditure. The measures which had already been enacted for promoting agrarian reform (expropriation for reasons of 'social utility' against compensation by public loan bonds) were reaffirmed.[22]

Industrial production was entrusted predominantly to private initiative, though account was taken of the important part played by the nationalised sector and the State retained the power to take over the monopoly of certain activities if they were considered essential for 'reasons of national security or with the aim of organising activities that cannot be effectively developed under a competitive, free initiative system'.[23]

Freedom of association in professional bodies or trade unions was guaranteed to workers, who were also authorised to collect trade union dues. Voting at trade union elections was made compulsory.[24]

Workers also received the following rights under Article 165 of the Constitution:

1. A minimum wage sufficient to meet the normal needs of the

worker and his family under living conditions appropriate to each region.
2. Family allocations for dependants of the worker.
3. Discrimination by reason of sex, colour or civil status in regard to wages or conditions of employment was forbidden.
4. Night work was to be paid more highly than day work.
5. Workers were to be integrated into the life and development of the enterprise, to share in the profits and in exceptional, defined cases and under conditions to be laid down, in the management.
6. The working day must not, except in certain specified cases, exceed eight hours with a rest period.
7. A paid weekly rest day and payment on non-working civil and religious holidays in accordance with local traditions.
8. Paid annual holidays.
9. Proper conditions of safety and hygiene at work.
10. The employment of children under twelve years of age and of women, and at night time, of young people under eighteen, in industries unhealthy for them, was prohibited.
11. Paid maternity leave before and after childbirth, without detriment either to the employment or the wages.
12. Fixed percentages of Brazilian workers to be employed in public services for which concessions were granted and in the workplaces of certain branches of trade and industry.
13. Stability of employment involving compensation to dismissed workmen or an equivalent guarantee fund.
14. Recognition of collective work agreement.
15. Medical, hospital and preventive medical assistance.
16. Social security in case of sickness, old age, inability to work or death; unemployment insurance, industrial accident insurance and maternity assurance met by contributions from the State, the employer and the employee.
17. It was forbidden to make distinctions between manual, technical and intellectual work or between workers in the corresponding trades.
18. The State maintained holiday homes and rest homes, sanatoria and convalescent homes under terms laid down by law.
19. Right of retirement for women after thirty years' service, on full pay.
20. The right to strike, subject to the provisions of Article 162 (this article forbids strikes in the public services and 'essential activities' listed in the law).[25]

It is interesting to note that with regard to individual liberties a new offence was added to the existing reasons for suspension of civil rights (civil incapacity and penal conviction) namely, 'the abuse of individual or political rights with the object either of subverting the democratic régime or of *corruption*'.[26] Thenceforward the suspension of civil rights required a decree of the Supreme Court and could be imposed for a period ranging from two to ten years.[27]

If the accused was an elected person at federal level he could not be proceeded against unless the institution to which he belonged raised his immunity, as suspension of civil rights carried with it, for the period involved, the loss of any public elective mandate, responsibility or function.[28] The fullest rights of defence were guaranteed to everybody.[29]

Lastly, although it was still within the power of military tribunals to judge civilians in cases of endangering national security, their decisions were subject to appeal before the Supreme Court.

On 25 February 1967 Castello Branco put the finishing touches to his work on the institutions by supplementing the Constitution by Decree Law No. 200 dealing with reform of the federal administration.

This text, which has seventeen chapters[30] and 215 articles, constitutes a fundamental recasting of the procedures of the body politic in Brazil[31] and cuts pitiless swaths into the jungle of vested interests.

Planning was made an absolute rule,[32] and all activity thenceforth had to fit into a programme extending over several years which covered the national, regional and sector plans. The latter were to be revised each year within the framework of the detailed programme budget, department by department. At the federal level, co-ordination and delegation of powers and responsibilities hitherto unknown in the administration became obligatory. A General Inspectorate of Finances was set up to monitor expenditure and in each civilian ministry there was a secretary general co-ordinating the activities of the various directorates. By a significant modification in their internal structure, ordinary ministries were limited to sixteen, distributed among five sectors, and a maximum of seven extraordinary ministries was authorised.[33]

The administrative code set the final seal on the concept of national security policy which since the Revolution had replaced the more restrictive concept of national defence. Worked out on the basis of a national strategic concept laid down by the National Security Council (C.S.N.) acting in a consultative capacity, the formulation and conduct of this policy were exclusive prerogatives of the President.[34] The President was assisted in this field by three bodies reporting directly to him, the Armed Forces High Command, the Armed Forces General Staff and the National Intelligence Service (S.N.I.). This last 'supervises and co-ordinates throughout the national territory the intelligence and counter-intelligence activities and in particular those concerned with national security'.[35] To assist it in executing its task, the S.N.I. had to establish a listening post in each ministry entitled the Security and Intelligence Division.[36]

In the purely administrative field, a new set of rules for civil servants was drawn up. It provided for the elimination of 'unoccupied' officials, of which ministries were often full, and for competitive recruitment and a revamping of the civilian personnel administrative department. Furthermore, all public contracts were in future to be put out to tender, with certain specified exceptions.

Some unrest among the urban population might have been anticipated. But in fact argument about the measures was only perfunctory. Perhaps the general apathy can be explained by the experience of 1937, when Getúlio Vargas had imposed a dictatorial Constitution, under which Brazil had lived for nine years. Yet the people remember that period not as one of dictatorship but as the one during which social legislation took shape in Brazil.

27 The Political Reforms which Flowed from the Plan

The new Constitution and the decree on the reform of the administration are useful pointers to the progress that had been made since 1964. In less than three years Castello Branco, 'analytical and objective',[1] had succeeded in endowing the country with modern institutions which explicitly conferred upon the future Federal Government the powers it needed to carry out a coherent policy of growth.

Parallel to this, and no doubt motivated by the same concern to create a framework within which Costa e Silva would have to act, he caused Roberto Campos to lay down a new Ten-Year Economic and Social Development Plan due for publication just before his term of office came to an end.

This Plan had been prepared by E.P.E.A. (Escritório de Pesquisa Econômica Aplicada do Ministerio do Planejamento), a specialised institution within the planning ministry, assisted by various consultants including a group from the University of California at Berkeley, led by Professor Howard S. Ellis from 1965 to 1967 (financed by U.S. aid) and experts lent by the United Nations, by the Organisation of American States and by a number of European governments.

To avoid the mistake of planning from above which had often been held against the P.A.E.G. of 1964, Roberto Campos had arranged to receive advice from various quarters. For example, the studies of the 'co-ordination groups' of CONSPLAN, on the model of the French 'plan committees', formed the basis of the sectorial analysis.

The Plan itself set out a number of steps to be taken. The objectives and strategies were formulated for the period 1967–76, and a five-year investment plan was submitted. It is unnecessary to go into the details here, as the Government of Costa e Silva abandoned the overall project, though it retained the main features of the investment plan for the first three years.

None the less, apart from the generally interesting macro-economic aspect of the Ten-Year Plan, it made a decisive contribution to future planning under the three following aspects:

(a) It was the first contribution to micro-economic planning supported by models specially constructed with the object of integrating the sector plans within the framework of monetary and fiscal options and options concerning foreign trade. A number of possible strategies were analysed and compatibility tests were applied to harmonise the objectives of growth and of stabilisation, of employment and of keeping the balance of payments in equilibrium.

(b) It was an attempt to interpret social problems born of growing inter-disciplinary collaboration between economists, students of politics, sociologists and experts in public administration. For example, the objectives set for education were for the first time fixed with reference to the requirements for manpower and the needed specialist trades instead of being studied within the traditional framework of teaching of the humanities and the population forecast. Again, investment in building and construction, regarded as a factor in social stability and as a source of unskilled jobs, received detailed study.

(c) Thirdly, the Plan was concerned to a large extent with agricultural production, a matter usually disregarded by planners, regarding it as a basis for bringing the balance of payments into equilibrium and as a means of containing inflation.

The discussions between these various specialists brought out on the one hand the need for a much greater effort on the part of the governmental team to communicate with those sections of public opinion that wished to have a share in shaping their future and on the other hand two main areas of conflict – the contradiction between stability and development and that known as nationalism versus foreign domination.

The first of these contradictions was explained by a widely held view that in a developing country inflation is a necessary by-product, if not a cause, of development. Although Brazil's experience from 1963 to 1964 had shown that stagnation can go hand in hand with inflation if the inflation is not home-made,[2] the question was far from being settled.[3]

The second was caused by the intense nationalism of Brazilians – nationalism, not xenophobia or anti-Americanism. However poor he may be, the man in the street, with his roots deep in his immense 'Brazilian Brazil',[4] feels instinctively that his country has a great economic future; hence he is not a prey to the antagonism born of fear which is so common among peoples living under the shadow of a great power.

This special form of nationalism, which is easily exploitable, may in certain circumstances act as a brake. With regard to foreign investment for instance, some of the politicians, officers, intellectuals, students and local business heads, motivated by different drives, were united in one and the same emotional reaction against control by foreigners, and their attitude was reflected among the urban masses. Consequently very many Brazilians were suspicious of economic dependence and therefore tended to reject even such foreign contributions as, judiciously controlled, could help to accelerate growth as long as Brazil was not yet in a position to mobilise locally all the resources needed for rapid development.[5]

Castello Branco and Roberto Campos opposed this trend of thought vigorously and their efforts met with some success, but only at the cost of their personal popularity, and the Minister of Planning, whom certain deputies accused of selling the country down the river, only just escaped appearing before the parliamentary Committee of Inquiry in 1966.

In retrospect, notwithstanding the tensions created by the options that were chosen, there is no doubt that Castello Branco's régime sought its vindication at the bar of history in the necessity of establishing a systematic programme for modernising the economy.

For the first time in Brazil, all political activity had been harnessed in the service of the Plan, thus standing on its head the traditional order of things, under which the Plan would have been subservient to politics. Indeed, planning had become 'the programme of the Revolution'.[6]

This phenomenon can be explained by the fact that the Military who seized power did so as an organised body and not as individuals. As such, they were relatively close to Weber's ideal:[7] as a technically based bureaucracy, the Armed Forces cannot fulfil their task and develop unless they have at their disposal a planned framework of decision.

During the first three years of Castello Branco's Government, public opinion evolved sufficiently to accept planning as an indispensable condition of the modernisation of the nation that it wished for[8] and in March 1967 the divergences related more to the choice of objectives than to the principle.

But in order to reach that point Castello Branco had thrown off the constraints of out-dated administrative institutions and had steadily imposed, by force where necessary, the establishment of plans formulated by the all too rare civilian representatives of Weber's bureaucratic élite, at a time when the civil service in Brazil was still at the 'prismatic' stage.[9]

The gap becomes even more apparent in the provisional definition of the role of the Administration just after the Revolution, given by Robert Daland:

> to provide a channel for upward mobility for the educated middle class,
> to provide permanent income for that portion of the middle class which provides support for the régime ...
> to provide opportunities for private entrepreneurship based on the powers attaching to certain offices.[10]

Since, under the provisions of the law of 'security of office' instituted by Vargas, officials were not within the power of the existing government, they were virtually isolated from the shocks of politics (unless of course a revolution took place) and led a life that was independent of the executive, protecting their own vested interests without being obliged to prove to anybody how productive they were.

As soon as they felt themselves to be threatened by the reforming ardour of the new régime, the civil servants instinctively set the weight of their inertia against all efforts to bring about change. In order to defend their interests better, they made common cause with the groups of which the former political system was composed, whose spokesmen, although they gave lip service to the idea of the Plan, questioned its viability and the usefulness of a central planning body.

But Castello Branco had come down decisively on the side of a rational scientific and centralised system. He considered that the planner should be given responsibility for carrying out the plan, and it is no exaggeration to claim that Roberto Campos was more a prime minister than a maker of blueprints.

This authoritarian planning was probably inevitable because it was necessary to impose at one and the same time short-term sacrifices, the redistribution of existing resources and a revision of the methods by which the resources were distributed. But such planning presupposed a professionally able bureaucracy whose actions were subject to logical and effective supervision, and the Government went vigorously to work at building just such a bureaucracy.

However, the fact that at least in its early days the political colour of the Government of the new régime was not altogether clear was a cause of division, and this absence of consensus led to a permanent need for supplementary powers to do away with obstacles, neutralise political reaction, inevitable though they were, and enable the Plan to be executed. Hence it is not surprising that under Castello Branco the element of political choice centred upon putting the P.A.E.G. to work rather than involving it.

This situation confirms that oft-quoted conclusion of Albert Waterston:

> When a country's leaders in a *stable* government are strongly devoted to development, inadequacies of the particular form of planning used – or even the lack of any formal planning – will not seriously impede the country's development. Conversely in the absence of political commitment or stability, the most advanced form of planning will not make a significant contribution towards a country's development.[11]

In theory a hybrid choice of 'centralised planning with its execution monitored but decentralised' would have been possible; but this was rejected probably because after the excesses of the Goulart régime, by a kind of swing of the pendulum the military who decided to assume full responsibility for order throughout the national territory did not see how this objective of political stability could be dissociated from their method of action in the economic sphere.

Hence, sensing the practical impossibility of achieving the main objective he had in view within the constraints of the situation inherited by the Revolution (for the President refused to devote the greater part of his time, energy and influence to assembling the wherewithal to govern) Castello Branco launched into a whirlwind of reforms.

These then were a *consequence, a necessary condition* and not an aim in themselves. Were they also a *sufficient condition* as his advisers tended to believe? The question may at any rate be asked, as in the words of the sociologist Fernando Henrique Cardoso:

> How effective is a decisional system that is not connected to the channels of political participation ... to push on with development? Is the success of formal rationalism and even possibly the existence of results that are impressive and yet do not carry the

accent of the main groups engaged in the economic and social activities of a developing country, sufficient reason to weaken the social controls such as freedom to criticise, a freely working press and an unfettered flow of information, which are necessary conditions for the formation of a participating public opinion?'[12]

However this may be, a long road has been travelled. And although the sociologist Hélio Jaguaribe considers that the model adopted since 1964 is a 'colonial-fascism',[13] other critics such as the political scientist Antonio Cândido Mendes de Almeida[14] rather agree with our opinion in attributing to the Castello Branco régime, after a systematic analysis, a 'high index of coherence in his actions'. He speaks of the real grasp of strategy which enabled the minority of technocrats to bring about 'for the first time a coherent group of changes undertaken from a rigid ideological view of the Brazilian reality'[15] with the object of 'establishing a coherent and vigorous economic system'.[16]

Nevertheless, in terms of a certain conception of democracy, the price paid was high. It need not be doubted that Castello Branco paid an even higher price: having accomplished his titanic labours he withdrew, misunderstood and unpopular for having agreed to be the 'guardian of the bankruptcy' of Brazil, a task which he had never sought.[17] On 15 March 1967 'the little shabby god', as Carlos Lacerda called him, was left alone to await the verdict of history.

28 The Attempt at Humanisation

In March 1967 Costa e Silva inherited a Brazil that was irrevocably committed to the path of modernisation and in which the military, still forming a 'twilight' régime, shared part of the power with certain civilian sectors. Compared with Castello Branco he had the advantage of being popular, for the average Brazilian thought he could recognise himself in this humanising President. Without expecting miracles, majority public opinion thought it could look forward to a government better than the previous one.[1]

'Good-natured, simple, understanding, willing to do deals which from time immemorial have smoothed so many paths in the political life of Brazil',[2] Costa e Silva tried to bring about a rebirth of democracy, but his attempt was frustrated by the onrush of the forces that the previous President had tried to dam and, by a cruel paradox, led to a real dictatorship after twenty months.

His Cabinet, which took office on 15 March 1967, contained eight officers on the active list, two military men on the reserve list, six civilian technicians and three politicians, counting both the Heads of the Civil and Military Households and the Head of the National Intelligence Service, all of ministerial rank.[3]

The military ministers represented a spectrum going from a right-wing extremist to a 'Nasserian' and included a representative of the 'Sorbonne', four pillars of the hard line, one of no clear views, a clever political manipulator and a prototype of the uniformed manager.[4] Of the civilians, the Minister of Justice was so far identified with the hard line that he has been described as a 'soldier in civvies'.[5]

The Government team had three characteristics: first it contained not a single member of the preceding Cabinet; secondly, all the posts directly linked to the activation of the development policy were held by military men; and thirdly a fresh orientation had been given to the ministers dealing with economic affairs (finance, planning and industry). Henceforward these were to be regarded as a co-ordinated team, led by the Finance Minister who thus took over the part previously played by Roberto Campos. This change justifies the conclusion that the President had been convinced by the arguments of those who were in favour of the policy of economic management closer to the daily life of Brazilians in contrast to ivory tower planning. He was more empirical than Castello Branco and sought to conduct a very flexible policy, and his choice shows that he would always come down on the side of pragmatism rather than that of theory.

The first few months of the new Government seemed to be characterised by some lack of a sense of direction. Statements and counter-statements[6] abounded, and it looked as if the President was not taking any decisions. This comparative inactivity was all the more striking to a public which had been accustomed for some time to Castello Branco's frantic legislative pace.

The opposition led by Carlos Lacerda was looking for changes and wanted rapid action. They called for three things to be done at once:

> an amnesty or at least a revision of the lists of those deprived of their civil rights;
>
> a change in the constitution reintroducing direct elections, a

strengthening of the powers of parliament and the repeal of the laws on the Press and on national security;

a more generous wages policy and an easing of the policy of austerity introduced by Roberto Campos.

Was Costa e Silva's silence due to political skill or lack of it? This question became a burning topic of discussion at the time. The doubts were fuelled by the tension which existed between ministers in office and the leaders of the previous Government. The latter, gathered in what was called by the press 'the phantom cabinet of the republic of Ipanema'[7] were indeed keeping a vigilant watch on how the Government was making out.[8]

As the opposition was trying to make capital out of the potential unrest, Castello Branco left Brazil and embarked upon a long tour of Europe as soon as he became aware of the perils the situation represented for the unity of the Revolution. As for the members of parliament, instead of taking the chance presented to them and making their mark as a constructive force, they dissipated their energies in senseless strife which only helped to discredit them.[9]

Meanwhile, the opposition's motions for repeal of the laws relating to national security and the amnesty remained open for discussion. These vain arguments were the cue for the Minister of the Army to say on 21 April to the officer corps which was asking what was the use of ARENA and of Parliament, that there could be no question of going back on the penal measures that Castello Branco had taken, and to warn the Upper and Lower Chamber against taking any hasty action in the matter.

Vice-President Pedro Aleixo immediately contradicted him and notwithstanding the controversy which then arose, Costa e Silva did not break his silence. He even added to the confusion by authorising the return of those who had been exiled. Ex-President Kubitschek and ex-Governor Adhémar de Barros[10] took advantage of this to return to Brazil where they immediately took up once more their political contacts.

With the object of goading the President to make his position clear, Carlos Lacerda published in the *Tribuna da Imprensa* some articles signed by his successor in the editorship of this daily paper, Hélio Fernandes, whose civil rights had been suspended and who in consequence had no right to publish anything. Nevertheless when legal proceedings were taken this political journalist was granted a non-suit judgment, and in spite of the clamour of the hard liners the court authorised him to continue to exercise his 'only profession'.

Signs of discontent multiplied on every hand. Starting in March 1967, bombs were exploded in the Ministry of Education and students demonstrated with increasing violence in several cities including Rio de Janeiro, Belo Horizonte, São Paulo and Brasilia.

In May the trade unions demanded the right of complete freedom of action and took the opposition line as regards their purchasing power, the amnesty and the abolition of some of the laws passed by the former Government.

During this same month, the press published the conclusions of the Commission of Inquiry appointed by the Legislative Assembly of the State of Rio Grande do Sul to determine the exact reasons for the death of ex-Sergeant Raimundo Soares, who had been arrested for subversion and found drowned on the previous 24 August. The report denounced the extortions committed and openly accused the military men who had been in charge of the inquiry.[11]

Finally on 24 May Costa e Silva, considering that there was a risk of things going too far, broke his silence. And he came out unreservedly on the side of the hard line: 'The revolutionary process', he said, 'will continue along the road to complete eradication of the distortions, mistakes and misunderstandings of the past until new methods of administration and a new system of national politics have been established.'[12] But this statement did not fully satisfy some hard-line colonels led by their colleague Colonel 'Tito'[13] Boaventura Cavalcanti Jr, brother of the Minister of Mines and Energy, who had just been appointed Commander of the Fort of São João at Rio de Janeiro. On 23 June, one of them, Colonel Amerino Raposo, Head of the National Intelligence Service in the city of Rio de Janeiro went so far as to call in the Minister of Finance for official interrogation. The same impertinent procedure was meted out to other members of the Government. The President reacted immediately against this attack on discipline and the hierarchy. He would have deprived the colonels responsible of their rank but in view of the protests raised in certain military circles he did no more than transfer them.

29 The New Economic Objectives

By the choice of his Minister of Finance, Professor Antonio Delfim Netto, Costa e Silva let it be known that the economic policy he intended to pursue would incorporate some changes.[1]

The directives of the Strategic Development Programme which were announced by the Planning Minister Hélio Beltrão on 27 June 1967 were published in July.[2] They were the prelude to the Strategic Development Programme (P.E.D.) which was to appear the following year. This text declared that economic and social development was the basic aim of the Government and that thenceforth national policy both at home and abroad was to be subordinated to it.

The economic system selected was based on five main criteria: strengthening of the private sector, gradual stabilisation of prices, increased Government responsibility for infrastructure investment, multiplication of job opportunities, and the consolidation and enlargement of both the home and foreign markets.

Compared with the views of the previous Government, the factors had been placed in reverse order. The fight against inflation yielded priority to expansion. This development, which was wanted by some sections of the business community, originated in the discussions on the P.A.E.G.[3] These discussions had highlighted the way in which Roberto Campos' fight against inflation had led to a sharp fall in production due to a lack of purchasing power, whereupon demand–pull inflation had turned upside-down and changed into cost–push inflation. According to this line of thought the situation could be reversed by re-stimulating the economy and for this purpose a stimulus had to be given to the private sector, always an excellent agent of growth when motivated by realisable profits. Delfim Netto, a 'Paulista' (i.e. a native of São Paulo) and former secretary of the employers' association, clearly shared this point of view.

The Strategic Programme was presented as a national development project the object of which was to prove that development in Brazil was viable, and it claimed to represent a general consensus of opinion. The aim was still to increase productivity by rationalising the system of distributing the limited available resources, and the main themes of the Ten-Year Plan which the previous Government had prepared were taken over, namely the marketing of agricultural products, administrative reform, construction, public health and education. But more emphasis was placed on transport, communications and industrialisation.

As a starting point, after having noted the increasing share taken by the public sector in the national economy, the P.E.D. recalled that the dynamic phase of growth by import substitution had reached its limit, thus reducing easy outlets for new investment.

It attributed this slowing down of industrialisation to insufficient investment. For the authors of the P.E.D. investment decisions of entrepreneurs were no longer, at least in part, conditioned by keeping or obtaining market shares in markets already existing, since these were saturated for the time being, but by the growth forecasts for the sectors concerned. But since the deflationary policy of the Castello Branco Government had resulted in some under-employment of the available factors of production, new investment appeared neither essential nor immediately profitable, and was therefore deferred. Consequently the authors of the P.E.D. thought that growth of demand should be stimulated without delay by a massive injection of investments both public and private.[4]

To finance the private investment the policy of income redistribution should have as a priority aim the activation of the propensity to save, while still encouraging balanced growth of the demand for goods and services. Hence the redistributive option chosen was aimed at an overall reactivation of industrial growth, not at total justice for the individual.

With this in view, managers of traditional businesses which generally employed large numbers of workers were to be helped by the State to compensate for the technology gap and to increase the profitability of their factories.

The distortions that have already been mentioned were enumerated again, but emphasis was also placed on two points that Roberto Campos had preferred not to spell out because of their political implications:

First, the unfavourable economic consequences of Vargas' labour legislation which, by considerably increasing the cost of the labour factor, had given an impetus to the adoption of modern technologies imported from abroad. These technologies, which consumed large amounts of capital, enabled productivity to be increased but did so by providing fewer jobs. This was one of the factors involved in the relative contraction of the consumer market capable of participating in an industrialised economy, and so it made the gap still wider between the dynamic and the traditional sectors of the economy.

In the second place, there was the very high opportunity cost of the large part of the national economy given over by populism to the public sector of which 'the efficiency in the use of resources is low compared with that of the private sector'.[5]

The New Economic Objectives

The P.E.D. did give Roberto Campos credit for having accomplished a difficult task by managing to change the habits and behaviour of the economically active population.[6]

It was this 'reversal of expectations' which prepared the way for the renewed expansion of which the new Government was to be the champion. To achieve this, it was planned to allocate a certain period of time to a preparatory phase during which a 'transitional strategy' would be applied. During this period, the men who held responsibility for the economic policy would have to exhibit great adaptability in order to maintain a balance between two incompatible pairs of objectives. On the one hand they must couple an increase in demand and liquidity with a gradual reduction of the rate of inflation, and on the other hand they must bring about a reduction in the percentage of the G.N.P. going to the public sector whilst at the same time increasing infrastructure investment. This predevelopment phase was to last until the end of 1972 at which time it was planned that the level of economic activity would have practically reached full employment of the available factors and since actual production would be close to productive capacity, it would be able to grow in accordance with 'a long-term vector of dynamic equilibrium'.[7]

For this purpose about 80 per cent of investment would be concentrated on the infrastructure in order to obtain 'maximum marginal social production', or in other words to allow the external economies created by basic investment to be exploited by other concomitant investments.[8]

The P.E.D. published a diagnosis that was at first sight paradoxical for a developing country, and it attracted a good deal of comment. According to this diagnosis, internal capital formation did not pose insurmountable problems in Brazil; what was lacking however were financial institutions capable of directing these savings – which were adequate in real terms – towards productive investment. The same was true, *mutatis mutandis*, as regards the external sector where it was thought that the bottleneck was due rather to a deficit in the balance of payments than to a real lack of funds, and that this bottleneck was due to the supply of hard currencies, not to the volume of home savings.

The new direction taken by economic policy was to have profound repercussions on the country. For it involved setting up financial institutions, channelling savings and, in order to make money 'productive', interesting the man in the street in economic matters, which was done by revitalising the Stock Exchange.

The immediate task was to identify the sectors that were suffering from under-utilisation of their productive capacity and to stimulate demand for their products by fiscal and monetary means.

It would also be necessary to improve the earnings of private sector investment, to encourage it to carry out voluntarily the task assigned to it under the P.E.D. plan. Since the Government had to increase the sums which it allocated to infrastructure investment without increasing taxation, it became imperative to reduce State expenditure on personnel which meant that it must certainly be prepared for political tension.

In truth, the strategic programme required a fundamental change in the relations between the capital factor and the labour factor, and this had to be brought about by a change in the relative cost of the factors of production (in practice by the temporary freezing of wages) and by tax advantages given primarily to methods of work that were labour-intensive.[9] This new formulation of the Government's economic policy may not have won over the working class at once but it did meet the wishes of the dynamic sector of the economy and disposed top management more favourably to the régime.

The flexibility of this policy[10] added to the reforms previously undertaken, enabled the Brazilian economy to show results very soon, and by the end of 1968 the annual rate of growth reached 8·4 per cent (industry having advanced by 13·2 per cent) whereas the cost of living rose by only 22 per cent compared with 41·3 per cent in 1966 and 30·4 per cent in 1967.[11]

30 Failure of the Enlarged Front

On 18 July 1967 Castello Branco, just back from Europe, was killed in an air accident near Fortaleza, the capital of his State of Ceará.[1] News of this fatality put an end to the expectancy of the preceding months. It increased Costa e Silva's freedom of action by enabling fresh alignments of strength to take place and, paradoxically, it brought about the dissolution of the 'Enlarged Front' owing to the excesses of Carlos Lacerda.

The spark which caused the explosion was struck by the journalist Hélio Fernandes, whose right to practise his profession had recently been restored by a court decision. The day after the accident he published in the *Tribuna da Imprensa*, a daily paper reflecting Lacerda's opinions, an unusually violent editorial:

> Humanity has lost little or nothing by the death of Castello Branco. With the ex-President a cold, insensitive, vindictive, implacable, inhuman, calculating, cruel, frustrated man has disappeared without greatness or nobility. A being cold within and without with a heart like the Sahara Desert. Throughout his life Castello Branco neither loved nor was loved. The death of such a man can only arouse indifference. How can we weep for one whose whole existence was marked by mistrust and surly isolation, without the least fibre of emotion, without a moment's greatness, without an instant of pity, meditation or humanity?[2]

The insult was too serious to remain unanswered. The Army called for punishment and Costa e Silva lost no time in having 'the author of this infamy' arrested and deported to Fernando de Noronha, a small volcanic island covering 26 sq. km, four degrees south of the equator.[3] To make it quite clear that he was acting in the name of the whole Revolution, the President based his decision on Institutional Act No. 2 which had lapsed, rather than on the wording of the laws in force.

This event finalised the break between the régime and Carlos Lacerda, who announced that he would run for the 1970 presidential elections, thus justifying those who thought that the Enlarged Front, which had been a talking point for months but which had never succeeded in formulating a definite programme, was simply a springboard designed to serve the ambitions of the ex-Governor of Guanabara.

Putting an end to the armistice which he had more or less observed, Lacerda loosed off at the Government, and at the Minister of Justice in particular, a series of his usual intemperate articles. Costa e Silva begged his minister not to reply, as the Enlarged Front was already enjoying a great deal of publicity caused by the number of attacks that had appeared in the newspaper *O Globo*.[4] They were written by General Augusto Cézar Moniz de Aragão, who had been President of the Military Club[5] since 1964 and was a member of the 'Sorbonne' who enjoyed considerable popularity among the officers.

This quarrel between Lacerda and Aragão became so embittered, not merely nationally but personally, that the protagonists threatened to take to fisticuffs.

On 28 August 1967 Carlos Lacerda was refused the right to appear on television and on the thirtieth Aragão was ordered by the Chief of the General Staff of the Armed Forces, General Orlando Geisel, to stop publishing his articles.

However, Lacerda desperately sought to gather beneath his

banner all the opposition elements in order to break up the régime from within. With this in view he stated that the Enlarged Front was not a new party but a civil movement, open to anybody to join. On 24 September he went to Uruguay where he concluded with ex-President Goulart, previously his implacable enemy, the Pact of Montevideo, and when he returned on the twenty-fifth he announced that the formative phase of the Enlarged Front was completed and that action could now commence.

Lacerda, as usual, had chosen the date for publishing his message with care. On the same day the Twentieth Meeting of the Governors of the International Monetary Fund opened at Rio de Janeiro, and in recognition of this sign that Brazil once more enjoyed the confidence of the financial world, the authorities did not take action against the ex-Governor for fear of giving the impression of a divided country.

Nevertheless, the Goulart–Lacerda–Kubitschek alliance[6] was too unusual to attract the masses of the people. The trade unions and former members of the Brazilian Workers' Party were more inclined to turn to the militant nationalism of the Minister of the Interior, Albuquerque Lima. And he stated, on 2 October, that he rejected the Enlarged Front which he called a 'movement aimed at restoring the state of affairs that existed before the Revolution'.[7] In spite of the growing opposition from the hard liners, who resented Carlos Lacerda's treason all the more because they had at one time been his fanatical admirers, Costa e Silva announced that he would not take any action against the Enlarged Front so long as the movement did not cause a breach of the peace.

The former Governor of Guanabara decided to concentrate his activity on combating the wages policy and on forming closer links with the student bodies. With this in view he launched into a veritable crescendo of verbal violence. Even his own supporters, after having warned him several times, left the Enlarged Front because they no longer considered it capable of forming a bridge between civilians and the Military.

On 16 December, speaking at the University of Porto Alegre, Lacerda accused the Army of having usurped power and incited youth to fight. 'Nobody is against the Military,' he said, 'but everybody ought to be against militarism, most of all the Military themselves... corruption among the Military or protected by the Military is the worst corruption there can be, because it is armed.'[8] On the twenty-sixth and twenty-seventh he renewed his attacks, at Rio de Janeiro and at São Paulo. One month later, on 26 January 1968, he said at São Paulo while addressing some young economists that certain ministers had been bought by foreign interests and that the Military had 'espoused the decadent oligarchy'.

That was too much, and the First, Second and Third Armies were put on a state of alert, apparently with the dual object of intimidating the opposition and of holding the most excitable hard-line officers in check. But Carlos Lacerda's repeated insults finally wore down even the most patient among the Military. After some other skirmishes,[9] Instruction No. 177 issued on 5 April 1968 by the Minister of Justice, forbade any demonstrations by the Enlarged Front, the existence of which had only succeeded in still further dividing an opposition which was already incapable of uniting for any positive purpose.[10]

31 Humanisation Comes to a Dead End

After the new session of Parliament had opened, the two official parties ARENA and the M.D.B. were each looking for a way forward. The opposition, which had at first tended towards a *rapprochement* with the Enlarged Front, divided into four schools of thought. The first was opposed to Lacerda for personal reasons, the second supported him, the third considered that the movement could not survive within the existing legal framework of the country and the fourth held aloof for fear of unleashing action by the Military which would put an end to the last formal vestiges of democracy in Brazil. At last, on 27 October 1967, the executive of the M.D.B. distributed a handout to the press in which it was said that though the party applauded the efforts put forward to reintroduce democracy into the country, it was not prepared to support the Enlarged Front.

For their part the ARENA deputies still wanted to make their voices heard. They had no intention of being regarded as puppets and they called for direct elections, changes in the electoral code, a return to a multi-party situation, the reduction of military expenditure, the abolition of the laws on national security and an economic policy allowing more freedom of movement on the wages front.[1] They went so far in a kind of electoral auction with the Enlarged Front that on 5 October Costa e Silva called them together and told them that neither the Constitution nor the wages policy was open to change.

At the same time the President strengthened the position of his ministers dealing with economic affairs. He rejected both the demands of his Minister of Labour who wanted an increase in wages, those of his Minister of the Interior who tried to obtain supplementary credits for Amazonia and the north-east, and those of the Foreign Minister who as part of his nationalist foreign policy was trying to force an entry into the atomic club.[2]

It is a curious fact that since the death of Castello Branco the attitude of the President had enabled those ministers most identified with Castello's thought to achieve a predominant place in his Government, over and against the nationalist elements led by Albuquerque Lima.

Nevertheless Lima himself was becoming increasingly popular and his name was often mentioned as a future candidate for the presidency of the Republic. This was largely due to his activities in promoting 'national integration' through the SUDENE and SUDAM,[3] which were development authorities for the north-east and Amazonia, and also for promoting the setting up of a 'free zone' of Manaus,[4] the establishment of SUDECO (Superintendência do Desenvolvimento da Região Centro-Oeste)[5] and for having launched on 14 December the Rondon Project[6] whereby students could work in the frontier regions of Amazonia to become acquainted with the problems of those regions.

Costa e Silva himself was convinced of the need to catalyse the interest of Brazilians for the vast open spaces in the interior of the country. In order to make a psychological impact he decided to go together with his whole ministry at regular intervals into a provincial city, which thus for a time became promoted to Capital of the Republic.

The first city to receive such a visit was Recife, and it became the seat of Government from 8 to 12 August 1967. The next year Belem and Manaus were similarly visited and exalted.

But however much this habit may have aided the cause of dialogue, it did not make it any easier to administer a country whose nominal capital, Brasilia,[7] was in 1967 comparatively isolated from the *de facto* capital Rio de Janeiro, where most of the ministers still functioned.

In November, under the influence of the political fight being waged by the Enlarged Front, Parliament, against the wishes of the Government, voted to convene itself in an extraordinary session for January and February. It also rejected, for the first time, a presidential decree reducing the rights of municipalities, and tried to get round the article in the constitution which forbade any initiative involving fresh expenditure for the State. At the end of the month a draft amendment to the Constitution reintroducing direct suffrage, which was laid by the M.D.B., was rejected by the Chambers but, significantly, twenty-nine ARENA deputies voted with the opposition.

On 6 February 1968 at the instigation of Luiz Vianna Filho, Governor of Bahia and formerly Head of the Civil Household of Castello Branco, Costa e Silva accepted the idea of reaching a *modus vivendi* with Parliament whereby the deputies of the two parties would undertake to support the administrative policy of the Government while retaining their freedom of action ideologically. But he refused to have any contact with Carlos Lacerda or with the Enlarged Front as an organised movement. On the thirteenth Senator Oscar Passos, President of the M.D.B., rejected these terms and the project was buried, much to the delight of those favouring the hard line who were very much against such a compromise. The end of the first year of Costa e Silva's Government was marked by one last passage at arms. Parliament kicked over the traces once more when a decree[8] was presented to it which consolidated the acts in force relating to the powers of the National Security Council and also somewhat enlarged them, especially as regards the powers of its secretary general, which post was held by the head of the Military Household of the President.

The President's proposal was finally approved in February, but the members of parliament queried the real role of General Portela, Head of the Military Household, and the influence exercised by the hard liners over his 'super ministry'. At the end of the year some more clouds were visible on the horizon of Costa e Silva's humanisation policy. Usually on the look-out for unwelcome action by the hard liners among the Military, he was taken by surprise when an attack came from the opposite wing. For Admiral José Santos Saldanha da Gama, a minister[9] on the supreme military tribunal, twice elected in 1965 and in 1967 as President of the Naval Club, protested in an interview given to the journal of the Naval College, *Galera*,[10] against the 'excessive part played by the Armed Forces in the life of the nation'. He referred specifically to the fact that the State Militia, which until the Revolution had been completely autonomous, had now been brought under central control. Since he had already, in April, expressed in the same publication bitter criticisms of the Government which under colour of the national security 'had become the enemy of the civil population' and on 9 December a large circulation weekly[11] had attributed yet more criticisms to him, the Admiral was compelled to resign from the presidency of the Naval Club.[12] For good measure, the admiral commanding the Naval College,[13] who was responsible in the last resort for articles that appeared in *Galera*, was relieved of his functions. These punishments, balancing out those administered a little earlier to the hard-line colonels, were very revealing as to the cracks which were appearing in the military monolith.

'Humanisation' suffered a further loss of credibility when on 27 November 1967 General Moniz de Aragão restarted the anti-Communist campaign[14] and accused the Church of helping subversive groups,[15] among which he included practically all the unauthorised opposition, from Catholic students to the radical left, naturally without forgetting the Brazilian Communist Party which had been illegal since 1947.

32 The 'Unauthorised' Opposition

Thus the Military were confronted by an unauthorised, extra-parliamentary opposition. In 1967 its active components consisting of students, workers, guerillas and clergy were still without any cohesion, but they could mount a political apparatus sufficiently powerful to threaten the régime. This possibility led Costa e Silva to bring humanisation to a halt and to harden his line of action before the end of 1968.

The reply of the Brazilian students was in line with a long tradition of left-wing radicalism. Organisationally the political action of the students was based on U.N.E. (União Nacional dos Estudantes), a nation-wide union set up under Vargas' dictatorship in 1938. It was organised at three levels, those of the university, the provincial state and the Federal State, and was financed directly by the Government. U.N.E. had mounted its first political demonstration during the 1940s.

In 1947 the organisation was dominated by radical elements some of whom called themselves 'Marxist reformers'.[1] When Marshal Dutra was President from 1946–51 they clashed quite often with the police. Towards the autumn of 1950 it elected leaders who were less radical but just as nationalist. The establishment of Petrobrás[2] in 1963 was evidence that this trend of thought had won. There was comparative quiet until 1956 when the students of Rio took part in a violent demonstration by workers to protest against an increase in tram fares. President Kubitschek ordered the Militia out; there were some wounded and about 150 arrests.

From 1956 to 1964 U.N.E. became an important hotbed of agitation. In 1958 it stated that it was 'fundamentally an entity of political representation of the university class'[3] and included among its aims 'the clarification of national problems for the workers and the people'.[4]

When John Foster Dulles arrived at Rio in 1958, U.N.E.'s headquarters on the Botafogo Beach was draped in black and demonstrators shouted: 'The U.S. has no friends, only interests!'[5] Two years later, when President Eisenhower went to Rio after the Cuban revolution, the banner over the building read: 'We like Fidel Castro!'

From 1962 onwards U.N.E.[6] concentrated on the 'politicisation of the masses' and tried to bring about a tripartite alliance between students, workers and peasants. With the aid of large funds from the Federal Government, U.N.E. set up its own publishing house, the Editora Universitária, and developed the organisation of 'popular culture centres' which soon became centres of political propaganda.

In the same year a strike which lasted two months in aid of a reform at universities which would give students one-third of the votes in the faculty councils, gave rise to several violent incidents. The strike was not successful, but it enabled the leaders of U.N.E. to demonstrate their capabilities as militants.

In January 1963 U.N.E. took part in the plebiscite campaign for João Goulart and six months later it joined with the group of left-wing parliamentarians forming the Nationalist Parliamentary Front (F.P.N.), with the General Workers' Command (C.G.T.) and with certain peasant leagues, to form a radical left pressure-group.

However, when the Revolution took place some right-wing sympathisers set fire to the building on Botafogo Beach. Several student leaders were arrested and the President of the U.N.E. and two members of his committee had to seek refuge in the Bolivian Embassy.

Thereupon some moderate presidents of the branches in some provincial states formed a provisional committee, but U.N.E. did not succeed in being reorganised. It was abolished on 9 November 1964 by the new law on national education which forbade student organisations to engage in any political activity.[7] U.N.E. was then replaced by a National Directory of Students (D.N.E.), a creature of the Government which rapidly fell into desuetude.

According to a recent survey carried out by Americans, students consider themselves to be members of a privileged group, the only élite in Brazilian politics that is impartial and uncorrupted. 'Consequently, they not only feel a sense of mission to change and improve the nation but also assume a role of defending the national interest against domestic and foreign exploiters.'[8] This idealistic self-definition is not shared by the rest of the community, which takes but little notice of their demonstrations.

The left radical ideal of university youth is however sometimes shared by the intellectual or politically attentive section of public opinion, which calls the students the 'public loudspeakers who represent rebellion and reform' destined to 'awaken the sense of responsibility in Brazil'.[9]

There were some 38,000 university students in 1948, and by 1966 their numbers had risen to 121,000; about 10 per cent of them were married.[10] The most popular faculties, in decreasing order, were: law, philosophy, social science and letters, engineering schools, economic science, medicine, dentistry, agronomy, architecture, etc. About 25 per cent of the students were women, who were mostly to be found in the philosophy faculties. In 1962 about 75 per cent of the students were registered in universities in the most developed states (Guanabara, São Paulo, Rio Grande do Sul, Minas Gerais and Paraná). Many of them were living away from their families, often in student hostels. Their average age was relatively high; an inquiry made in 1960 showed that the average age for law students was about twenty-six. They came mostly from the middle classes (in 1960 when 2500 students were sampled, 83 per cent of them claimed that as their background).

The financial difficulties which stand in the way of higher education explain the almost complete absence of representatives of the poor classes (less than 1 per cent of university students questioned in the above sampling replied that their fathers were illiterate). Various surveys have shown that 66-75 per cent of students do some work in order to finance their studies.

In this environment, politics is a form of social promotion and until the Revolution took place it was easy for a student leader to project himself nationally. Nevertheless, political activists are only a small minority. A very careful study made in five cities early in 1964 highlighted the comparative strengths of the various opinions among students in nine Brazilian universities. The survey showed that there were three major streams of political thought – conservative, reformist and revolutionary. It divided the students into two groups, active and passive, in accordance with the results of tests, surveys and interviews. The first group included only 15 per cent of the total whereas the second formed 85 per cent of the student body. Of the complete sample, the passive wing contained 15 per cent conservatives, 60 per cent moderate reformers and 10 per cent revolutionaries. Also as a proportion of the total, the active stream represented 3 per cent conservatives, 7 per cent more-or-less moderate reformers and 5 per cent revolutionaries. Thus 15 per cent of all Brazilian students were potential revolutionaries but only 5 per cent were actively standing for their ideas.[11]

But they were ready to make sacrifices for their convictions and to take part in activist movements. Therefore, as the sociologist Glaucio Soares observes, 'if one tries to estimate the real extent of student radicalism by mass demonstrations, severe distortions are bound to appear as the radical leftist groups are likely to be greatly over-represented among demonstrators'.[12]

Although student opinion found small means of expression during the first few years of the régime, it gradually recrystallised. In July 1966 the National Student Union (U.N.E.), which was officially dissolved, succeeded in holding its Twenty-Eighth Congress illegally at Belo Horizonte in spite of police supervision. It seems that Militants of Popular Action, a movement founded in 1961 by members of Catholic Action, was responsible for this initiative. The delegates lodged privately and did their work in secret in the cellars of a Franciscan convent, where they prepared an offensive against the agreement between Brazil and USAID aimed at reforming higher education[13] which had been signed a short while previously.

In August 1967 the Twenty-Ninth Congress of U.N.E. was held in secret for three days at Campinas near São Paulo in a Benedictine monastery.[14] About 400 young people took part and the resolutions approved ranged from denunciation of the 'plot' designed to enable imperialism to get a stranglehold on education in Brazil, to condemnation of the Government's wage freeze policy. This meeting cemented the alliance between the student movement, the progressive wing of the Church and the radical left, subversive or non-violent, which would tend to show that General Moniz de Aragão had good informers.

On 28 March 1968 during a rather minor demonstration at Rio de Janeiro caused by the closure of a university canteen,[15] a squad of State police which intervened and was met by a hail of stones, opened fire and killed an eighteen-year-old boy.[16] The student cause had been presented with a martyr, and his body was carried into the Legislative Assembly, where the M.D.B. had the strongest representation.

U.N.E. called a nation-wide strike. There were demonstrations at Salvador, Belo Horizonte, Goiás and Porto Alegre, which were the occasion of deaths and arrests. On 31 March about 20,000 persons attended the funeral of the victim. Although the Head of the Military Household, in agreement with the Minister of Justice, had announced that public order must be safeguarded but without resort to fire-arms, the Governor,[17] overwhelmed by the turnout, called in the Army, and in the demonstrations which followed the burial at least one person was killed and sixty wounded, and 200 arrests were made.[18]

On 4 April the Mass celebrated on the seventh day after the funeral (even more important than the actual funeral in a tropical country) took place at the Candelaria, the central church of Rio de Janeiro. Troops, mounted police and armoured vehicles encircled the area ready to stamp on any incipient violence. The clergy, some of whom were still dressed in their liturgical regalia, prevented the worst from happening by spontaneously placing themselves between the opposing elements. Nevertheless there was trouble, and it is said that 700 people were arrested.

Then the student unrest quietened down somewhat, partly on account of the police activity and also of the very widely drawn terms of Instruction 177 which was published on 5 April and placed the Enlarged Front under interdiction.

Five weeks later on 14 May General Meira Mattos[19] officially presented the report he had been commissioned to make on the situation in the universities. In it he acknowledged that there were many gaps in the education offered and he recommended the necessary reforms and drew the attention of the President to the fact that 'undue repression results in increasing radicalisation of demands'. Without waiting for publication of the report, the Minister of Education announced an increase in the budget for the federal universities and relieved all his heads of departments, including the Director of Higher Education, of their duties.[20]

But the calm did not last long. The student explosion that took place in Europe in the summer of 1968 was inevitably echoed in Brazil. At the end of May, after a demonstration, about 150 students were arrested at the School of Medicine at Belo Horizonte. On 22 May, in order to reinforce the powers of the police, minors (persons less than eighteen years old) were declared to be legally responsible in the event of certain specified criminal acts, including crimes against national security.[21]

On 19, 20 and 21 June the army was placed on the alert when barricades were erected in the streets of Rio de Janeiro by the students. In the extremely violent clashes that followed, more people were killed and wounded.[22] The city centre was paralysed and about 400 students were detained for questioning.[23] On 22 June the Federal University of Rio de Janeiro suspended its courses for an indefinite period and the State Government sent all schools on holiday before the due date.

Four days later a march of students and professors for the purpose of protesting against police violence was authorised. Known as the 'march of the 100,000', this demonstration went through the city without incident. The student marchers were accompanied by delegates from the workers and also by intellectuals and artists, and about a hundred priests officially accompanied them.

The President then made a fresh attempt to recommence in some measure the dialogue with the students. On 28 June he signed a decree making available to the Rondon Project[24] the funds required for its development. On 2 July 1968 he agreed personally to receive a representative delegation of students to present four demands to him: the freeing of students who had been arrested, the reopening of the Calabouço Restaurant, the ending of all repression by the police and the abolition of the censorship on art.

But these requests were unacceptable[25] to the hard liners, and the President rejected them. The National Security Council held two meetings[26] and decided to ratify the ban on all marches or demonstrations which the Minister of Justice had made on 5 July. It instructed the Minister to take all necessary measures to suppress the 'counter-revolutionary state' which was making its appearance in the country, with the aid of the military ministers.

Public opinion, which did not like violence in the streets,[27] supported this energetic attitude. The increasing effectiveness of the repression[28] soon put an end to public demonstrations of any size, as the generality of students was no longer willing to take part in them. More localised police drives were still taking place.[29] Sometimes the police took the initiative, as happened at the University of Brasilia on 30 August.[30]

On 12 October the forces of order organised a raid on Itabira where the Thirtieth Congress of U.N.E., still outlawed, was being held; 712 students were arrested. Save for about a dozen of the leaders they were all released, but in the meantime dossiers had been compiled and photographs taken. The student movement was broken. After a few last flings during which students took over the former headquarters of U.N.E. at Rio de Janeiro and occupied it for twelve hours, the demonstrators gave in to the superior forces deployed against them. On 26 October 1968 the last student leaders announced that thenceforth they were abandoning violent action in favour of discussion meetings in the faculties. Those who did not share that point of view came together for the terrorist activity which developed later.

Whereas force had triumphed, Costa e Silva set himself to satisfy some of the aspirations of the student body. On 27 September he signed seven decrees concerning higher education. They included one authorising the engagement of university assistants and reviewed the salary scale of full-time and part-time professors, a move which affected some 7000 teaching staff. Another decree forbade any reduction in the budget for national education for

1969–70. On 1 October the President sent to Parliament an important message concerning reform of the universities which embodied a practical answer to many of the problems that had been noted.

The student agitation was reflected to some degree among the working population. But partly because of the persuasive gifts of the Minister of Labour Colonel Jarbas Passarinho, who found a way of making himself popular among trade unionists, and partly owing to some arrests, the violence was largely muted. On 31 March 1968 a new minimum wage, increased by 23 per cent, came into force.[31] This increase was immediately reflected throughout the scales of payment for labour.

But this decree did not give satisfaction to the wage earners because it was still not enough to bring their real purchasing power up to that of the previous year, which itself had been less than the year before. On 22 April there was a strike in Minas Gerais where about 6700 metallurgy workers stayed away for three days. They were claiming an increase of 25 per cent, but went back to work after having been threatened with the application of the laws of national security and the loss of their jobs. On 1 May Costa e Silva announced that a supplementary emergency bonus of 10 per cent would be paid to workers.[32] He also took the opportunity of publishing his decision to bring forward the plans providing for distribution of uncultivated land in the north-east.

On 16 July 3000 metal workers of one of the outlying districts of São Paulo, Osasco, occupied six factories. Their trade union was placed under federal intervention and about sixty strikers were arrested including a French priest, Père Pierre Wauthier, who was expelled on 26 August 1968.[33] About 600 workers, including fifteen out of the twenty-five trade union leaders, were dismissed from their jobs as a result of this demonstration.

Costa e Silva tried once more to take action. On 10 September he received a list of complaints from the main workers' federations. He passed the papers to his Minister of Labour but the file was closed almost at once, since to accede to the demands of the workers would have meant abandoning the economic policy on which the Government had embarked. On 27 September there was another strike, this time of metal workers in Belo Horizonte, and this time the bank employees followed suit. The Rio de Janeiro bank staffs fell into step as well. The strikers obtained a number of increases but the police forces were again on a state of alert and arrests, interrogations and dismissals began again.

All things considered, however, these rumblings among the workers' organisations remained fairly muted and the Minister of Labour Jarbas Passarinho had some success in maintaining a dialogue with the representatives of the workers.

The Brazilian Communist Party, which had been outlawed since 1947, was badly affected by the repression. But it was used to covert action and at the end of 1967 its leaders, once more taking their courage in both hands, decided to hold their Sixth Congress of which they had been speaking for a very long time. The main resolutions passed at this clandestine meeting were published in the press,[34] which had its humorous side in view of the laws on freedom of expression mentioned earlier.

The orthodox Muscovite Party of Luiz Carlos Prestes considered that the Brazilian masses were not sufficiently keyed-up to make a socialist revolution feasible. He therefore confined himself to preaching national and democratic revolution. For this purpose he tried to bring together all possible movements opposing the régime, for action.

The themes that were put over in public included tributes to the progressive elements in the Church, exploitation of the fight against the wages policy with the object of winning over the petit bourgeois side of the proletariat, the definition of nationalism as an effective catalyst in setting up an enlarged opposition, and the view that the workers had become less militant since the Fifth Congress that was held in 1960. Congress also ratified the expulsion of 'adventurers of the left',[35] who had embarked on guerila action 'in contempt of the organisation of the masses' and condemned the Communist Party of Brazil.[36]

It is interesting to compare these resolutions with the attitude of the future Che Guevara of Brazil, Carlos Marighela, who left for Cuba in August to attend the OLAS Conference (Latin American Solidarity Organisation) in defiance of the instructions of the Central Committee of the Brazilian Communist Party, which he accused of having given up 'its independence'.[37]

When he returned to Brazil towards the end of the year he launched a campaign of armed revolutionary action. In a letter to Fidel Castro he set out his position as follows: 'The road I have chosen is that of guerila warfare which has to be unleashed in the countryside and through which I shall finally take my place within the Latin American revolution. I consider guerila warfare to be the only way to unite Brazilian revolutionaries and to bring our people to power.'[38]

In 1968 a new phenomenon appeared in Brazil – urban terrorism. From January onwards a number of armed attacks were committed in Rio Grande do Sul, and to obtain money the terrorists carried out hold-ups in many different places.[39] On 28 April the building of the *Estado de São Paulo*, which also houses a luxury hotel, was shaken by an explosion. On 26 June 1000 lb. of dynamite were stolen in São Paulo, and a few days later the headquarters of the Second

Army was the target for an attack. On 20 September a sentry was killed at the same place, and on the twenty-seventh three bombs exploded in Rio de Janeiro.

On 12 October a former American captain, Charles Chandler, a scholarship student at the University of São Paulo, was assassinated. A note found near the body stated that this was an act of vengeance for the participation of the United States in the death of Che Guevara. On 14 October a bomb exploded in Rio de Janeiro in front of a publishing house specialising in the publication of works of political argumentation. On 8 November the windows of the Sears Roebuck store at São Paulo were blown out, followed by those of the *Jornal do Brasil*. On 2 December a bomb exploded in the doorway of an *avant-garde* theatre in Rio de Janeiro.

Other similar incidents occurred, and although not very numerous they succeeded in creating a certain atmosphere of disquiet among civilians and of rousing the fury of the Military. In fact it was scarcely possible to know whether these acts were the work of left-wing or right-wing terrorists, since both extremes make use of the bomb and the sub-machine gun.

Two right-wing organisations in particular hit the headlines: the C.C.C. (Communist-Hunting Commando), and the 'Death Squad'. Consisting partly of former policemen, these mobile groups went in for a kind of instant justice, for they killed those whom they considered guilty.

On the left there were very many small groups but they lacked co-ordination. Carlos Marighela, the main revolutionary leader in Brazil, tried to make better use of the rebellion potential of the country through Action for National Liberation (A.L.N.). However, all the apparatus of military repression had not submerged Brazil, which retained its characteristics as a country of the sun, since on 25 September 1968 the *Jornal do Brasil* published a long manifesto by Marighela.

In it, Marighela came out in favour of guerilla warfare as the only viable revolutionary strategy and frankly announced the aim he had in view – to transform the political crisis into an armed conflict.

> ... by letting loose both in the cities and in the countryside such a large number of armed incidents that the Government will be compelled to change the political situation of the country into a military situation. But that is bound to displease the masses who will then rise against the police and the Government soldiers whom they consider to be responsible for this state of affairs. The alliance between the masses and the guerilla vanguard will end with the destruction of the bureaucratic and military apparatus of the State and with the seizure of power.[40]

The international press has not always given due weight to the ideological drive behind the phenomenon of the urban guerilla in Brazil, which was stated in the following terms by Carlos Marighela: 'It is a class war and as such a life or death matter.'[41] There is no place in his declarations for the argumentative romanticism which it has sometimes been described as in Europe. It is not at all a reaction against the misdeeds of a military régime, but a freely chosen option, chosen with the very object of provoking such misdeeds to provide an excuse for the popular rising through which 'power would pass to the armed people'.[42]

The rules of the game are laid down in his manual of the urban guerilla,[43] of whom he writes that he

> is an implacable enemy of the Government; he systematically seeks to undermine the authorities and the men who dominate the country and wield power. His main task is to outwit, discredit and harass the Military and all forces of repression, to destroy or pillage goods belonging to North Americans, heads of foreign businesses or the Brazilian upper classes.
>
> The urban guerilla does not shrink from dismantling and destroying the economic, political and social system in force.[44]
>
> In the context of class war, the sharpening of which is as inevitable as it is necessary, the armed struggle of the urban guerilla has two aims in view: (a) the physical liquidation of the heads of the Armed Forces and the police and their subordinate officers, (b) the expropriation of arms or goods belonging to the Government, the big capitalists, the large landowners and imperialists.[45]

Among the specific objectives Marighela mentions:

> To weaken the base of support of the State and of North American domination . . . constituted by the triangle of Rio–São Paulo–Belo Horizonte . . . for it is within this area that the huge industrial, financial, economic, political, cultural, and military complex of the country, in other words the decision centre of the nation, is situated.
>
> To weaken the security system of the dictatorship by forcing the enemy to mobilise his troops for the defence of this support base without ever knowing where, when or how he will be attacked.
>
> To compel the Army and the police . . . to leave the comfort and quiet of the barracks and of routine and to keep them constantly in a state of alarm and nervous tension or to draw them into blind alleys.[46]

Noting that 'one of the most important requirements of the present Government relates to the collection of very high taxes', the guerilla in order to obtain the support of the people 'will thereupon concentrate on attacking the fiscal system of the dictatorship and preventing it with all the weight of revolutionary violence from working properly'.[47]

This scorched-earth policy was to have a definite aim:

> The Government will be compelled to intensify repression and this will make life intolerable for the citizens. Homes will be broken into, police raids will be organised, innocent people arrested and channels of communication shut down. Police terror will be set up and more and more political assassinations will take place; there will be massive political persecution ... by such action we will prevent the reopening of Congress and the reorganisation of either the Government party or that of the tolerated opposition ...
>
> This is how the guerillas will win the support of the masses, overthrow the dictatorship and shake off the North American yoke.[48]

These apocalyptic counsels of Marighela were partly carried out, but by their very absolutism the guerillas, who mostly had but little contact with the poorest classes, did not succeed in making the urban masses follow them.[49]

There was a wave of repression. From 1969 onwards a great number of people[50] including priests and other religious workers were arrested. Cases of physical or psychological torture began to be more and more frequently exposed.[51]

Use of the iron fist was successful notwithstanding some spectacular successes by opposition groups, including ten hijackings of aircraft[52] and four successful kidnappings (against four unsuccessful ones).[53] On 4 November 1969 Marighela walked into a trap laid by the police in São Paulo.[54] Without leaving him time to apply one of the precepts of his Manual ('if the guerilla doesn't fire first he is likely to lose his life')[55] they shot him down then and there.[56]

On 27 November the Communist leader 'Capivara' was arrested and a terrorist cell near Brasilia was destroyed. In December, nine cells were eliminated in Rio de Janeiro and in January an important network was put out of action at São Paulo. On 3 May Juarez Guimarães de Brito, one of the leaders of the Revolutionary Peoples' Avant-Garde committed suicide just as he was being captured. In May and June a group of rural guerillas was run to earth on the frontier between the States of São Paulo and Paraná. The leader, ex-Captain Lamarca, just managed to escape but was rediscovered and shot while armed on 18 September 1971 in the north of the country. In October Marighela's successor, Joaquim Câmara Ferreira, was arrested, and died in prison after a few days.[57] On 17 October 1970 the São Paulo regional cell of the VAR-Palmares Revolutionary Avant-Garde was destroyed and twenty four of its members put in prison. In June 1970 it was sufficiently clear that the Military had won for an anti-Government commentator to say: 'The urban guerilla movement appears to be nearing its end after two years of disasters, both politically and in terms of personnel.'[58]

Another analyst arrived at the same conclusion. His verdict was that in Brazil there was

> a situation characterised by the will of the Armed Forces to take matters into their own hands. We are not witnessing an instrument manipulated by an oligarchy or a group of capitalist interests, but a force that is committed and determined... that type of army has little in common with, for example, the Army which Batista commanded. This being so, it would appear to be specially difficult in Brazil to establish a countervailing power based on guerillas.[59]

The people of Brazil rejected violent action; a survey carried out in Rio de Janeiro in July 1969 showed that 79 per cent of the Cariocas (inhabitants of Rio) condemned terrorism.[60] True, this was the year during which subversion took an acute form[61] which led certain observers to speak of a 'incipient civil war'.[62]

During this period a great deal was published in the European press about torture in Brazil. Little was said about the murderous aspect and the ideological motivations of subversion which we have just mentioned, and the terrorists were more often than not depicted as innocent defenders of a just cause. Sometimes action by the Army and police was equated with that of the 'Death Squad', a group originally founded to combat common law banditry and which practised summary justice. Although there is no doubt that this organisation also went in for counter-terrorist action and that some of its members were bent policemen, for all that it was not an official government service.[63]

At the end of 1969 the reporting went on to include other accusations.[64] One French daily even published statistics purporting to show that the victims were made up of '35 per cent students, 28 per cent workers, 15 per cent members of the liberal professions and 12 per cent white-collar workers'.[65]

Though this campaign may have been exaggerated at the time, it was nevertheless based on actual facts,[66] and it achieved the result of first compelling the Government to break its silence and then to state its position with increasing clarity. When giving his first press conference on 2 December 1969 the new Minister of Justice claimed that he had no knowledge of any torture and promised to punish the guilty persons if any such facts should be proved. He repeated these statements[67] at least twice, but when confronted with proven facts the authorities changed their attitude and Jarbas Passarinho, the Minister of Education, finally admitted: 'It would be untrue to claim that torture does not exist in Brazil, but to say that it is practised as a system of government is mere vilification.'[68]

On 24 July 1970 the International Commission of Jurists at Geneva passed on to the Inter-American Commission for Human Rights of the Organisation of American States an allegation concerning violation of human rights dealing with the treatment of political prisoners. At its meeting on 3 May 1972 the Inter-American Commission decided that 'it has not been possible to obtain absolutely conclusive proof of the truth or untruth of the allegations but that the evidence collected leads to the persuasive presumption that in Brazil serious cases of torture, abuse and maltreatment have occurred to persons of both sexes while they were deprived of their liberty'.[69]

In July 1970, following a complaint by the President of the Assize Court of São Paulo, President Médici threatened the Governors of the five states in which executions had been carried out by the Death Squad that the Federal Government would intervene unless immediate steps were taken to prevent this group 'from committing crimes on the pretext of eliminating outlaws'.

On 1 July the federal police were effectively instructed to put an end to the activities of the Death Squad and on 18 August the Ministry of Justice speeded up the inquiries that had been started. In October, sixteen policemen were accused of murder by the Procurator-General of São Paulo. On 22 October inquiries were opened against Sérgio Fernando Paranhos Fleury, said to be the head of the Death Squad. The case was a thorny one since this was the man who, as Commissioner of Police at São Paulo,[70] had arranged the ambush in which Marighela had been shot down.

Together with seven other policemen he was accused of murder and of brutal treatment of prisoners. On 16 February 1971 he was placed in preventive detention. The criminal inquiries, during which he was given conditional freedom, lasted until the end of August 1972 and resulted in thirty-one auxiliary policemen being found guilty.

The four principal accused were charged with ninety-one murders, twenty of which were attributed to Fleury.[71] The cases were likely to last until the end of 1973 but as far as the press was concerned, judgement had already been given. One journalist commented: 'As regards São Paulo, the Death Squad has ceased its killings.'[72]

At the end of 1971, President Médici called upon the right-wing extremists in the Air Force to answer for their actions. His minister, Air Marshal Marcio de Souza e Mello, who was a hard liner and an advocate of violent repression, tendered his resignation. This led the way to a purge of the Air Force, one faction of which had been in the forefront of the fight against subversion since 1968. Led by Air Brigadier João-Paulo Burnier, at that time Chief Secretary at the Air Ministry, this faction had taken an active part, in particular, in harassing the student leaders. For this purpose it used elements from the first squadron of the PARA-SAR, a group of parachutists specialising in rescue operations, which protested at being used for missions of this sort. One of its founders, Captain Ribeiro de Carvalho, had also publicly denounced[73] a plan whereby the PARA-SAR would have been instructed to seize certain opposition leaders and to throw their bodies into the sea after having liquidated them. This accusation was confirmed by the Head of the Air Traffic Department, Air Force Major-General Itamar Rocha. The matter had been swept under the carpet at the time, but at the beginning of 1952 after the Cardinal-Archbishop Dom Eugenio Salles had reopened it in a detailed report, Médici insisted upon a thorough inquiry. Shortly afterwards, six generals and four colonels, some of whom held important commands, were superseded by presidential decree.

To say this is not to deny that atrocities occurred,[74] but it does show that the Médici Government appeared to be determined to put down excesses,[75] and it throws very considerable doubt on the views of those who have tried to present cases of brutality[76] that have occurred in Brazil as systematic acts of the power held by 'armed forces transformed into an almost monolithic praetorian guard of big money'.[77]

Among the 'unauthorised' opposition voices, those of some of the clergy aroused most attention. The Church plays a dominant part in 'the largest Catholic country in the world'.[78] For a long time it had been one of the pillars of the establishment,[79] but even before 1964 it had developed considerable awareness of the country's social problems, one of the clerics most associated with this awakening being the Auxiliary Bishop of Rio de Janeiro, Mgr Helder Câmara, who just before the Revolution was promoted Archbishop of Olinda and Recife.

Although this liberal and reformist wing of the Church was in the minority, it set the tone and was dominant in the sense that all the other trends within the Church defined themselves by their attitude to this wing. Its members included about thirty bishops, or about the same number as the 'ultra-conservatives', whereas the hierarchy comprised 5 cardinals, 32 archbishops, 122 resident bishops, 37 auxiliary bishops, 41 prelates and 7 apostolic administrators. Of these 65 were foreigners.[80] In 1967 the census showed that there were about 12,970 priests, 10–15 per cent of them being foreigners, serving about 86 million inhabitants. But only about 5000 of these priests were working in parishes.

When the Revolution took place the Church was less than wholehearted in its support of the régime, though it did not take up an opposition stance. The Church endeavoured to assert its right to intervene in questions concerning respect for human personality, the defence of social justice and the implementation of reforms, while at the same time showing that it wished to avoid a final break with the State. Since the Military too were anxious to avoid a break, the story of the relations between the spiritual and the temporal power has been marked by a succession of ups and downs.

On 3 July at São Paulo the police raided a university dormitory and arrested some students, who resisted removal. As one of the group was a priest, the Cardinal Archbishop, Dom Agnelo Rossi,[81] protested against unnecessary brutality on the part of the police.

In August 1967 Dom Helder Câmara proclaimed before the Legislative Assembly of Pernambuco 'the need for a free Latin America not only politically but also economically', and stated his conviction that 'only the social action of the Church will be able to halt violent revolution in the north-east'.

In November the Bishop of Cratéus, speaking in Ceará, praised the régime in Cuba and in the previous month the bishops in the north-east had published a manifesto calling for 'social justice which is threatened by the economic policy of the Government'.

On 5 November 1967 at Volta Redonda, Brazil's main steel-producing centre, four members of the Catholic Workers' Youth, including a French deacon, Guy Thibault,[82] were arrested while in possession of subversive tracts, in a vehicle belonging to the bishopric which the army immediately searched. Several priests who opposed this search were imprisoned. The conflict which followed between the Bishop of the city, Dom Valdir Calheiros, and the military authority rapidly came to resemble a trial of strength.

On 30 November the central committee of the C.N.B.B. (National Conference of Brazilian Bishops) published a manifesto which, while condemning subversion, stated: 'We are bound to express our solidarity with our brother bishops, priests and laymen who are the victims of misunderstanding and injustice while carrying out true apostolic work.' After denouncing 'misuse of economic or political power for personal gain', the prelates affirmed that 'any attempt to shackle the teaching mission of the Church when she is trying to defend human values is tantamount to promoting camouflaged paganism'.[83] They dwelt upon the need for 'a just social order' and while recognising that adults could not have the vitality of youth they stressed the need to 'accept the gift of dynamism which they bring'. They ended by warning the Government against 'the folly of causing youth to despair by adopting rigid attitudes'.[84]

Realising that this was a serious crisis in which the Church had clearly set itself apart from the régime, Costa e Silva[85] received a representative of the C.N.B.B., and in order to 'clear up misunderstandings' the priests who had been arrested were released, but the French deacon was expelled.

This easing of the situation did not last long, for the Church was still seeking to find a balance between the traditional majority of its clergy and the extremely active minority of its committed prelates. But in 1968 it was the latter who dominated the scene, and the cleavage between Church and Government became increasingly marked.

The priests reasoned not in terms of economic units but of human needs. From this standpoint, the situation of the masses left much to be desired; it is therefore not surprising that some members of the Church who were in daily contact with the underdogs spoke up on behalf of that section of the population on which the internal logic of the growth model was imposing the heaviest immediate sacrifices.

As early as January 1968 hostilities were resumed by the Bishop of Santo André, an industrial suburb of São Paulo, and he drew the fire of the economic and military authorities when he publicly declared that armed revolution by the people could 'be justified when oppression rules and famine wages are paid'.[86]

In February, Dom Helder Câmara took up the same theme and condemned the feudalism of the north-east, at the same time proclaiming his faith in the inevitable march of socialism, to which the Church can offer 'the mystique of universal brotherhood, incomparably greater than the narrow mystique of historical materialism'.[87]

On 19 July the Ninth Assembly of the C.N.B.B. closed with an appeal for reforms, non-violence, and a return to freedom for the individual.

On 1 October Dom Helder Câmara announced that under the new title of Action, Justice and Peace his movement, formerly known as Moral Pressure for Liberation would 'support peaceful popular movements and justified strikes'. On the same day the Cardinal Archbishop of São Paulo, Dom Agnelo Rossi, did something which caused a furore. For 'pastoral reasons' he refused the Grand Cross of the Order of Merit which the President was to confer upon him the following day. And he made matters no better by also letting it be known that he approved of an organisation known as Collective Action for Justice which had been formed in

São Paulo to bring the Church closer to the workers in the metallurgical industry and to form a link with Action, Justice and Peace. In connection with this organisation the Bishop serving the steelmaking centre of Volta Redonda, Mgr Valdir Calheiros, suggested on 7 October that a great procession of the people should take place on 2 December at Rio de Janeiro to 'break with the social structures which are keeping the people in slavery'.[88]

Reactions were not slow in coming, and on 24 October 1968 Dom Helder Câmara's residence in Recife was machine-gunned and covered with vengeful slogans just at the time when the central committee of the C.N.B.B. was meeting in Rio de Janeiro. This committee decided to set up a body with instructions to maintain close contact with the Government in order to 'reduce political tensions whenever this seems necessary' and it did not contest the remark of one of its counsellors[89] to the effect that 'the proliferation of extremist groups is very largely due to the blindness of the present rulers who are completely out of touch with national life'.[90]

The conflict took a turn for the worse when on 21 November the police looking for Carlos Marighela explicitly accused Mgr Antonio Fragoso, Bishop of Cratéus, of being an agent of subversion and maintaining contacts with the terrorist who had gone into hiding. Two days later the Archbishop of Fortaleza[91] stated publicly that 'any action against the person of the Bishop of Cratéus would create a political–religious crisis without precedent in Brazil'.[92] On 28 November one of the auxiliary bishops of Rio de Janeiro[93] gave a press conference in which he stated that Mgr Fragoso had been accused because he 'took up the defence of the weak against the strong'.

But these declarations no longer availed to halt the march of events. On the same day at Belo Horizonte three French priests who were taking part in an evangelistic campaign for the Working Christian Youth which had taken up a revolutionary stance since June were accused of subversion and arrested, together with a Brazilian deacon. They were held incommunicado, threatened with torture and interrogated at length. On 14 December 1968, despite protests, two more French priests and a Uruguayan priest were taken into custody at Santos and accused of collusion with the three who were first arrested. On the sixteenth, two American priests were arrested at Recife. Writs were served on the former and the latter were sent back to the United States.

By these actions the Government was proving that it had no intention of allowing the Church any scope for setting itself up as an arbiter between the aspirations of the masses of the people and the requirements of its own economic policy.[94] By the press campaign that was orchestrated with the arrests it endeavoured to sow doubts as to the political probity and the religious vocation of the progressive priests, many of whom were foreigners. In order to make its arguments more credible, the Government tuned them to nationalistic themes that would be readily understood by public opinion.

In 1969 this repression appeared to have paralysed the Church. Nevertheless the episcopate reacted again early in the year and in February Cardinal Jaime de Barros Câmara and Mgr Aloisio Lorscheider were received by Costa e Silva. On 18 February the central committee of the C.N.B.B. even published a statement in which it affirmed the right of the Church to support 'the principles of true development which may be anti-capitalist but are not therefore either subversive or Marxist' and called upon the Government to put in hand immediately measures of 'redemocratisation'.[95]

Also worthy of notice are the reserved statements of the central committee of the C.N.B.B. dated 18 January, the inflammatory remarks made in New York by Dom Helder Câmara between 23 and 28 January, the closure of the churches in Fortaleza (Ceará) during the Whitsun celebrations in protest against the penalty of a year's imprisonment inflicted upon the priest accused of scurrilously attacking the Army, the statement by the Cardinal Archbishop of Porto Alegre on 20 May that Christian social doctrine permitted resort to arms for the overthrow of tyrannical governments, the murder on 27 May of Father Henrique Pereira Netto, almoner of the Recife students and a collaborator of Dom Helder Câmara, by a group of right-wing extremists, the arrest of a priest on a charge of subversion on 9 June at Belo Horizonte, and the sentencing of a priest accused of the same misdemeanour at Botucatu (São Paulo) on 24 June 1969.

And yet there was a lessening of tension. The tenth Assembly of the National Conference of Brazilian Bishops concluded on 30 July with a vote of the bishops which rejected by 135 to 60 the basic document on 'relations between Church and State in Brazil', and this was considered to be a victory for conservative and moderate elements. Already on 16 July the desire for dialogue had been shown by the visit made by the five Brazilian cardinals to Costa e Silva during which the problems of agrarian reform were discussed. Dom Agnelo Rossi said to the assembly that his colleagues and he had made known to the President 'the anxieties and grievances of the people'.

The episcopate seemed to be in a state of indecision and the affair of the Dominicans accused of active complicity with Marighela increased still further the disquiet within the Church.

In 1970 the episcopate gave battle with the object of rescuing the priests and the religious which the Government was arresting in large numbers. On 27 May the Eleventh General Assembly of

C.N.B.B. spelt out its determination to stand side-by-side with the victims and said that it was called to mount 'firm opposition... in loyalty and dignity'.

On 25 August the C.N.B.B. issued a printed declaration concerning the activities of two priests who had been arrested in the State of Maranhão[96] who, it claimed, had been tortured. The document stated that efforts made by religious people towards social advancement of the people should not be equated 'as the large landowners and certain politicians do, with subversion, agitation and Communism'.

On 1 October Cardinal Jaime de Barros Câmara, who was known for his moderation, was received by President Médici and on 10 October the two priests were acquitted by a military tribunal. Six days later the central committee of the C.N.B.B., disturbed by fresh arrests, unequivocally condemned arbitrary acts of police repression which it said were 'preparing the ground for subversion'.[97] On 18 October the newspapers announced that President Médici had let it be known that in future no Church members could be arrested without the specific agreement of the Minister of Justice.[98]

In the address which he gave on 21 October 1970 the Pope took up the themes that the bishops in Brazil had been developing for several months; two days before making the speech he had received two of their representatives.[99] In a reference to torture 'which is said, not always without some political undertone, to be centred in a great country striving hard to make economic and social progress', he stated: 'Torture, which means the use of cruel and inhuman methods to extract confessions from prisoners, is to be absolutely condemned. Such methods are not tolerable nowadays, even with the object of doing justice and defending public order. They are not to be tolerated even when carried out by subordinate bodies.'[100] But he also emphasised that 'violence and terrorism used as normal means for the overthrow of the established order' or 'hijacking of aircraft, kidnapping of people and armed theft are just as improper'. He ended by saying, 'the so-called theology of revolution is not in accordance with the spirit of the Gospel'.[101]

Immediately upon his return from Rome on 20 October Mgr Agnelo Rossi issued to the Brazilian press a statement which was published in full the following day. In it he said:

> I can state without equivocation that Pope Paul VI maintains an unshakeable confidence in the destiny of Brazil... he fully appreciates the sincere and Christian efforts which the President of the Republic and other members of the Government are making to further the development of the nation and to oppose subversion and the intense international campaign of systematic

vilification that has been launched against Brazil... The members of the Government and the bishops of Brazil who are devoted to the good of the Brazilian people must unite their efforts in brotherhood as becomes Christians, and under the flag of Brazil as our patriotism requires. The Pope is also aware that there are always tares mixed with the good seed everywhere among men, whatever position they hold.[102]

It was a time for unfreezing relations between the Church and the Brazilian authorities. And so, after nearly six years during which the Church had used its prestige to act as the conscience of the Government, it had succeeded in finding a *modus vivendi* between the conflicting pressures of its own ways and the military power. The régime had now evolved to a point at which the Church felt that it could renew the 'sincere and loyal dialogue in an atmosphere of independence'[103] offered to it by the Government.

Although this was the interpretation placed on the situation by the episcopate in Brazil, it was not shared by everybody. One of the contributors to the review published by the Fathers of the Company of Jesus reached a different conclusion: 'The Church is timidly withdrawing to concentrate on its own internal problems. Some of its members (bishops, priests and Catholic Action militants) are resisting the claims and manoeuvres of the Government, but the majority is silent through lack of understanding and through fear. The weakness of the Church strengthens the extraordinary powers of the Government.'[104]

33 Costa e Silva between Two Fires

By the end of his first twelve months at the head of the Government, during which Costa e Silva had amply learnt the bitter lesson that the ways of power are full of pitfalls, all hope of humanisation had been dissipated by the social, economic and political realities. Nevertheless, in the speech which he made on 15 March 1968, Costa e Silva promised to ensure that the November municipal elections would be held 'in a climate of freedom'.

He was caught between two fires, and his position was far from easy. If he tried to gain the support of the parliamentary deputies by offering them a civilian successor as they wished, he would lay himself open to a military coup; and if on the other hand he tried to satisfy the extremists among the officers, who had no understanding of the relativities of politics, he would have to cease treading the road of legality à la Castello Branco and set up a *de facto* dictatorship. He none the less tried for a further nine months to tread a middle way, making concessions to the civilians whenever he could, provided that national security was not thereby jeopardised.

This dualism of action might have had a chance of succeeding eventually, if the reforms of Castello Branco had had time to take root. But the conflicting constraints of a parliamentary system too artificial to be truly representative and a military power too inexperienced to be tolerant, were too much for it. The more Costa e Silva had to cope with rebellions, the more heavily he would rely on his technicians of the economy, giving them ever wider powers, in the hope of bringing about the economic miracle which, when it came, might swing public opinion in favour of the Government.

Having made this choice, he was compelled to make common cause with the only section of the nation which had the ability to revitalise the economy – namely the heads of businesses. And although they reserved judgment on some measures by which they felt themselves to be threatened,[1] they did support the Government because they respected its firmness and admired its effective pragmatism.

On 5 July 1968 for instance the employers for the first time sent a delegation to assure the President of the full co-operation of the employers' organisations which they represented. And on 26 October another delegation handed him an address praising the working of the economic and financial system, while deploring the unrest in the ideological sphere which was preventing business from going full steam ahead. They appreciated in particular the flexible style of Delfim Netto who, stout though he was, always seemed to make a nimble turn when events called for the exercise of imagination whether orthodox or unorthodox. Such trouble as they experienced through the wrong-headed application of some of the Government legislation did not blind them to the systematic efforts of the government towards a sound economy[2] or prevent them from supporting the process of administrative reform.[3]

They were still more pleased when on 29 October the National Bank for Economic Development was authorised to finance the circulating capital requirement of businesses. Nor were other sectors forgotten, and helpful decisions were taken in a number of areas.

For instance, the literacy programme that had been virtually closed down since the Revolution owing to the political form it had been taking,[4] was restarted under the name of MOBRAL.[5]

A fresh department was set up in the Ministry of the Interior called CHISAM[6] with the task of organising the rehousing of the people living in the *favelas* or shanty towns around Rio de Janeiro and giving them dwellings at rents they could afford. As a result of an inquiry, three directors[7] of the Institute for Agrarian Reform (I.B.R.A.) were convicted of illicit use of funds and were relieved of their functions, and the task of restarting the programme was given to a Special Task Force for Agrarian Reform.[8]

On 10 September 1968 Costa e Silva caused a Council for the Defence of the Rights of the Human Person[9] to be set up with due ceremony, to ensure respect for liberties laid down in the Constitution and in the Universal Declaration of Human Rights; but although this was a gesture intended to reassure public opinion, in practice it had only symbolic value.

Dialogue with Parliament was begun on 20 March 1968 with an appeal to the deputies by the Planning Minister, who emphasised that the execution of the Strategic Development Programme depended on the right political conditions, over which the deputies exercised decisive influence. He therefore asked them to support the efforts of the Government by creating a 'national consciousness' in favour of this project which 'was capable of achieving the pacification of the country'.[10]

On 17 April Costa e Silva, addressing a group of ARENA deputies, stated that he 'wanted to see a constitutionally based civilian government, although there was no shortage of people advising him to take strong measures to deal with the crisis'.[11] But the members of parliament themselves were caught between the past and the future, between the old system and the one that, although due to replace it, was not yet electorally speaking a tangible reality. Two episodes which bore the marks of this dualism were indicative of the approaching crisis between the politicians and the President.

The first concerned the bill containing a list of those municipalities that the Government wished to classify as 'of interest for national security'. Under the Constitution these municipalities would lose the right to elect their mayor, who would be nominated by the State Governor as was done for the State capitals. Originally the military wished to include 236 communes out of the 3940 existing in the country in 1967[12] in their strategic concept. But as a result of protests by the opposition and by ARENA the official draft which was submitted on 18 April retained only 68 obviously well-chosen ones. The deputies refused to agree to this selection and on 30 April a faction of ARENA[13] published a manifesto opposing this increase in the powers of the executive as being 'uncalled for in present circumstances'.

The President had no more room for manoeuvre and he therefore vetoed the proposed amendments. The ARENA leadership, seeing the danger that its own troops would defect, resigned itself to an artifice. It caused its deputies to leave the meeting so that voting would have to be postponed for lack of a quorum, and the leader of the opposition declared in disgust that it would be better to close down Parliament than to indulge in antics of this sort. On 4 June, as no vote had been taken on the bill, the time limit allowed to Parliament had expired and Costa e Silva promulgated the law in its official form.

The second episode concerned the law on assimilation. The bi-partite régime worked well at federal level but was not suited to the needs of regional politics, and therefore local interests were allowed to voice their views by linking these sub-groups to the national party under a system known as 'sublegenda'. The Government regarded this simply as a technical procedural matter, but the parliamentary deputies saw it as affecting their whole political future. So although they were prepared to leave the economy to the technocrats, they had no intention of allowing them to draw up the rules of the electoral game.

Discussion on this law began in May 1967 and was of course very lively. For, when applied to the proportional vote (which was how deputies to the Federal and State parliaments were elected) the law had the effect of increasing the number of deputies belonging to the most powerful party; whereas in voting by simple majority, which is how senators were elected, it might cause one party to be eliminated by giving all the seats in a state to the candidate who had obtained a majority. And in fact in two large states, Guanabara and Rio Grande do Sul, the opposition had previously defeated ARENA!

After various convulsions (including the refusal of the M.D.B. to take part in the debate on the bill when submitted in its final form on 26 April 1968, the official proposal by the M.D.B. deputies in Minas Gerais to dissolve the party,[14] and the resignation of the President of ARENA[15] in protest against the manoeuvre of those members of his party who wanted to abstain from voting) the text was approved by a narrow majority notwithstanding the fact that a large number of deputies were absent.[16]

Three days later the opposition party published a commentary denouncing 'a military minority who endeavouring to put the Brazilian nation in leading strings with the support of a political group (ARENA) which is more out of touch with reality every day... has transformed the myth that national security is incompatible with sovereignty of the people into a dogma'.[17]

Some of the Military, although they enjoyed some material advantages hitherto denied them,[18] at times took a different line from Costa e Silva, often for opposite reasons. For instance Marshal Mario Poppe de Figueiredo, who although retired still had considerable prestige in military circles, demanded that the President should be a civilian, that deputies should again be chosen by direct elections and that an 'uncompromisingly nationalist' development plan should be drawn up.[19] Then again on 10 July Minister Jarbas Passarinho in the course of a press conference denounced the radicalisation of student agitation, which he said was due to the 'paternalist attitude of the President of the Republic' which so irritated the Army.[20]

On 23 August during a meeting of the National Security Council convened to discuss the 'concept of national strategy', the Minister of the Interior, General Albuquerque Lima, disagreed violently with his colleagues the Ministers of Finance and Planning because his order of priority for investments differed fundamentally from the one they proposed, which he considered to be too much oriented in the direction of internationalism and monetary policy.[21]

He confirmed this attitude in an address which he gave to the Superior War College in October in which he demanded the formation of a National Development Council[22] in which the Military would have the predominant say, which would give them active participation in all the modern social-economic sectors connected with development. His speeches and writings on the subject of economic nationalism became so positive that they were transformed into an electoral platform for the presidential elections of 1970.

But the use of the theme 'We need another ten years of revolution in order to meet our growth objectives' as the opening shot in a campaign was not at all popular with Costa e Silva who described the step taken by his minister as 'inopportune'. The wheel had come full circle since Castello Branco had used the same phrase in speaking of Costa e Silva.[23]

On 1 November the press published a manifesto signed by 385 captains[24] who were on a training course, deploring the situation of the country and demanding immediate changes. They also attacked the corruption which they said existed in high quarters.[25]

In such an atmosphere it is hardly surprising that a relatively minor incident sufficed to set off an explosion that had been building up for some time. Just before the National Independence celebrations, when the President of Chile, Eduardo Frey, was making an official visit to Brazil and preparations were being made for a grand patriotic ceremony, a young deputy who was one of the most virulent members of the opposition, Marcio Moreira Alvès,[26] twice spoke in the Chamber, on 2 and 3 September. He called for a boycott of the ceremony, asked parents not to let their children take part in the military procession on 7 September, and also asked young women who were 'lovers of freedom' to refuse to go out with officers. Another M.D.B. deputy, the journalist Hermano Alvès, made the same points in a series of provocative articles.[27]

The Army regarded these attacks as scurrilous, and on 13 September the three military ministers demanded the punishment of those responsible. Costa e Silva acknowledged that 'irresponsible and intolerable offence and provocation' had been given,[28] but he prevaricated and, for the sake of reaching a compromise, was ready to agree to the idea of his Foreign Minister who suggested that Parliament should pass a mollifying motion. But he was already too isolated to be able to offer much resistance, and on 9 October the Minister of Justice, faithful to his hard-line ideas, notified the leaders of ARENA that the Government proposed to commence proceedings for suspending the civil rights of the two dissident deputies.

On the sixteenth, after holding a number of consultations, the Chairman of ARENA[29] informed Costa e Silva that in his opinion and that of his party the deputies were covered by their parliamentary immunity and that in any event the step proposed would be 'politically inopportune'. The leader of the M.D.B., Senator Oscar Passos, supported this view though he said that, as a reserve general, he did not share the views expressed by the deputies concerned.

On 21 October the President held a meeting behind closed doors with the Military High Command. It was understood from leaks that the attitude of the Army had hardened. Two days later Marcio Moreira Alvès, quite unruffled, again spoke in the Chamber and complained about police brutality at student demonstrations.

Next day Parliament passed an enthusiastic vote of confidence in the Armed Forces on the occasion of Aviation Week, in the hope of smoothing over the dispute, but on 29 October Carlos Lacerda complicated the situation still further by publishing in the *Tribuna da Imprensa* an article violently attacking the Military, whom he described as 'a radical neo-fascist minority'.

Hostilities were suspended during the celebrations organized in honour of Queen Elizabeth and the Duke of Edinburgh who were on an official visit from 5 to 10 November 1968.[30] The truce also continued during the municipal elections held on 15 November,[31] in which ARENA received about 75 per cent of the votes, following a campaign during which the electors were entirely free to demonstrate their disillusionment.

Meanwhile the Supreme Court had placed before the Chamber on 6 November the demand for the suspension of privilege and the Chamber had passed the request to its competent committee. As this committee was hesitating to issue a decision, nine of its members who were ARENA deputies considered to be lukewarm were replaced by others on the orders of the party managers. Even so, the commission did everything possible to avoid giving a decision before the ordinary session ended.

But the manoeuvre was unsuccessful, for the President forced the hand of the deputies by convening an extraordinarry session of Parliament for 2 December. This put the committee on the spot and it voted that the case should be submitted to the full assembly. The fateful appeal was heard on the twelfth. Those deputies who attended were about to take a decision of major importance and they were in no doubt as to what was at stake, as they were well aware of the violent reaction of the Military to the decisions of the Supreme Court on the tenth and eleventh, when the Court had granted habeas corpus to 79 student leaders who had been arrested.[32]

When the voting was analysed, the Chamber had rejected the suspension of immunity by 216 to 114 with 15 abstentions, and 94 representatives of the governmental party had voted against the motion. The Military considered this to be desertion in the face of the enemy.

On the next day, 13 December 1968, Costa e Silva signed Institutional Act No. 5 and its Supplementary Act No. 38 in order to secure the continuity of the Revolution. These acts caused Parliament to go on vacation for an indefinite period, renewed the possibility of political sanctions not subject to scrutiny by the judges, and gave full power to the President.

It is worth noting that while citing the essential needs of national security, the preamble to Institutional Act No. 5 emphasised the need to reach the objectives of the Revolution 'in order to find the indispensable resources for the work of economic, financial, and political reconstruction of Brazil'.[33]

The Finance Minister immediately highlighted the importance attributed by the Government to this factor when during a press conference on 18 December he stated: 'Institutional Act No. 5 will enable us to take the necessary steps to reduce the treasury deficit and to contain the inflationary process with the object of securing the development of the country.'[34]

The following day the President himself took up this theme when, speaking to the Superior War College, he said: 'In this way the Government will be better equipped to carry out the Strategic Development Programme.'[35]

On 31 December, after various practical measures relating to the stock exchange and taxation had been announced, the Constitution was modified in seven points dealing with the authority of the federal government in economic matters. These amendments were intended to enable the fight against inflation to be carried on more effectively and to give the government powers to require provincial states and the federal administration to carry out changes in economic and financial matters.

It was the end of the semi-representative phase of the régime that Castello Branco had tried to set up under laboratory conditions but which had not been able to withstand the stresses of everyday realities. Addressing 198 generals, Costa e Silva later said in reference to this fact: 'The Government tried to tread the path of tolerance. When it strove for magnanimity it was accused of weakness. It then looked for political support, only to be betrayed by widespread lack of patriotism.'[36]

This disillusioned phrase well expresses the insecurity of a military élite which, having a share of power too great for popularity yet too little to enable it to impose modernisation at the pace which the development of the country required, was compelled by an opposition, itself given to violent excesses, to take by force an authority which it lacked. A judge in its own cause since 1964, the Army no longer had the moderating power and since then no one has been able to fulfil this arbiter's role, which is none the less necessary to the balance of powers within a traditional democratic framework.

So on 13 December 1968 the wish expressed by ex-President Jânio Quadros was to be fulfilled. For had he not said, before being placed under house arrest:[37] 'What we need is either a return to democracy or a dictatorship, for what we now have in Brazil is no good to anybody!'[38]

PART FOUR

An Appraisal of Modernising Authoritarianism

Now that it had the fresh powers which it thought it needed, would the Government at last find the way forward? This question was fated to remain unanswerable as, harassed on all sides, Costa e Silva suffered a cerebral thrombosis on 31 August 1969 and had to leave the reins of power in the hands of his military ministers. It is however legitimate to conclude that initially the régime tried to ensure order by the use of dissuasion rather than punishment, for it assembled a panoply of legal weapons enabling it to act harshly, but it did not deploy them.

The President even preferred to delegate to the Minister of Justice and his three military colleagues responsibility for suppressing terrorism and suspending civil rights and other sanctions,[1] while he concentrated his efforts on the economic and political aspects of government. The first list of suspensions of civil rights was published on 30 December 1968. Carlos Lacerda, accused of having wanted to overthrow the Government, was deprived of his political rights for ten years. The two protagonists of the crisis, Marcio Moreira Alvès and Hermano Alvès,[2] together with nine other deputies, one of whom belonged to ARENA, suffered the same penalty. The lists which followed[3] cut a swath through Parliament, which on 29 April 1969 was deprived of four senators and 95 deputies from the two parties (out of 409). The M.D.B. in fact lost 40 per cent of its representatives; nor was insubordination among the judges overlooked. Five Supreme Court judges[4] were retired early as was one of their colleagues on the Supreme Military Tribunal, General Pery Constant Bevilacqua, also accused of having adopted too liberal an attitude.

Suddenly the pace quickened until by the end of July some 500 persons had suffered various penalties. Besides the members of parliament, they included members of state assemblies or municipal councils, journalists, soldiers, diplomats, doctors, lawyers and many professors.[5]

164   *An Appraisal of Modernising Authoritarianism*

The concentration of powers was carried out by means of a series of institutional acts – which thus ceased to be exceptional in character – and of supplementary execratory acts. The former ensured a docile Supreme Court by reducing the number of its members (which had been increased to sixteen by Castello Branco) to eleven and restricting its powers.[6] The following acts[7] reduced the emoluments of deputies in the legislatures and cancelled the electoral calendar. They speeded up administrative reforms, restarted agrarian reform, regulated political sanctions[8] and lastly fixed a new electoral calendar under which elections were due to be held on 15 November 1969. On 8 February 1969 the General Commission of Inquiry was reconstituted in order to search out the authors of subversive or counter-revolutionary acts.

34 Nationalist Inflexibility

A decision of major importance for economic policy was taken at the beginning of the year. With the object of intensifying the fight against inflation, which was still proceeding at a high rate, the Finance Minister announced on 15 February 1969 large reductions in the budgets in order to reduce the State deficit by one half. Only the Ministry of Education was spared. This measure particularly affected the Minister of the Interior Albuquerque Lima whose means of acting on regional imbalance were severely curtailed.[1] And the theme of accelerated national growth even at the cost of more inflation was one of the main planks in the electoral platform of this candidate for the succession to the presidency.

He therefore decided to endeavour to force Costa e Silva's hand, and on 24 January he submitted his resignation. He took the opportunity of publicly arraigning a Government which according to him was too soft and was dodging the main problems of the nation, which were immediate agrarian reform, the integration of Amazonia, the development of the north-east and of the under-privileged regions, and suport for Brazilian business and industrial firms. But this attempt misfired, for the fiery general had too quickly forgotten that the President was bound by the economic choices that had been made, in as much as the aid sought from abroad[2] implied some appreciable control of inflation and the catalytic role given to industrialists and exporters of agricultural products involved, encouraging them to take risks in the hope of profiting from successful business deals. He was therefore unable successfully to change his target or to plunge into a vast programme for land redistribution, which would at once have lost him the goodwill of the entrepreneurial class who had close links with the landed proprietors.

Costa e Silva knew what he was doing, and he accepted the resignation of his Minister of the Interior without taking any further action.[3] Nevertheless the affair did cause some stir and the heads of the development agencies for the north-east and for Amazonia, SUDENE and SUDAM, resigned in the wake of their superior.[4]

However, nationalist themes were very popular among the hard-line military men and the intellectual élites. The former were quite strongly impressed by the experiment begun in October 1968 in Peru, while the latter were influenced by the debate on the de-nationalisation of Brazilian firms and the formulation of the sub-imperialist theory, 'the form which dependent capitalism takes when it reaches the stage of monopolies and financial capital'.[5]

The President, clever tactician that he was, anticipated the inevitable protests of the hard liners by replacing Albuquerque Lima by the Minister of Mines and Energy, Colonel Costa Cavalcanti, the brother of one of the leading hard liners,[6] and reassured those who feared that foreign capital might get a stranglehold on Brazil's mineral wealth by entrusting the vacant ministry to Professor Antonio Dias Leite, one of the most brilliant protagonists of enlightened nationalism.[7]

Thereupon the Finance Minister Delfim Netto, who was now incontestably the key personality in the cabinet, immediately gave fresh proof of his political adroitness by having the Government take up again the most popular themes of Albuquerque Lima, suitably sweetened up, and adopting them wherever this could be done without endangering his development strategy.

This manoeuvre did not in fact present any major difficulties, since it was mainly concerned with the allocation of investments, which Delfim Netto directed preferentially towards sectors dear to the hearts of the nationalists. However, he did not interfere either with the wages policy or with the basic principle of growth stimulated by the private sector, both Brazilian and foreign.

For example, on 30 January he announced that more money would be paid out in the states of the north and the north-east in order partially to compensate for their loss of income. On the same day Supplementary Act No. 45 forbade non-resident foreigners to purchase rural property. On 24 March a list of priority projects relating to ten large regions was published, and on 18 April during a meeting with the trade unionists, the Minister of Labour said that the opportunity would be taken on 1 May of promulgating a decree whereby a start was made on social security in country areas.[8]

On 25 April agrarian reform was once more set in motion by Institutional Act No. 9, which declared that zones in which social tension existed were to be priority areas.[9] It stated that expropriation compensation would be paid in special national debt bonds repayable in twenty years and subject to monetary correction. The accompanying decree law however stipulated that in the event of disagreement as to the value of the land, compensation would be based on the valuation made in the cadastral survey.[10] On 15 May a further decree instructed the Executive Group for Agrarian Reform (G.E.R.A.)[11] to co-ordinate the activity of the two existing organisations I.B.R.A. and I.N.D.A. To hasten the process still further an additional decree published on 21 July accorded I.B.R.A. a period not exceeding thirty days in which to submit a practical programme of operations, and on 26 August the names of the 198 communes in which the Government would take priority action was made public.[12]

Important steps were also taken in regard to education, the only sector not to have been affected by the budgetary restraints; in addition to the normal credits, the President allocated to it on 31 March 1969 Crz. 107 million (about $25 million). He also announced on 6 June that secondary, middle and primary schooling would be reformed and on 14 June he allocated $64 million in the budget to finance this reform.[13] Also with immediate effect, physical culture and civic instruction were made compulsory for university students, a measure which aroused some stirrings among the intellectuals but which accorded with the views of the Military.[14]

Achievements followed in rapid succession on the industrial front. One of the most important was the inauguration of work on Latin America's largest petrochemical complex[15] which, according to the Minister of the Interior, was to 'bring about an economic upswing that can only be compared with that initiated by the starting up of the automobile industry'.[16]

And yet the birth of this technologically advanced sector disturbed businessmen, for the volume of investment required called both for increasing participation by the State and for the import of foreign know-how and capital. They could already foresee the pressure towards mergers that was to make itself felt during the next few months. In vain did the President assure a delegation from the employers' association which he received on 10 July that 'the aim of the Revolution is to give the Brazilian people with the help of top management the peace and quiet necessary for production'.[17] Top management remained sceptical.

Their anxiety was increased when on 15 August a semi-public company, Minerobrás, was set up with the object of rationalising the prospecting and extraction of minerals; by the concentration of State powers and by their extension into the Merchant Navy (SUDANAM) and into steelmaking, which had always been one of the avowed aims of Professor Dias Leite. This unease was sufficiently widespread for the review *Visão*, which was read by the wealthy section of the popluation, to turn over most of its special number of 29 August 1969 to a feature entitled 'Who's who in the Brazilian economy'.

The former Finance Minister Octavio Gouvêa de Bulhões, a spokesman for banking circles, said that although there were encouraging instances of co-operative effort on the development front between the State and private industry, 'this is not always a common effort'. For this he blamed the State which, outstepping its co-ordinating role, fell into the extreme 'either of omission or of paternalism. In the first case private initiative is wastefully spread over the whole economy, and in the second case the whole of the economy debilitates private initiative.'[18] He cited as a case in point the Stock Exchange, where the Government did not intervene to put down speculation, and that of the mining industry where the authorities had decided to assume the technical and financial risk. He ended by saying: 'Between these two extremes there is the vast range of possible collaboration between the State and individuals in the interests of economic and social progress... such co-operation must be resolutely sought... so as to avoid the swamping of private initiative by State paternalism.'

The Vice-President of the Federation of Industries of the State of São Paulo, Luis R. Rossi, after reminding his audience that it was 'impossible not to be aware of the very important part played by small and medium-sized businesses... which have been responsible for installing industrial equipment which made a significant contribution in Brazil' and going on to speak about 'the difficulties of all kinds that have latterly been encountered [by these firms] in relation to taxation, credit, technology, quality, administration and human relations',[18] demanded more Government financial help. He said that the State was neglecting them in favour of the giant concentrations.

An employer who had many contacts among foreigners, Paulo Reis de Magalhães, whose chairmanships included that of the Rhodia Group, said that in his opinion the unco-ordinated flood of laws which was submerging the country – including the limitation on the purchase of land by foreigners, the restrictions imposed on mineral exploitation by foreign companies and on the work of public works or engineering companies – represented 'a step backwards which must inevitably have its effect on capital which might otherwise be interested in investing in Brazil'.[20] Eduardo Prado, another of the São Paulo patricians, also shared this view, and said that 'the bureaucratic difficulties and the shoal of regulations (often of short duration) cause less worry to foreign investors than outdated, meaningless laws such as those on land and on minerals, which impose restrictions on the activities of foreigners'.[21] Summing up these opinions, the managing director of *Visão*, Saïd Farhat, wrote in his editorial:

> Brazil must in the end decide where it is going as an economic entity, either by choosing the road of increasing State control, thus unnecessarily taking on the risk which is the very essence of private initiative, or by continuing to provide for private initiative the conditions it requires in order to become stronger and to expand. To choose the second option would be to free official funds for many other sectors such as education or public health, where there is still so much that urgently needs to be done.[22]

35 The End of Costa e Silva

But the main subject of discussion at that time was still a return to normality in politics, which Costa e Silva wanted but which the hard-line element in the Army neither wanted nor thought necessary.

After a long hesitation waltz the two largest groupings, ARENA and M.D.B., were retained.[1] The legal requirements for transforming them into properly constituted political parties were facilitated[2] and the guarantees were given to secure freedom of choice for everybody.[3]

A draft constitutional reform was produced by a high commission of which Costa e Silva himself was Chairman, and which met from 14 to 17 July.[4] Nevertheless before giving his final approval the President decided to consult once more the Federal Supreme Court and above all the National Security Council.

What had happened to make Costa e Silva feel the need of this additional control by the Military? It cannot be explained by any particular event, but seems to have been due to the growing tension within the Armed Forces. For the first time since the Revolution, generals were being criticised by their immediate subordinates such as Colonel Francisco Boaventura Cavalcanti, a brother of the Minister of the Interior, who was at once transferred to the reserve of officers on 19 May 1969 for 'failing in his duty and loyalty towards his superiors in the Armed Forces'.[5]

When the detailed report of the commission of inquiry into the case was published in the press, the crisis which had been smouldering underground for some months, burst into open conflagration. It took a dangerous turn for the continued existence of the régime when General Augusto Cézar Moniz de Aragão, responsible for army supplies, attacked his superior Lyra Tavares, Minister of the Army, for his decision concerning Boaventura Cavalcanti in confidential letters, copies of which were circulating comparatively freely. In it he accused, *inter alia*, Costa e Silva of favouritism towards his Transport Minister, of hushing up some questionable business dealings of his son who was himself a colonel, and other misdemeanours.[6]

Aragão was relieved of his post on 1 July, but his attitude was the more revealing of the state of mind of the higher Army echelons in that he wanted to speak on behalf of his cadets, those discontented officers who, if they could not have a 'pure, austere and effective' government such as they demanded, 'may well unleash a storm which will carry us all to chaos and unforeseen events'.[7] The public thought there was unlikely to be smoke without fire, and there was open talk about a possible 'colonels' coup' aimed at replacing Costa e Silva by a younger, more energetic general.[8]

This crack in the Military edifice was obvious enough, for the press release issued on 21 July concerning the forty-second meeting of the Army High Command stated that business had included 'an analysis of the various aspects of the problems resulting from terrorist activity and from recently discovered efforts to weaken the discipline and unity of the Army'. During the meeting 'the fundamental need to safeguard the cohesion of the Army by channelling all effort through the chain of command and through discipline was unanimously affirmed'.[9]

It was in this strained atmosphere, made even worse by a fresh wave of terrorism,[10] by the conflict with the Church and by student demonstrations,[11] that on 13 August Costa e Silva was struck down by a cerebral thrombosis from which he died on 17 December 1969 without having recovered either the use of his limbs or the faculty of speech. And so the steersman was swept from the wheel while the storm was still brewing.

36 The Military Triumvirate

On the afternoon of 31 August 1969 the three military ministers[1] informed the Brazilians of the seriousness of the President's condition. They also announced by Institutional Act No. 12, which was signed immediately, that they were taking over the ruling power for the time being. Rio de Janeiro was temporarily promoted to being the capital of the Republic.

The suddenness of this news[2] bursting upon the uncertain political situation then prevailing,[3] led some to suspect that the President had been forcibly retired. An illness of which people were not convinced looked like a convenient explanation. Jibes were hurled at the Government and jokes were being bandied about right up to the time at which the medical bulletins confirmed[4] that Costa e Silva was seriously ill and that he would recover only slowly, if at all.

The Military had no intention whatever of allowing the constitutional successor, Vice-President Pedro Aleixo, to assume power. He himself was sufficiently conscious of the precariousness of his situation in the equilibrium of forces to agree with the way in which the Foreign Minister put it to the press on 2 and 3 September when he said that the military triumvirate was acting 'with Costa e Silva's powers but not in substitution of him'.

A comparison of this politics of the strongest with the observance of the proprieties practised by Castello Branco shows how the aspect of the Armed Forces had changed between 1964 and 1969. Nor did the change stop there: the doctrine of the Superior War College had taken a fresh turn with the years, and it was becoming increasingly difficult to distinguish between the original hard liners and the members of the 'Sorbonne'.

One reason for this trend is to be found in the changes that had come about in the high echelons of the Army. Some Army generals had retired, their juniors had taken their places, the best of the colonels had become one-star generals, and many majors and captains had been promoted. Moreover, the exercise of power had produced a kind of amalgam of the two schools of thought in a direction at once more nationalist and less patient of discussion. Thus in international affairs anti-Communism had been almost wholly abandoned (except as regards Cuba) and Brazil had taken an independent foreign-policy line, less aligned with that of the United States.

A similar shift had taken place in regard to private enterprise, and while the Military sought to encourage greater participation of top managers in the life of the nation in place of the former political class,[5] they were increasingly hostile to the very idea of capitalist profit. In practice, for fear of what they called the 'economic power' of the private sector, in spite of saying that they were supporting it, they were always calling on the technocrats and the nationalised sector.[6]

Several of the younger officers in the higher ranks[7] went further, and although they realised that Nasserism was not a choice which could be adapted to an economic system as complex as that of Brazil, were following with interest the experiment begun in October 1968[8] in Peru and did not hesitate to question the sacrosanctity of private property or the infallibility of the hierarchical principle.[9]

This group took an ever-deepening interest in social problems such as agrarian reform, the taxation system, income distribution, subversion, etc., which they saw as obstacles along the road leading to political stability which was the basis of national security – obstacles which had to be overcome.

These professional officers who had been moulded by a Brazilian outlook cut off from the traditional democratic patterns from which their elders drew their inspiration, thought of the military government not as an organisation artificially superimposed upon the national society but as the crystallisation of all the aspirations of the nation, and that its moral authority was a substitute for the popular vote.

This was another area in which this group, which consisted of hard liners, held different ideas from the leaders who assumed power in 1964. It is difficult to estimate their strength accurately, but the group was quite a large one if the warnings given by General Augusto Cézar de Castro Moniz de Aragão were to be believed. Aragão had become their spokesman since his suspension from his command for opposing the Minister of the Army in the affair of Colonel Cavalcanti.[10] The aims which this group had concerning the defence of the national interest and the creation of social harmony were to be highlighted some years later in the speech which Aragão made when he was retired in August 1972. Although he had spent fifty of his sixty-six years in uniform he nevertheless could say to his audience, which included forty-three generals; 'The Military should come into action when the elected representatives, in exercising their governmental powers, openly, expressly and flagrantly commit acts against the national interest; or ... when justice is no longer dispensed wisely and in the interests of social harmony.'[11] He ended by defining discipline in the following words: 'Stars and decorations by themselves express but a sham illusory hierarchy. Only moral prestige calls forth admiration and respect, which is the essence of real obedience.'[12]

Those who held these views also gave up the theory of the inevitability of a confrontation between the United States and the Soviet Union leading to a third world war, which seemed to give the lie to peaceful coexistence. It was replaced by a concept of accelerated development as the foundation of the doctrine of 'national security' of which the Army was the custodian.[13]

Thus, although it was taking a harder line, the Army was in a state of unstable equilibrium between different views at the time when Costa e Silva's health failed. The kidnapping of the United States Ambassador Charles Burke Elbrick at Rio de Janeiro on 4 September 1969 was to upset this balance further still, even while the triumvirate was still in the midst of its consultations. The revolutionary commando which carried out the operation[14] let it be known that it would free its hostage if the Government agreed to release fifteen political prisoners[15] and to publish a communiqué in which the existence of an opposition to the Government was admitted.

Although Washington exerted strong diplomatic pressure[16] the core of 'nationalist' officers set their faces against any compromise which would endanger the 'national honour'. They wanted the prisoners whose release the terrorists were demanding to be summarily shot, even though this meant that the Ambassador would lose his life.

The triumvirate was divided. Its oldest member, Admiral Rademacker, was a right-wing hard liner who was not disposed to yield. General Lyra Tavares was an intellectual who believed in the primacy of law. He came from a good family and had commanded the Superior War College in 1966–7; he had been a member of the Brazilian Expeditionary Force in Italy and had represented Brazil in the occupation force in Germany. His experience of the Americans and his training at Fort Leavenworth disposed him to an understanding attitude towards the position of the United States. Air Marshal Marcio de Souza e Mello, who had also passed through the E.S.G., had been Chief of the Staff of the Armed Forces (E.C.E.M.E.). He was a hard liner whose anti-Goulart sentiments had been so strong that he had gone on leave for more than a year between 1963 and 1964. In the present case his view of the situation inclined him rather towards the American side, because at that time Brazil was in no position to afford the luxury of a break with the United States or to risk the success of its economic policy for the sake of a matter of prestige.

The Government[17] agreed to wait until later before expunging the insult put upon it by the terrorists, and on 5 September 1969 it gave in to their demands[18] and had the controversial manifesto broadcast over the radio.[19] Next day the political prisoners were flown to Mexico in a Brazilian military aircraft which had to be given special protection as some Naval and Air Force officers were suspected of preparing a surprise attack. The American Ambassador was put into circulation again twenty-four hours later.

The crisis between Brazil and the United States had indeed been avoided[20] but discontent in the Army had increased: on 7 September during a football match at Rio de Janeiro a group of officers seized the microphone of a sports commentator and broadcast criticism of the Government's capitulation to the terrorists.[21] The Government immediately took a number of stern measures with the twofold object of cooling tempers and giving proof of its will to deal with the problem of armed subversion:

Institutional Act No. 13 which was published on 8 September 1969[22] provided for the banishment of persons whose presence was a danger to state security, and Supplementary Act No. 64 which accompanied it made the penalty applicable to the fifteen ex-prisoners who had taken refuge in Mexico.

Institutional Act No. 14[23] modified the wording of Article 115, paragraph 11 of the Constitution and allowed the death penalty or life imprisonment to be inflicted in case of 'psychological opposition, warfare, revolutionary war or subversive struggle'.

On 18 September the new law on National Security[24] which reinforced the preceding law by incorporating in it all the emergency regulations that had been adopted since it was passed, decreed that anybody who was condemned to death would be shot unless within thirty days the President commuted his penalty to life imprisonment. By the same law the Government tightened its control on the press by punishing with prison sentences ranging from six months to two years the propagation either of 'false and tendentious news' or of true facts 'half-told or distorted'.[25]

The Army combed all areas intensively and unmitigated repression was the order of the day; according to the *Estado de São Paulo* about 1800 suspects were arrested. More people were deprived of their civil rights and those affected included nine members of the Federal Parliament and one senator.[26] Administrative sanctions were also applied. For example, fourteen professors at the University of Belo Horizonte were summarily retired.[27] Dialogue had virtually ceased, and to circumvent any political risk, most of the elections that had been fixed by Costa e Silva were adjourned *sine die*,[28] as were also the dates for the national conventions of the two political parties.[29] It looked very much as if a praetorian régime might be on its way.

37 The Succession

Active though the Military were as legislators, they still found time to give close attention to the problem of the presidential succession, despite the protests of Minister Andreazza, who may still have cherished the hope that his protector would be reinstated in power.

On 16 September an official note announced that Costa e Silva would now definitely have to be replaced and that the triumvirate, after having repeatedly consulted the Army High Command had instructed a committee of three members[1] to consider all the possible options concerning the succession. The committee was also instructed to give a judgment about another matter on which the Army was divided, namely how long the new President should remain in power. For whereas one faction wanted the tenure of the head of government to be only temporary, serving out only the remaining period of Costa e Silva's mandate which was to end on 15 March 1971, another faction wanted him to have a five-year term of office.[2]

Too much was at stake for the decision to be left to four generals, and the committee decided to engage in wide-ranging discussions which would give all the higher officers of the three services from colonel upwards the opportunity of expressing their choice among the eight leading candidates.[3] Each arm was to draw up a list of three candidates in order of preference. These lists would then be considered together and merged into a single list of three names from which the successful candidate would be nominated by the three military ministers, the Chiefs of Staff of the three arms and the Chief of Staff of the Armed Forces meeting in council. This procedure was weighted in favour of the votes of the 'administrative' generals with offices in the ministries at Rio de Janeiro, who were more heavily represented than generals having an operational command.

In the end Castello Branco's and Costa e Silva's supporters united in support of Garrastazu Médici, who was also the favourite of the higher-ranking field officers. In this way they blocked Albuquerque Lima who was close behind Médici on the lists of the operational staffs but did not gain the votes of his colleagues in the ministry. On 7 October 1969 the press office of the presidency announced the choice of the Military, which was to be ratified by ARENA.

To counterbalance the neutralism of General Médici, who was above politics, Admiral Augusto Rademacker Grünewald was placed on the same ticket as Vice-President; he was well known as having extreme-right leanings. Agreement at the highest level was further strengthened by the semi-official nomination of General Orlando Geisel as Minister of the Army and the decision to have Marcio de Souza e Mello as Minister of Aviation and to retain General Muricy as Chief of Staff of the Army.

The Brazilian press was too closely watched to be a sounding board for discordant voices (in particular that of Albuquerque Lima) but echoes were heard under the signature of Joseph Novitski in the *New York Times* on 6 October.[4] However, disagreement must have gone deeper than was generally known, since on 14 October the triumvirate was authorised by Institutional Act No. 17 to transfer soldiers who 'have endangered the cohesion of the Armed Forces or who might do so'[5] to the reserve of officers, either for a specified or an indeterminate period.

In his first radio and television address[6] the general who was the successful candidate reminded his listeners that 'Brazil is still far from being a developed country' and that they were living under a régime which 'could not be considered as fully democratic'. He said that Brazil needed 'free universities, free parties, free trade unions, a free press and a free church' but he nevertheless warned troublemakers that they would be severely punished.

He also confirmed that once elected he would carry on the economic and financial policy of the preceding government, with improvements in the fields of public health, education, the development of the underprivileged areas of the country and a fairer distribution of the national wealth.

He came down too on the side of those who were advocating a readiness to entertain links with East European countries[7] when he said that exports should be sent to all countries where they could be sold irrespective of ideological differences.

On 14 October Institutional Act No. 16 officially declared the presidency and the vice-presidency to be vacant[8] and fixed 25 October as the date for election by Parliament. By means of two supplementary acts[9] Parliament was reopened and the deputies and senators were reconvened to Brasilia for 22 October. On the following day the M.D.B. decided to attend officially but to abstain from voting in the election. On the twenty-fifth General Emilio Garrastazu Médici and Admiral Augusto Hamann Rademacker Grünewald were elected President and Vice-President of the Republic respectively for a period running from 30 October 1969 to 15 March 1974, by 293 votes[10] and 76 abstentions.[11]

Meanwhile on 17 October the Military High Command had promulgated the amendment to the Constitution which had been promised several months previously and on 21 October it adopted three more codes, the penal code,[12] military penal code and the code of military penal procedure, as well as a law on the organisation of military tribunals. By this revision of the Constitution all the emergency regulations promulgated since 1967 were assimilated into the Constitution, including the right of the executive to suspend civil rights under the terms of Institutional Act No. 5, which now became permanent.[13] Interestingly enough, this step did not appear to cause a stir among Brazilian citizens.

A public opinion test carried out in Rio de Janeiro showed that 50 per cent of the 'Cariocas' replied 'don't know' as regards the maintenance of this act, 28 per cent with the decision of the Government and only 22 per cent were against it.[14] The federal legislature was further weakened[15] both as regards the prerogatives left to members of parliament and also as regards the number of deputies. For in future they were to be elected not on the basis of the number of inhabitants, but in proportion to the number of electors.[16]

The powers of the National Security Council were set out. It was to be 'the top-level body with the task of assisting the President of the Republic in formulating and executing policy on national security'.[17]

Then on 23 October a decree law was passed which regulated the reasons for ineligibility in such a way that a good number of politicians from the pre-1964 period would never again be able to stand for election.

The new President[18] was comparatively little known. None the less it does not appear that the time he spent as head of the National Intelligence Service (S.N.I.), the files of which contain innumerable pieces of information, had damaged his reputation with public opinion. Regarded as a new man, he even enjoyed predisposition in his favour and was considered 'sincere', 'firm' and 'capable of breadth of vision'.[19] The question of how representative he was did not arise, since it was clear to all that he owed his position to the Army, of which at the date of his election he was the highest common denominator. As this was well understood, nobody expected miracles but they hoped for 'an improvement'.[20]

Médici was himself aware of the limits imposed upon him by this situation and he charted his course in such a way as to avoid hasty alignments of any sort. He proved to be moderate, prudent and realistic and his keen intelligence sought to go beyond the slogans of the struggle against subversion to an understanding of its causes. This inevitably led him on to a study of the reforms that were needed in the economic and social structures of the country, as he stated in the speech he made on 7 October 1969.

This concern of the new President recalls the question which Governor Nelson Rockefeller asked in the report on his journey through South America submitted to President Nixon on 9 November 1969: 'The critical test, ultimately is whether the new military can and will move the nation with sensitivity and conscious design toward a transition from military control for a social purpose to a more pluralistic form of government which will enable individual talent and dignity to flourish.'[21]

38 The Path Chosen by President Médici

President Garrastazu Médici returned to the method of government by 'authoritarian centralism' which Castello Branco had begun. He was also influenced by many of the other political principles of the late President, though he adapted them to the new situation in Brazil. For instance, although he welcomed the influx of foreign capital he was more selective in doing so. While still remaining a convinced internationalist, he nevertheless steered the doctrine of global economic interdependence toward what might be called a vision of 'sovereign interdependence' by adding to it elements of national self-protection. He spoke of the need to encourage democracy, yet did not hesitate to resort either to force in order to restore order disturbed by terrorist acts or to punish the excesses which sometimes accompanied such repression.

He outlined the path he was going to follow in his inaugural speech to Parliament on 30 October 1969, which is a veritable declaration of faith:

> I believe in the miracles that men perform with their own hands and in those of the collective will... I believe in the generous soul of youth, in my country and in my people. I believe in bringing the future nearer, in the potential and the economic viability of Brazil. I believe in development as a universal phenomenon... and in the steady growth of industry in Brazil ... I believe in a world without technological frontiers in which scientific progress will offer humanity the option of an open society... I believe that we shall see a world without ideological frontiers in which each nation will respect the way of life of others... I am a man of the Revolution... and I believe in the renewing, innovating dynamic of its ideas and... I believe it will become more active and more progressive.

To put this faith into practice, Médici brought in seven civilian technicians[1] who were sent to assist Delfim Netto and Dias Leite, each of whom had kept his ministerial post. There were virtually no changes in the Military ministries and they were allocated in accordance with the decisions that had been taken when the President was chosen.

However, one significant change in the allocation of tasks calls for comment: Senator (and ex-Colonel) Jarbas Passarinho gave up the Ministry of Labour and took the portfolio of National Education where he was able to exercise fully his gifts as an organiser and negotiator. To underline the importance he attached to cohesion among his team, the President created the function of 'general co-ordination' reporting directly to him, and in this post he placed a young economist Marcus Vinicius Pratini de Morães.

No changes were made in the Cabinet for more than two years,[2] with one exception – Fabio Riodi Yassuda, the Minister of Industry and Trade, resigned on 23 February 1970 after a dispute between the 'pure nationalist' wing which he represented and the 'flexible nationalists' of which Delfim Netto was the epitome.

It is worth pausing to examine this crisis because the way in which Garrastazu Médici handled it – he came down on the side of the flexible nationalists against the rigidity of the pure – is characteristic. The antagonism surfaced because of two related events each of which touched, in different degrees, on national prestige. The first resulted in the cancellation on 11 December by presidential decree of the International Exhibition Commemorating the 150th Anniversary of the Independence of Brazil, which was to have been held in 1972.[3] The money already earmarked for this prestige event was to be used for building the campus of the Federal University of Rio de Janeiro, work on which had stopped even before the Revolution. The new Minister of Education had lost no time... The second was even more important since it concerned coffee, that basic constituent in the economic life of the country, which gave employment to more than one million people.[4]

Ever since 1966 the National Coffee Association of the United States had been worried about the increasing sales in America of soluble coffee produced in Brazil[5] at a price which was low compared with that of ground coffee;[6] and the Association was demanding protection against this competition which it described as unfair.

The two countries began a lengthy series of talks and the matter was discussed at meetings of the International Coffee Organisation in London from 1967 onwards. The discussions became more and more acrimonious, and the Employers' Organisation of the Soluble Coffee Industry in the State of São Paulo published newspaper articles denouncing 'the colonial-type pressures to which Brazil is being subjected'.[7]

But in spite of this, on 23 April 1969 Delfim Netto, who was then a minister under Costa e Silva, had given some ground and had introduced a tax[8] on exports of soluble coffee to the United States, which came into force on 1 May.

This decision was regarded in Brazil as an 'out-and-out capitulation... which is a direct affront to principles of national sovereignty... because, under pressure from a group of United

States industrialists, the Washington Government has succeeded in imposing in Brazil a tax on the export of a manufactured product'.[9]

Nevertheless, as its author had foreseen, the tax, which was really quite a small one, did not make much difference to the market penetration of soluble coffee from Brazil in the United States. But the big North American food groups were by no means satisfied and in January 1970 the largest American producer, General Foods, requested its Government to persuade Brazil, where Médici was now President, to impose a higher export tax.[10]

It was at this juncture that the new President of the Brazilian Coffee Institute[11] decided to replace the marketing manager of the Institute after having obtained the agreement of the Minister of Industry and Trade; and on 18 February he appointed to this post, which was of critical importance in the negotiations, Monsieur Wander Batalha, from whom a more nationalist attitude was expected.

Next day, at the request of Delfim Netto, the President of the Republic removed the new manager from his position. Minister Yassuda had to give way and he submitted his resignation, which was at once accepted. Marcus Vinicius Pratini de Moraes, who held the post of general co-ordinator in the presidency, was appointed to replace him.[12]

The appointment of this thirty-four-year-old technocrat set the seal on the victory of the two technical ministries (Finance and Planning) over the political ministry of Industry and Trade. Under the previous Government Macedo Soares had made it the representative body of top business management, and with the appointment of Morães it became an instrument of execution and co-ordination.

Once more Delfim Netto had a free hand and the policy line on coffee which he followed won its first victory in May, when the National Coffee Association adopted a resolution deploring both the intervention of the United States in the problem of the Brazilian tax on the export of soluble coffee and the introduction of a protective tariff in America on imports of this product.[13]

It was a short-lived victory, for General Foods did not give up. Following further representations[14] the Ways and Means Committee of the House of Representatives chaired by the Democrat Wilbur Mills passed a resolution which was an ultimatum demanding that the Brazilian tax should be increased from 13 to 30 cents per pound of soluble coffee before 1 April 1971 at latest.[15]

Certain other measures that were taken by the United States during this period[16] are indicative of a hardening of American policy with regard to Brazilian exports and in the end it was only with difficulty that an agreement on soluble coffee was concluded in April 1971.

This agreement provided for the abolition of the export surtax. In consideration of this Brazil authorised the export to the United States of 560,000 bags (60 kilograms per bag) of green coffee annually[17] (for American manufacturers of soluble coffee) free of a 'contribution quota' which was the new name given to the foreign exchange withholding.[18] This latter condition represented for the Brazilian Coffee Institute a loss of revenue of something like U.S. $10–12 million yearly;[19] this should however be set against the U.S. $312·2 million earned by exporting coffee to the United States in 1970.[20] Another consequence of the agreement, implicit but none the less important, was the renewal by the United States of the International Coffee Agreement. For it should be borne in mind that the American legislation authorising the application of these rules, which had regulated the world-wide distribution of coffee since 1962, was due to expire in June 1971; and every year from 1968 to 1971 Brazil had exported between 17 and 19·5 million bags.[21] The Chairman of the Ways and Means Committee changed his tune and recommended the House of Representatives to extend the agreement until 30 September 1973, and this was done in October by 200 votes to 99.[22]

It can be stated without fear of contradiction that these results would not have been obtained by negotiators who preferred nationalist harangues to a rational analysis of the situation. This agreement, which resulted from realistic negotiations between trading partners, was probably the first sign that Brazil had passed from adolescence to maturity in its dealings with the United States.[23]

The impression was confirmed by the arrival of Garrastazu Médici in Washington on 7 December 1971. He was received at the White House where together with President Nixon he laid down the main lines for future relations between the two countries. In these, two main themes are discernible.

1. Brazil was accepted as being the leading power in the southern hemisphere, thus ending an American political fiction according to which Latin America formed a whole composed of equal members.
2. Brazil was recognised as the main ally of the United States in Latin America and its Government was to be supported and recognised whether elected by direct suffrage or not.

President Nixon specifically stated: 'Where Brazil goes, Latin America will go.'[24] This statement called forth reactions throughout the South American continent, and particularly in Argentina.

A large part of Brazilian public opinion took no interest throughout the arguments about coffee, and this striking absence of reaction was observable in other cases too such as the development of

Amazonia, the extension of territorial waters[25] or the question of nuclear power. It was as though the country was content to hand over the solution of problems that were considered as technical to the specialists, and that no burning desire was felt for a more active participation.

It is always difficult to know the opinion of the silent majority, but an opinion test that was published in July 1970[26] was very revealing concerning what was on the minds of the Brazilians.

39 The Opinion of the Silent Majority

This opinion poll[1] was based on a sample of 500 persons of both sexes grouped by socio-economic strata taken from the inhabitants of five of the main cities in Brazil – São Paulo, Rio Janeiro, Brasilia, Recife and Porto Alegre.[2]

The results constitute a background which shows up some of the characteristics of the state of mind of the city dwellers of Brazil after six years of military government. For example, when asked about the progress of their standard of living according to subjective criteria, 57 per cent of the respondents agreed that their situation had improved either 'a little'[3] or 'a good deal'[4] – only 3 per cent spoke of an appreciable lowering of their standard of living; 68 per cent said they had increased job opportunities[5] and 63 per cent thought that social assistance to wage earners had greatly improved;[6] 68 per cent also thought that handouts by the Government amounted to more than it had taken back in additional taxes;[7] 62 per cent of the replies were favourable to an official policy of birth control (whereas the Church and some of the Military were opposed to this).

One characteristic concerned the part which the respondents thought the State should play in the economic life of the country: 65 per cent thought that the Government should intervene in all areas of the economy, 3 per cent thought the State should take no part and 6 per cent did not know. The lower the educational standard of the respondent the more they thought it necessary for the State to intervene economically; the percentage went from

74 per cent of persons who had only attended a primary school to 42 per cent among those with university education.

As regards private business and industry, only 47 per cent of replies attributed a 'very important' role to such industry in the development of Brazil whereas 38 per cent hardly conceded it a 'normal' role.[8] On this question, 57 per cent of the well-to-do classes were in favour while only 45 per cent of the middle and poor classes were in favour.

Opinions concerning the role of foreign capital in the development of Brazil were symptomatic of the division of the country; 44 per cent of all replies were favourable while 47 per cent were opposed to the admission of foreign capital (54 per cent of women voted against it, compared with only 40 per cent of men). The higher the level of education the more ready were the respondents to approve the calling in of foreign capital – 66 per cent of university educated against 55 per cent of primary-school educated. The same opinion shifts were found according to levels of income. Surprisingly, in view of their Germanic origin, the inhabitants of Porto Alegre were the most negative, 69 per cent of them replying 'no'.

Nobody expressed concern about the future of the country and 52 per cent replied that Brazil would be a great power as early as the year 2000; 56 per cent of the total sample thought that football was 'important to the individual' and this included 62 per cent of the men.[9] Lastly, the population showed a relative unconcern with terrorism in that only 54 per cent said that they felt themselves to be directly affected from a security aspect.[10] The poorer sections of the community felt themselves to be more at risk (58 per cent) than the middle classes (53 per cent) or the well-to-do (41 per cent), possibly because they often had direct contact with the phenomena of terrorism and repression.

The city dwellers in Brazil considered that the most important problems were social inequality, illiteracy, shortage of schools, inflation, the rise in the cost of living and the scarcity of medical and general hospital services.

In brief, after six years of military government city dwellers in Brazil thought that their own standard of living had improved and that employment opportunities had increased. They thought that social security was working, that education made it easier to rise in the social scale and that the country was passing through a phase of renewal which would bring Brazil to the status of a great power by the end of the century.

Finally, 'although they realised that there were still problems to be overcome, they thought that these would soon be solved'.[11]

40 Towards Political Normalisation?

By the second half of 1971 political debate was already sufficiently free[1] for General Rodrigo Octavio Jordão Ramos to be able to say: 'The present moment is favourable to the institutional normalisation of Brazil.'[2]

The review *Visão* even devoted a part of its special annual number[3] to a forum on the subject of 'Development – freedom – national security'. Of the ten questions that were asked the most interesting is the following: 'What steps do you suggest should be taken in order that the country should reach a stage of political–institutional reconciliation in which the alternatives of revolution or counter-revolution should give place to creative actions which, oriented towards our future, should lead towards an open political society?'[4]

According to Luiz Gonzaga do Nascimento e Silva, a lawyer and industrialist, formerly Castello Branco's Minister of Labour, it was necessary to 'maintain and strengthen the present economic growth strategy based upon an open and flexible model' because 'without an active and developing private sector ... it will not be possible to create a truly open democratic society'. Politically, 'a demarcation of areas between what is essential for the survival of the institutions and what is only subsidiary would be very useful'.[5]

Dom Helder Câmara took a contrary view when he wrote:

> It is urgently necessary for the Revolution to opt for real, courageous, firm and effective reforms. We think we are correct in observing some changing attitudes ... I must have the confidence and the courage to say that I do not see any hope for Brazil, for Latin America or for the Third World along the lines of capitalism or neo-capitalism. Obviously I can no more see a solution ... along the lines of the current Communist models. We have to find a model of growth along the lines of socialisation ... But it is essential ... that it should really give human beings their rights, and not become a dictatorship of government or party.[6]

The leader of the opposition group in Parliament, lawyer Oscar Pedroso d'Horta, claimed to be a 'simple citizen who, with all his limitations, is opposing a bad government'. To him it was obvious that any search for a solution involved 'untrammelled freedom of information ... For if, as is now the case in Brazil, it is suppressed, the people can only move with the halting steps of the blind and deaf, neither hearing nor seeing.'[7]

Bresser Pereira, who was an economist and leading businessman, thought that 'Brazilians in general are not looking for extremes, and therefore... neither the extreme left nor the extreme right will be able to achieve democratic success'.[8]

The sociologist Florestan Fernandes saw the problem from another angle. He wrote that:

> In Brazil... a privileged *status* has been created within civilian society for businesses and entrepreneurs. Private initiative has always been at hand to claim its share and to impose on the State patterns for action which exalt business growth above the well-being of the people or the growth of the nation. That is why the break with democratic principles can be traced back to the interest of heads of businesses... The democracy perceptible through this philosophy is always the same one, giving total priority to the rights of business and to national policies which keep Latin America under the wing of *restricted democracy*.[9]

The Vice-President of the National Federation of Industry, José Mindlin, did not agree. He considered small and medium-sized businesses

> an essential element in the defence of democracy... a development unilaterally imposed by the small body of technocrats... can hardly lead to an economic democracy and still less to a political democracy... if it is necessary to put down any abuses of freedom that may take place, it is just as important to prevent the instruments of security from being misused... without confusing argument or criticism with subversion, and without regarding the exercise of basic liberties as potential threats to the Government.[10]

Luiz Vianna Filho, a man of letters and former Head of the Civil Household of Castello Branco and Governor of Bahia until 1971, noted that 'it has from the beginning been an assumption of the Government that in order to survive democracy had to be prosperous... The important thing is that the most responsible leaders of the Revolution have never believed either that development is an end in itself or that dictatorship can be an ideal form of government.'[11]

Roberto Campos, the first architect of economic recovery, thought that

> during the process of modernisation, acute tensions, structural modifications and social disequilibria make their appearance, and

in some circumstances an authoritarian framework may be needed in order to restore harmony. Once the stage of modernisation has been reached, the instincts of freedom which are truly necessary to ensure the survival of creativity in advanced societies, revive.[12]

In presenting a summary of the forum the writers in the review observed that 'hitherto maintenance of the revolutionary system appeared to be better served by the total elimination of controversy. But henceforward it will depend on the very existence of controversy'.[13] They advocated the setting up of a Brazilian model which 'had the courage to recognise the fact that no modern political régime can ignore the problem of representation, and that it could not for long deny that universal suffrage was here to stay ... for if a recession was to occur what would happen to a régime based only on the legitimacy of success and efficiency?'[14]

We shall now briefly review the hesitant steps along this road that have been taken since President Médici took office. After the municipal elections of 30 November 1969 which confirmed the relative stability of the existing positions, and following the reopening of Parliament in December, the Government agreed with the heads of the two parties, ARENA and M.D.B., the arrangements for the next elections by direct voting, due to take place on 15 November 1970.

From March 1970 onward, the Legislative Assemblies of the states were also reopened one after another and their members were called upon to elect the new governors.[15] Here again this was only a formality, since the President had selected the future governors with great care. There was but a single candidate in each state, and when voting took place the opposition simply made up the quorum but either sent in blank papers or did not vote.

Since the State of Guanabara was an M.D.B. stronghold the President accepted the candidature of a member of that party, Antonio Chagas Freitas.[16] All the twenty-one other governors belonged to ARENA.[17]

In view of the careful screening that had been done, Médici justly hoped to have an 'ideal' group to support the Government. But something happened which disturbed this fine optimism. On 23 November 1971 the press carried the news that the Governor of Paraná, Haroldo Leon Peres, had resigned. Although it received little publicity, the federal departments had found a number of irregularities during the brief period of office of the Governor and the President had insisted on his immediate retirement. But instead of admitting that it had made a wrong choice of candidate, the Government seized copies of the review *Veja* which carried the story in its issue of 1 December[18] and which drew the following conclusion: 'Having taken from the people the right to choose their governors because they are not considered sufficiently mature, the Government thought it had made quite sure of the integrity of all future holders of the office. This supposition is not destroyed, but since last week it has been shown that the probability of error is at least one in twenty-two.'[19] On 15 December 1970, 29,140,554 electors went to the voting boxes to elect a number of mayors and deputy mayors, municipal councillors, the 721 members of the state legislative assemblies, the 310 federal deputies[20] and 46 senators (out of 66).[21] When the votes were counted ARENA had won 220 seats in the Federal Parliament whereas the M.D.B. had only 90. In the Senate, counting senators who did not have to be re-elected, ARENA controlled 59 seats whereas M.D.B. had only seven. The opposition had won the three Guanabara seats but many of its most distinguished senators including the president and treasurer of the party,[22] had lost their seats.

The results of these elections were as expected, and relatively few new faces went to Brasilia. Those who had obtained the largest number of votes bore names well known to the electors, such as the sons of Adhémar de Barros, Faria Lima,[23] or Aloisio Alvès.

But although the leadership of ARENA was confirmed, the vote also showed that one party in the electorate had refused to take part. Although voting was compulsory, the total of abstentions, unmarked and spoilt papers varied between 30 and 50 per cent (whereas traditionally they amount to 15-20 per cent). This trend, which was already noticed in 1966, had become more marked and the principle of bipartite conduct in Parliament, as practised, was called in question.

Confronted with this phenomenon, the Military were forced almost inevitably to reconsider the problem and modify some of their ideas concerning the institutions of the Government.[24] Although they were sometimes exasperated by the excessive use of the word 'openness' they allowed a wide-ranging debate to begin which although it took place only among the intelligentsia, quickly spread across the nation.

Until about November 1971 the Government allowed the discussion to gather substance. Then, in view of the divergent opinions that were expressed even within ARENA,[25] it appeared to take fright and revert to silence. It was then, for example, that the right of legislating by secret decrees on matters concerning national security was given to the President.[26] The former Vice-President Pedro Aleixo, seconded by the press, rightly pointed out how absurd this measure was: 'In so far as citizens share responsibility for the security of the country, they cannot be asked to defend it without knowing the laws which govern it.'[27]

Confronted with refusal of information, of which the Peres case was a glaring example, some newspaper writers even questioned whether 'the Government is already so weak that it has to fall back on the myth of infallibility'.[28]

Why then did Médici resort to these 'blackout' measures? Paradoxically, they were brought in just when his personal popularity was at its highest, according to public opinion polls.[29] It therefore appears that the hypothesis of a hardening of attitude due to fear can be discounted; rather have such measures been due to the existence of divided opinions among the Military which civilians would not know about.

It was in fact a reopening of the struggle between the 'Sorbonne' party and the hard liners. The latter were opposed to readiness to listen to fresh opinions, whereas the former looked for a wider participation of civilians, as they considered that some complex problems, mainly concerning the choices in the economic sphere, ought to be debated outside the immediate circle of power. They were thinking mainly of the integration of territory (Amazonia and the north-east), the rate at which incomes should be redistributed, and wages policy. In other words they admitted that discussion at a certain level was necessary, but refused systematic debate or any questioning of the established constitutional order.

This way of thinking had two main emphases: according to the first, the right to discussion and information should be confined to the executive (the Cabinet and the federal administration). Its supporters nevertheless favoured the bringing in of business heads and certain experts who would take part in the discussion in *ad hoc* committees. This procedure would naturally favour the high-income classes, who would be the only ones able to make their opinions heard. Those who favoured this theory recognised that differences to which expression was given might give rise to tension if they went outside the framework laid down, but they thought that this dialogue would provide for accurate appreciation of the resistances and would give an opportunity for compromise solutions to be worked out.

Partisans of the second trend wanted to go further and include Parliament in the circle of consultation. For this purpose they wanted some legislative powers to be restored to the two Chambers. But they were insistent upon protecting the development model that had been chosen by the Government and in stifling at birth any incipient basic disagreement between those members of parliament who had been elected by popular vote and the military régime; for that reason the right to suspend elective mandates that was given to the executive by Institutional Act No. 5 would be retained and would always be suspended like the sword of Damocles above the deputies and senators.

The uncertainty and lack of political definition were such that in March 1972 Senator Filinto Muller, one of the former *tenentes* of 1922, was instructed by Garrastazu Médici to become the President of ARENA. His task was to transform the electoral college into a united, disciplined and if possible a renewed group, a fact which shows that the new régime was conscious of its failure in this area.[30]

Apart from the inherent slowness in any process of renewal, two facts will give some appreciation of the extent of the problem: in the first place the electoral system itself and the inclination of the electors to abstain from voting played into the hands of the old guard of the established parties.[31] Secondly, the loss of prestige by Parliament often repelled the younger officials in the technostructure; they preferred to be administrators possessing actual executive power rather than representatives of the people, honorific no doubt, but without any real authority and, moreover, liable to be suspended if ever they stepped out of line.

Obviously some time would be needed before the paralysing effect of these contradictions could be overcome, but Médici took two immediate steps that were interesting. First of all, to stop any intrigue at source, he forbade the question of the presidential succession to be raised.[32]

In his speech on television commemorating the eighth anniversary of the Revolution on 31 March 1972 he said: 'It would be an ill service to the country to open this political question while the date of such an event is still far distant. Only in the second half of next year will the parties be called upon to express their opinions as to the presidential succession.'[33] As Médici had power to suspend civil rights and to annul parliamentary mandates, everyone knew that he had the power to secure obedience, and the political marriage-brokers held their peace.

Clearly, by taking this step Garrastazu Médici was endeavouring to circumvent any repetition of the politics of the *fait accompli* whereby Costa e Silva had been able to climb into power. Profiting by experience, he wanted to eliminate the risk of seeing the loyalties of the military prematurely divided between a president nearing the end of his term and a potential president as yet without power, as had happened under Castello Branco. The question remains, to whom was his forthright message addressed? Certainly not to the political parties; the M.D.B. knew that it had no chance of nominating a candidate and that ARENA did not aim to do so.

One is forced to conclude that his remarks were aimed at the circle of his own ministers or councillors with the rank of ministers, both civil and military. By enjoining them to silence he emphasised that he wanted to see them working as a team in solving the immediate problems of the country, instead of wasting their energy in speculating about the future. The date he had set for the opening of the discussion, 1 July 1973, allowed possible candidates exactly fifteen days to give up the official posts that they were occupying at that moment, since the legal period barring office holders from candidature ran from the fifteenth of that month.

The second measure was taken on 3 April. On that day the President informed the leaders of the congress that by virtue of Constitutional Amendment No. 2 which he had just enacted, Article 13, chapter 9, paragraph 2 of the Constitution was changed. The consequence was that the election of governors due to be held in October 1974[34] would not take place 'under universal suffrage, by secret and direct votes'[35] but by indirect voting. Among the considerations mentioned in the preamble were the need to 'preserve the atmosphere of calm confidence and work which are essential for the consolidation of the social and political institutions'.[36]

This decision was a reply to the feeling created by the M.D.B. which since January 1972 had been endeavouring to cement its unity by embarking on an electoral strategy aimed at winning the largest possible number of governorships. The strategy was to make the M.D.B. candidates the mouthpieces of all the latent discontents, by presenting the coming elections as the first opportunity given to the people since October 1965 of voting against the régime, and by choosing members of the executive branch of government from the opposition.[37]

Faced with the presidential ukase, the parties were hard put to it to retain a semblance of internal cohesion. ARENA had to resort to the clause concerning 'loyalty to the party'[38] (which obliged its representatives to vote in accordance with the decisions of its executive) in order to ensure that the constitutional majority of two-thirds voted for the amendment when it was submitted to Parliament.

One wing of the M.D.B. which felt that it had been swindled demanded that the party should dissolve itself. But after an internal vote taken during the night of 6 April the opposition members of parliament decided against this futile gesture and to continue instead for good or ill with the task of verbal censor which had fallen to them. This phlegmatic philosophy reflects Brazilian good sense which popular imagery expresses in this fable: 'My son, if when walking in the fields you see a tortoise balanced on a fork stuck into the ground, don't tip it off. First ask yourself who put it there. Tortoises don't climb up forks by themselves, you know . . .'[39]

In fact, the M.D.B.'s electoral ploy had done no more than hasten a decision which the Government had been preparing to take for some time. Observers agree in considering that the party had no chance of success in its undertaking, and that to have won in a quarter of the states of the federation would have required a miracle. Unfortunately, by an unforeseeable coincidence, the opposition campaign got under way just when the health of the Vice-Governor of Paraná[40] took a serious turn for the worse. He was the one who, under normal procedure, had replaced Governor Haroldo Peres when the latter was found guilty of improprieties. But in the event of the death or long-term incapacity of the governor's successor, direct elections would have to be held within thirty days, and this would inevitably have caused political demonstrations in Paraná which Médici wanted to avoid.

Thus it was that the threat of a public debate starting up before the intended time and the possibility that notwithstanding the efforts of the Government to bring about renewal, certain individuals hankering after the old order might be elected as governors[41] (whose rights would include that of scrutinising the economic policy carried out by the federal government) set off the self-protective reflex of the Military, which back in 1965 had been responsible for Institutional Act No. 2 and in 1968 for Institutional Act No. 5.

This reaction shows once more how quick the Government was to put an end to any attempt at dialogue as soon as such debate might enable persons outside the Government to question the official concept of accelerated development.[42]

These cautious tactics may be justified if they really lead to the renovation of the system in due time. If not, they turn into a vicious circle. It is therefore important to look carefully at the decisions taken thereafter by the Government in order to distinguish temporary tactical stoppages from irreversible steps to close down dialogue.

It is still too early to make a final judgment, although in May 1972 two events revived the hopes of those who wanted open debate.[43] First, with the agreement of both parties the Government modified the electoral law so as to facilitate recruitment by ARENA and M.D.B. and to reinforce the part they would play in the coming municipal elections – even though it has to be admitted that few of the voters took much interest in them.

Secondly, in an attempt to define its task as a government party ARENA sought the aid of the doyen of Brazilian sociologists, Gilberto Freyre. With the assistance of an inter-disciplinary committee[44] Freyre submitted to the party managers an analysis in which he stated that traditionally political parties in Brazil have suffered from an excess of legal and political rules imported from abroad, and had consequently been out of touch with the concrete realities of Brazil at the psycho-social and socio-cultural level.

Emphasising that the essence of democracy is not a particular method of election but 'respect for love of freedom, appreciation of diversity and a feeling for tolerance, all of which are intrinsic parts of our traditions',[45] he considered that the task of ARENA was to bring about a new alliance between politicians and intellectuals, together seeking for ways of action that would bring about 'participation by a growing number of Brazilians in the forms of political and social life that are now coming to birth'.[46] How far this programme can become official ARENA policy and to what extent such an alliance if it came about could make an effective contribution to resolving the problems now facing the present coalition of military men and technocrats, has yet to be proved.[47]

41 The Distortions still to be Overcome

Eight years after the Revolution the economy has made such impressive strides that observers speak of a 'miracle'.[1]

Expressed in concrete terms, the gross domestic product[2] increased by an average of 9·8 per cent per annum between 1968 and 1971, reaching 11·6 per cent[3] in 1971, a rate which has been maintained into 1974. Industrial production grew by 80 per cent between 1965 and 1971, exports increased from U.S. $1·3 billion in 1963 to U.S. $2·9 billion in 1971, and of these totals U.S. $763 million were in respect of manufactured products which reached a growth ratio of 20 per cent compared with 1963.[4] The budget deficit fell to 0·3 per cent of G.D.P. and the balance of payments was favourable to the extent of U.S. $536 million at 31 December 1971. Also at that date, Brazil's international reserves amounted to U.S. $1723 million.

The message of all these figures is that the economy was doing well. Nevertheless there were still a number of unanswered questions, of which the three main ones were the following.

First, the question of inflation, which after a spectacular fall[5] had levelled out around 20 per cent per annum since 1969.[6] Government policy was partly responsible for this situation which was caused by the combined effects of four sources of resistance:

(a) The mechanism of monetary correction which injected a fair amount of reinflation into the system, although this cannot be exactly quantified. It affected production costs in that it was pre-set[7] for most monetary operations. It had an almost total impact on cash rents, housing and public services which were automatically adjusted, but a lesser effect on the compulsory minimum wage, which increased more slowly than did the cost of living.

(b) The development model selected, giving priority to growth rather than to stabilisation. Because of this, the Government could not risk even a limited crisis by controlling too strictly the expansion of the means of payment.

(c) The operational and administrative cost of the banking system, which in some cases was as high as 20 per cent of the total deposits;[8] it was so high that it hindered the Government's efforts to force down rates of interest.

(d) Fluctuations in agricultural production; in theory these should have resulted in prices either rising or falling but in practice as regards Brazilian domestic consumption, they generally tended to rise.[9]

In order to break the 20 per cent inflation barrier, and excluding recourse to the lowering of real wages which would have been socially unjust and politically dangerous,[10] the Government found that it had to use the conventional monetary weapons and to grapple with the problem of costs.

On 31 March 1972 President Médici, speaking at a meeting celebrating the eighth anniversary of the Revolution, laid it down that all his ministers must join him in the fight against inflation. He announced categorically 'that the Federal Government had taken a fresh stance . . . with the object of reducing inflation . . . to a level that would not threaten the prosperity of the country or worsen the living standards of the people'.

He set the tolerable inflation rate[11] at 15 per cent for 1972 and gave notice of his intention to bring it down to 10 per cent before the end of 1974, while still maintaining the annual growth target at 8–10 per cent as set out by the First National Development Plan.[12] Ministers were told that they would be held personally responsible for balancing their budgets,[13] and those responsible for nationalised enterprises were thenceforward compelled to submit any increase in prices for the prior approval of the watchdog body, the Interministerial Price Council.[14]

This objective was all the more ambitious in that the cost of living had risen by as much as 6 per cent during the first quarter of 1972, but it was not impossible because the harvest promised to be a very good one. Bearing in mind the efforts made by the Government to improve the system of distributing agricultural products, their retail price could be expected to fall, which would have an immediate effect on the cost of living index.[15] To make quite sure, the authorities had reserved the right to import free of customs duties any foodstuffs and raw materials which might be required for stabilising the market.

Still on the question of costs, the banks were informed that they would have to reduce their operating costs and that for 1972 interest rates must not include an inflationary residue of more than 15 per cent.

In April about a hundred leading industrialists were called to a meeting in Brasilia by the Finance Minister. During the meeting they were told that the Government intended to use every means in its power to achieve the aims set by the President. In order to get prices moving downwards, foodstuffs were exempted from manufactured products tax.[16] In return business heads would have to keep their prices unchanged unless the Inter-ministerial Price Council specifically allowed a rise, even if thereby their profit margins were reduced.

The second handicap to the development model in Brazil was the unequal distribution of incomes, which showed a trend towards concentration. The model of growth selected, centring on the development of dynamic industries, capital intensive and using advanced technology, called for the creation of a market able to absorb the goods produced by these enterprises which were usually durables or semi-durables.

To this end the Government both encouraged exports,[17] with excellent results, and also created a domestic market by concentrating the distribution of incomes on those strata of the population which could rapidly become users of such goods, rather than aiming at an equitable distribution among all citizens. No doubt if they had done so the standard of living of every Brazilian would have been raised, but not enough to absorb the products of the modern factories which therefore would have been unable to prosper. In practice this result was obtained by freezing the minimum wage and allowing the incomes of skilled workers and capitalists to rise.

There has been heated controversy on this subject, and those economists who deny the validity of the Brazilian model[18] express doubts as to the possibility of maintaining for long the rates of growth that have been achieved. They point to three critical areas: the restricted volume of demand, the increasing share of investment coming from abroad and the small extent to which industrial workers are being absorbed.

And yet as the years passed and the prophesised stagnation did not set in the argument imperceptibly shifted its ground from economics to social justice. For example, a study made by the U.N.-

The Distortions still to be Overcome

sponsored FLACSO (Latin American Faculty of Social Sciences) notes that although the concentration of incomes is socially unjust it nevertheless allows the market to expand sufficiently to stimulate the advanced industries. The authors add:

> Capitalism in Brazil appears to have succeeded, after a considerable break in its political model, in making the best use of its power to control the key variables, capital formation and modernisation. It has even succeeded in carving out for itself a modest but relatively privileged place in the new distribution pattern of regional and international markets which is being brought about by the multinational companies.[19]

This analysis, which runs counter to some structuralist arguments, notes that 'the size of a market depends less on the number of persons in it than on the amount of the available economic surplus'.[20] It is the way this surplus value is spent that will determine real demand. This is confirmed by stimulation[21] carried out recently, which in the specific case of Brazil have given the following results:

(a) The variation in the distribution of income parameters within the plausible limits of the Brazilian market economy do not cause a significant variation in the structure of growth;

(b) Within the predicted framework of 'technological' industrialisation, job opportunities will increase at least in proportion to the population increase.

(c) The share of foreign investment will show a slight tendency to rise but the rate of growth is quite insensitive to variations in the distribution of income.

Nevertheless, lacking the results of the 1970 census, the economists were without recent statistical data with which to support their theories. To enable the matter to be settled the Finance Ministry commissioned a survey, the preliminary results of which were published in June 1972.[22] The author, who had had access to all the basic documents of the 1970 census[23] and to the tax declarations, chose to highlight two factors, the level of education and the income declared. The four tables given below, taken from this study, make it clear that there was no systematic pauperisation of the Brazilian people. They prove that although some concentration of incomes certainly took place, and though some groups benefited more than others from the material advantages of development, *nobody* was disadvantaged.[24]

To sum up, between 1960 and 1970:

(a) All the income categories increased their purchasing power with the exception of illiterates whose incomes expressed in real terms remained practically the same.

(b) The degree of skill of the wage-earning population[25] increased and the number of persons educated to beyond primary level more than doubled.
(c) Incomes were more unequally distributed in cities than in the country.
(d) Concentration of incomes was linked to the level of education and not only to the social class. In other words, persons with qualifications received a larger share of the national product. This development reflects the increased requirement for skilled workers in enterprises using advanced technologies. Thus education become the main instrument of social mobility and the investments made in this sector augur well for the future. It was estimated that by 1974 there would be 35 per cent more primary education, 100 per cent more secondary and 90 per cent more higher education available.[26]
(e) The concentration coefficient for the dynamic industries was higher than that for the traditional industries, but the average wage[27] paid by the former was 75 per cent higher than that paid in the traditional industries.

The third category of problems to be solved, which is a result of the second, is that of the concentration of businesses. This phenomenon is not peculiar to Brazil but it had become more acute there than elsewhere owing to the combined influence on the one hand of the efforts of the Government, which systematically sought to promote industrial mergers and concentration[28] and on the other hand of the financial and technological contribution made by the large multinational companies.[29]

In the main there were three avenues for this concentration: State enterprises, whether monopolies or mixed economy companies, a number of large Brazilian companies, and the foreign groups.[30] It did not affect small and medium-sized local businesses which have declined in relative importance.[31]

This trend was denounced by the Rio de Janeiro Charter which was adopted by the Third National Conference of the Producing Classes just before Easter 1972. In this document, drawn up to be sent to the authorities, the employers said: 'The tendency for the State and foreign capital to dominate large enterprises cannot be attributed to insufficiency of private saving, which is one of the main sources of finance and of capital formation in the country... What private savings lack is not overall volume but the cohesive power required for the formation of giant companies.'[32]

Just before the conference a large financial merger had been announced. The two main banks, which were privately owned, merged in an effort to become the major conglomerate in Latin

TABLE 1 INCOME DISTRIBUTION BY SECTOR AND EDUCATIONAL STANDARD

		Percentage of wage-earning population*			Monthly income in 1970 cruzeiros†			Gini‡ coefficient		
		1960	1970	+/-%	1960	1970	+/-%	1960	1970	+/-%
Sector	Rural	46·56	40·05	−13·98	129	138	+7	0·43	0·44	+2·32
	Urban	53·44	59·95	+12·18	273	378	+38	0·48	0·55	+14·49
Educational level	Illiterate	39·05	29·75	−23·81	111	112	—	0·42	0·39	−7·14
	Primary	51·71	54·47	+5·34	211	240	+14	0·42	0·46	+9·52
	Middle	5·16	8·03	+55·62	440	482	+9	0·44	0·51	+15·90
	Secondary	2·67	5·24	+96·25	536	688	+28	0·42	0·50	+19·05
	Higher	1·40	2·51	+79·28	1123	1706	+52	0·46	0·46	—

Source: Tables 1–4: *Veja*, no. 196 (7 June 1972), 68–70.
* Total in 1960: 19,404,421 persons; in 1970: 26,079,743 persons (according to declarations).
† U.S. $1 = Crz. 4·63 (1 September 1970).
‡ The Gini (or Lorenz) coefficient is the concentration index for a given distribution. It is always between 0 and 1. A coefficient of 1 indicates a total concentration whereas a Gini of 0 shows a complete absence of concentration.

TABLE 2   DISTRIBUTION BY INCOME CATEGORY AND IN RELATION TO THE TOTAL NUMBER OF RESPONDENTS

Monthly income category (1970 cruzeiros) Cruzeiros	Approximate U.S. $ equivalent	Number of respondents 1960	1970	Percentage of total number of respondents 1960	1970
Up to 98	21	4,899,932	7,452,929	25·2	28·6
99–154	33	3,318,008	5,707,926	17·1	21·9
155–210	45	2,534,189	4,682,106	13	17·9
211–280	60	2,955,074	1,580,858	15·2	6·1
281–466	100	3,247,010	3,166,785	16·7	12·1
467–934	200	1,776,356	2,167,000	9·1	8·3
935–2333	500	569,267	1,038,199	2·9	3·9
Above 2334	500	104,585	283,940	0·5	1·1

Average monthly income: Crz. 206 (U.S. $45 approx.); Crz. 282 (+37 per cent) (U.S. $61 approx.).
Average per capita income: approx. Crz. 154 per month.

TABLE 3   BREAKDOWN OF THE EXTREMES IN THE INCOMES PYRAMID (PERCENTAGE OF TOTAL DECLARATIONS)

	Share of total income	Education Illiterate	Higher	Under 20 years of age	Agriculture	Sector Industry	Services
40% of respondents at bottom of scale represent:	10	50	0·01	25	64·5	7·4	28·1
20% of respondents at top of scale represent:	62·24	3·6	9·1	1·2	9·3	27·2	63·5

TABLE 4   CONCENTRATION BY TYPE OF INDUSTRY, IN 1970

Type	Sector	Average monthly wage*	Gini coefficient
Traditional low-paid industries with low income concentration	Foodstuffs, civil construction, textiles	260 300 315	0·34 0·34 0·38
	Average†	291	—
Dynamic highly-paid industries with high income concentration	Engineering, electrical and electronic equipment, automobile	412 608	0·41 0·42
	Average†	510	—

* 1970 cruzeiros.   † Unweighted.

America, controlling investments to the value of some U.S. $1·5 billion.[33] But the Government, anxious to avoid such a powerful concentration, did not allow the project to go through in its entirety. Nevertheless, the principle of concentration for banks was not itself called into question, and in July 1972 another giant grouping, managing something like U.S. $300 million of deposits, was born.[34]

Although it was what they wanted, this concentration of economic power nevertheless worried the heads of businesses and in their Charter they expressed their disquiet in view of the possibility of 'situations of monopoly and oligopoly',[35] to which there was no effective check in the form of anti-cartel legislation with teeth in it. While warmly praising their Government and congratulating it on the results obtained, the industrialists also appealed for discussion on the philosophy of development in Brazil to be thrown widely open.

The Rio Charter constitutes an attempt by the employers to form a common front *vis-à-vis* the Government and it is perhaps not surprising, in view of the flexible nature of the economic policy that was in force, that some of their demands were favourably received.[36]

The industrialists were also worried about the part played by multinational companies which controlled the most dynamic sectors in Brazilian industry and hence came to occupy a key position in the exports of manufactured products. They had in fact 'reacted much more quickly than the purely Brazilian companies',[37] contrary to the theory of those who believe that multinational enterprises by dividing up world markets to suit their interests, prevent the growth of exports of manufactured products from developing countries. It is true that by so doing so they benefited both from fiscal advantages accorded by the government to exporting industries and from economies of scale which access to foreign markets enabled them to achieve.

The Finance Minister did not share the distrust felt by representatives of the traditional industries. He thought that 'exports play an extremely important role in enlarging the domestic market'. He explained this paradoxical saying as follows:

> The main concern of the Government is with the problem of the domestic market. Exporting is a simple means of increasing the domestic market. A local producer who doesn't know where to sell his product is only a demographic unit. When we beat a path to him... and supply him with the credit he needs, he becomes within two years fully involved in the economy... Similarly, when we give this unit an outlet to exports, we link it up with the total economic system. That is how Brazil is being unified... Overseas markets are essential to the continuity of development.[38]

This problem is directly connected to that of Brazil's external indebtedness. For although there was a favourable balance of payments in 1971, the trade balance showed its largest deficit since 1947 (minus $325 million).[39]

The main reason for this situation was the increased quantity of imports sucked in by the intense industrialisation drive and the poor harvest in 1971. If this were to happen every year it could imperil expansion in Brazil as the country would have simultaneously to provide for its rate of growth and service its foreign debt. And this debt rose from U.S. $3·2 billion in 1963 to U.S. $5·295 billion by 31 December 1970,[40] to reach U.S. $6·6 billion before the end of 1972.

Bearing in mind the further investment needs arising from the national objectives from 1972 to 1974,[41] it would appear that Brazil must unavoidably incur still further indebtedness with a resultant increase in debt servicings. This prospect would be alarming if the capacity of the country to carry the debt were not increasing at the same time. But if we extrapolate the mean data for the years 1969 to 1971[42] we see that assuming an increase in export receipts of 10–15 per cent annually, Brazil would be able by 1975 to service an external debt of $8–10 billion.[43]

As Alain Vernay remarked in September 1972:

> It is a frantic race against the clock between development and poverty, resignation and resentment. And this leads to a doctrine based on this simple syllogism: everything that conduces to growth is good for Brazil; foreign capital means growth, therefore foreign capital is a good thing.
>
> This apparently simplistic argument is based on complex calculations which may be very briefly summarised as follows: assuming depreciation at 4 per cent per annum and mean annual interest at 8 per cent, foreign capital borrowed for five years creates in Brazil in two years the income needed to repay it and can always be repaid in less than three years.[44]

Continuing his enquiry into recent economic developments in Brazil Vernay adds:

> A closer examination reveals that for an input of 100 dollars the G.N.P. increases by 64, imports by 4·5 per cent, interest transfer by 12 per cent (the legal maximum that can be repatriated without punitive rates of tax), which represents therefore a total increased expenditure on foreign exchange of 16·5 per cent, which has to be neutralised by a growth of exports representing 25 per cent of the increase in the G.N.P. (16·5/64 = 25 per cent). And this is just what happened.
>
> But is there not a threshold beyond which even profitable

indebtedness becomes dangerous? Is not this threshold reached when servicing the debt – which amounts to $6·6 billion – represents 10 per cent of actual exports, to which has to be added a further 11 per cent in respect of credits on the import of capital goods? The reply of the Brazilian rulers was that there was no danger in the delay in so far as, given the structure of the debt and taking into account its term, they only needed to borrow each year from abroad about two-thirds of its total amount.

The technocrats of Brasilia say that it is easy on two conditions, both of which are fully met: on the one hand a steady growth in exports and on the other hand confidence on the part of the international community in the financial policy of Brazil such that, if Brazil gets into debt, it can still go on borrowing in order to repay the debt. This confidence was won and maintained by reducing the rate of inflation from 86 per cent per annum in 1964 to 24 per cent in 1968, 20 per cent in 1971 and probably 15 per cent in 1972.

But might it not be thought that Brazil needs foreign investments as a drug addict needs morphine? The answer is 'No', to judge by the following figures, which it was not easy to come by. The total amount of foreign capital invested in Brazil on 31 December 1970 (after deducting foreign exchange reserves, of course) amounted to $6442 million, which made a contribution to the G.N.P. of $4123 million (6442×0·64) leaving $2327 million after transfer for repayments and interest on the debt, and for transfer of profits. Since in 1971 the G.N.P. amounted to $41 billion, the contribution made by foreign capital to its formation represented only 5·7 per cent – a marginal amount.

Nevertheless, since the population of Brazil at that time was 94·7 million, the average income per capita was $430 and the contribution made by foreign capital was $25. This is not negligible and could not be disregarded in a country that was still so poor.

Indeed, these 25 dollars become more significant compared with the amount of investment which, in Brazil, with a rate of 17·5 per cent of G.N.P. (comparable to that in Britain and slightly higher than in the United States) represented $66 in 1961 compared with $340 per capita in Britain, $780 in the United States and $700 in France at the same date.

Although it was not said in so many words, it appeared to us that the Brazilian authorities would not be unduly disturbed if the share of foreign capital in the country's G.N.P. were to increase from 5·6 per cent to 8 per cent.

This tranquillity calls for an explanation. A favourite saying in Brasilia is that one should not be caught out by mistaken generalisations. One should not behave as though foreign capital came in a single packet of dollars controlled from afar by a great big computer. It was not even considered a reason for alarm if there was a very considerable concentration of foreign capital in certain key sectors. The view taken in Brasilia is that even though 40 per cent of investment may still come from America, it no longer is preponderant when compared with those of the great multinational European companies and even more, Japanese companies, which go in for larger projects than anybody else. In any event, Brazilians have become past masters at the art of stimulating competition among powerful groupings.

Their confidence is based finally, and above all, on the fact that Brazil has made sure that the State controls the commanding heights of the economy such as steelmaking and energy production, and that it is banking on the development of a Brazilian capitalism, protected by the installation of increasingly effective methods of surveillance of foreign capital in the commercial banks and by a watchful eye on credit policy, so that it is no longer possible for anybody to borrow from abroad just as he pleases.[45]

So strangulation can be avoided, but achievement of this aim depends on export receipts. Hence to achieve the objective Brazil has to carry out a policy with the object of 'dismantling the protectionist barriers which directly or indirectly affect exports from developing countries both of raw materials and manufactured goods'.[46] As regards coffee, energetic steps have been taken to form a 'group of producer nations' powerful enough to counteract the demands of the importing countries.[47]

According to Brazilian projections, export sales of manufactured products were to reach a value of U.S. $1 billion in 1972, U.S. $2 billion in 1975 and U.S. $3.2 billion[48] in 1977, and in regard to these products they favour a return to liberalisation: Delfim Netto unashamedly admits this about-turn in commercial procedures in Brazil. During a luncheon at the São Paulo Exporters Club in July 1972 he said unequivocally: 'Nowadays it suits Brazil to be a free trading nation, just as we were ultra-protectionist during the 1950s and somewhat protectionist during the 1960s.'[49]

It is interesting to note that this conversion could claim such respectable authority as that of Professor Jacques L'Huillier who wrote back in 1969:

> This development is the more plausible in that over the last twenty years or so a considerable effort has been put forth in many other developed countries to build up a strong economic infrastructure. It had been somewhat fancifully supposed that an

industrial superstructure would providentially take its place on this base; but for the most part such hopes have proved false. If the developed countries were to open their markets freely, this might provide just the fresh impetus which would at last enable full use to be made of this infrastructure.[50]

In a manner of speaking, what Brazil has now to do is to leave the amateur league of exporters and become a professional.[51] Prizes are not given for nothing, and to get into that class Brazilians will need all the foreign collaboration they can muster. They will not be able to do without the assistance of foreign capital and know-how during this transitional phase and must continue to call in aid the results of foreign saving in order to promote their own domestic development.[52]

Brazil's management team, aware of this need, has opened the economy to foreign investment whilst also taking some precautions aimed at preventing Brazil from falling into industrial dependence on other countries.[53]

This choice, which was a direct result of Brazil's intention of keeping the country as 'one of the ten Western nations having the highest gross domestic product, taking the eighth place' and of 'breaking the $500 per capita income barrier[54] in 1974' obviously places certain limits on the Government's freedom of action politically and economically in international relations.[55] But these limits were freely chosen by Brazil, and have nothing to do with a so-called 'sub-imperialism'.

On the domestic front also, the final success of the modernisation initiated by Castello Branco is still the result of decisions freely taken and will depend upon the speed with which the régime succeeds in overcoming the domestic distortions which are still hindering the harmonious development of the country. And one can agree with Max Link's conclusion: 'These achievements do not justify us in speaking of a "Brazilian miracle"... but the results achieved since 1964 are convincing and justify the optimism which, for the first time in the changing history of this country, is evident on all sides.'[56]

CONCLUSION

Integration through Practical Achievements

In this analysis of the modernising régime we have given special attention to the participation of non-military elements in the power structures. By our scale of values we have implicitly assumed that the ideal towards which any political system ought to tend is democracy, understood as being a method of popular government, a system designed for the peaceful settlement of conflicts within a certain consensus of the people.

As Rustow says,[1] this concept requires that 'conflicting interests be expressed rather than suppressed but also that the participants acquire experience in the arts of settling conflict'. Like other modern techniques, it combines continuity and change and hence it presupposes the existence of a relative abundance of skilled administrative and political personnel to enable a team to be changed without bringing about a temporary stoppage in the mechanism of government. Otherwise, how could it ensure a smooth transfer of power between one temporary majority and another?

In a country that is still developing, these conditions are not yet all fulfilled. This means that it is probably impossible to achieve the rapid rate of growth which the nation wills except by agreeing that for the time being political continuity must take precedence over a change of political rulers, in view of the risk noted above. In practice this may result in a 'twilight' military régime, such as has existed in Brazil since 1964. But it is clear that if the aim is the one which was noted at the beginning of this chapter, the sacrifice will make sense only if the twilight régime remains sufficiently open to discussion and innovation to refrain from inhibiting the training of the new leaders who will be required and to prepare itself to face up to the thorny problems of transition.

Brazil has been fortunate in that for the last 150 years it has had national unity in the geographical, linguistic and racial sense.

After the period of anarchy in the late 1950s, a new principle of authority has been forged since 1964 and generally accepted by the nation. In terms of Rustow's sequence it still remains to achieve equality of opportunity for its citizens, but this ideal cannot be imposed from above, it must be based on a civilian and military administrative infrastructure. 'If this growing bureaucracy is recruited from increasingly wider social strata, trained for impersonal public service, promoted according to some objective system of merit, and dedicated to the rule of the law, then it can at later stages promote integration.'[2] Since 1964 such a bureaucracy has been rapidly coming into existence.

Hence, in order to bring about its transition the régime should learn to look beyond itself and find means of setting up an adequate organic link between the governors and the governed, to enable it to phase out while ensuring continuity for the method whereby political succession is effected. In the nature of things, this link is bound to take the form of a political structure.

Is this road still open in the Brazil of 1972, when the régime has already weathered the first five or six years in power, probably 'the most vulnerable period'?[3]

Nothing in the development that we have endeavoured to retrace seems to have finally ruled this out. On the contrary, three achievements which do not directly concern the political parties but which do affect equality of opportunity lend credibility to this view. First is the Social Integration Programme (P.I.S.) that was instituted in September 1970.[4] It is designed to give workers a share in the surplus value arising from industrial development. The Government set up a 'participation fund' administered by the National Savings Fund into which more than a million firms had to pay two types of contributions. One is based on the amount of profits tax (2 per cent in 1971, 3 per cent in 1972, 5 per cent from 1973 onwards); the other, which has been payable monthly since 1 July 1971, is indexed on the gross turnover achieved (0·15 per cent in 1971, 0·25 per cent in 1972, 0·4 per cent in 1973 and 0·5 per cent from 1974 onwards). A similar fund has also been set up for public servants.[5]

The system is managed like a mutual investment fund, and thus the whole of the money collected, which is scheduled to reach a billion dollars a year from 1974 onwards, is recirculated into the economy. All workers whether temporary or permanent are automatically members of the fund, though on a non-contributory basis. An account is opened for each individual and regularly credited with an amount calculated at a proportion of his or her wages and according to the number of years during which the employee has been working.[6] Members of the fund, who numbered more than 13 million in 1971, may if they wish withdraw each year the profits made by the fund on their proportional share (such as monetary correction, interest, etc.) and can withdraw the capital itself in specific circumstances such as marriage, retirement, permanent sickness, death or the purchase of a dwelling. Since the fund is not geared to participation in the profits of a business but is an overall system, workers are entirely free in respect of their present employer and are not dependent upon the fortunes of the company for which they work.[7]

The second of these three schemes, the National Integration

Scheme (P.I.N.)[8] was announced in June 1970 and started work in September. Its main objective is to exploit the natural wealth of Amazonia which covers some $3\frac{1}{2}$ million square kilometres, an area comparable to that of Western Europe but having a population of only 1·03 inhabitants per square kilometre.[9]

This project was conceived in 'socio-economic'[10] terms and claims to be a 'national adventure' capable of mobilising and firing with enthusiasm all the vital forces of the country. Opening up Amazonia, whose vast potential in mineral wealth is still relatively unknown,[11] should both enable some of the problems of the inhabitants of the north-east to be solved by giving them the opportunity of settling there as colonists; it should also thereby create an enlarged market for manufactured products, as well as adding strength to Brazil's economy by making available to it fresh sources of raw materials which are much in demand in world markets.

A budget of two billion cruzeiros (about U.S. $500 million) has been set up for this purpose covering the period 1971–4.[12] Part of this sum is to be used for financing the settlement of the first colonists[13] as well as to making a topographical and geological survey of two million square kilometres by aerial photogrammetry using a very advanced radar system,[14] and to irrigating 100,000 acres of semi-arid land in the north-east and improving the port infrastructure of the region.

However, most of the money that has been allocated is to be used in constructing two great trunk roads. The first, the Trans-Amazonian route, will be about 3200 miles long[15] and will connect the most easterly point in Brazil, João Pessoa near Recife, with the road network of Peru.[16] The other route, cutting at right angles to the former, will start from Cuiaba[17] in the centre of Brazil and will go as far as Santarem on the Amazon. There will also be connecting roads to Manaus and Venezuela. Work began in September 1970 and by 1972 some 500 miles of the Trans-Amazonian road[18] had been completed and some colonists settled in about thirty '*agro-villes*'.[19]

The third measure was promulgated in May 1971.[20] Known as the Rural Workers Aid Programme it brought agricultural workers within the scope of social security benefits. This was a further step along the road of assimilating the least-privileged section of the population of Brazil into the family life of the nation. It was supported by other efforts, such as the revamping of the agricultural reform procedures[21] and the creation of PROTERRA.[22] The last-named organisation is responsible for helping small producers (especially the landless ones and smallholders) to obtain economically sized holdings. For this purpose land formerly belonging to certain expropriated areas is being sold to them through long-term credits.[23] PROTERRA was intended to become the equivalent in agricultural terms of SUDENE and SUDAM (the organisations through which development of the north-east and Amazonia respectively was channelled), and to encourage agricultural development in the regions concerned.

Finance is also being made available for setting up industrial-scale rural undertakings able to supply products for export. To facilitate the marketing of these harvests, the State will assist in developing the agricultural marketing network.

These decisions indicate that the Médici Government attaches due importance to the rural sector, in which production increased by 12·2 per cent in 1971 compared with 5·6 per cent in 1970.[24] And yet progress along the road of agrarian reform is still very slow because, at least for the moment, the Government appears to be trying to avoid the confrontation inherent in any radical reform. It was warned of the strength of the resistance to change which landowners would show during the parliamentary debate occasioned by the announcement at the beginning of August 1972 of the first steps in application of the land redistribution plan, modest though they were. Did not a senator from Pernambuco say during the debate that the *Fazendeiros*[25] in his state were ready to take up arms to prevent the programme from being carried out?[26]

So although the way to the establishment of new arrangements is still open, the question how long the present mixed phase will last is also open. Present indications point to the probability that the successor to President Médici in 1974 will again be a military man.

Yet, hard though it may be to see just how the régime will develop between now and then, one may hazard a guess that it will tread even more firmly the path of reform and national modernisation. For since the end of July 1972 the High Command of the Army has been almost completely re-staffed as a result of retirements and promotions. Nine of its eleven members were still colonels in 1964, and have received their fourth star under the Médici Government.[27] This college of new military cardinals holds the keys of power, and their attitude in the past points to the likelihood that they will hasten the movement towards professionalising the Army and the administrative structure of the country, both measures favouring greater social equality.

In order to maintain contact with the officer corps, the High Command has introduced a kind of 'democratic' sampling on a semi-permanent basis. In a return to the procedure that was used when Médici was 'elected', officers of the three arms from the rank of captain upwards are often asked which of a number of choices they would favour on matters of future policy. The procedure differs from case to case, but in principle each voter has one vote whatever his rank. Sometimes the vote is not secret and consequently the results can be analysed according to rank, regions and military units.

Thus it appears that the present régime which, let us remember, is an emanation of the middle class, seems to have set its feet firmly on the road that leads to modernisation. President Médici said as much to the pupils of the Superior War College when, speaking about economic development, he said: 'The first step towards developing Brazilian man to his full stature is to involve everyone in the national effort.'[28] The same theme is set out even more clearly in the four necessary conditions for development as formulated by his Government:

> Wide distribution of the results of economic progress, which should reach all income groups and all areas.
>
> Social change to modernise institutions, accelerate growth, give a better distribution of incomes and underpin an open society.
>
> Political stability, in order to achieve development under a democratic régime.
>
> National security at home and abroad.[29]

In view of the importance which the Military attach to raising per capita incomes, the present transitional phase might be considerably shortened by adopting a policy of birth control and by widening the distribution of wealth.

Indeed, the standard of life could be more quickly raised by a systematic campaign aimed at reducing the annual birth rate from 2·9 per cent to 2·3 per cent by the end of the next decade,[30] though both the Church and some of the Military are against this; and the domestic market could be quickly enlarged by an increasingly wide distribution of the accruing surplus value, which would enable a steadily increasing number of Brazilians to take their place within the money economy.

This process had a slow beginning,[31] but now that new generals have come on the scene it is likely to gather speed, and the privileged classes in Brazil must expect their material advantages gradually to diminish.[32] To avoid endangering economic growth, which at present requires higher rates of capital formation,[33] the Government will no doubt avoid doing this suddenly or unceremoniously.

If its past conduct is anything to go by, the Government will probably feel its way empirically in an attempt to sense how far it can go without the wealthy classes ceasing to invest, to produce locally and to increase trade rather than succumbing to the temptation to expatriate their capital either legally or otherwise. Nevertheless, as an institutional élite the Military would be able, should the need arise, to mount an all-out attack on the privileges of the middle and upper classes.[34]

We have now reached the end of this study, and our finding is that the modernising régime which was born of the 1964 Revolution has carried through, within an authoritarian framework, a considerable task of prompting human and economic welfare. Would a liberal régime really have been incapable of achieving the same results in eight years? More and more Brazilians seem inclined to think so.[35]

Even though the strategy selected has not always met the criteria of intellectual purists as regards distributive justice or democratic liberty,[36] the accelerated growth model has already borne fruit as far as a large part of the population is concerned. Even if it cannot yet be said with certainty whether a sufficiently strong impetus has been given to ensure continued development, it would seem impossible to turn back now.[37] If this growth is maintained, Brazil will indeed become an industrialised nation on the American model, 'The youngest of the giants'.[38]

Notes

Author's Note
1 Throughout this book we shall make use of official Brazilian terminology without trying to qualify it, as do certain authors who prefer the expression 'coup d'état' or 'counter-revolution'.
2 On the idea of 'Populism' in Brazil, which has not yet been thoroughly analysed, see, for example, Weffort, Francisco, 'Populism', *Les Temps Modernes*, 23rd year, no. 257 (Oct 1967) 624–49; Lopes, Juarez, R. B., 'Some Basic Developments in Brazilian Politics and Society', *New Perspectives of Brazil*, ed. Eric N. Baklanoff (Nashville: Vanderbilt Univ. Press, 1966) pp. 59–77.
3 Article 177 of the Constitution of 1946: 'The task of the Armed Forces is to defend the country and to guarantee the constitutional powers, law and order.'
4 Rustow, Dankwart A., *A World of Nations: Problems of Political Modernization*, 3rd ed. (Washington, D.C.: Brookings Institution, 1968).
5 Almond, Gabriel A., *Political Development: Essays in Heuristic Theory* (Boston: Little, Brown & Co., 1970).
6 Huntington, Samuel P., *Political Order in Changing Societies* (New Haven, London: Yale Univ. Press, 1968).
7 Rostow, *World of Nations*, p. 3.
8 Ibid., p. 5,
9 Ibid., p. 3.
10 Ibid.
11 Ronald Schneider, who for eight months in 1962 was assistant to the American Ambassador in Rio, Lincoln Gordon, before becoming a professor, prefers for example to distinguish eight phases. Schneider, Ronald M. *The Political System of Brazil, Emergence of a 'Modernizing' Authoritarian Regime 1964–1970* (New York, London: Columbia Univ. Press, for the Institute of Latin American Studies, Columbia University, 1971) pp. 109–10.
   We have found this study valuable and are glad to acknowledge here our debt to Professor Schneider. We would like also to express our gratitude to all those who have helped us to discover Brazil, as well as to Senhor Luiz Aranha Corrêa do Lago and Senhor Vasco Medina Coeli who have kindly undertaken the task of assembling part of the documentation for this work.
12 This is the third term of Rustow's ideal sequence: 'Unity–Authority–Equality'.
13 Rustow, *World of Nations*, pp. 199–200.

Introduction
1 The territory of Brazil covers 3,275,000 square miles. It is the world's fifth largest country, after the U.S.S.R., Canada, China and the United States. By way of comparison we may note that the area of Switzerland, 15,940 square miles, is approximately the size of the island of Marajó in the mouth of the Amazon. Three statistics will illustrate the country's continental dimensions: length from north to south, 2700 miles; length from east to west, 2750 miles; Atlantic seaboard, 4630 miles.
2 According to the preliminary results of the census taken on 1 September

1970, the total population was 94·5 million persons of whom 54 per cent were urban and 46 per cent rural (a revised estimate, published by the Getúlio Vargas Foundation in September 1971, gave only 92,763,000 inhabitants) and the population has been growing at a rate of 2·7 per cent since 1960; 52·64 per cent of the population was under the age of 20. Average population density is eleven inhabitants to the square kilometre. However, there is a great deal of variation, ranging from 0·18 in the Roraima territory to 3182·7 in Rio de Janeiro city. Besides São Paulo with 6 million inhabitants and Rio de Janeiro with 4·3 million, three cities – Belo Horizonte, Salvador and Recife – have passed the million mark. Six other towns have more than half a million inhabitants – Porto Alegre, Fortaleza, Nova Iguaçu, Belem, Curtiba and Brasilia. There are large inter-regional differences. For instance, the five southeastern states – São Paulo, Guanabara, Rio de Janeiro, Minas Gerais and Espirito Santo – cover 22·08 per cent of the area of the country and have 42·7 per cent of the population, but they account for about 85 per cent of industrial production, employ some 70 per cent of the labour force and pay 81 per cent of federal taxes. (*Source*: *Sinopse Estatística do Brazil, 1971*, Instituto Brasileiro de Estatística, Rio de Janeiro: Fundação I.B.G.E., 1971 (hereafter cited as *Sinopse*).
3. Politically, the Federal Republic of Brazil is made up of 22 states, 4 territories, and one Federal District (Brasilia). Brazil celebrated the 150th anniversary of its independence on 7 September 1972.
4. For example, Fernando Henrique Cardoso, Luciano Martins, Hélio Jaguaribe, Octavio Ianni and Celso Furtado.
5. See Martins, Luciano, *Industrialização, Burguesia Nacional e Desenvolvimento* (Rio de Janeiro: Editôra Saga, 1968); Cardoso, Fernando Henrique, *Política e Desenvolvimento em Sociedades Dependentes* (Rio de Janeiro: Zahar Editores, 1971).
6. Martins, *Industrialização*, p. 95.
7. Freymond, Jacques, 'Réflexions sur la structure du système mondial', *Gazette de Lausanne* (17 Aug 1972) 3.
8. Gosset, Pierre and Renée, 'Cent millions de Brésiliens: Pour réussir? Il faut voir trop grand', *Journal de Genève* (29 Aug 1972) 1.
9. A term used by Galbraith, John K., in *The New Industrial State* (London: Hamish Hamilton, 1967) pp. 60–71.
10. An address to the *Swiss Conference on Technical Cooperation*, Bern, 1 June 1972.
    In a recent book, Tibor Mende develops this idea in a slightly different context: 'It would be better if those who have not yet demonstrated their ability to give really effective aid would show sympathetic consideration towards those who voluntarily undertake to exchange their hitherto pointless sufferings for sufferings having a defined goal.' Mende, Tibor, *De l'Aide à la Recolonisation – Les Leçons d'un Echec* (Paris: Editions du Seuil, 1972) p. 230.
11. 'The great national objectives of development in Brazil are: first to place Brazil within the space of a generation among the developed countries ...' *Primeiro Plano Nacional de Desenvolvimento Econômico e Social (P.N.D.) 1972/74*, República Federativa do Brasil, I.B.G.E. (Dec 1971) 14 (hereafter cited as *P.N.D.*).

PART ONE

1. In 1500 Pedro Alvares Cabral landed on the north-east coast of Brazil, having been blown off course while endeavouring to reach the Indies

by the western route. He thus became the official 'discoverer' of Brazil. Their are in fact three claimants to this title – Jean Cousin from Dieppe, who is said to have reached Brazil as early as 1488, the Spaniard Vicente Pinzon, who reached Cabo São Agostino in 1493, and Cabral, to whom historians award the title.
2. Raids by pirates, a French expedition led by Paulmier de Gonneville in 1503, another by Villegaignon in 1567, the Batavian occupation of Bahia and Pernambuco in 1624, among others.
3. From 1549 onwards the Portuguese monarch delegated to Brazil a governor-general with the task of ensuring recognition of Portuguese sovereignty, which the first captains were unable to secure.
4. Capture of Lisbon by Junot's army in 1807.
5. *'Deus é Brasileiro'*. Niedergang also calls attention to this confident attitude among Brazilians. Niedergang, Marcel, *Les vingt Amériques Latines*, rev. and enlarged ed. (Paris: Editions du Seuil, 1969) vol. 1, p. 30.

Chapter 1
1. *Source:* quantified data calculated by the author on the basis of official documents, censuses and electors.
2. Article 147 of the Constitution of 1967: illiterate persons, soldiers and persons not speaking Portuguese are not entitled to vote.
3. The federal referendum held on 7 February 1971 dealt with the introduction of women's suffrage into Switzerland. There were 1,654,708 on the electoral register out of a total population of 6,269,783 inhabitants (1 Dec 1970). When voting took place only 955,321 electors, or 15·2 per cent of the population, expressed an opinion. *Source: Annuaire Statistique Suisse,* 79th year, Federal Statistical Office, Bâle (Editions Birkhäuser, 1971) pp. 13, 546–7.
4. Vianna, Oliveira, *Instituções Políticas do Brasil* (Rio de Janeiro: Livraria José Olympio Editôra, 1949) vol. 1, p. 145.
5. Such as the municipal parliaments in each region, where the 'men of quality' deliberated, and the Senate of the Chamber, composed of the élite which enjoyed the privileges recorded in the 'book of the Nobility'.
6. Article 98 of the Constitution of 25 March 1824.
7. This phenomenon is partly connected with the prohibition of the traffic in negroes in 1850, with the 'law of the free womb' of 1869, after which children born to mothers who were slaves were themselves free, and finally with the abolition of slavery in 1888.
8. Scantimburgo, João de, *Tratado Geral do Brasil* (São Paulo: Companhia Editôra Nacional, Editôra da Universidade de São Paulo, 1971) p. 101. However, the states do still depend partly on a subsidy from the Federal Government to balance their budgets.
9. *Sinopse,* pp. 56, 58, 68.
10. A rebellion by junior officers of a somewhat romantic kind but with a programme calling for a radical transformation of the country, which undoubtedly has left its mark on contemporary thinking in Brazil.
11. Averaging the 1940 and 1950 censuses.
12. The implicit growth model is characterised by the concentration of investment in manufacturing industry, the setting up of large-scale undertakings in the primary industries, and by relative stagnation in the agricultural sector.
13. Until quite recently there were virtually no professional managers in the traditional Brazilian family firms, as distinct from companies of foreign origin.

14 'Charismatic', to use Weber's term.
15 After General Enrico Dutra (1946) the presidents of the populist era were Vargas (1951) who committed suicide in 1954; he was followed by Kubitschek, the only president to run his full term of office; he was followed by Jânio Quadros who resigned in August 1961 a few months after his investiture, and was replaced by João Goulart, the Vice-President, who was deposed in March 1964.
16 According to the Constitution of 1946, illiterate persons and military personnel up to and including the rank of sergeant, and some other specified cases, could neither vote nor be elected.
17 In 1960 the urban population numbered 32 million (*Sinopse*, p. 62).
18 *Novos Rumos*, for the P.C.B. and *A Classe Operária* for the P.C.D.B.
19 União Nacional dos Estudantes and Ação Popular.
20 Such as the Comando Geral dos Trabalhadores, a *de facto* trade union federation, the Comando de Greve, the Pacto Sindical de Unidade e Ação, whose members were railwaymen and port workers, or the 'Peasant Leagues'.
21 For example in 1962 in the State of Pernambuco, which had always been a stronghold of the rural aristocracy, Miguel Arraes, the candidate for the post of governor, was elected by a left-wing coalition led by the P.T.B., but his campaign was financed in part by one of the richest industrialists of São Paulo, José Ermirio de Moraes, who received in exchange the support of the P.T.B. for his candidature for the senate, to which he was elected as representative for the State of Pernambuco on the P.S.D. ticket.
22 Furtado, Celso, *Les Etats-Unis et Le Sous-Developpement de l'Amérique Latine* (Paris: Calmann-Lévy, 1970) pp. 172, 173.
23 On this subject an American author has written: 'As long as enough clients are satisfied to permit election, the politicians can take as their principal goal the cultivation of their individual careers and prestige.' Leff, Nathaniel H., *Economic Policy-Making and Development in Brazil, 1947–1964* (New York: John Wiley, 1968) p. 121.
24 Furtado, *Les Etats-Unis*, p. 178.
25 See in particular 'Uma Caraterização do Sistema', *O Estado de São Paulo* (17 and 24 October 1965).
26 Schmitter, Philippe C., *Interest Conflict and Political Change in Brazil* (Stanford Univ. Press, 1971) p. 378.
27 Jaguaribe, Hélio: 'Stabilité social par le "colonial-fascisme" ', *Les Temps Modernes*, 23rd year, no. 257 (Oct 1967) 636–7.

Chapter 2
1 Buescu, Mircea, *Historia Econômica do Brazil* (Rio de Janeiro: APEC, 1970) p. 88.
2 Skidmore, Thomas E., 'Toward a Comparative Analysis of Race Relations Since Abolition in Brazil and the United States', *Journal of Latin American Studies*, vol. 4, pt. 1 (May 1972) 25.
3 Ibid. The two extremes are the north (27·3 per cent) and the centre-west (40·7 per cent). It should however be noted that these two regions together employed only 7·4 per cent of the total number of slaves in Brazil.
4 *Sinopse*, p. 56.
5 Klein, Herbert S., 'The Colored Freedmen in Brazilian Slave Society', *Journal of Social History*, III, no. 1 (autumn 1969) 36.
6 Immigrants from Europe (about 5 million between 1820 and 1950) have obviously influenced this statistic. The important part played also by Japanese immigration is noteworthy; those of Japanese descent represent

about 0·6 per cent of the population. It should also be noted that starting with the 1960 census, the question as to racial origin was deleted from the questionnaires, a fact which deprives us of recent statistics but is evidence of a definite will to regard the Brazilian nation as a whole from this aspect.

7 This expression has been taken from Thomas E. Skidmore, whose work on this subject has formed the basis for this brief outline. See Skidmore, 'Toward Comparative Analysis', pp. 1–28.

8 Neither the attempt made in 1920 nor the latest one inspired by Abdias do Nascimento after the war was able to gather supporters.

9 Whereas in 1940 66 per cent of economically active persons were employed in the country, by 1950 this figure had fallen to 60 per cent, to 54 per cent in 1960 and 44 per cent in 1970 or in absolute figures, 9,725,693, 10,254,245, 12,163,057 and 13,071,385 respectively. (*Source: Tabulações Avançadas do Censo Demografico* (Rio de Janeiro: I.B.G.E., 1971) p. xxix.

10 Introduction of the minimum guaranteed wage for urban workers in 1940 and the Consolidation of the Labour Laws in 1943.

11 The rate of urbanisation (i.e. the ratio of urban to rural population) developed as follows:

Year	Percentage	Approximate number
	Town dwellers	
1920	23	7,000,000
1940	31	12,880,182
1950	36	18,782,891
1960	45	32,004,187
1970	56	52,904,744

This development has been most marked in the south-eastern region where most of the industry has been established, but it is noticeable throughout the country, as the following figures show:

	1 Sep 1960 %	1 Sep 1970 %
North	37·8	45·2
North-east	34·2	41·8
South-east	57·4	72·8
South	57·6	44·6
Centre-west	35·0	48·2

(*Source:* calculated from *Sinopse*)

The definition adopted for the official Brazilian statistics is misleading in fact, since it includes villages with less than 200 inhabitants, which are in no sense urban. Nevertheless, even if we use the rigorous criterion of centres housing more than 20,000 inhabitants, the rate of urbanisation in Brazil is still impressive. For in 1970 it had reached 36 per cent whereas according to D. C. Lambert who applies that criterion, it is 16 per cent for Asia and 13 per cent for Africa – or was in 1960. (*Source:* Lambert, Denis-Clair and Martin, Jean-Marie, *L'Amérique Latine, Economies et Sociétés*, Collection U, Economic science and management ser. (Paris: A. Colin, 1971) p. 134.

12 Furtado, *Les Etats-Unis*, pp. 174–5 (my italics).

13 Marini, Ruy Mauro, *Sous Développement et Révolution en Amérique Latine* (Paris: François Maspéro, 1972), p. 172.

14 There appears to be a hiatus between the degree to which the 'enlightened minority' is really aware of the historical process and the degree of awareness acceptable at the level of practical politics which the class itself has reached. The Brazilian Communist Party, conscious of this gap, has historically taken up a reformist position, favouring a policy of collaboration between the classes, which an apologist of the revolutionary left denounces as an 'ideology falsely identified with Marxism'. (Marini, *Sous-Développement*, p. 119.)

15 Vinhas, M., *Estudos Sôbre o Proletariado Brasileiro* (Rio de Janeiro: Civilização Brasileira, 1970).

16 Ibid., p. 224.

17 Ibid., p. 126.

18 Ibid.

19 Ibid., p. 121. This quotation has been translated from Lenin, V. I., Complete Works (Buenos Aires: Editorial Cartego, n.d.) vol. 4, p. 200.

20 Bresser Pereira, Luiz Carlos, *Desenvolvimento e Crise no Brasil*, 2nd ed. (Rio de Janeiro, Editôra Brasiliense, 1970) pp. 83, 86.

21 Ibid., pp. 84–7.

22 Ibid., pp. 57–8, 79.

23 *Exame* (Nov 1971) pp. 42–7.

24 The concept of a minimum wage (paid to an adult for 30 days or 240 hours of work) may be misleading. It is often forgotten that Brazil is divided into 23 regions, in which the minimum wage may vary considerably. On 1 May 1971 there were six monthly minimum wages in force going from Crz. 151·20 (Piauí, Céara, etc.) to Crz. 225·6 (Rio, São Paulo), a difference of 49·2 per cent. (Decree No. 68,576 dated 1 May 1971).

25 The idea of a minimum wage should be considered as an indicator of a relativity between the income of different groups. It is not an indicator of the standard of living, since it does not take into account non-monetary income such as social security, the social and financial advantages of the wage-earning classes, the subsistence cultures of rural workers, etc., which nowadays play an important part in the life of the nation. It is therefore dangerous simply to convert these figures into their foreign currency equivalents; they should be taken with the reserve mentioned above. Even so, it is interesting to note that between July 1940 when it was introduced by Getúlio Vargas and 1 May 1971, the highest minimum wage rose from U.S. $13 to U.S. $43·7 per month.

26 Leff, *Economic Policy-Making*, p. 128.

Chapter 3

1 Part of the State of Pará was also affected by the rubber fever. If this state is included in the population count, population rose from 333,000 in 1872 to 695,000 in 1900 (*Sinopse*, p. 55).

2 The average annual production of coffee between 1821 and 1830 was 317,800 bags (1 bag = 60 kgs). Between 1851 and 1860 it rose to 2,652,530 bags and between 1891 and 1900 to 7,449,100. Between 1951 and 1960 it reached something like 23 million bags. Scantimburgo, *Tratado Geral*, p. 286; Baer, Werner, *Industrialization and Economic Development in Brazil* (Homewood, Ill.: Richard D. Irwin, 1965) p. 258.

3 It is estimated that there were then 300,000 workers in industry in Brazil. Scantimburgo, *Tratado Geral*, p. 289.

4 'The take-off in the more advanced South American nations can be dated from the mid-1930s, although elements of modern industry were introduced earlier.' Rostow, Walt W., *Politics and the Stages of Growth*

(Cambridge Univ. Press, 1971) p. 292. Rostow classifies Brazil among the countries beyond the take-off stage, in *The Stages of Economic Growth*, 2nd ed. (Cambridge Univ. Press, 1971) addendum B, p. 235.

5 Furtado, *Les Etats-Unis*, p. 163.
6 We are adopting the main features of the classical analysis by Celso Furtado whilst bringing in certain correctives that have been fashioned by Professor Pereira Bresser. See Furtado, Celso, *História Econômica do Brasil* (Rio de Janeiro: Editôra Fundo da Cultura S.A., 1959); *Dialética do Desenvolvimento* (Rio de Janeiro: Editôra Funda da Cultura S.A., 1964); and *Les Etats-Unis*.
7 In 1925 Brazil exported 13,482,000 bags and in 1933, 15,459,000 bags. Yet production rose from 14,801,150 bags in 1925 to 29,610,000 bags in 1933. During the whole of this period exports increased by only about 5 per cent. Between 1921 and 1930 they reached 140,520,000 bags and from 1931 to 1940, 146,680,000 bags. But production, which rose from 115,229,390 bags in 1921–30 to 140,036,660 bags in 1931–40, showed a growth of 22 per cent. Baer, *Industrialization ... in Brazil*, p. 258.
8 Furtado, *Les Etats-Unis*, p. 164.
9 This is of course only an *ex post facto* justification. The Government simply wished to avoid having the mainstay of the Brazilian economy crumble. Only later was it realised that in so far as the value of the coffee destroyed was less than the income generated by the coffee industry, this policy was in fact an application of Keynesian theory before it was formulated.
10 When industrialisation is at an early stage and is selectively protected, it only needs quite small financial investments to bring about a large increase in product, or put another way a high marginal product/capital ratio, either directly or by bringing about external economies.
11 It should be noted that even though the State buys their coffee at a price above that of world markets, it does not pay them sufficient to counterbalance the real drop in the value of exports.
12 Bresser, Pereira, *Desenvolvimento e Crise*, p. 39.
13 Furtado, *Les Etats-Unis*, p. 39.
14 Industrial production, which had increased by 49 per cent between 1934 and 1939, rose by only 37 per cent between 1940 and 1944. Bresser, Pereira, *Desenvolvimento e Crise*, p. 41.
15 In 1930 cruzeiros were 8·3 to the dollar, and in 1939 they were 18·7. It was legitimate to maintain this parity in 1945 going by the experience of the preceding years, which showed that if the cruzeiro was devalued the price of coffee on world markets fell.
16 In 1946 Brazil's reserves amounted to U.S. $700 million, of which U.S. $350 million were held in gold and U.S. $262 million in partially blocked pounds sterling. These sums were considered at the time by Brazilian economists as enormous but they were small in comparison with the foreign exchange reserves which Brazil had in July 1972, lodged with the I.M.F., amounting to U.S. $2600 million. (For 1946 see Gudin, Eugênio, 'The Chief Characteristics of the Postwar Economic Development of Brazil', *The Economy of Brazil*, ed. Howard S. Ellis (Berkeley: Univ. of California Press, 1969) p. 6; for 1972 see *Veja*, no. 205 (9 Aug 1972) 84.)
17 Gudin, 'Chief Characteristics', p. 6.
18 Bresser, Pereira, *Desenvolvimento e Crise*, p. 43.
19 From 1954 to 1963 this foreign currency withholding represented on average 38·7 per cent of the total value of exports of coffee, equal to an average tax of U.S. $306 million annually on these exports. (Calculated

by the author on the basis of data submitted by Leff, *Economic Policy-Making*, p. 189.)
20 From 1948 to 1961 the import of consumer durables as a percentage of total imports fell from 9·8 per cent to 1·2 per cent, and that of non-durable consumer goods from 7·5 per cent to 6·2 per cent. Gudin, 'Chief Characteristics', p. 4.
21 The 'register of similar products' in which Brazilian manufacturers who were asking for tariff protection could have their products entered was first set up in 1911. The officials who had to apply protective measures had for a long time done so with flexibility, allowing the import of goods which were considered necessary for development. But in a period of crisis in the balance of payments, these rules were interpreted strictly. The barriers thus created encouraged non-Brazilian companies to obtain a direct foothold in Brazil in order to retain their market.

Not until August 1972 was this protective wall breached by Decree No. 1236 which authorised the transfer to Brazil of complete factories (second-hand machinery) even if some of the machinery so imported was already locally manufactured. This was subject to two conditions, (a) that the productive unit should be in working order, and (b) that the production should be destined 'mainly' for export.

The object of this operation was to attract to the country industrial companies capable of increasing in the very short term Brazil's hard foreign-currency earnings. Some observers say that it was partly designed to attract industrialists operating at that time in Formosa who, disturbed by the changes in the Asian policy of the United States, were looking for other countries in which to carry on their activities.
22 Bresser, Pereira, *Desenvolvimento e Crise*, p. 46; Gudin, 'Chief Characteristics', p. 4.
23 American Chamber of Commerce, *Weekly News Letter*, São Paulo no. 43 (27 Oct 1966).
24 Ibid.
25 Simonsen, Marío Henrique, *A Estrutura Econômica Brasileira*, Ensaios Econômicos da E.P.G.E. no. 3 (Rio de Janeiro, 1971) duplicated, p. 22.
26 Ibid., p. 23.
27 *Programa de Ação Econômica do Governo 1964–1966 Sintese*, Ministry of Economic Planning and Coordination (Rio de Janeiro, 1964) p. 19 (hereafter cited as P.A.E.G.).
28 P.A.E.G., p. 19. Also quoted in Bresser, Pereira, *Desenvolvimento e Crise*, p. 58.
29 Gudin, 'Chief Characteristics', p. 17.
30 Instruction 113 in particular allowed foreign investors wishing to set up or modernise an industrial undertaking that was considered useful to the Brazilian economy to import the necessary equipment under certain conditions without having to obtain cruzeiros on the official market. Since the exchange was not covered, they were required in consideration of this to agree to the investment being paid for in the form of a share in the capital of the local business. This measure stimulated investment by foreigners and between 1954 and 1961 foreign risk capital invested in Brazil amounted to U.S. $1018 million whereas from 1947 to 1953 the total had amounted to only U.S. $422 million. (Figures quoted by Medina, Rubem, *Desnacionalização, Crime Contra O Brasil?* (Rio de Janeiro: Editôra Saga, 1970) p. 47.)
31 Gordon, Lincoln and Grommers, Engelbert L., *U.S. Manufacturing Investment in Brazil 1946–1960* (Boston: Harvard Univ., 1962) p. 147.
32 *Journal de Genève* (15 Aug 1972) p. 5.

33 For example: machine tools, + 125 per cent; metallurgy, + 78 per cent; chemicals, + 106 per cent.
34 Programa de Metas based on the creation of 'growth centres'.
35 Simonsen, *A Estrutura*, p. 6.
36 Ibid., p. 9.
37 The treasury deficit rose from 0·7 per cent of G.D.P. in 1954 to 5·1 per cent in 1963. Gudin, 'Chief Characteristics', p. 16.

Chapter 4

1 The terms 'military', 'army', 'officers', etc. here refer to all the Brazilian Armed Forces including the Navy and Air Force.
2 Article 14 of the Constitution of 1891; Article 162 of the Constitution of 1934; Articles 176 and 177 of the Constitution of 1946; Articles 90 and 91 of the Constitution of 1967.
3 These were as follows: October 1930, fall of the Old Republic; October 1945, end of the *Estado Novo*; August 1954, suicide of Vargas; October/November 1955, abortive move by the Military against the investiture of the President-elect, Juscelino Kubitschek (the military candidate, Juarez Tavora had been beaten); Augst 1961, under the provisions of the Constitution, the unexpected resignation of President Quadros laid the presidency open to Vice-President João Goulart who was known to have pro-Communist sympathies. The Army tried unsuccessfully to prevent him from taking office.
    These events are described in detail in Skidmore, Thomas E., *Politics in Brazil, 1930–1964. An Experiment in Democracy* (London: Oxford Univ. Press, 1967).
4 *Nouveau Larousse Universel* (Paris: Librairie Larousse, 1949) vol. 2, p. 215 (my italics). An encyclopaedic dictionary in two volumes.
5 *Nouveau Petit Larousse* (Paris: Librairie Larousse, 1971) p. 654.
6 This training is becoming ever longer and more costly, *pari passu* with improvements in military technology and the increasing complexity of the administrative knowledge required to run a modern army.
7 Huntington distinguishes corporateness (i.e. corporate self-interest), expertise, responsibility and a sense of career as hallmarks of military professionalism. Huntington, Samuel P., *The Soldier and the State, The Theory and Politics of Civil Military Relations* (Cambridge, Mass.: Belknap Press of Harvard Univ., 1957).
8 Nunn makes use of a similar idea which he calls 'professional militarism'. Nunn, Frederick M., 'Military Professionalism and Professional Militarism in Brazil 1870–1970: Historical Perspectives and Political Implications', *Journal of Latin American Studies*, vol. 4, pt 1 (May 1972) 29–54.
9 Rustow, *World of Nations*, p. 190.
10 It should be noted that modern military education began earlier still: the Royal Naval and Military academies were founded in 1810. The Army was reorganised in 1856.
11 Calogeras, João Pandia, *Formação Histórica do Brasil*, 4th ed., coll. 'Biblioteca Pedagógica Brasileira', no. 42 (São Paulo: Companhia Editôra Brasileira, 1945) pp. 341, 342.
12 Bandits operating in the *sertões* of the north-east. The mystical rising of Canudos has been admirably described by Euclides da Cunha in his work which is a classic in Brazil, *Os Sertões*.
13 A network of roads and bridges, the telegraph, the Rondon mission to the Indian territories, etc.
14 Nunn, 'Military Professionalism', p. 37.

15 In 1904 the training of the most powerful of these militias, that of São Paulo, was entrusted to French instructors. In 1965, a year after the military Revolution, the São Paulo militia still contained 30,000 men and possessed light armoured vehicles; that of Rio Grande do Sul still had 15,000 men. (*Source:* Stepan, Alfred, *The Military in Politics. Changing Patterns in Brazil* (Princeton Univ. Press, 1971) p. 17.)

16 Decree No. 13,415 dated 29 January 1919.

17 This training comprises the following stages: four years at the military academy (Academia Militar das Agulhas Negras, A.M.A.N.), one year at the officers' school (Escola de Aperfeiçoamento de Oficiais, Es. A.O.), then, after an entry examination in which three-quarters of the candidates fail, three years at the general staff school (Escola de Comando e Estado Maior do Exército, E.C.E.M.E.). Thereafter, apart from specialist courses and training periods spent abroad, colonels and brigadier-generals should spend one year at the Superior War College (E.S.G.) which was founded in 1949.

Undoubtedly this intensive training, which is given in the Navy and Air Force as well as the Army, will widen the gap which separates army 'professionals' from the vast majority of civilian administrative and political officials, because the latter do not have the advantage of a comparable training sequence.

18 Naturally, officers who have received their training since the war are more specialised than most of their elders and have also enjoyed a wider intellectual stimulus. It is however worthy of note that already by 1964, 40 per cent of the generals on active service had passed through one of the advanced schools (Es. A.O., E.C.E.M.E., or E.S.G.) earlier in their careers. Stepan, *Military in Politics*, p. 51.

19 Between 1950 and 1967, 646 civilians and 630 military, most of them colonels and brigadier-generals (or of the equivalent rank in the other arms) gained their passing out certificate. Fragoso, General Augusto, 'A Escola Superior de Guerra', *Segurança e Desenvolvimento: Revista da Associação dos Diplomados da ESG*, year XVIII, no. 132 (1969).

Looking at these figures, one may well be surprised to find in a book published by François Maspero the following passage: 'With this ugly little man, almost neckless [Castello Branco], there arrived in power an *organisation closed to civilians* and even to most of the military – the Superior War College'.

Pau de Arara, 'La Violence militaire au Brésil', Cahiers libres 215–16 (Paris: François Maspero, 1971) p. 46 (my italics).

20 Probably of set purpose, there were no representatives of the working class.

21 The Government of the United States usually invites participants to visit certain military or industrial centres as a group. The programme often includes a short meeting with the President at the White House.

22 This organisation is said to have spent between U.S. $200,000 and U.S. $300,000 between 1962 and 1964 to gather information on the activities of Communists and to distribute it regularly to officers in key positions in the country. Stepan, *Military in Politics*, p. 154.

Another anti-Communist organisation, the Instituto Brasileiro de Ação Democratica (I.B.A.D.), which played an important part in the 1962 electoral campaign, had already prepared the ground. The leader of this organisation, M. Ivan Hasslocher, at present lives near Geneva.

23 In particular General Golbery de Couto e Silva, a famous geo-politician who became under Castello Branco the first head of the National Intelligence Service (S.N.I.), the President's new security, intelligence and information organisation. It would appear that the press campaign in

which the name of Castello Branco was launched as a 'non-political' candidate for the presidency was the work of I.P.E.S.

24 In practice, this was a long-term objective. The immediate priority for the E.S.G. was the problems of development as they affected economic growth, and it therefore attacked the privileges of the rural or urban oligarchy when and where they were seen to be a hindrance to such growth. For example, in the case of agrarian reform, the measures that were planned were aimed rather at increasing productivity than at a redistribution of land in terms of social justice.

25 It should be noted that the corps of serving officers in Brazil corresponds to that of a modern army. In 1964 it showed the following breakdown compared with the American Army.

	Percentage of total serving officers	
	Brazil	U.S.A.
Generals	1	0·4
Colonels	4·2	4·7
Lieutenant-Colonels	9·7	11·3
Majors	15·7	17·4
Captains	29·9	32·9
First Lieutenants	23·1	18·4
Second Lieutenants	16·4	14·9
	100	100

Source: Stepan, *Military in Politics*, p. 50.

26 Ibid., pp. 30–56.
27 The sons of skilled workers (lower-middle class) rose from 1·5 per cent in 1941–3 to 8·6 per cent in 1962–6.
28 In 1962–6, 6·7 per cent of the total, being orphans, did not state their father's occupation; hence the total adds up to 93·3 per cent.
29 In 1964 there were about 10 million schoolchildren in primary schools and 1·9 million receiving secondary education. (*Source: Sinopse*, pp. 396, 400.)
30 Even taking into account the non-monetary advantages of soldiers.
31 The states included in SUDENE (the development organisation for the north-east).
32 The population figures quoted come from the 1960 census.
33 Stepan, *Military in Politics*, p. 39.
34 Ibid., p. 41.
35 The number of cadets coming from São Paulo which has a relatively advanced school system, rose to more than 15 per cent of the total in 1969. Schneider, *Political System of Brazil*, pp. 252, 253.
36 Many present-day small townships have grown up around garrisons or military administrative centres.
37 The First Army, traditionally the best equipped, plays a special part in the political happenings in the country as it controls Rio de Janeiro. The Third Army is the largest, since it guards the frontiers with the traditional enemies, Argentina and Uruguay.
38 Military service is compulsory but as the age classes due for call-up cannot all be accommodated within the military budget, the call-up is applied selectively.
39 Stepan, *Military in Politics*, p. 13.
40 To quote an example, in 1967 the Third Army (Rio Grande do Sul) had

approximately the following percentages of gauchos (inhabitants of Rio Grande do Sul): conscripts, 100 per cent; career corporals 95 per cent; sergeants 70–80 per cent; officers 50–60 per cent. *Source:* ibid., p. 14.
41 According to some military estimates, the spread goes from 1·5 per cent in the artillery to 10 per cent in the infantry. Ibid., pp. 16–17.
42 In 1963 the Army represented 0·41 per cent of the total population in Peru; in Argentina at the same date it represented 0·51 per cent of the total population (0·56 per cent in 1969). For the period 1966–9 the military budget was 2 per cent of G.N.P. in Argentina and an average of 3 per cent in Peru; for the same period it was 2·4 per cent of the G.N.P. in Switzerland (U.S. $66 per inhabitant) and 3·8 per cent for NATO less the United States (U.S. $67·7 per inhabitant). Nun, José, 'A Latin America Phenomenon: The Middle Class Military Coup', *Latin America Reform or Revolution?* ed. J. Patras and M. Zeitlin, Political Perspective ser. (Greenwich, Conn.: Fawcett, 1968) p. 158. *Notes et Etudes documentaires,* Paris: La Documentation française, Sécretariat général du Gouvernement, Direction de la Documentation, no. 3812–14 (12 Sep 1971) 83 and Table III (hereafter cited as *Notes et Etudes*).
43 This was said by Ambassador Juracy Magalhães, who was himself a general, at Washington on 16 February 1965.
44 Nun, *Latin America Phenomenon*, p. 181.
45 Institutional Act No. 1, preamble, translated in *Notes et Etudes,* no. 3749–3750, p. 28 (hereafter cited as Institutional 1).

PART TWO

1 For a detailed analysis of the events that led to the fall of President Goulart, see Skidmore, *Politics in Brazil.* For a 'committed' view, see for example Ianni, Octavio, *Os Idos de Março e a Queda em Abril,* Alberto Dines *et al.* (Rio de Janeiro: José Alvaro Editôr, 1964); Stacchini, José, *Março 1964: Mobilização da Audácia* (São Paulo: Companhia Editôra Nacional, 1965); Jurema, Abelardo, *Sexta Feira 13: os últimos dias do governo Goulart* (Rio de Janeiro: Editôra O Cruzeiro, 1964).
2 Institutional 1, preamble: 'The victorious revolution as a constitutive power is self-legitimating'.

Chapter 5

1 Ibid.
2 Ibid.
3 Ibid.
4 Ibid., Article 7, p 1.
5 Ibid., Article 10. We should mention at once that according to the *Correio da Manhã* for 1 April 1965, 378 persons had had their civil rights suspended between 18 April and 15 June 1964 under the provisions of this Institutional Act. They included three former presidents of the Republic, Senhor Goulart, Senhor Quadros and Senhor Kubitschek, six state governors and 55 members of parliament (out of 475). One American author cites more detailed data, but does not specify his sources. He speaks of 378 cases of suspension of political rights, 116 of which were elected mandates cancelled and he adds that there were 544 compulsory retirements for political reasons, 1528 dismissals, 555 forced military retirements, 165 involuntary transfers to the reserve and various other punishments, making a total of more than 3500 persons affected at federal level. He estimates that at least an equal number of individuals were

Notes

affected at state and municipal level. Schneider, *Political System of Brazil*, p. 199.
6 A reform of Portuguese orthography entailed the abolition of some double consonants and the dropping of certain letters such as 'y'. Proper names therefore can be written either in the new style or in the old one, which we use here in order to conform with the way in which these persons signed their names.
7 *Jornal do Brasil* (Rio de Janeiro: 2 April 1964).
8 *Estado de São Paulo* (5 April 1964).
9 Manifesto of 3 April 1964.
10 Ibid.
11 Editorial of 5 April 1964.

Chapter 6
1 His wife, Dona Argentina Vianna Castello Branco, died within three days from the effects of a heart ailment in 1963 at Recife. They had been married for 41 years.
2 Among other foreign decorations he held the Bronze Star of the United States, the Croix de guerre from France, with palms, and the French medal of gratitude (silver-gilt).
3 These included: Marshal Oswaldo Cordeiro de Farias, 'Minister Extraordinary for Coordination of Regional Bodies' (Minister of the Interior); Marshal Juarez Tavora, Minister of Transport and Public Works; General Golbery de Couto e Silva, Head of the S.N.I., responsible for co-ordinating all aspects of national security (the National Intelligence Service was established by Decree No. 3431 dated 14 June 1964 and was directly attached to the President; it was of equal standing with the civil and military households); Ambassador Vasco Leitão da Cunha, then General Juracy Magalhães, Ministers of Foreign Affairs; General Ernesto Geisel, Head of the Military Household; and Air Force General Nelson Freire Lavanère-Wanderley, Minister of Aviation. (*Source*: 'Adesguianos no Governo', *Bulletin of the ADESG*, no. 103 (Mar/Apr 1964) 11–15. Roberto Campos, Minister Extraordinary for Planning and Economic Co-ordination, the work-horse of the Government, had not passed through the E.S.G., but he had averaged two courses per year since 1955.
4 Choosing about twenty parameters, Stepan has highlighted the salient characteristics in the careers of the 102 serving generals in the Army in 1964. Out of this 'complete universe' he extracted the ten generals who were indisputably at the heart of the Castello Branco régime. In comparing the two groups, he noted that the members of the second shared the following characteristics: they had been members of the teaching body of the E.S.G., had passed through military schools abroad, had been first of their year in one of the three leading army schools, had taken part in the Italian campaign and they belonged to a technically advanced arm. Half of the ten 'Castellians' satisfied the first four parameters, and the others did so partially. Of the 92 remaining generals, only one had shared the same experience, a statistical probability of 1/1000. Stepan, *Military in Politics*, pp. 237–40.
5 We should not fail to notice the somewhat romantic nature of this wish of a general who had been brought to power by a military Revolution, and whose aim was to promote basic reforms in the political, economic and social structures of the country. This aspect has been stressed in a letter to the author from Professor Dalmo de Abreu Dallari. This lack of

political realism might even have had harmful consequences by allowing the thorny problem of the succession to be raised prematurely.
6 Rustow, *World of Nations*, p. 185.
7 This places the régime in the 'twilight' category of Rustow.
8 It will be remembered that this lieutenants' rebellion of 1922, which aimed at transforming the country, made a deep impression on contemporary thought in Brazil.
9 Among the military associated with this movement, Admiral Silvio Heck and General José Alberto Bittencourt may be mentioned.
10 *Correio da Manhã* (Rio de Janeiro: 19 Dec 1963). Also reproduced by Stacchini, *Março 1964*, pp. 20–2 and in translation quoted from Stepan, *Military in Politics*, pp. 251–2.
11 A State Petroleum Monopoly set up by Getúlio Vargas in October 1953 after a violent campaign between the 'nationalists' and the 'internationalists'.
12 It should be remembered that the corps of serving officers numbers only about 20,000 professionals or 0·022 per cent of the population.
13 The review *Veja* (24 Nov 1971) 37, attributes this phrase to Professor Ronald Schneider.

Chapter 7
1 See the list published by Morel, Edmar, *O Golpe Começou em Washington* (Rio de Janeiro, Editôra Civilização Brasileira, 1965), pp. 248–59. See also the *Diário Oficial da União* for 11 and 14 April, 17 May and 13 June 1964.
2 Since the purge of the *tenentes*.
3 Decree No. 53,897.
4 *Inquérito Policial Militar No. 709, O Comunismo no Brasil*, 4 vols (Rio de Janeiro: Biblioteca do Exército, 1966–7) (hereafter cited as *Inquérito 709*).
5 See, among others, Cony, Carlos Heitor, *O Ano e O Fato: Crônicaos Politicos* (Rio de Janeiro: Editôra Civilização Brasileira, 1964); Lago, Mário, *Primeiro de Abril: Estórias para a História* (Rio de Janeiro: Editôra Civilização Brasileira, 1964); Moreira Alves, Márcio, *Torturas e Torturados* (Rio de Janeiro: Editôra Artenova, 1966); Borges, Mauro, *O Golpe em Goiás: História de uma grande Traição* (Rio de Janeiro: Editôra Civilização Brasileira, 1965); Morel, *O Golpe Começou, Pau de Arara;* and Schneider, *Political System of Brazil*.
6 Faust, Jean-Jacques, *A Revolução Devora Seus Presidentes* (Rio de Janeiro: Editôra Saga, 1965) p. 86.
7 Law No. 4330/64 dated 1 July 1964.
8 Law No. 4320/64.
9 Law No 4390 dated 29 August 1964, modifying Law No. 4131 of 3 September 1962.
10 Baklanoff, Eric N., 'Foreign Private Investment and Industrialization in Brazil', *New Perspectives of Brazil*, ed. E. N. Baklanoff (Nashville: Vanderbilt Univ. Press, 1966) p. 133.
11 The documents consulted show that Castello Branco only agreed to this promulgation against his will. He had first to be convinced that the policy of economic austerity would not survive his departure as had happened under previous governments.
12 The *Archives of Marshal Castello Branco* (hereafter A.M.C.B.) are still very little known. There are three collections. The first, which was assembled by his son, is kept at his house at Rio de Janeiro (part was

transferred to Fortaleza (Ceará) in the mausoleum where since 22 July 1972 the ashes of the Marshal and of his wife have rested). The second is deposited at E.C.E.M.E., Escola de Comando e Estado Maior do Exército, also in Rio de Janeiro. It has to do with the military thinking of Castello Branco. The third was collected by the former Head of the President's Civil Household, the academician Luiz Vianna Filho, at Salvador (Bahia). The letter quoted belongs to the Paulo Castello Branco collection and a photocopy of it has been published. *Veja*, no. 187 (5 Apr 1972) 38.

Chapter 8

1 Magalhães Pinto, from Minas Gerais, Adhémar de Barros, from São Paulo, Carlos Lacerda from Guanabara, Ney Braga from Paraná, Mauro Borges of Goiás, Ildo Meneghetti from Rio Grande do Sul, Fernando Correia da Costa from Mato Grosso. During these meetings it became clear that a civilian president would not be acceptable to the military, but Costa e Silva would have liked the High Command, of which he was the president, to remain operative for 'some time yet', and that Adhémar de Barros supported the candidature of the Head of the Second Army (São Paulo), his friend General Amaury Kruel. The name of Castello Branco was then put forward by Carlos Lacerda.
2 At that time Goulart was Vice-President. The electoral law did allow the president to belong to one party and the vice-president to a different one, even though the latter was the successor appointed by the Constitution in the event of presidential incapacity.
3 *Pau de Arara*, pp. 49–50.
4 The Supreme Court put forward the argument that Borges' rank of governor enabled him to be judged by the Legislative Assembly of the State of Goiás, and not by a military tribunal.
5 Some observers considered that this was too neat a solution to have been arrived at by the Military. They wondered whether it might not have been thought of by Senator Pedro Ludovico Borges Texeira, the old fox of the political 'system' who might have decided to sacrifice the few remaining months of his son's term of office in order to safeguard the son's political future.
6 Natives of Rio de Janeiro.
7 Eduardo Gomes also played an important part in the fall of Vargas in 1945.

Chapter 9

1 Romão, Lucas, 'Perspectives de la lutte démocratique et nationale au Brésil', *La Nouvelle Revue Internationale*, 8th year, no. 2 (78), (Feb 1965) 98. See also Morel, *O Golpe Começou*.
2 See Skidmore, '*Politics in Brazil*', pp. 322–30. See also *Hearing Before the Committee on Foreign Relations on the Nomination of Lincoln Gordon to be Assistant Secretary of State for Inter-American Affairs*, Washington: U.S. Senate, 89th Congress, 2nd sess. (7 Feb 1966) specially pp. 9, 44–5.
3 Costa e Silva gave up this initiative when he became President.
4 But on one point, the Treaty of Non-Proliferation of Nuclear Arms, Castello Branco did not go along with North American policy. His successors also refused to sign the Treaty, in order to leave Brazil with the option of developing the new source of energy as her interests might

require. See Zoppo, Ciro Elliot, 'Brazil', *Technology, Politics, and Proliferation*, Arms Control Special Studies Program, ACDA/WEC-126, vol. x, prepared for the U.S. Arms Control and Disarmament Agency, Washington, D.C. (30 June 1968) duplicated, pp. 14–21.
5 A speech made on 31 July 1964 and published in *A Política da Revolução Brasileira* (Rio de Janeiro: Ministry of Foreign Relations, 1966) pages unnumbered.
6 Baklanoff, 'Foreign Private Investment', p. 133.
7 Ibid.
8 Since 1960 exports from Brazil fluctuated between 1·2 billion and 1·4 billion dollars per year.
9 We may note in passing that the Société de Banque Suisse which had been represented in Brazil since 1953, although it displayed prudence for fear of a moratorium, had not restricted its credit facilities to the Bank of Brazil. This attitude, which was rare among the international establishment, and was reinforced by the announcement immediately after the Revolution of the extension of the credit limits granted, resulted in Switzerland being privileged to be the first State with which Brazil resumed talks aimed at credit consolidation operations. Later on this 'confidence credit' given at the psychological moment in 1964, smoothed the way for certain financial discussions between the two countries.
10 World Bank: U.S. $80 million early in 1965; United States: U.S. $450 million under the Alliance for Progress Programme during 1965; International Monetary Fund: 'stand-by credit', U.S. $125 million in February 1965. These figures are quoted in Baklanoff, 'Foreign Private Investment', p. 135. Daland adds to the list the Inter-American Development Bank and makes a total of more than a thousand million dollars by the end of 1965. Daland, Robert T., *Brazilian Planning* (Chapel Hill: Univ. of North Carolina Press, 1967) p. 73.
11 *Notes et Etudes*, no. 3383 (19 Apr 1967) 47.

Chapter 10
1 Whose posts included that of Alternate Executive Director of the International Monetary Fund.
2 Decree No. 53,914 dated 11 May 1964.
3 Campos, Roberto de Oliveira, 'Outlook of the Brazilian Economy', address delivered at the Union Bank of Switzerland, on 4 September 1969; printed in Switzerland, April 1970, p. 3.
4 *Plano Trienal de Desenvolvimento Econômico e Social 1963–1965*, Rio de Janeiro: Presidency of the Republic (Dec 1962).
5 P.A.E.G., pp. 15–16.
6 Which has fallen to −1·1 per cent per capita in 1963 compared with an average of +6 to 7 per cent in previous years.
7 See, *inter alia*, on this discussion Simonsen, Mário Henrique, *Inflação: Gradualismo x Tratamento de Choque* (Rio de Janeiro: APEC Editôra, 1970).
8 We shall not deal specifically with the imbalances, which are studied in a doctoral thesis being prepared at the Graduate Institute of International Studies at Geneva under the direction of Professor Gilbert Etienne. Probst, Gisella, *La Développement économique régional et son Application à un cas pratique: le Nord-Est du Brésil*.
9 See Graham, Lawrence S., *Civil Service Reform in Brazil: Principles versus Practice*, Latin American Monographs no. 13 (Austin, London: Univ. of Texas Press, 1968).

10 The *Diário Oficial da União* for 7 July 1966 published a list of 207 enterprises controlled by the federal authorities, states or communes. The importance of this public sector is reflected in the percentage of the formation of fixed capital in Brazil. From 1947 to 1960 the share of the State (the government and mixed economy enterprises) rose from 15·8 per cent of the total to 46·2 per cent according to the data cited by Baer, *Industrialization . . . in Brazil*, p. 84. The main sectors in which the State took an interest were petroleum, steel, mining, electricity, transport and communications. Since the Revolution an aircraft industry sprang up under the aegis of the Air Force. The first aircraft, the twin turbo-prop *Bandeirante*, of which 150 were produced, designed and manufactured in Brazil, flew in July 1972.
11 Approximately 65 per cent in 1960.
12 This concept of increase of productivity is not defined in the P.A.E.G. and in practice it is extremely difficult to calculate accurately, especially where presumed work productivity is involved.
13 Assuming a 6 per cent growth of G.N.P. annually from 1965 onwards, and a constant speed of circulation of money.
14 Campos, Roberto de Oliveira: 'A Retrospect over Brazilian Development Plans', *The Economy of Brazil*, ed. H. S. Ellis (Berkeley, Los Angeles: Univ. of California Press, 1969) p. 334.
15 Between 1964 and 1966 receipts increased by 45 per cent in real terms whereas budgetary expenses fell by only about 8 per cent in real terms.
16 Martone, Celso L., 'Análise do Plano de Ação Econômica do Governo', *Planejamento no Brasil*, ed. Betty Mindlin Lafer (São Paulo: Editôra Perspectiva, 1970) p. 89.

Chapter 11

1 Roberto Campos is the one always mentioned, while little is said about the part played by Octavio Gouvêa de Bulhões, Finance Minister; but in fact the two men had close links even before joining Castello Branco's team.
2 A lecture at the Brazilian Seminar held in Zurich on 26 and 27 May 1971 under the auspices of the St-Gall Latin American Institute. It should however be remembered that Roberto Campos himself carries a share of responsibility for the 'catastrophes' of the pre-1964 years. He was a member of the team of advisers to Getúlio Vargas, was President of the National Economic Development Bank (B.N.D.E.) under Juscelino Kubitschek and served as Ambassador at Washington under João Goulart.
3 Law No. 4357/64, developing Article 57 of Law No. 3470 of November 1958.
4 Established by Article 205 of the 1946 Constitution, the Conselho Nacional de Economia had the task of studying the life and economic needs of the country and suggesting appropriate measures to the various governmental agencies. Its members were appointed by the President whose choice had to be approved by the Senate. It was abolished by Article 181 of the 1967 Constitution.
5 Bulhões, Octavio Gouvêa de, 'Financial Recuperation for Economic Expansion', *The Economy of Brazil*, op. cit., p. 162.
6 In fact the law on usury dating from 1933 forbade loans at interests of more than 12 per cent per annum. But even if all possible tricks were used, money gave a negative return when inflation reached 30·5 per cent in 1960, 47·7 per cent in 1961, 51·3 per cent in 1962, 81·3 per cent in 1963 and 91·9 per cent in 1964. (*Source*: general index of prices of

the Getúlio Vargas Foundation, a self-governing institution whose tasks included making up the national accounts of Brazil.)
7. Whereas in December 1963 the balance of governmental consolidated debt was Ncrz. 58 million, the balance of O.R.T.N.s in circulation in December 1969 was Ncrz. 6095 millions. Simonsen, *A Estrutura*, p. 32.
8. The previous law provided for tax at 10 per cent. The new law gave enterprises the option of not paying the tax provided they subscribed twice its amount in O.R.T.N. with a term of at least five years.
9. To avoid too great a fall in State receipts, this was not taken into account when calculating profits tax. But correction could be deducted in respect of the extraordinary tax on business profits as soon as they exceeded 30 per cent of the value of the capital and reserves, which until then had been brought into the accounts at historical value.
10. According to the economist Mario Henrique Simonsen this dualism between the historical cost of capital and profits expressed in current values made 'phantom gains' of 52·1 per cent to 74 per cent of profits made by limited companies in Brazil between 1958 and 1964. Simonsen, *A Estrutura*, p. 14.
11. Law No. 4380/64.
12. Law No. 4496/64.
13. Law No. 4595/64.
14. Law No. 4728/65.
15. Decree Law No. 157.
16. Whereas the holders of the electricity or telephone concessions, which were largely in foreign hands, were subject to these restrictions, port installations, whether nationalised or private, were not.
17. Roberto Campos stated his position as follows: 'The usual procedure whereby wages are raised proportionately to or beyond the cost of living is incompatible with the objective of disinflation without sacrificing development.' Thus Campos reached by another route the same conclusions as those of a young economist attached to the USAID–University of California Mission, sent to Brazil to assist in working out the ten-year development plan. This economist, noting that between 1962 and 1964 real average wages had increased at 13·1 per cent per annum whereas the average annual productivity increase was only 2·7 per cent, emphasised that among a number of distortions, the distortion produced by wages exceeding in value the marginal product of labour in a market in which labour was abundant 'seems to exist in Brazil'. Bergsman, Joel, *Brazil, Industrialization and Trade Policy* (London: Oxford Univ. Press, 1970) pp. 59, 176.
18. Law 4506 of 30 November 1964.

Chapter 12
1. Baklanoff, 'Foreign Private Investment', p. 134.
2. See Lacerda, Carlos, *Palavras e Ação* (Rio de Janeiro Distribuidora Record, 1965).
3. The title is 'Minister Extraordinary for Co-ordination of Regional Bodies'. Cordeiro de Farias, who was closely attached to Castello Branco, was Artillery Commander of the Brazilian Expeditionary Force in Italy.
4. *Visão*, vol. 40, no. 4 (28 Feb 1972) 70.
5. In actual fact, as regards electricity alone the installed power doubled, rising from 6209 million kWh in 1963 to 12,629 million kWh in 1971. Production increased from 29,094 million kWh in 1964 to 42,280 million kWh in 1971.

(*Sources:* 1963 *Conjuntura Econômica*, vol. 24, no. 1 (Jan. 1970) 131; 1964 *Sinopse*, p. 211; 1971 *Conjuntura Econômica*, vol. 26, no. 2 (Feb 1972) 33, 34.)

Chapter 13
1. *Estatuto da Terra*, Law No. 4504/64.
2. Ibid.
3. Preliminary results of the I.B.R.A. (Brazilian Institute for Agrarian Reform) survey completed in December 1965. Quoted by Chacel, Julian, 'The Principal Characteristics of the Agrarian Structure and Agrarian Production in Brazil', *The Economy of Brazil*, op. cit., p. 105.
4. Minifundium: a land parcel of less than 25 acres. Latifundium: generally a property covering more than 2500 acres (except in certain fertile or densely populated regions). See the definitions suggested by the Conference on Methods of Appropriation and Use of Land, Rio de Janeiro, 1953.
5. Between 1964 and 1969 2,500,000 acres were distributed to 47,000 families. *Source:* Lambert and Martin, *L'Amérique Latine*, p. 281. The establishment of 'Proterra' in 1971 hastened the process; (see above).
6. These figures, which are high by comparison with the censuses of 1950 and 1960, are due to the fact that it was no longer possible to obtain credits from State Banks through which the rural assistance programme (guaranteed prices, etc.) was operated without a certificate of registration with I.B.R.A.
7. Paraphrasing Lambert and Martin, *L'Amérique Latine*, p. 278.
8. It is true that the experience of some countries in Latin America has not always been a happy one. In Brazil, a crisis of this sort arose at the end of 1963, involving the Hanna Corporation managed at that time by one of the *bêtes noires* of the nationalist left, George Humphrey, formerly Secretary of the Treasury under President Eisenhower. This company had purchased on the London and New York stock exchanges the shares of a British company which had a mining concession in Brazil, that of São João del Rey. These transactions had been made behind the backs of the Brazilians (and without bringing any foreign currency into the country) and Goulart's government was on the point of revoking the concession just before the Revolution. A number of serious psychological errors committed by Hanna had done nothing to improve the situation. By contrast, ICOMI (Industria e Comercio de Minérios S.A.) the 'joint venture' of the Bethlehem Steel Corporation, with a 51 per cent capital participation by the Brazilian group Antunes, is a model of public relations and produces impressive profits.
9. At 31 December 1969, known and listed reserves were estimated at: crude oil, 852 million barrels; mineral coal, 2910 million tons (unfortunately with a bitumen content making it unsuitable for coke production); iron ore, 40,000 million tons graded at 58 to 59 per cent; manganese, at least 152·5 million tons; bauxite, 80 million tons, with an aluminium content of 45–50 per cent and less than 5 per cent silica; copper, 35 million tons of low grade (1·5 per cent); nickel, 25 million tons; calamine, 13 million tons with an 82 per cent zinc oxide content; galena, 1·5 million tons with a lead content of 11 per cent. Besides asbestos, chromium, dolomite, graphite, magnesite and tungsten already exploited, large reserves of cassiterite (tin), thorium, uranium, magnesium and niobium have already been located. And exploration of the territory is far from complete, as is shown by the discovery in 1972 of new deposits

of iron ore in the Carajas massif in Pará in the Amazon region. The catalogued deposits amount to 1600 million tons with 67 per cent metal content and reserves are thought to be of the order of 6600 million tons.
Source: 'O Brasil Cresce', *Realidade*, (July 1970) supplement, 176–8. *Veja*, no. 206 (16 Aug 1972) 60–72.
10 Source: 1964: 'O Brasil Cresce', *Realidade*, 177. 1970: iron ore, P.N.D., Table III; manganese, *Conjuntura Econômica* (Feb 1972) 29.
11 *Imagem do Brasil* (São Paulo: Editôra Banas S.A., 1971) p. 116.
12 'O Brasil Cresce', *Realidade*, 176. It is interesting to note that the mining port of Sepetiba 125 miles from Rio, which the 'Hanna Corp.' wanted to construct, will in fact be constructed by a company belonging to the Antunes Brazilian group, namely Minerações Brasileiras Reunidas. Cargo boats of 150,000 tons will be able to berth there and it will have transportation capacity for 10 million tons of ore per year. It will cost something like U.S. $140 million.

Chapter 14
1 Gasparian, Fernando, *Em Defesa da Economia Nacional* (Rio de Janeiro: Editôra Saga, 1966) p. 119 (an address made to the National Economic Council on 13 July 1965).
2 Also known as the 'Parliamentary Renewal Group'.
3 Forty-eight deputies of the P.S.D., the party of ex-President Kubitschek, and twenty-three deputies of the P.T.B., the party of ex-President Goulart. The latter were immediately expelled from the P.T.B.
4 It will be recalled that M. R. Mazzili, leader of the P.S.D., had been President for a few days just after the Revolution in accordance with the 1946 Constitution.
5 The population of São Paulo grew from 31,000 inhabitants in 1872 to 6 million in 1970. By 1965 it was about 4½ million. Today the population of Greater São Paulo is something like 10 million. *Sinopse*, p. 68.
6 Dias Leite, Antonio, *Caminhos do Desenvolvimento, Contribuição para um Projeto Brasileiro* (Rio de Janeiro: Zahar Editôres, 1966) p. 15.
7 Ibid., p. 171.

Chapter 15
1 The guerillas, led by ex-Colonel Jefferson Cardim de Alencar Ossorio, called themselves 'Armed forces of national liberation'.
2 Dias Leite, *Caminhos do Desenvolvimento*, pp. 194–5.
3 *O Debate do Programa de Ação*, Rio de Janeiro, Conselho Consultivo do Planejamento, Ministério de Planejamento e Coordenação Econômica (1965).
4 Gasparian, *Defesa da Economia*, p. 33.
5 Ibid., p. 10.
6 Ibid., p. 45.
7 Ibid., p. 109.

Chapter 16
1 The Government made great efforts to assist the nation's industry to modernise itself. But some time had to elapse before the new bodies became operational. They were:

The Industrial Machinery and Equipment Purchases Finance Fund (Fundo de Financiamento para a Aquisição de Maquinas e Equipamentos Industriais, FINAME), which was set up in 1964 to provide finance for both the sale and purchase of capital goods produced in Brazil. In its first four months of activity this fund provided loans to the value of 8000 million old cruzeiros (approximately U.S. $4 million) but the interest rate, which took account of monetary correction, was high.

The Fund for the Democratisation of Business Capital (Fundo de Democratização do Capital das Emprêsas, FUNDECE), set up in 1964 to supply industrial enterprises with any additional circulating capital they might need for the full employment of the means of production.

The Technico-Scientific Development Fund (Fundo de Desenvolvimento Technico-Cientifico, FUNTEC) set up in 1964 in order to support various post-graduate courses, to finance research programmes for basic industries and to give some skilled and highly skilled technicians a grounding in some of the exact sciences.

The Financing Fund for the Study of Projects and Programmes (Fundo de Financiamento de Estudos de Projetos e Programas, FINEP) set up in 1965, for financing programmes of economic development, including those aimed at increasing exports, import substitution or vertical integration between agriculture and industry.

The Financing Programme for Small and Medium Businesses (Programa de Financiamento à Pequena e Média Empresas, FIPEME) set up in 1965 to serve as a system for distributing assistance funds to small and medium-sized businesses, supplied by the Inter-American Development Bank.

All these governmental agencies were developed and incorporated in the new Brazilian financial system over the next few years.

2 Roberto Campos, a talk given at the Nacional Club de São Paulo. *Estado de São Paulo* (25 Apr 1965) 38.
3 Interview published on 21 August 1968 in *Jornal do Brasil* (Rio de Janeiro) 22.
4 This sanction could drive most of the firms producing capital goods into bankruptcy, since their order books depended very largely on the State or on state-controlled enterprises.
5 Dias Leite, *Caminhos do Desenvolvimento*, p. 185.
6 Ibid., pp. 185–6.
7 Gasparian, *Defesa da Economia*, p. 116.

Chapter 17

1 *Fôlha de São Paulo* (29 May) p. 3.
2 Arraes had been an 'advanced radical' advocating action by constitutional means; but in exile he changed his views and called for armed rebellion. See Arraes, Miguel, *Le Brésil, le pouvoir et le peuple*, coll. Cahiers libres, no. 155 (Paris: François Maspero, 1969).
3 Liga Democrática Radical.
4 The following clauses, among others, were retained.
  the exclusion of illiterates (the registration form had to be dated and signed in the presence of the responsible officer);
  electoral courts (with powers increased and specified);
  the principle of compulsory voting (on pain of monetary or administrative penalties);
  the role of the parties (which alone could submit candidates);
  the method of election (by majority vote for executive positions –

president and vice-president, governors and vice-governors, mayors and deputy mayors and for the Senate; proportional for members of the lower chamber).

Among the new features introduced apart from those already mentioned, were:

the institution of the single voting paper, a logical consequence of the 'freezing' of the lists;

persons deprived of their political rights were forbidden to participate in party life or to take part in electoral demonstrations;

definition of voting qualifications and of the eligibility of military personnel. Officers and under-officers were electors and eligible. Those who had served for less than five years would be taken off the active strength if they became candidates. Those with more than five years' service would be stood down on half pay for personal reasons. Those who were elected would be retired or placed on reserve;

the length of electoral campaigns was limited in that no candidate could be registered more than six months before any election.

5 (a) To have obtained at least 3 per cent of the votes at the preceding parliamentary elections, distributed among at least 11 states in each of which the party must have received 2 per cent of the votes.

(b) To have had in any event 12 federal deputies elected, spread over 7 states.

(c) To have organised at least 7 regional party organisations which must be made up of municipal party organisations, which in turn could not be formed unless the party had a minimum number of members, which varied from place to place. This system was workable because of the existence of a system of electoral courts which was particularly strong in Brazil. These courts were authorised to draw the boundaries for electoral constituencies, to register parties, to look after the distribution of the money intended to finance them, to examine and approve the eligibility of candidates, to organise the elections, to see to the correctness of the electoral registers and to declare the results of elections. The Supreme Electoral Tribunal consisted of 7 judges, two of whom were appointed by the Federal Supreme Court, two by the Federal Court of Appeal, two by the President and one by the Court of Appeal of the Federal District of Brasilia.

6 Electoral Code, Law No. 4737/65; Statute of Political Parties, Law No. 4740/65; Ineligibility, Law No. 4738/65.

7 *Estado de São Paulo* (17 Mar 1965) 7.

Chapter 18

1 São Paulo (Adhémar de Barros) was not involved because for the purpose of electing governors, the country is divided into two zones which vote alternately. One group consists of Alagoas, Goiás, Guanabara, Maranhão, Mato Grosso, Minas Gerais, Pará, Paraíba, Paraná, Rio Grande do Norte, Santa Catarina and the other group consists of Acre, Amazonas, Bahia, Ceará, Espírito Santo, Pernambuco, Piauí, Rio Grande do Sul, Rio de Janeiro, São Paulo and Sergipe.

2 The alliance was permitted because this election was decided by a majority vote.

3 Apart from Guanabara and Minas Gerais they were Mato Grosso (Pedro

Notes

Pedrossian), Rio Grande do Norte (Walfredo Gurgel) and Santa Catarina (Ivo Silveira).
4 In addition to the Brazilian dailies for the period, *Notes et Etudes*, no. 3247 (21 Dec 1965) 13–16, gives a 'chronological account' of the October crisis, on which we have drawn.
5 Led by admirals Sílvio Heck and Augusto Hamann Rademacker Grünewald, two hard liners who had been among the first of the revolutionaries.
6 *Correio da Manhã* (Rio de Janeiro: 7 Oct 1965) 2.
7 Ibid., p. 5. Discussion had been under way on most of these amendments since August in a bicameral committee.
8 Milton Campos, a distinguished lawyer, was Governor of Minas Gerais and U.D.N. candidate for the post of vice-president of Brazil in 1960; he was beaten by João Goulart.
9 He also withdrew his candidature for the post of president of the Republic.
10 Supreme Court judges had this title.
11 Cited by Rustow, *World of Nations*, p. 194.
12 Ibid., p. 200.
13 Ibid., pp. 199–203.

PART THREE
1 By so doing Castello Branco secured a favourable majority for the Revolution in the Supreme Court, without having to resort to annulling the mandates of federal judges.
2 Ten military men and five civilians appointed for life.
3 Article 12.
4 Before any of these exceptional measures were taken the National Security Council had to give an opinion, but they were not subject to control by the judges (Articles 14, 15, 16, 19).
5 Law No. 4740/65 (*infra*).
6 *Notes et Etudes*, no. 3300 (17 June 1966) 32–7, contains a French translation of Institutional Act No. 2.

Chapter 19
1 This lapidary phrase occurs in a manuscript in the President's archives: 'As to carrying out my mandate, I shall not desert; as to the period assigned, I shall not exceed it.' Source: A.M.C.B., collection ECEME, Rio de Janeiro, photocopy published by *Veja*, no. 187 (5 Apr 1972) 42.
2 *Jornal do Brasil* (Rio de Janeiro: 4 Apr 1966).
3 He did not begin to take such measures until the end of April 1966, but ex-President Kubitschek had thought it prudent to leave for New York on 10 November of the previous year.
4 Professor Bonavides even argues brilliantly that although in theory the situation in Brazil was apparently bipartite, it remained in fact a one-party system so long as certain sociological and political conditions were not fulfilled. Bonavides, Paulo, *A Crise Política Brasileira* (Rio de Janeiro: Editôra Forense, 1969).
5 'In order to make the two-party formula become a *de facto* reality, the

Government was almost obliged to *lend* two senators to the opposition party'. *Jornal do Brasil* (Rio de Janeiro: 18 June 1967) special supplement, p. 5. Since Supplementary Act No. 4 forbade the use of the names, initials or symbols of the former parties, the provisional groupings had to choose fresh names. Nevertheless the men were still the same and the new organisations were formed around the following nuclei.

	Deputies	*Senators*	*Source*
For ARENA	83	16	U.D.N.
	67	15	P.S.D.
	38	4	P.T.B.
	22	—	P.S.P.
	12	—	P.D.C.
For M.D.B.	73	13	P.T.B.
	40	5	P.S.D.
	6	1	U.D.N.
	6	—	P.D.C.

6 There is a French translation of Institutional Act No. 3 in *Notes et Etudes* no. 3300 (17 June 1966) 37–8.

Chapter 20
1 *Correio da Manhã* (Rio de Janeiro: 2 Apr 1964).
2 A.M.C.B., collection Paulo Castello Branco, Rio de Janeiro. *Veja*, no. 187 (5 Apr 1972) 42.
3 *Jornal do Brasil* (Rio de Janeiro: 19, 20 May 1966). It is interesting that General Alvès Bastos, like Costa e Silva, was one of the group of officers who, unlike the 'Castellians' had not taken part in the Italian campaign.
4 *O Estado de São Paulo* (26 July 1966). General Olympio Mourão Filho was the first officer to cause his troops to march against President Goulart in 1964.

Chapter 21
1 *Rouba mas faz*, quoted *inter alia* by Skidmore, in *Politics in Brazil*, p. 68. The public did not find this surprising. One of the ex-governor's apologists had written: 'In Brazil there is only one option open to a politician: either he does nothing and is honest or he achieves something and is taken for a rogue'. Ferreira, H. Lopes Rodrigues, *Adhémar de Barros perante a Nação* (São Paulo. Tipografia Piratininga, 1954) p. 305. The élite in São Paulo, among whom Adhémar had made many enemies while he was still Getúlio Vargas' 'hatchet man' from 1938 to 1941, shed no tears for him. One of them, for example, the owner of the great daily *O Estado de São Paulo* had since that time always referred to him as A. de Barros in his newspaper.
2 The latter appointed Antonio Delfim Netto, a young economist of humble origins, born in 1929, as financial secretary. Netto won a good reputation in this position and as Finance Minister under Costa e Silva and Garrastazu Médici became the principal architect of Brazil's economic recovery after the departure of Roberto Campos.
3 At that time it looked as though Costa e Silva had ambitions in that direction.

4 Costa e Silva was immediately placed on the reserve with the rank of marshal.
5 Even so three ARENA deputies handed in unmarked voting papers and Colonel Peracchi Barcelos, former Head of the State militia, was elected by only 23 votes.
6 The eleven states in which elections were due to take place under the electoral law, and Alagoas where a fresh election had become necessary because the results of the voting in October 1965 had been challenged.
7 Alagoas: Antonio Lamenha Filho; Amazonas: Danilo Areosa; Bahia: Luiz Vianna Filho; Ceará: Plácido Castelo; Espírito Santo: Cristiano Dias Lopes; Pernambuco: Nilo Coelho; Piauí: Helvídio Nunes de Barros; Rio Grande do Sul: Peracchi Barcelos; Rio de Janeiro: Jeremias de Matos Fontes; São Paulo: Roberto de Abreu Sodré; Sergipe: Lourival Baptista.
8 Mato Grosso: Pedro Pedrossian; Rio Grande do Norte: Walredo Gurgel; Santa Catarina: Ivo Silveira.

Chapter 22
1 According to the indices of the FIESP, Federation of Industries of the State of São Paulo, industrial employment with a base of 100 for December 1963 had fallen to 83·5 in July 1965 and then rose to 101 in July 1966 but fell once more to 94·7 in December 1966.
2 The term 'denationalisation' is used here as understood in Brazil, where it means loss of national identity for the benefit of foreigners.
3 Gasparian, *Defesa da Economia*, p. 179.
4 Medina, *Desnacionalização*, p. 14.
5 Report of the Federal Bank of Brazil for 1965.
6 There also existed a very active black market, the rate on which was much higher.
7 It was not possible simply to block them, since the State had to be in a position to repay previous 'swaps'. There was a first phase during which it was legal to extend them in so far as they were twinned with a 289 operation for an equal amount. On 31 December 1964 the total value of these operations had fallen to U.S. $313 million and by 31 December 1965 only U.S. $123 million remained.
8 This organisation was to become the nucleus of the new Central Bank.
9 Evidence given by Roberto Campos before the Parliamentary Committee of Enquiry, cited by its rapporteur R. Medina, in *Desnacionalização*, p. 66.
10 Ibid.
11 For a loan at a nominal interest rate of 7 per cent the fixed charges were: outward stamp duty: 1 per cent on the value of the contract; interest: 7 per cent, stamp duty on transfer of interest: 1 per cent = 0·07 per cent of the value of the contract; tax on transferred interest: 25 per cent + supplement of 10 per cent on the total of the interest and the tax = approx. 2·7 per cent of the value of the contract; foreign exchange buying/selling turn, stamp duty on the accounting slip, commission, etc.: about 0·23 per cent; return stamp duty: 1 per cent of the contract; giving a total of 12 per cent. To this must be added devaluation which was dependent on the date of repayment but which during this period was of the order of 20 per cent per annum. Therefore for a transaction of this kind the cost of the loan came to something like 32 per cent per annum for the borrower rather than the 7 per cent written on the operation 289 agreement recorded in the Central Bank!

238 *Notes*

12 These are in fact companies registered under Brazilian law but owned by foreigners.
13 Balance of the 289s: U.S. $141·3 million at 31 December 1965. *Report of the Central Bank for 1965*, p. 133.
14 Gasparian, *Defesa da Economia*, p. 182.
15 Ibid., p. 188.
16 The expression was popularised by Stefan Zweig, in *Le Brésil, Terre d'Avenir* (New York: Editions de la Maison Française, 1942).
17 Medina *Desnacionalização*, pp. 52–3. Mathematically the thesis is irrefutable; two of the public utility companies purchased by the State represent a 'renationalisation' of U.S. $231 million whereas the total input of foreign risk capital in 1964–5 amounted to U.S. $172 million.
18 The Central Bank keeps a computerised up-to-date list of foreign capital invested in Brazil. It is compulsory to register such funds for the purpose of dividend transfer etc. It had taken several years to compile a reliable listing, for inflation and reinvestment make it difficult to value past investment in terms of hard currency. Nowadays this is the only possible basis for serious figuring, since all other sources consist of subjective estimates of the undefined 'value' of foreign enterprises, and this inevitably introduces unverifiable distortion factors.
19 The rapporteur of the Committee of Enquiry, Rubem Medina, extracted this data from *O Capital Estrangeiro no Brasil* (São Paulo: Editôra Banas, 1961). The base year is 1960. This very haphazard study says that there were 2030 foreign businesses, including 118 Swiss ones. In *Imagem do Brasil*, p. 158, the value of foreign investments is estimated at U.S. $4100 million, but Switzerland is not specifically mentioned, whereas with something like U.S. $300–400 million' worth of investment in Brazil the country must come third or fourth.

Chapter 23

1 Fernando Gasparian, in a talk given on 21 March 1966 to students of the 1965 class in the Faculty of Economic and Administrative Sciences of the University of São Paulo. Gasparian, *Defesa da Economia*, p. 264.
2 Law No. 4388/64.
3 Law No. 4506/64.
4 Ibid.
5 Law No. 4729/65.
6 The system was brought up to date on 25 October 1966 in the *National Tax Code* (Law No. 5172/66) and incorporated in the new Constitution of 1967.
7 In such conditions, if a misdemeanour consists of a simple mistake in interpreting a provision, not of fraud, it can be tempting to 'come to an arrangement' directly with the inspector, who is often able to find a quick legal way out of the problem thus avoiding the very real risk of seeing his colleagues at other levels in the tax administration take it over, with their charge sheets at the ready (this provision was cancelled by the Constitution of 1967, Article 196).
8 The gross tax charge includes taxes, duties, social contributions of all kinds, special deductions (such as equipment capital, 'education wage') and from 1967 onwards payments to the F.G.T.S. (Workers' Pension Fund). The net charges obtained by adding together (a) receipts from indirect taxes after deducting the item 'subsidies' from the G.N.P. and (b) receipts from direct taxes minus the item 'transfer to consumers'. 'O Brasil Cresce', *Realidade*, 111.

9 *Imagem do Brasil*, p. 76, and 'Implicit Deflator' of the Getúlio Vargas Foundation, *Conjuntura Econômica*, vol. 25, no. 9 (Sep 1971) 92.
10 *Time* (24 Apr 1972) 17.
11 These compulsory contributions are mixed; the workers' share is withheld from their wages by the employer and if he then does not pay it in as he should, he can use it to assist his liquidity.
12 Medina, *Desnacionalização*, p. 71.
13 Ibid., p. 102 (my italics).
14 Under the name of 'Cia de Navegação Lloyd Brasileiro, Lloydbras'.
15 *O Estado de São Paulo* (9 Nov 1966) 4.

Chapter 24
1 Detrez, Conrad, 'Pour une stratégie de la guerre révolutionnaire', foreword to Marighela, Carlos, *Pour la Libération du Brésil* (Paris: privately published, 1970) p. 32.
2 This happened to the dockers' trade union, which was dissolved in June 1966, among others.
3 The compulsory trade union tax, equal to one day's working pay per year, is automatically deducted from the pay of all blue-collar and white-collar workers. It provides a means of financing trade union activity through the intermediary of the Ministry of Labour which distributes the money to registered and approved organisations only.
4 From the name of the sheepskin that was placed for comfort between the saddle and the horse by horsemen in South Brazil.
5 Weffort, Françisco C., 'Education et Politique', preface to Freire, Paulo, *L'éducation: pratique de la liberté* (Paris: Les Editions du Cerf, 1971) p. 26.
6 The best known is Oswaldo Pacheco, who was elected to Congress on the list of the Brazilian Communist Party, which was then still legal, in 1945.
7 A group of Marxist students tried to take control of A.P. in 1963–4.
8 'We [the leaders of the Brazilian Communist Party] did not understand that the offensive of the Single Front and the relative strengthening of positions by the forces of the people imperilled reactionaries to unite and to press on faster with preparations for the coup d'Etat'. Romão, 'Perspective de la Lutte', p. 102.
9 *O Estado de São Paulo* (15 Aug 1964) 16.
10 Some figures may throw light on the problem of the trade unions: from 1964 to 1966 the number of national federations of workers together with that of the liberal professions rose from seven to eleven. They comprised 128 federations grouped under types of activity, five of them being for the liberal professions (in 1964 the corresponding figures were 122 and four). The trade unions making up the federations rose in number from 1879 to 2173 of which 124 represented the liberal professions. Unionised urban workers increased from 1,497,000 in 1964 to 1,683,000 in 1966 (including 55,000 engaged in the liberal professions). Since at the same time a count of urban workers showed about 8 million, those of them who were unionised represented only 21 per cent of the total.

Turning to the situation in the countryside we find that in 1969 the newly formed National Federation of Agricultural Workers (CONTAG) had 825 trade unions with a membership of only 120,000 agricultural workers. As there were more than 7 million rural wage-earners the proportion unionised was less than 2 per cent. Thus, taking Brazilian wage-earning classes as a whole, less than 15 per cent were unionised. Yet when the Revolution took place something like 45 per cent of industrial workers were already organised, which explains the attention that had to be given to them by the Government. Vinhas, *Estudos Sôbre*, pp. 259–61. The statistics quoted by Vinhas relate to 1964, 1965, 1966, 1967, 1969 and 1970, and not all of them are strictly comparable.

11 The up-dating of the social law (Decree Law No. 5452 of 1 May 1943) known as the *Consolidação das Leis do Trabalho* (Rio de Janeiro: Livraria Freitas Bastos S.A., 1950) was the work of one of the most faithful lieutenants of Getúlio Vargas, his Minister of Labour, Alexander Marcondes Filho.
12 Ibid., Articles 477, 478, pp. 80–1.
13 Ibid., Article 492, p. 83.
14 Ibid., Article 496, p. 84.
15 Ibid., Articles 497, 498, 501, pp. 84–5.
16 The Minister of Labour, Arnaldo Lopes Sussekind, described the situation which the Government proposed to correct in the following words: 'In the past the Brazilian worker did not realise the need for a trade union, because his individual rights were guaranteed by state action. He did not understand that in order that this legislation should progress, it was essential that a class organisation of his own should exist and consequently he was not attracted to it.' Address to the sixth Basic Course on Trade Union Management, São Paulo, 1965, quoted by Scantimburgo, *Tratado Geral*, pp. 247–8.
17 These measures include:

The law regulating the right to strike dated 1 July 1964 (Law No. 4330/64) whereby a strike, to be legal, must have been approved by a simple majority voting in secret, by a full meeting of a recognised trade union convened with at least ten days' notice and attended by two-thirds of the members at a first summons and one-third at a second summons. Once the resolution to strike had been approved, the employer (or the employers' organisation concerned) must be notified in writing of the decision and of the demands of the workers. A period of five days during which the employer and the trade union were to endeavour to reach agreement was compulsory before the strike could be started. In the case of essential services (public utilities, transport, funerals, hospitals, hotels, the food industry, chemists and key industries for the national defence, etc.) this period was extended to ten days. If however the reason for striking was non-payment of wages or non-compliance with a decision handed down under the labour laws, it was reduced to three days. Employers were forbidden to operate a lock-out, and if a foreign employer did so he could be expelled from the country.

The law introducing wage readjustment criteria (Decree No. 54,018 of July 1964) supplemented by Law No. 4725 of 13 July 1965 and Decree Law Nos. 15 and 17 dated 1 August 1966.

Law 4749 dated 12 August 1965 which laid down that the 'thirteenth monthly wage' which had been compulsory since 1962, would no longer be paid at the end of the year but in two equal parts, the first being payable between January and November (or if the employee preferred, just before his annual holidays of 20 working days) and the second part at the end of the year. These provisions avoided the liquidity crisis which was apt to hit most businesses at the end of December.

Law No. 4923 dated 23 December 1965 whereby a register held by the Ministry of Labour was instituted in which all engagements and dismissals of workers had to be entered. This information had to be supplied by businesses before the fifteenth of each month. This law also authorised companies temporarily to reduce working hours in crisis situations in association with the trade unions. But the pay slip must not be more than 25 per cent lower and then only on the strict understanding that the total remuneration of management was reduced by the same proportion.

A number of measures extending the application of the Labour Code to seamen and railwaymen (April 1966), developing assistance to those on strike (April 1966) and unifying the different agencies charged with administering social security into a single agency, the I.N.P.S., Instituto Nacional de Previdência Social (November 1966).
All these labour laws were consolidated by Decree Law No. 229 of 28 February 1967.

18 Fundo de Garantia do Tempo de Serviço.
19 Corresponding in round figures to the preceding rule of one month's wages per year of service.
20 'O Brasil Cresce', *Realidade*, 18. *Conjuntura Econômica*, vol. 26, no. 2 (Feb 1972) 180.
21 Individual voluntary agreements could be entered into with 'stable' workers based on at least 60 per cent of their existing rights; all such agreements had to be submitted to the Labour Courts for approval. In other words an employee who, for example, had 35 years' service and earned £100 per month could negotiate his hypothetical right of 35 × 2 months of his highest wage, equal to £7000, for a cash sum of at least 60 per cent of this entitlement, i.e. £4,200.
22 The Getúlio Vargas Foundation has published a study in which the cost to the employer of the social legislation adopted by Castello Branco is quantified. It should be noticed that in practice there were very few cases in which all the items detailed below applied cumulatively to the same employee.

First group	Percentage of wage
1. Social Security	8
2. SESI or SESC (social service)	1·5
3. SENAI or SENAC (apprenticeship)	1
4. INDA (National Agricultural Development Institute)	0·4
5. Social security on thirteenth months' salary	0·6
6. Family allowances	4·3
7. Education wage	1·4
8. Accident insurance	3
9. Length of service guarantee fund	8
	28·2

Second group	
10. End of week wage	18·4
11. Annual holidays	7·1
12. Official holidays	3·5
13. Notice in case of dismissal	2·2
14. Sickness payment	1·9
	33·1

	Percentage of wage
Third group	
15. Thirteenth monthly salary	10·6
16. Supplementary payment in the event of unfair dismissal	1·1
	11·7
17. Total incidence of groups 1 and 2	9·3
Total	82·3

Source: *A Guide to Investing in Brazil*, Washington, Brazilian Embassy (Mar 1969) p. 46.

23 Such as for instance the ideas of the sociologist Octavio Ianni which may be summarised as follows.
The aim of the labour policy of the new régime is:
  (a) To exclude the wage earning classes and in particular the proletariat from overall political decisions. With this object to do away with or radically reduce the involvement of 'trade unionism' in political events at federal, state and municipal level.
  (b) To control or destroy the possibility for bourgeois opposition groups of using the wage-earning class as a power base or acting as its spokesman.
  (c) To restore the control of the ruling class on the behaviour of the 'basic' factor of production by manipulating as far as possible the relative cost of the working force. For this purpose the principle of 'stability' was transformed into that of 'unemployment insurance' thus freeing businesses from a fixed, permanent charge. In other words, 'wage confiscation' was reintroduced by means of rigid, centralised control of wages policy and the trade union movement.
  (d) In sum to do away with 'mass politics' both as a technique for supporting the former régime and as an essential expression of populist democracy: 'For this purpose the law on strikes is changed by strictly limiting the extent to which it can be used as a weapon in support of economic or political demands, and class relations are recast legally and politically in new terms, thus changing the definition that prevailed before 1964.'

Ianni, Octavio, *O Colapso do Populismo no Brasil* (Rio de Janeiro: Editôra Civilização Brasileira, 1968) pp. 211–12.
24 In fact the correct date is 1966.
25 *Pau de Arara*, p. 69.
26 B.N.H., activity report for 1971. *Conjuntura Econômica*, vol. 26, no. 2 (Feb 1972) 179. At 31 December 1971, U.S. $ = Crz. 5·60 (buying) (ibid., p. 53).
27 Decree No. 54,018 of July 1964, Article 7: 'The readjusted wage will be calculated in such a way as to equal the average real wage for the last 24 months, multiplied by a coefficient representing the estimated increase in productivity during the preceding year, plus the amount allowed by the Government's financial programme to compensate the expected residual inflation.' Text supplemented by Law No. 4725 of July 1965. *A Economia Brasileira e suas Perspectivas* (Rio de Janeiro: APEC Editôra S.A., July 1967) p. 8.
28 *Fôlha de São Paulo* (2 Aug 1966) 9.

29 *Conjuntura Econômica*, vol. 24, no. 1 (Jan 1970) 18.
30 *A Economia Brasileira e suas Perspectivas*, pp. 8–9.
31 The author requested but was not granted the right to quote the source of the duplicated document dated 22 January 1971, vol. 1, 'Summary and Conclusions'; p. iii, par. 7, which is marked 'restricted circulation'.

According to Celso Furtado, 'from 1964 to 1970, on average, real minimum wages fell by 4 per cent per annum whilst average productivity (income per capita) rose at approximately 3 per cent per annum. Consequently in terms of its own productivity the cost of labour fell by approximately 60 per cent during the period.' Furtado, Celso, *Analise do 'Modelo' Brasileiro*, 2nd ed. (Rio de Janeiro: Editôra Civilização Brasileira, 1972) p. 38, note 27.
32 Maracãna, Rio de Janeiro, 170,000 places; Morumbi, São Paulo, 153,000 places; Mineirão, Belo Horizonte, 140,000 places; Beira-Rio, Porto Alegre, 120,000 places.

Chapter 25
1 The same cannot be said of the impression that he made on the thinking élite of the country, as was made clear to us in several interviews.
2 252 deputies of ARENA; one who had crossed over from the M.D.B. and was later expelled from the party: two outgoing deputies without party affiliation; 40 ARENA senators. 136 M.D.B. deputies and senators expressed their opposition by not being present when the vote was taken, and 39 by abstaining. Two ARENA senators, Afonso Arinos de Mello Franco and Mem de Sá, who was Castello Branco's Minister of Justice, were among the 41 abstentionists. The 255 deputies who voted for Costa e Silva had obtained 4·6 million votes in 1962, whereas the 136 'silent opposition' had gained 2·8 million.
3 Abraão had replaced Kubitschek who had been deprived of his position in 1965.
4 *Jornal do Brasil* (Rio de Janeiro: 4 Oct 1966).
5 In connection with these preparations he again went on a journey abroad where his engagements included being received by Pope Paul VI on 5 January 1967, giving rise to hope of an improvement in relations between the Government and the Church.
6 Or approximately 27 per cent of the population compared with 24·6 per cent in 1962. This proportion was as high as 39 per cent in the city of Rio de Janeiro and was more than 30 per cent in the State of São Paulo which has about 5 million electors. Two new factors explain the general increase in registered electors: the higher literary rate of those citizens who had reached the age of 18 since 1962 and the introduction of compulsory voting by women not in paid employment. (Women have had the vote since 1946, but until then voting was not compulsory except for women in jobs.)
7 He replaced Octavio Bilac Pinto who was appointed Ambassador to Paris.
8 Shortly afterwards Audoto Cardoso was nominated as a judge of the Supreme Court by Castello Branco.
9 Inquerito No. 709. The I.P.M. was led by Colonel Ferdinando de Carvalho.
10 By Law No. 4961/66 dated 4 May, Institutional Act No. 3 of 5 February 1966 and various supplementary acts.
11 Which avoided the traditional avalanche of electoral stickers, posters stuck all over the place, slogans hastily sketched and banners stretched across the streets.

12 Including the falsification of electoral lists or organised collection of electors.
13 Abstentions represented 22·8 per cent of the electoral body, a normal rate (it was 25 per cent in 1962); spoilt voting papers represented about 7 per cent of the votes which may be partly explained by the introduction of the single voting paper for the three ballots, an arrangement which may have confused electors; there were as many as 14 per cent voting papers not marked.
14 ARENA: 1·41 million votes; M.D.B.: 1·22 million votes.
15 For an analysis of the votes, published under the direction of Professor Orlando M. Carvalho, see *Revista Brasileira de Estudos Politicos*, nos 23, 24, July 1967 and January 1968.
16 *Guanabara*: M.D.B., 40; ARENA, 15. *Rio de Janeiro*: M.D.B., 34; ARENA, 28. *Rio Grande do Sul*: M.D.B., 28; ARENA, 27.
17 Normally one-third of the senate, or 22 senators, come up for re-election (one per state) but owing to the death of a senator from Ceará, the electors of this state had to choose two candidates instead of one.
18 Mendes de Almeida, Cândido A., 'O govêrno Castello Branco: paradigma e prognose', *Dados*, no. 2/3 (1967) 84–5.
19 Ibid., p. 85.
20 Ibid., p. 89. The successful M.D.B. candidate, Antonio Chagas Freitas, who obtained a majority of votes in the State of Guanabara (157,000 out of a total of 696,258 given to his party), is the owner of the largest chain of popular journals in Rio. In 1970 he became Governor of Guanabara.
21 Ibid., p. 87.
22 Ibid.

Chapter 26
1 The total number of cases of suspension of civil rights during the validity of Institutional Act No. 2 amounts to about 250.
2 Levi Carneiro, Themístocles Cavalcanti, Miguel Seabra Fagundes (who resigned on 5 August) and Orozimbo Nonato.
3 *Correio da Manhã* (Rio de Janeiro: 25 Aug 1966) special supplement.
4 Carlos Medeiros da Silva, co-author of the first Institutional Act with Francisco Campos, who also drafted the Constitution of 1937. This Constitution, which was also authoritarian, had been imposed by Getúlio Vargas without prior consultation.
5 In accordance with this law a mixed commission of seven senators and eleven deputies appointed on the proposal of heads of parliamentary groups in proportion to the number of representatives of the political parties (and hence with a clear majority from ARENA) was given 72 hours to approve or reject the draft. Next, four days were given to the two Chambers meeting in common session to discuss and adopt or reject the recommendation of the mixed commission. Only after this preliminary line up and after a period of five days, could amendments if supported by at least a quarter of the two Chambers be submitted to the commission which then had twelve days to give its judgment and a further twelve days for discussion in joint session. Voting had to take place without fail on 1 January and the law had to be promulgated on the twenty-fourth.
6 The town chosen by Kubitschek, who on 4 October was formally accused of corruption by a Brazilian tribunal, as his permanent residence. The text of the *Pact of Lisbon* was published on 19 November 1966 in the Brazilian press.

7 *Frente Ampla*.
8 The Brazilian Communist Party led by Luiz Carlos Prestes planned this formation. This caused Carlos Marighela, who later became leader of the A.L.N. (National Liberation Action) to resign from the executive committee of the Central Committee in December 1966. In a letter addressed to his 'Dear Comrades' he wrote: '... I wish to state publicly my will to fight as a revolutionary side by side with the masses; I signify also thereby my contempt for political bureaucratic and conventional chicanery, which is entrenched at the centre of affairs.' Marighela, *Pour la Libération*, p. 48.
9 Only two measures had been enacted before then. The first derived from Institutional Act No. 2 of 27 October 1965, Article 24 of which made the same judges responsible for investigating and sentencing offences committed by the press and it increased the period of time that had to elapse before such offences could no longer be investigated. Article 12 of the same act stated that the offence of 'subversion of the established order' named in paragraph 5 of Article 141 of the Constitution of 1946 could exist even though there had been no resort to 'violent meaures'. And Article 16 laid down that persons who had been deprived of their civil rights were not allowed to take part in 'demonstrations of a political nature'. Furthermore Supplementary Act No. 1 of 27 October 1965 set out the penalties for these offences, which could also be inflicted on the owners, managers and editors of information media in which any writings caught by these laws had been published. The second, a curious law, No. 5089 of 30 August 1966, forbade on moral grounds 'the printing and circulation of any publication likely to be read by children or adolescents which contains or exploits themes of crime, terror or violence.'
10 Article 150, paragraph 8: 'The publication of thoughts, political or philosophic convictions and the dissemination of information is free and not subject to censorship, except in the case of public shows and amusements, and everyone is responsible under the terms of the law for any misuse of this freedom. The right of reply is guaranteed. The publication of books, newspapers and periodicals does not require government authorisation. Nevertheless, propaganda in favour of war, subversion of order or race or class prejudice will not be tolerated.'
11 Article 166: 'The following are forbidden to earn or administer journalistic undertakings of any kind whatsoever, including television and radio broadcasting:

I foreigners
II companies with bearer shares
III companies whose shareholders or associates include foreigners or corporate bodies, with the exception of political parties.

Paragraph 1. Only Brazilians born in Brazil may exercise overall responsibility or give intellectual administrative policy guidance in enterprises to which this article refers.

Paragraph 2. While maintaining freedom of thought and information, the law may set out other conditions for the reorganisation and operation of journalistic radio broadcasting and television organisations in the interest of the democratic régime and the fight against subversion and corruption.'

12 At that time the written press was governed by Law No. 2083 of 12 November 1953, whereas radio and television were subject to the Telecommunications Code Law No. 4117 of 27 August 1962.

13 Costella, Antonio F., *O Contrôle da Informação no Brasil* (Petrópolis: Editôra Vozes, 1970) p. 136.
14 In order to avoid that under existing legislation the law was automatically promulgated in its original form by the President, it was necessary for Parliament to have voted on the new text before midnight on 22 January. As the fateful hour approached, all the clocks in Parliament were temporarily stopped and were only started again after the vote had been taken; so in strict accuracy it was taken very early on the twenty-third. The law was numbered 5250 and was published on 9 February 1967.

Shortly afterwards a new paragraph was added to Article 3 of this regulation, which reproduced Article 166 of the Constitution word for word and by a decree-law. This new paragraph made it possible for foreigners to become owners or managers of journalistic undertakings dealing exclusively with the 'scientific, technical, cultural and artistic spheres'.

This decree caused some reactions, because the *Time-Life* affair (in which that American group took a camouflaged investment in the holding company of *O Globo* dealing with press, radio and television) had touched public opinion on the raw and led to the establishment of a commission of inquiry on 'the infiltration of foreign capital into the information media'. But Castello Branco thought that his decree was needed in the interests of the scientific and technical development of the country, and he did not revoke it.
15 Law No. 5250 of 9 February 1967, Article 23.
16 This decree-law, No. 314 dated 13 March 1967, gives the state powers to watch very closely activities considered to be subversive. Such activities include the dissemination of false reports which may imperil the good name, the authority, the credit or the prestige of Brazil; insults against the President or the Federal Government; incitement to class war, to collective disobedience to the laws, to hostility towards the armed forces, to the commission of crimes against national security or to paralysing the public services. These offences were made subject to investigation and punishment by military tribunals which would prevail over any other courts even if the offences had been committed via the press, radio or television.
17 Nobre, José de Freitas, *Lei da Informação* (São Paulo: Editôra Saraiva, 1968) p. 3.
18 The author came to this conclusion as a result of several interviews with the representatives of the press at Rio de Janeiro and São Paulo and it is confirmed by the following quotation from one of the leading Brazilian journalists working for the *Jornal do Brasil*, Antônio Callado (who was deprived of his civil rights in April 1969): '... Nevertheless, until 13 December 1968 [when Institutional Act No. 5 was issued] they [the military] had allowed freedom of the press'. Combret, François de, *Les Trois Brésil* (Paris: Editions Planète, 1971) p. 43.
19 In this vote there were 223 yes's and 110 no's in the Lower House and 37 yes's, 17 no's and 7 abstentions in the Senate. 107 ARENA deputies, while having to vote for the motion, expressed their reserve by demanding the right to introduce amendments as soon as the first session of the new Parliament (to which they had also been elected) opened on 15 March 1967, the date on which the Constitution came into force.
20 A.M.C.B., Paulo Castello Branco Collection, Rio de Janeiro. Photocopy published by *Veja* (5 Apr 1972) 39.

This same publication photocopied extracts of the twenty handwritten pages of Castello Branco containing the 99 notes made by the President on the preliminary draft of the Constitution, belonging to the Luiz Vianna Filho Collection at Salvador. A part of the fifteenth note is revealing as to Castello Branco's deep convictions: on the part played by the National Security Council, a consultative body, he wrote, 'It advises the President but he, after listening to its recommendation, may take a decision contrary to the unanimous opinion of its members. This arrangement is very arbitrary and could become a weapon for authoritarian, personalist rule. We shall have to discuss this.' (ibid.)

21 The case of Adhémar de Barros (below) was not an isolated one and according to the Finance Minister, in 1966 the Federal Government had to pay out more than 150 million cruzeiros (about U.S. $67.6 millions) abroad and 'several hundred millions' inside Brazil over and above the budget in order to meet obligations entered into by states. Moreover in order to cope with the administrative excesses of the latter, the Central Bank and the Finance Ministry paid Crz. 143.6 million (about U.S. $64.7 million) since otherwise 'the banking illiquidity of 1966... would have provoked a banking crisis'. Bulhões, 'Financial Recuperation', pp. 165, 166, 186.

22 These bonds were subject to monetary correction and they had a term of twenty years. *Constituição da República Federativa do Brasil, de 24 de Janeiro de 1967, Emenda constitucional no. 1*, no. 1116, Departemento de Imprensa Nacional (1969), Article 161.

We should state here that in order to simplify reading we refer directly to the revised edition of the Constitution after the incorporation of the amendments of 13 December 1968 (Institutional Act No. 5, Article 2, par. 1) and of 14 October 1969 (Institutional Act No. 16, Article 3). There is a French translation of the Constitution of 1967, in its original form, in *Notes et Etudes*, no. 3512 (31 Oct 1968).

23 *Constituição de 1967*, Article 163.
24 Ibid., Article 166.
25 Ibid., Article 165.
26 Ibid., Article 154 (italics added). We would stress that this fight against dishonesty in any form was particularly close to Castello Branco's heart and he would have liked to go even further. In a handwritten note which he sent to the Minister of Justice he asked the following question: 'Can unlawful self-enrichment be punished by the death penalty?' A.M.C.B., Luiz Vianna Filho Collection, Salvador, photocopy published by *Veja*, no. 187 (5 Apr 1972) 37.
27 *Constituição de 1967*, Article 154.
28 The immunity of parliamentarians and other elected persons was erased from the Constitution by the amendment of 17 October 1969 after incidents that took place in Parliament in December 1968 (see above).
29 *Constituição de 1967*, Article 153, par. 15.
30 I The federal administration. II basic principles. III planning programme budgets, a financial programme. IV ministerial supervision. V auxiliary activity systems. VI the Presidents of the Republic. VII ministers and their respective spheres of authority. VIII national security. IX the armed forces. X administrative, financial and accounting procedures. XI civilian personnel. XII standards for the award of tenders. XIII administrative reform. XIV special co-ordination measures. XV general arrangements. XV general arrangements. XVI temporary arrangements. XVII final arrangements.
31 The text was somewhat modified, especially as regards national security, by Decree Law No. 900 of 29 September 1969.
32 Roberto Campos' extraordinary ministry was promoted to a full ministry

and thereafter constituted by itself a complete sector under the title Ministry of Planning and General Co-ordination. The I.P.E.A. Foundation (Instituto de Pesquisa Econômico-Social Aplicada) was established to put in hand studies, research and analyses in the economic and social spheres, required for planning.

33 Political sector: justice (which controlled the civilian police forces); foreign relations.
Planning sector: planning and overall co-ordination.
Economic sector: finance; transport; agriculture; trade and industry; mines and energy; internal.
Social sector: education and culture; labour and social security; health; communications.
Military sector: Army (as the War Ministry was now called); Navy; Air Force.
There were also four extraordinary ministries: administrative reform; science and technology; supply; and defence (charged with preparing for the amalgamation of the three ministries in the military sector).

34 Decree Law No. 200 of 25 February 1967, Article 40.
35 Ibid., Article 44.
36 Ibid., Article 29, par. 3.

Chapter 27

1 *Estado de São Paulo* (6 Jan 1970), quoting Roberto Campos.
2 'Stagflation', which has been experienced in other countries as well.
3 The fact is that fiscal and monetary measures adopted with the object of checking inflation are almost bound to result in temporary unemployment and in a decrease of production in those branches of the economy that were artificially boosted by inflationary prices or by excess demand caused, either by the formation of speculative stocks or by defensive purchases on the part of the consumer anxious to protect himself against decreases in the value of his money. Since any austerity policy while re-establishing confidence in the currency inevitably causes demand to contract in such a situation, supply is compelled to come into line and unit costs of production increase. At that point demand inflation is changed into cost inflation, which leads to a change in the measures required to effect recovery. And although the government economists and their detractors were both agreed on the theory of the matter, they differed in their evaluations of the point in the cycle that Brazil had then reached; it was undeniably difficult to appraise the exact moment at which the change of treatment should in fact be introduced. The issue is further clouded by the groans of the producers who, before resigning themselves to the often painful sacrifices entailed in adapting to the existing demand, exert whatever pressure they can to persuade the politicians to end the restrictive measures, on the pretext of saving the country from a stoppage of the economy.
4 'Aquarela do Brasil', a popular song by Ary Barroso.
5 See Fiechter, Georges A., 'Critères d'évaluation des effets des investissements privés suisses sur le développement', *Les investissements privés suisses dans le Tiers Monde*, duplicated (Geneva: Graduate Institute of International Studies, 1971) pp. 98–104.
6 Daland, *Brazilian Planning*, p. 199.
7 The ideal characteristics of bureaucracy according to Weber can be summarised as follows: rationality, hierarchical authority, absence of personality cult, formalism, obedience to rational roles, a sense of pur-

pose, legitimacy, professional training, a career-ideal based on public service, a monistic philosophy of administrative relations and a faith in the bureaucratisation of society.
8 The Military also saw in it a means of achieving the 'integration of the territory' and the 'colonisation of unoccupied land' which are basic elements in the doctrine of national security.
9 See Riggs, Fred A., *Administration in Developing Countries: The Theory of Prismatic Society* (Boston: Houghton Mifflin, 1964).
10 Daland, *Brazilian Planning*, p. 210.
11 Waterston, Albert, *Development Planning: Lessons of Experience* (Baltimore: Johns Hopkins Press, 1965) p. 6.
12 Cardoso, Fernando Henrique, 'Aspectos Políticos do Planejamento', *Planejamento no Brasil*, ed. Betty Mindlin Lafer (São Paulo: Editôra Perspectiva, 1970) pp. 183, 184.
13 Jaguaribe, 'Stabilité Sociale', pp. 603–23.
14 A. Cândido Mendes de Almeida was a councillor of President Jânio Quadros.
15 Mendes de Almeida, 'O govêrno Castello Branco', pp. 64–5.
16 Ibid., p. 67.
17 See letter from Castello Branco to his son and his grandchildren, below.

Chapter 28
1 An opinion survey carried out in the five main urban centres of the country. *Manchete* (11 Mar 1967).
2 *Notes et Etudes*, nos 3749–50 (30 Dec 1970) 7.
3 The composition of this cabinet was known from 17 February onwards:

Serving officers
Army: General Aurelio de Lyra Tavares, born in 1905. Former Commandant of the Superior War College, he was useful as a bridge between the 'Sorbonne' and the hard liners.
Navy: Admiral Augusto H. Rademacker Grünewald, born in 1905. He was one of the three members of the revolutionary High Command which enacted Institutional Act No. 1 in April 1964.
Air Force. Air Marshal Marcio de Souza e Mello, born in 1906. Passed through the Superior War College; left Castello Branco's cabinet rather than accept the President's decision concerning the Fleet Air Arm.
Transport: Colonel Mario Andreazza, born in 1920, had passed through the Superior War College and had been working together with Costa e Silva since 1964.
Interior: Major-General Affonso de Albuquerque Lima, born in 1909. Had passed through the Superior War College, was formerly Director-General of Engineers and Signals, and represented the nationalist wing of the Army.
Labour and Social Security: Colonel Jarbas Gonçalves Passarinho, born in 1920. He was one of the rising stars of the régime and his popularity had ensured a brilliant performance in the senatorial elections in November 1966 for the State of Pará.
Military Household: Brigadier Jaime Portela de Melo, born in 1911. He was one of Costa e Silva's co-workers at the War Ministry.
National Intelligence Service: Major-General Emilio Garrastazu Médici, born in 1905. Formerly Military Attaché in Washington, he was called

to this key post as being a personal friend of the President. He replaced the well-known General Golbery whom Castello Branco had just appointed to the 'Cour des Comptes' and nobody foresaw that he would replace Costa e Silva in the presidential palace.

Reserve Officers

Mines and energy: Colonel José Costa Cavalcanti, born in 1918. Former Military Attaché in Washington and deputy for Pernambuco (ARENA).

Trade and industry: General Edmundo de Macedo Soares, born in 1901. His credentials were remarkable; he had been the work-horse of the Brazilian steel industry, Governor of the State of Rio de Janeiro and was elected President of the Federation of Industry both in 1964 and 1966.

Technicians

Finance: Professor Antonio Delfim Netto, born in 1929. A brilliant unmarried man who had been Financial Secretary to the State of São Paulo after Adhémar de Barros' departure.

Planning and general co-ordination: Helio Marcos Penna Beltrão, born in 1916. Director of a department store in Rio de Janeiro with countrywide ramifications, he headed the administrative planning of Carlos Lacerda's government in the State of Guanabara.

Justice: Professor Luis Antonio da Gama e Silva, born in 1913. He was Minister of Justice during the few days before the Castello Branco government was set up. Rector of the University of São Paulo, this international jurist was also a judge at the Permanent Court of Arbitration at the Hague.

Agriculture: Ivo Arzua Pereira, born in 1925. Civil engineer who had been Mayor of Curitiba, the capital of Paraná, until 1966.

Health: Dr Leonel Tavares Miranda de Albuquerque, born in 1903. He was doctor and on very friendly terms with the President.

Communications: Professor Carlos Furtado de Simas of the Polytechnic College of Bahia. He had been Director of Telephones at Salvador.

Politicians

Foreign affairs: José de Magalhães Pinto, born in 1914. A nationalist banker, formerly Governor of Minas Gerais for which state he was a deputy (ARENA, ex-U.D.N.).

Education and culture: Tarso de Morais Dutra, born in 1914. A lawyer, deputy for Rio Grande do Sul (ARENA, ex-P.S.D.), appointed in compensation for having been prevented by Castello Branco from standing as a candidate for the post of governor of his state.

Civil Household: Rondon Pacheco, born in 1918. He was secretary of ARENA and Deputy of Minas Gerais (ARENA, ex-U.D.N.).

It is noteworthy that Costa e Silva made virtually no use of the extremely wide political experience of Vice-President Pedro Aleixo, born in 1901 and formerly leader of the majority and Minister of Education; no doubt Costa e Silva considered that he was too strongly identified with the old régime.

4 In the above order they were, Ministers Rademacker, Passarinho, Lyra Tavares, Albuquerque Lima, Souza e Mello, Cavalcanti, Portela, Médici, Macedo Soares, Andreazza.
5 Schneider, *Political System of Brazil*, p. 270.
6 For instance, the Minister of Labour promised to increase the workers'

purchasing power and to revoke Decree No. 293 of Castello Branco which had given 'industrial accidents insurance' to the private sector, but the Minister for Industry would have nothing to do with this. The Education Minister said that he would allow all candidates who had passed the university entrance exams to be admitted to the University, although there were neither sufficient places nor sufficient teaching staff. The Minister of Mines and Energy wanted to set up an atomic power station and his colleague the Minister of the Interior announced huge investments in the north-east and in Amazonia. Meanwhile the Minister of Transport revived the idea of a bridge joining Rio de Janeiro to the town of Niteroi, capital of the State of Rio de Janeiro and wanted to have the road between Brasilia and Belem surfaced with asphalt.

Delfim Netto, who on 17 April and 2 May 1967 took steps to lighten the incidence of tax and to reduce interest rates, retorted that these projects would not be allowed to proceed unless they could be financed by loans from abroad.

7 Ipanema is the district of Rio de Janeiro in which Castello Branco lived.
8 For example, stung by Roberto Campos' criticism of his views, Delfim Netto said at this time: 'Putting an economic policy into practice calls for a fair amount of luck, a great deal of skill and very hard work. When one is using solutions based on hypotheses it is only reasonable to admit that there are margins of error. One cannot help being worried about people who believe they alone know the way of salvation.' *O Estado de São Paulo* (21 Apr 1967).
9 The question was who should preside over the joint sessions of the Chamber and the Senate. Was this the task of Vice-President Pedro Aleixo or that of the President of the Senate Auro de Moura Andrade? Even if some people saw in this dilemma a chance to open discussion on revision of the Constitution, the obscure by-ways of the dispute and the differences that blew up within ARENA rightly alienated public opinion. The hard liners saw in them arguments in favour of closing down Parliament. Finally Auro de Moura Andrade was posted to Madrid as ambassador, and this settled the question in favour of Pedro Aleixo.
10 Adhémar de Barros went into exile again, and died in Paris on 13 March 1969.
11 *Jornal do Brasil* (Rio de Janeiro: 9 Sep 1966, 17 May 1967). See also the book by the journalist Moreira Alvès (who was elected Deputy for Guanabara for the M.D.B. in 1966) whom the Government sought to prevent from taking his seat: Moreira Alvès, Márcio, *Torturas e Torturados* (Rio de Janeiro: Editôra Artenova, 1966).
12 *Jornal do Brasil* (Rio de Janeiro: 25 May 1967).
13 Francisco.

Chapter 29

1 Delfim Netto was secretary of the Associação Comercial de São Paulo (the employers' trade association) before becoming Financial Secretary to the State of São Paulo in 1966 and Minister of Finance in 1967. His diagnosis of the Brazilian economy is set out in a work that had been published the year before: Delfim Netto, Antonio, *Planejamento para o Desenvolvimento Econômico* (São Paulo: Editôra Pioneira, 1966).
2 Ministerio do Planejamento e Coordenação Geral, *Diretrizes de Govêrno, Programa Estratégico de Desenvolvimento* (Rio de Janeiro: July 1967), followed by *O Programa Estratégico de Desenvolvimento, 1968–1970* (Rio de Janeiro: June 1968). For an interesting comment see Alvès,

Denysard O. and Sayad, João, 'O Plano Estratégico de Desenvolvimento (1968–1970)', *Planejamento no Brasil*, pp. 91–109.
3 See below.
4 These investments were quantified in total, having regard both to the limits of the capacity for saving and imports and to the need for reconciling expansion with a reasonable rate of inflation, by means of a compatibility model. The results were then broken down into sectors.
5 Alvès and Sayad, 'O Plano Estratégico', p. 97.
6 Prepared by the technicians of I.P.E.A. (which was set up by Roberto Campos), the *PED* made considerable use of the experience acquired in working out the Ten-Year Plan. One important innovation was the setting up of a system of monitoring results which enabled those responsible to react quickly and to rectify their aim in case of need.
7 Growth was at first estimated at about 6 per cent per annum and then increased to 7 or 8 per cent.
8 This is by no means certain, the more so as the *PED* does not rank the priority 'investment blocks' in any hierarchy of value.
9 The long-term viability of this project also required that the ample labour available should not consist only of 'hands' but of 'workers' who had had a minimum of industrial training. The *PED* did not have a large enough education investment programme to meet this requirement. Nevertheless this gap was not in practice important because it was filled by President Médici's plan *Metas e Bases para a Ação de Governo* (Rio de Janeiro: Presidencia de Republica, I.B.G.E., Sep 1970).
10 Delfim Netto was a past master in acting on the economic situation in ways that would take effect immediately. He made brilliant use of the possibilities with which monetary policy provided him, and he juggled cleverly with instruction regarding credit and the incidence of taxation. His ability to do this was still further strengthened by the appointment on 6 February 1968 of his direct collaborator Ernani Galvêas as President of the Central Bank, followed on 10 February by the appointment of the right-hand man of the Minister of Planning, João Paulo dos Reis Velloso, to head up one of the departments in the Central Bank.

For example, to give satisfaction to the nationalists he caused the Central Bank to publish Resolution 53 on 11 May 1967, compelling the financial institutions to reserve at least half of the total value of their credit operations for Brazilian individuals or companies with a majority of Brazilian shareholders; to increase the flow of working capital and to reply to attacks against Instruction 289, Instruction 63 was issued on 21 August authorising both investment and commercial banks to make direct borrowings abroad and reflect them into Brazil; to help finance agriculture, he had Resolution 69 approved by the National Economic Council on 22 September 1967. This compelled the banks to invest 10 per cent of their total deposits in rural credit operations. (On 2 May he lowered the maximum rate of bank interest from 36 per cent per annum to 24 per cent, but for such credits the rate was not to exceed 12 per cent, or 10 per cent in the case of agricultural co-operatives.) To halt the outflow of foreign exchange, the Resolution of the Central Bank dated 17 August 1967 also required every purchaser to identify himself and submit his tax receipt so that a check could be made to see that the amount asked for and the income declared were in agreement. On 29 December the rate of exchange of the dollar was raised from Crz. 2·70 to Crz. 3·20, a devaluation of 18·8 per cent. (The previous devaluation had taken place on 8 February 1967.) On 3 January 1968, by Resolutions 81–4 and by Circular 111, the Central Bank closed the Bureaux de

Change (which were operating a black market in foreign exchange) and allowed thereafter only banks which met certain criteria to operate in the exchange market. The most important step in this field was taken on 21 August 1969 when Delfim Netto adopted the policy of flexible rates for the cruzeiros which he had just subjected to a fresh devaluation of 13.4 per cent, and secured the agreement of the I.M.F. to this step. Thenceforward, Brazilian currency moved at irregular intervals (between 30 and 60 days) in step with the development of the cost of living (in accordance with indices weighted by a number of factors including the rate of inflation of so-called hard currencies). These mini-devaluations virtually eliminated speculation on the exchanges (which certain informed persons had previously used to enrich themselves) and allowed exporters to expand their sales and receipts.

11 *Conjuntura Econômica* (Jan 1970) 5, 18, 33. (Index of cost of living in the State of Guanabara.)

Chapter 30
1 The light plane in which he was returning from the estate of the writer Raquel de Queiros was struck by a jet T-33 trainer which however managed to land safely after the accident. By an irony of fate, the military aircraft was piloted by the son of General Alfredo Souto Malan, a 'Sorbonnard' of long standing and a close friend of the President. Castello was 67 years old.
2 *Tribuna da Imprensa* (Rio de Janeiro: 19 July 1967), Castello Branco had suspended the civil rights of Fernandes just before the 1966 parliamentary elections, thus depriving him of a seat in parliament for Guanabara which he would undoubtedly have won.
3 He was later transferred from the island to the backwoods of the State of São Paulo. For his self-justifying version of these events see Fernandes, Hélio, *Recordações de um Desterrado em Fernando de Noronha* (Rio de Janeiro: Editôra da Tribuna da Imprensa, 1967).
4 A leading conservative daily paper published in Rio de Janeiro.
5 Election as president of the Army, Navy or Air Force Club is indisputable proof of an officer's popularity with his companions in arms.
6 Kubitschek, who had returned to Brazil, thought it better to leave the country again on 12 September after having refused to reply to a summons from the Federal Police (which was issued with Costa e Silva's agreement) asking him to state the reasons for his political activity in connection with the 'enlarged front'. He returned a few weeks later but lived under the threat of house arrest if he engaged in political activity again.
7 *Dados*, no. 4 (1968) 212.
8 *Jornal do Brasil* (Rio de Janeiro: 17 Dec 1967).
9 Among which may be mentioned two interviews between Carlos Lacerda and the United States Ambassador, John W. Tuthill, which disturbed the nationalists and a speech made by Lacerda on 15 March, the first anniversary of the Costa e Silva government, in which he accused the Head of the Military Household, General Jaime Portela, of having usurped power on behalf of the Army and of being the real head of state.
10 Before being deprived of his civil rights in April 1969, Antonio Callado wrote that the left in Brazil 'paradoxically managed to be non-existent and divided'. Speaking about the two leaders in the north-east, Miguel Arraes and Francisco Julião, who were neither allies nor friends before the military imprisoned them together for six months in the same cell,

he added: 'This is almost like a fairy story ... military tyrannies nourish a stupidity so stupendous that it borders on the creative.' He also referred in this publication, which was written in March 1967, i.e. after the new press laws, to 'five-star animals' who finally seized power on 1 April 1964. Callado, Antonio, 'Les Ligues paysannes du Nord-Est brésilien', *Les Temps Modernes*, 23rd year, no 257 (Oct 1967) 751, 752, 756.

Chapter 31
1 See on this subject: Castello Branco, Carlos, 'Como Pensa O Congresso (e Como Votaria Se Pudesse)', *Realidade* (Dec 1967) 30–42. The author, who is not related to the former President, was undoubtedly the best informed political commentator in Brazil. He was attached to the *Jornal do Brasil* office in Brasilia.
2 Costa e Silva then used his authority to make his Minister of Mines and Energy responsible for all questions concerning nuclear power.
3 Superintendência do Desenvolvimento do Nordeste and Superintendência do Desenvolvimento da Amazônia. The opening up of Amazonia, which represents 60 per cent of the territory of the Republic and yet has no more than 5 per cent of Brazil's population, is one of the foremost preoccupations of the nationalists among the Military. Albuquerque Lima appeared to believe that foreign powers would do anything to gain control of those regions and he gave expression to his views in the Chamber on 13 March 1968 when he condemned the plan presented by Herman Kahn's Hudson Institute involving the creation of a network of large lakes in Amazonia.
4 This zone of 10,000 sq. km was established by decree on 25 August 1967 and on the twenty-ninth of the same month Costa e Silva set out the statutory prerogatives it would enjoy. It quickly became one of the most active centres of contraband traffic in Brazil, while slowly moving towards the goal for which it was designed – industrialisation of Amazonia.
5 Development Organisation for the West-Central Region (States of Goiás and Mato Grosso) set up on 1 December 1967.
6 Named after Marshal Cândido da Silva Rondon who founded the Indians' Protection Department. Members of the Rondon Order pledge themselves to protect the Indians and to help in preserving them. The Rondon Project was a definite success among students and was extended to other parts of Brazil. Since 1969 about 10,000 young people have taken part.

Pierre and Renée Gosset describe the Rondon Project as follows: 'From now onwards each university in a coastal city sends its boy and girl students in small groups with a teacher for one month a year in what are given the high-sounding name of Campuses of the Interior, which are in fact rudimentary centres in areas which hitherto have been remote from progress, to carry out limited projects in health, education, medicine or agriculture. It is the practical down-to-earth complement to their university training, free of any paternalistic bias that would only be a hindrance to progress ... And it really seems as if these young city dwelling undergraduates have taken to it. Not a few, having discovered for the first time what the interior of their own country is like and how vast is its potential, have decided to go back and live there. Others, after having worked in the locality with the Army or the pioneers or in agricultural co-operatives, schools or rural hospitals, return with very different views on Brazil and its problems.' *Journal de Genève* (1 Sep 1972) 17.
7 When the Revolution took place it looked as if the Government might give up Brasilia notwithstanding the enormous investment which the

building of the city had called for (about 1000 million dollars). A reliable source has told the author in confidence that when Castello Branco was questioned on this subject by some civilian leaders who wanted to stay in Rio de Janeiro he simply replied: 'As an officer I have always exercised my command from the headquarters of my unit. Well, I believe that Brasilia is the capital of this country. So we shall go there.' This good military logic is said to have saved Brasilia which at 1 September 1970 had 546,015 inhabitants. *Sinopse,* p. 56.
8 Myhr, 'Brazil', p. 259.
9 A title given to judges.
10 15 December 1967, reproduced by *Ultima Hora* (Rio de Janeiro: 20 Dec 1967) 8.
11 *O Cruzeiro* (9 Dec 1967).
12 We may note in passing that in Brazil the Navy is considered as an arm mainly reserved for the 'sons of good families'.
13 Alexandrino de Paulo Freitas Serpa.
14 See *O Globo* (Rio de Janeiro: 27 Nov 1967).
15 A first group of urban guerillas, taken by surprise whilst training, was destroyed in April 1967 on the frontier of Minas Gerais. A second group was destroyed in September in similar circumstances. In June, the headquarters of the Second Army at São Paulo were attacked, and one death resulted. In September a soldier was killed, also at São Paulo.

Chapter 32
1 Myhr, Robert O., 'Brazil', *Students and Politics in Developing Nations*, ed. Donald K. Emmerson (New York: Praeger, 1968) p. 265.
2 Until 1964 Petrobrás was one of the main sources of the 'special fund' of U.N.E. Ibid., p. 265.
3 Ibid., p. 266.
4 Ibid.
5 Ibid.
6 The part played by secondary school pupils who were members of the União Brasileira dos Estudantes Secundários (U.B.E.S.) should also be noted.
7 Law No. 4464 of 9 November 1964. It was known as the Suplicy Law after the name of the Minister of Education, and was soon regarded with considerable disfavour by a good number of students.
8 Myhr, 'Brazil', p. 259,
9 Ibid.
10 All these statistics are taken from ibid., pp. 256–60.
11 Wedge, Bryant, *Problems in Dialogue: Brazilian University Students and the United States* (Princeton, N.J.: Institute for the Study of National Behaviour, 1965) pp. 154–5.
12 Soares, Glaucio A. D., 'The Active Few: Student Ideology and Participation in Developing Countries', *Comparative Education Review*, x, no. 2 (June 1966) 212.
13 The programme that was suggested looked towards lessening the traditional preponderance of the humanities and concentrating investment on scientific and technical training. Although some of the students were against it, this plan meets the needs of a modernising government, which must have enough technically trained manpower to bring about economic growth since, as Alfred Sauvy has observed, 'It costs much less to train a sociologist than to create the economic sub-structure needed to give him employment'. *Le Monde* (Paris: 8 Aug 1972) 12.

14 The prior, Frei Chico (Rev. Francisco de Araujo), and a number of priests including some American citizens were afterwards arrested and then freed.
15 Calabouço.
16 Edson Luis Lima Souto. About twenty people were also wounded. The state military police was on a full alert as students had promised that violent demonstrations would take place to mark 1 April, the anniversary of the Revolution.
17 Negrão de Lima who was himself a member of the M.D.B.
18 *Jornal do Brasil* (Rio de Janeiro: 31 Mar 1968) special illustrated number.
19 This loyal friend of Castello Branco who was appointed a general in March 1968 was shortly afterward placed in command of the 200,000 men in the twenty-two State militias before heading up the Military Academy of Agulhas Negras. He was a specialist in politically delicate missions such as the closure of Parliament in 1966. His report is divided into two parts: (a) relations between the government and the students; (b) gaps in education.
20 12 and 16 April respectively.
21 Law No. 5439.
22 At least one policeman and two civilians. Nobody who experienced these demonstrations will ever forget how tense they were. In the central artery of Rio de Janeiro, Avenida Rio Branco, drowned in clouds of tear gas, groups of students with great mobility (and seemingly well trained) infiltrated between the ranks of the police. Perched on the roofs of some buildings, some of the more excited ones bombarded the mounted police squadrons with whatever missiles came to hand, stones, directories, bottles and even typewriters, while the horses slipped on marbles thrown down between their feet by the demonstrators.
23 Including Jean-Marc von der Weid, a Brazilian of Swiss origin who became the leader of U.N.E. after being freed. He was later arrested again and tortured.
24 See below.
25 The interview given by the President of U.N.E., Luis Travassos, published under the title 'They want to overthrow the Government' in the July number of the review *Realidade* of São Paulo, did not make the atmosphere any less tense.
26 On 11 and 17 July 1968.
27 For instance on 21 August the Chamber of Deputies rejected by 198 votes to 145 a bill for giving an amnesty to students and workers who had been arrested for involvement in the demonstrations.
28 The police had taken photographs of many of the demonstrators during the preceding months and by various means had obtained some information from the students who had been arrested. One of the leaders of the March movement, Vladimir Palmeira, the son of an ARENA senator, was arrested on 2 August with some of his friends. On the fifteenth the Supreme Court refused to grant him Habeas Corpus, which was however granted on 12 December 1968. About 300 students were arrested in São Paulo on 4 August and 500 at Rio de Janeiro on 6 August. On 30 August the University of Belo Horizonte was closed after the police had raided it.
29 For example on 8 October clashes with the police took place in São Paulo and Rio de Janeiro and resulted in one dead and several wounded. On 22 and 23 October in Rio 'protest days' resulted in at least three deaths (a student and two workers).
30 The police occupied the university and dealt brutally with students,

professors and some members of parliament who went there to try to get their children out. The Rector, Caio Benjamin Dias, handed in his resignation but this was not accepted by Costa e Silva who instructed the head of the S.N.I., the future President Médici, to carry out an inquiry. Parliament appointed its own commission which concluded on 28 December that what had happened amounted to a 'premeditated show of force', an 'undue use of firearms' and a 'violation of parliamentary immunities and of the Constitution'.

31 Decree No. 62,461 of 25 March 1968. The last readjustment of the minimum wage had taken place on 12 February 1967. From January to December 1967 the cost of living in the city of Rio de Janeiro rose by 30·4 per cent (index given by the Getúlio Vargas Foundation). Inflation itself had been at the rate of 25 per cent during this period according to data supplied by the Finance Minister to the Chamber of Deputies on 28 March.

32 On the same day, to avoid this new payment being reflected in the cost of living, Delfim Netto persuaded the governors of the industrial region of the centre-south to reduce the rate of tax on transmission of goods, for which they were responsible, by 1 per cent. Also, to lighten the financial burden on business, the Government decided to finance 70 per cent of the increase at a favourable rate through the I.N.P.S. (Social Security).

33 There were many demonstrations in his favour.

34 *Jornal do Brasil* (Rio de Janeiro: 31 Dec 1967) 16.

35 These 'adventurers', tiny opposition groups, were scattered and disunited; the main ones were:

POLOP, the workers' political organisation which even before the Revolution had supported revolutionary action by the workers. In September 1967 some of its members decided to engage in armed activity in the countryside. These breakaway members then split into a number of groups:

POC, Workers' Communist Party, was a Trotskyist group trying to integrate the struggle in all its forms into a single strategic programme for socialism. The 'red' wing of the Communist Party of Brazil supported this trend.

V.P.R., Revolutionary Avant-Garde of the People, consisted mainly of members of the Military who had been deprived of their civil rights by the Revolution and had come together under the sign M.N.R., National Revolutionary Movement. The leader of the group was ex-Captain Carlos Lamarca.

COLINA, Commando for National Liberation, which is hardly distinguishable from the V.P.R.

VAR-Palmares, the result of a merger between some sections of the above mentioned groups.

M.R. 8, Revolutionary Movement of 8 October (the anniversary of the death of Che Guevara) and M.R. Tiradentes who openly left their trademark on terrorist acts they committed in the cities. Then there was A.L.N., Action for National Liberation which, led by Carlos Marighela and his successors, sought to promote unity among the revolutionary forces.

36 It may be recalled that the Chinese wing of the party seceded and formed the Communist Party of Brazil in 1962. Later, its left wing joined the Trotskyist group, Communist Workers' Party (POC).

37 Marighela, *Pour le Libération*, p. 52.
38 Ibid. (letter written at Havana on 18th August 1967) p. 62.
39 The newspapers reported 26 bank hold-ups in 1968.
40 'Algumas Questões Sobre as Guerrilhas no Brasil' published in Havana in October 1967. Quoted by Conrad Detrez in Marighela, *Pour la Libération*, p. 34.
41 Marighela, *Pour la Libération*, p. 131.
42 Ibid., p. 85.
43 Ibid., pp. 82–138. The Manual dated June 1969.
44 Ibid., p. 85.
45 Ibid., p. 90.
46 Ibid., pp. 110, 111.
47 Ibid., p. 134.
48 Ibid., pp. 134, 135.
49 Several observers agree on this point. For example:
Dom Helder Câmara: 'I respect the views of those who have taken the way of obedience but there are few of them. Revolution will only be made by the masses ... These men [the masses] have not enough to live for to have anything to die for'. Quoted by Laurentin, René, *L'Amérique Latine à l'heure de l'Enfantement* (Paris: Editions du Seuil, 1969), p. 94.

Jarbas Passarinho, Brazilian Minister of Education, on 17 March 1970: '80 per cent of the terrorists come from university circles and of the latter 70 per cent from the social science and philosophy departments'. *Notes et Etudes*; no. 3749-50, p. 78.

Nicole Salle: 'The members of the revolutionary groups constitute only a small proportion of the workers'. Salle, Nicole, 'La Lutte Révolutionnaire au Brésil', *Notes et Etudes*, no. 3749-50, p. 44.
50 On 18 July 1970, General Muricy, Chief of General Staff of the Army, admitted that about 500 persons were in detention for subversive acts.
51 *Brésil 69 – Torture et Répression*, Bulletin de Documentation published by the Association Internationale des Juristes Démocrates, Brussels, duplicated (Nov 1969) pages unnumbered; *Dagens Nyheters* (Stockholm: 11 Dec 1969) 1, 18 (report by Kjell A. Johansson to Amnesty International published in London on 20 March 1970); Black Book: 'Terreur et Torture au Brésil', *Croissance des Jeunes Nations*, no. 94 (Dec 1969) 19–34.
52 On and after 20 October 1969 hijacking, 'a crime against national security', was punishable by twenty years' imprisonment.
53 The unsuccessful attempts were those against the Secretaries of the Security Organisations of the States of Guanabara and São Paulo and the United States Consuls in Recife and Porto Alegre.

Successful attempts were made on Ambassador Elbrick of the United States; the Japanese Consul General in São Paulo who was abducted on 11 March and freed after five political prisoners had arrived in Mexico, including the Mother Superior of a convent in São Paulo, Maurina Borges da Silveira, accused of having sheltered guerillas; the German Ambassador Ehrenfried von Holleben, who was abducted on 11 June 1970 and released on 17 June after the liberation of forty political prisoners who were flown to Algeria, and the broadcasting of a statement denouncing the régime; the Swiss Ambassador, Giovani Enrico Bucher, on 7 December (his bodyguard was killed during the kidnapping). He was held by his captors for forty days and was not freed until the following 16 January. For the first time the Government flatly refused to give in and after complicated negotiations seventy adult prisoners together with the three children of one detainee were expelled to Chile. They included the student leaders Apolôneo de Carvalho and Jean-Marc von der Weid. However the authorities retained those prisoners who were on the list of the guerillas' demands but who had already been sentenced to long prison sentences and those who preferred to remain in prison in Brazil rather than be banished abroad. They also refused to publish the statement put out by the kidnappers, though it was in fact published in the press.

54 Apparently the ambush was laid after two A.L.N. sympathisers, Brother Fernando and Brother Yves from the Dominican Convent at São Paulo, had been arrested – one of whom is said to have been used as a bait to catch Marighela. Another version of the story has it that the police had already arrested and killed the A.L.N. leader before the ambush and the official scenario was mounted using Marighela's body to discredit the Dominicans.
55 Marighela, *Pour la Libération*, p. 97.
56 Two other persons were also killed and one seriously wounded.
57 Officially from heart failure.
58 *Pau de Arara*, p. 110. In the countryside too, although the drought in the north-east led to risings by groups of famished peasants, it did not work as a catalyst for the rural guerilla movement.
59 Mercier Vega, Luis, *Technique du Contre-Etat* (Paris: Pierre Belfond, 1968) p. 160.
60 *Jornal do Brasil* (Rio de Janeiro: 27 July 1969) MARPLAN/J.B. Survey.
61 Between 1964 and 1970 290 armed attacks by 'subversive' groups are reported, causing 193 wounded and 44 dead.
62 'Der Unterschwellige Bürgerkrieg in Brasilien', *Neue Zürcher Zeitung* (5 July, 1970) 6.
63 The real status of Operation Bandeirantes, a temporary organisation set up by the Army and the police of São Paulo to co-ordinate anti-terrorist action is harder to define; it was not officially recognised but the press reported openly on it. Its premises were used for interrogation of persons suspected of armed subversion with the object of obtaining as much information as possible leading to the arrest of the largest possible number of their comrades.
64 Others include: Cava, Ralph della, 'Torture in Brasil', *Commonweal*, xcii, no. 6 (24 Apr 1970) 135–41; Niedergang, Marcel, 'La Guérilla et la Torture au Brésil', *Le Monde* (Paris: 24–25 May 1970) 5; *Rapport concernant la répression policière et les tortures infligées aux opposants et prisonniers politiques au Brésil*, Press release, International Commission of Jurists, Geneva, document S. 2827, duplicated; *Dossier Brésil*, bulletin published by the Association Internationale des Juristes Démocrates, Brussels, duplicated (Apr 1971).
65 'It is said that doctors took part in torture sessions inflicted on political prisoners'. *Le Monde* (Paris: 16 May 1970) 3.
66 It should not be forgotten that these excesses were repeatedly mentioned in the Brazilian press as well.
67 8 May and 1 August 1970.
68 'Passarinho: Repressáo não é causa e sim efeito do terror', *O Globo* (Rio de Janeiro: 2 Dec 1970) 11.
69 *The Review*, International Commission of Jurists, no. 8 (June 1972) 4.
70 He was attached to the DEOPS (Departamento Estadual da Ordem Politica e Social).
71 *Veja*, no. 206 (16 Aug 1972) 29.
72 Ibid., p. 30. On 16 September 1972 the first member of the 'death squadron' to be convicted, former policeman José Alvès da Silva, known

as 'Zé Guarda' was sentenced to nineteen years in prison, eleven years to be with hard labour.
73 *O Cruzeiro* (7 Apr 1968).
74 In a report published in September 1972 and covering the period from 13 December 1968 to 15 July 1972, Amnesty International listed by name 1081 persons mentioned in documents that had been submitted to it 'as having been subjected to torture, having been murdered by police or military, or having disappeared whilst held in prison'. *Report on Allegations of Torture in Brazil*, duplicated (London: Amnesty International Publications, [Sep 1972] pp. 1–40, ch. v, appendix 1. On 13 September 1972 *Le Monde* in Paris published on page 4 an inaccurate summary of this document under the heading 'Damning report by Amnesty International'.
75 The dossier compiled by François Maspero (*Pau de Arara*) confirms that most of the cases quoted were in fact publicly denounced either in the press or before commissions of inquiry.
76 According to Maspero's publication, altogether thirteen urban guerilla militants died in Brazilian gaols. Exact figures of those who were tortured are not given.
77 *Pau de Arara* (jacket). In a reference to some of these events Henri Gilliéron writes: 'The purge that had just taken place explains the definite decrease in cases of torture'. *Tribune de Genève* (6 June 1972) 12.
78 In view of the great variety of forms of worship in use in Brazil, this much-used phrase is only statistically true.
79 This trend of thought supports a strong traditionalist movement, the T.F.P. (Brazilian Society for the Defence of Tradition, Family and Property). This organisation played an important part in mobilising public opinion against Goulart in 1964. In 1966 its campaign against the institution of divorce gathered a million signatures in fifty days. In 1968 a petition addressed to Pope Paul VI requesting him to take action against 'Communist infiltration in the Brazilian clergy' obtained 1,600,368 signatures in two months. Antoine, Charles, 'L'Episcopat brésilien Face au Pouvoir, 1962–1969', *Etudes*, vol. 333 (July–Dec 1970) 92.
80 Meyer, Jean A., 'L'Eglise Catholique au Brésil', *Notes et Etudes*, no. 3749–50, p. 49.
81 This prelate of very humble birth was later appointed by the Pope, on 22 October 1970, as Cardinal Prefect of the Holy Congregation for the Evangelisation of Nations.
82 Some observers thought that the whole affair was arranged by the Military to compromise the Church. Antoine, 'L'Episcopat brésilien', p. 98.
83 Ibid., pp. 94–5.
84 Ibid., p. 96.
85 It will be recalled that Costa e Silva had been received by the Pope on 5 January 1967.
86 *Notes et Etudes*, no. 3749–50, p. 15.
87 Ibid.
88 Ibid., p. 63.
89 Mgr José de Castro Pinto, auxiliary bishop of Rio de Janeiro.
90 *Notes et Etudes*, no. 3749–50, p. 64.
91 Mgr José Delgado, responsible for Crateus.
92 *Notes et Etudes*, no. 3749–50, p. 65.
93 Mgr José de Castro Pinto.
94 This wish is expressed for example in a document issued by Workers'

Catholic Action of the North-East of Brazil: 'Governments are under obligation to make laws which satisfy the real aspirations of the people, and thereafter to require these laws to be applied, more particularly when their object is to reform out-of-date, unjust and inhuman structures ... the common good can be understood only as the good of all. This places an obligation on governments to take action to correct injustices in the existing state of things...' Câmara, Dom Helder, *Le Tiers Monde Trahi* (Paris: Desclée et Cie, 1968) p. 222.
95 *Notes et Etudes*, no. 3749–50, p. 53.
96 A Frenchman, Gilles de Maupeou, and a Brazilian, J. A. Magalhães de Monteiro.
97 President Médici began anew a regular dialogue with the Church. He sent as representatives to the 11 General Assembly of the C.N.B.B. his Educational Minister, his Minister of Justice and the Head of his Special Consultative Council, Colonel Miguel Pereira Manso Neto, who also observed the work of the Central Committee. In 1972 Colonel Manso Neto was appointed as Military Attaché of Brazil in Berne.
98 It appears however that this decision has not invariably been obeyed.
99 The Cardinal-Archbishop of São Paulo, Mgr Agnelo Rossi, and the Secretary General of the C.N.B.B., Mgr Aloisio Lorscheider.
100 Translation from *L'Osservatore Romano*, French ed. (30 Oct 1970).
101 Ibid.
102 *Jornal do Brasil* (Rio de Janeiro: 21 Oct 1970) translated in *Notes et Etudes*, no. 3749–50, p. 59.
103 *Centro de Informaçôes Ecclesia* (São Paulo: 19 Oct 1970).
104 Antoine, 'L'Episcopat brésilien', p. 103.

Chapter 33
1 Such as, for example, the price control measures – on corn, of 16 April and on textiles, of 27 May (when the Government threatened to drive the employers' leaders in this branch into bankruptcy by blocking the credits advanced to them by the Bank of Brazil); in regard to foodstuffs, on 10 December (the Government arranged for a chain of 100 supermarkets which were forcing down prices to be financed in São Paulo by the Federal Savings Bank); also measures compelling finance companies to invest 50 per cent of their resources in consumers' credit at specified rates of interest; and those whereby on 20 September 130 large companies found guilty of offences against general regulations of price control were punished, and those which on 19 June reinforced the tax inspection machinery and set up at the Finance Ministry a central register of private persons liable to pay tax.
2 Including the establishment of an Inter-ministerial Price Council which although armed with wide powers of intervention in the economy was better adapted to reality than the former system (28 August); the transformation of the National Finance Directorate into the Federal Secretariat for Receipts (21 November); the reactivation of the provisions of Decree 157, stimulating the purchase of shares in companies whose capital was freely open to public subscription (30 March); the bill for eliminating value added tax (I.P.I.) on goods destined for export (19 April); the abolition of customs duties on capital goods defined as necessary for the development of the national economy (28 June); and the 20 per cent increase in all the credit lines granted to the private sector (6 July).
3 Decree No. 63,500 of 30 October 1968.

4 See Freire, *L'Education*, pp. 105–54.
5 'Movimento Brasileiro de Alfabetização', Decree No. 62,455 dated 22 March 1968. The movement got off to a slow start but then went ahead rapidly. Its aim was to educate 1½ million Brazilians each year from 1970 onwards in order to lower the illiteracy rate to 10 per cent by 1975. The budget for 1970 was U.S. $13 million. The basic course lasted five months and was administered by about 80,000 educators, some of whom gave their services free. They taught reading, writing and arithmetic and also imparted general knowledge. The effort was very decentralised and was also aimed at informing participants about the resources and potentialities of the district in which they lived. With Professor Mario Henrique Simonsen as chairman, MOBRAL made nearly 4 million Brazilians literate in two years, about half of them in 1972 alone. For this achievement Simonsen was acclaimed by UNESCO. *Veja*, no. 210 (13 Sep 1972) 59.
6 'Coordenação de Habitação de Interesse Social na Área Metropolitana', established by Decree No. 62,654 dated 6 May 1968.
7 Cesar Cantanhede, José Pires de Castro, Arilson Tompson de Carvalho.
8 4 September 1968.
9 This council was set up on 16 March 1964 by the Goulart government under Law No. 4319 but this law had remained a dead letter and the by-laws of the council were set out in Decree No. 63,681 of 22 November 1968. Consisting of the Minister of Justice, the President of the Federal Council of the Order of Advocates, the President of the Brazilian Press Association, the President of the Brazilian Education Association, leaders of the majority and minority parties in the Senate and a professor of constitutional law, its aim is to:
(a) Promote inquiries, research and studies to ensure respect for the rights of human beings.
(b) To make known the meaning and content of each of these rights.
(c) To promote inquiries to look into the causes of violations of these rights and to ensure their full exercise.
In practice this body awakened no public interest because its discussions took place in secret and it was dominated by government representatives. Nevertheless it was considered to have done sufficiently useful work on behalf of persons who had been persecuted by the police for the Federal Council of the Order of Advocates to decide to continue to be represented on it in May 1972 by 22 votes to 2.
10 Beltrão made a similar statement to the state governors when they met on 15 March.
11 *Dados*, no. 8 (1971) 155. It will be recalled that on 5 April the 'Enlarged Front' had been prohibited by decree.
12 *Sinopse*, p. 420.
13 The so-called 'independants' formed in January 1968 under the leadership of Rafael de Almeida Magalhães, a reforming parliamentarian who was Vice-Governor of Guanabara under Carlos Lacerda.
14 5 May 1968.
15 Senator Daniel Krieger, who was nevertheless re-elected at the National Convention of the Party.
16 177 votes to 22 against with 8 abstentions. ARENA had 220 deputies in the Chamber.
17 *Dados*, no. 8 (1971) 159. It may be pointed out that on 10 June the Commission for the Constitution and Justice of Parliament rejected a proposed M.D.B. amendment granting a wide-ranging political amnesty and looking towards a return to direct election of the president.

18 The number of serving officers had been increased. Compared with 1955 there were added: 2 major generals, 3 brigadier generals, 13 colonels, 35 lieutenant colonels, 78 majors, 136 captains and 225 first lieutenants (Schneider, *Political System of Brazil*, p. 260). Pay had been raised on a number of occasions (including a readjustment of 20 per cent with effect from 1 September) and thenceforth the military were allowed to engage in various well-paid occupations in the public and private sector.
19 *Jornal do Brasil* (Rio de Janeiro: 24 Mar 1968).
20 *Dados*, no. 8 (1971) 161.
21 *Jornal do Brasil* (Rio de Janeiro: 24 Aug 1968).
22 A kind of pendant to the National Security Council.
23 But Albuquerque Lima was only a three-star man and did not have the advantages which Costa e Silva had in 1965. He was not the senior in service among the generals and did not control the Ministry of War. Moreover, others besides him were setting their sights on the office of president, including General Jaime Portela, Head of the Military Household, and Colonel Andreazza, Ministry of Transport, who went on to the reserve strength of his own free will in October. But his most dangerous competitor was General Sizeno Sarmento, this 'civilian in uniform' who commanded the First Army and thus controlled Rio de Janeiro. However, Albuquerque Lima tried to secure backing for himself by suggesting that a Fifth Army, responsible for Amazonia, should be created and that he should then command it.
24 There were 2481 captains on the active strength. *Correio da Manhã* (Rio de Janeiro: 1 Nov 1968).
25 Next day the *Jornal do Brasil* mentioned a draft of the text couched in even stronger terms, which was said to have mentioned certain ministers by name as being suspected of corruption.
26 The author of *Torturas e Torturados*.
27 In the *Correio da Manhã*, Rio de Janeiro.
28 An address at the Headquarters of the Second Army in São Paulo on 22 October 1968. *Dados*, no. 8 (1971) 165.
29 Senator Daniel Krieger.
30 The Queen arrived at Recife on 1 November, but the official visit did not begin until the fifth in Rio de Janeiro, after a stay at Salvador.
31 In ten states, 15 million electors chose 1273 municipal councillors and 1381 mayors. It will be recalled that the mayors of capital cities and those for municipalities affecting national security were appointed by the governors.
32 On the twelfth the two student leaders who were most under attack, Vladimir Palmeira and Luis Travassos, were also accorded the protection of this measure.
33 A translation in *Notes et Etudes*, no. 3749–50, p. 30. Article VIII of the Act is revealing as to the moralising propensities of the Military: 'After inquiry the President of the Republic may decree the confiscation of the goods of anybody who has enriched himself illegally while in the exercise of official duties or office, including the duties and offices of private and public enterprises and of mixed economy companies, without prejudice to the appropriate punishments under criminal law.'
  On 17 December 1968 Decree Law No. 359 set up a General Committee of Inquiry charged with opening summary inquiries with the object of bringing about the seizure of the goods of persons caught by Article VIII, and on 27 January 1969 Supplementary Act No. 42 (complemented on 7 February by Article 1 of Decree Law No. 457) included within its powers legal action against dishonest public works contractors,

bookmakers, pimps and bodies corporate which had enriched themselves illicitly.
34 *Dados*, no. 8 (1971) 208.
35 Ibid., p. 170.
36 Ibid., p. 171. A banquet given in honour of Costa e Silva on 28 December 1968.
37 In April 1968, wishing to fill the vacuum caused by the proscription of the 'Enlarged Front', Jânio Quadros, on his return from Europe, made some political statements, some of which were quite sensible. But as he had been deprived of his civil rights the hard liners demanded that the law should be applied, whereas Costa e Silva tried to avoid an unnecessary crisis. Quâdros was simply placed under house arrest in Corumba in Mato Grosso for 120 days, thus gaining his halo as a persecutee relatively cheaply.
38 Translated in *Notes et Etudes*, no. 3749–50, p. 11. Unlike Marighela, Quardros would certainly have wanted the military to choose the first term of the alternative rather than the second.

PART FOUR

1 Supplementary Act No. 39 of 20 December 1968 and Decree No. 63,888 of the same date.
2 Hermano Alvès took refuge in the Mexican Embassy on 10 January 1969 and obtained a safe conduct to Mexico on 19 April.
3 Issued on 16 January, 8 February, 13 March and 29 April 1969. The *Correio da Manhã* which had published opposition articles was forbidden on 27 February to publish for five days. Its directress and proprietor, Mme Niomar Moniz Sodré Bittencourt, whose civil rights had been suspended, was taken into protective custody together with five persons holding responsible posts on the newspaper, from 27 February to 12 March. On 14 May 1970 she was acquitted of charges of subversion by the Supreme Military Tribunal.
4 Ministers Victor Nunes Leal, Hermès Lima, Evandro Lins e Silva, Antonio Carlos Lafayette de Andrada and Antonio Gonçalves de Oliveira.
5 Including three atomic scientists as well as the sociologists whose teaching is known as the school of São Paulo.
6 Institutional Act No. 6 of 1 February 1969 which 'to reinforce its position as an eminently constitutional court' removed from it the power to decide as an appeals court in cases of civilians sentenced by military tribunals and all cases resulting from the application of Institutional Act No. 5.
7 In order of enactment they were Institutional Act No 7 of 26 February, No. 8 of 2 April, No. 9 of 25 April, No. 10 of 16 May and No. 11 of 14 August.
8 For example, persons subject to punitive measures could no longer work either in enterprises coming under public services or in state research or teaching institutions. Since there is virtually no private research, this decision was a far-reaching one for researchers.

Chapter 34

1 State receipts had already been reduced by a federal decision which on 31 December 1968 reduced their share of the 'fiscal participation fund' from 20 to 12 per cent and compelled them to use this money in accordance with a pre-established set of priorities.

2. Between April 1964 and December 1968 the United States granted Brazil aid worth U.S. $1·1 billion and on 25 December 1968 the I.B.R.D. announced a loan of U.S. $204 million for building 1880 km of roads in nine states of Brazil. *Notes et Etudes*, no. 3749–50, p. 87.
3. On 3 April Albuquerque Lima returned to his desk in the Ministry of the Army, heading the Armaments Department.
4. 27 January 1969.
5. Marini, *Sous-développement et Revolution*, p. 177.
6. Colonel Francisco Boaventura Cavalcanti Jr.
7. He championed the 'national development model' which he vigorously defended in the CONSPLAN, see below. When appointed he was managing the Companhia Vale do Rio Doce, a State-controlled undertaking which was the principal exporter of iron ore.
8. Decree Law No. 564 of 1 May 1969, *Plano Básico de Previdência Social para os Trabalhadores Rurais*, and regulations for applying it dated 1 September 1969. In the initial phase this plan was applied only to sectors already partially industrialised, such as sugar or meat.
9. Rio Grande do Sul, Ceará, the State of Rio de Janeiro, Minas Gerais and Pernambuco.
10. On 7 May the Minister of Agriculture announced in this connection that 40,000 acres were being distributed to 650 families near Porto Alegre in the State of Rio Grande do Sul.
11. Its composition, announced on 1 March, shows the importance attached to it by the President. Its members were representatives of the ministries involved, Finance, Planning, Interior and Labour; of the National Security Council; of the Central Bank; of the I.B.R.A.; of the Agricultural Employers Confederation and the Agricultural Workers Confederation.
12. Resistance was widespread and it was symptomatic that on 10 June 1969 the Minister of Agriculture stated during a press conference which he gave at the National Police Academy that 'Among the economic and political forces which pressurise the Government in order to obtain support and favourable tax treatment, the rural sectors are generally at a disadvantage owing to the aggressiveness and high-powered nature of the associations of rural proprietors, bankers and industrialists which through their capital have access to the media which form public opinion.' *Dados*, no. 8 (1971) 220. On 4 August, the Minister of the Interior for his part preferred to reassure these same landowners by stating in Porto Alegre that agrarian reform would not affect the structure of their properties except in cases where land had been left uncultivated (Ibid., p. 226). That was not the opinion of the Chairman of I.B.R.A., General Carlos de Moraes, who on 26 August, speaking to the Third National Congress of Agricultural Economics, came out in favour of a widespread use of the principle of expropriation in the interests of social justice (Ibid., p. 228).
13. Half of this was financed by USAID (Ibid., p. 181). Another agreement signed with USAID on 1 July provided training for instructors specialising in export and business administration.
14. One of the sources of finance for all these programmes was the profit made by the State on a kind of football pool – the 'Loteria Esportiva' – for which a plan had been submitted to the President on 26 May 1969. As Brazilians love games of chance, this type of lottery immediately caught on and traders even complained that people were spending so much money on it that their takings suffered. The profits were divided according to the following scheme: sport, 30 per cent; social service activities (L.B.A.), 40 per cent; education, 30 per cent.

15 Petroquimica União was inaugurated by Costa e Silva on 11 April at Santo André near São Paulo in the presence of eight of his ministers. The investment, worth 72·5 million dollars, was partly financed from abroad (mainly by France and the International Finance Corporation). The State had a majority holding. Annual production was scheduled to reach 700,000 tons of basic petro-chemical products by 1975. Investments of the order of 600 million dollars were scheduled until 1980 and the project was expected to give employment to 40,000 more people. The first production unit was inaugurated on 15 June 1972 in the presence of President Médici. It cost U.S. $126 million. At that time 40 per cent of the capital of the enterprise, whose chairman was Eduardo Paes Barreto, was under the control of the State (Petrobrás-Petroquisa). The rest was divided between the World Bank (International Finance Corporation) which had 10 per cent and the Brazilian group Unipar with 50 per cent. This latter group was owned by Refinaria União with 28·1 per cent; the Moreira Salles group, 25·5 per cent; Hanna Corp., 14·1 per cent; private shareholders, 32·3 per cent (*Visão*, vol. 35, no. 5 (29 Aug 1969) 175–82 and *Veja*, no. 198 (21 June 1972) 75–6).
16 *Visão*, vol. 35, no. 5, p. 180.
17 *Dados*, no. 8 (1971) 183.
18 *Visão*, vol. 35, no. 5, p. 33.
19 Ibid., pp. 139–40. In fact the statistics of the 1960 census show that medium-sized businesses represented 31 per cent of industrial establishments in Brazil, gave employment to 63·3 per cent of the workers and supplied 65·1 per cent of the product (whereas the comparable figures for large companies with more that 500 employees were 0·5 per cent; 25·3 per cent; and 27·6 per cent). Ibid., p. 133.
20 Ibid., p. 173.
21 Ibid., p. 172.
22 Ibid., p. 25.

Chapter 35
1 Some of the hard liners wished to put a truly revolutionary party, the Brazilian Revolution Party in place of ARENA. Nevertheless the whole leadership of ARENA was renewed after its president and his executive commission had resigned on 7 January 1969.
2 Supplementary Act No. 56 of 18 June 1969.
3 The Minister of Justice who had given both parties the opportunity to broadcast on television on 25 June officially declared the next day that people could join the parties without 'fear of being leaned on'. Nevertheless, the 'permitted opposition' was not allowed to take issue with the régime in the talks they gave on this occasion.
4 The first draft was prepared by Vice-President Pedro Aleixo who on 21 June submitted a 'range of proposals'.
5 *Jornal do Brasil* (Rio de Janeiro: 20 May 1969).
6 Schneider, *Political System of Brazil*, deals with this in detail, particularly on p. 290.
7 Letter from Moniz de Aragão to Lyra Tavares dated 17 June 1969 (ibid.).
8 See for example *Visão*, no. 4 (15 Aug 1969).
9 *Dados*, no. 8 (1971) 185.
10 According to the press there were 65 bank raids between 1 January and 20 August 1969, carried out by terrorists who made off with 765,000 dollars. From 22 March onwards these attacks were regarded by the law as attacks on national security. The outstanding occurrences also included

the destruction of three television stations in São Paulo on 14 July and the explosion of a bomb at the residence of the Cardinal Archbishop of São Paulo on 5 August. Repression was tough and effective. In addition to many arrests resulting in 67 persons being charged on 2 July in connection with the movement Revolutionary Avant-Garde of the People, led by ex-Captain Carlos Lamarca, there was the breaking up of M.R. 8 reported on 26 July and the liquidation between 8 and 20 August of an incipient guerilla movement in the region of Angra dos Reis between Rio and São Paulo.

11 On 30 April about a thousand students, after demonstrating in São Paulo against measures taken against their teaching staff, were arrested. On 6 May a fresh strike broke out for the same reason. On 19 May the Federal University and the Catholic University in Rio de Janeiro were occupied by the police. On 26 June Vladimir Palmeira, the student leader, was condemned to 30 months' imprisonment.

Chapter 36
1 General Aurelio de Lyra Tavares (Army), Admiral Augusto Rademacker Grünewald (Navy), and Air Marshal Marcio de Souza e Mello (Air Force).
2 The newspapers simply announced on 28 August that Costa e Silva was suffering from a severe bout of influenza; he was struck by partial paralysis in the aircraft taking him from Brasilia to Rio de Janeiro on the twenty-ninth.
3 The banks and the Stock Exchange even closed for a day.
4 To put an end to rumours, the triumvirate sent for a French specialist, Professor François Lhermitte, who arrived from Paris on 12 September to give his opinion on the seriousness of the case.
5 See on this subject, *inter alia*, the *Jornal do Brasil* (Rio de Janeiro: 17 July 1969), 'Uma presença adequada de empresários na politica' and 'O papel das forças armadas no apoio a iniciativa privada'.
6 This trend was foreseen by the political writer Oliveiro S. Ferreira. Ferreira, Oliveiro S., *O Fim do Poder Civil* (São Paulo: Editôra Convívio, 1966).
7 They are better trained than were their elders. They have passed through several officers' training courses in Brazil and abroad and were exposed a lot earlier to the arguments of the 'young old-boys' of the E.S.G. who in their turn had become instructors and who were thick on the ground at the Staff College (ECEME) and the Military Academy of Agulhas Negras (AMAN). Obviously the same thing happened in all arms.
8 See on this Einaudi, Luigi R. and Stepan Alfred C., *Latin American Institutional Development: Changing Military Perspectives in Peru and Brasil*, report prepared for the Office of External Research, Department of State, Santa Monica, Cal., R–586–DOS (The Rand Corporation, Apr 1971).
9 See the article by Pedreira, Fernando, 'O nosso Exército antes ae depois', *Correio da Manhã* (Rio de Janeiro: 11 Feb 1968).
10 See below. It was significant that Aragão, rehabilitated under Médici, became head of the new Army Training Department which gave him an opportunity of propagating his views among the young officers.
11 *Visão*, no. 206 (16 Aug 1972) 21.
12 Ibid.
13 The military ministers, after having modified the Constitution by Decree Law No. 900 of 29 September, changed Castello Branco's Decree No. 200, dealing with the reform of the federal administration, at several

points. The new version gave the Military the largest say in relation to national security, whereas this idea did not occur in the original text. Article 45 is couched as follows: 'The armed forces, *essential to the execution of the policy of national security*, have the task of defending the fatherland and of guaranteeing the constituted powers, law and order' (my italics).

14 It appears that a group of intellectuals – journalists and students – was responsible for this kidnapping, not so much guerillas as 'drawing-room revolutionaries' (called in Brazil *esquerda festiva* – 'the bank holiday left', or *whisquerda* – the 'whisky left'). It appears that their symbolic gesture was designed as a protest against the increasing prestige of the Government abroad.

15 They were mentioned by name. They included the Communist leader Gregório Bezerra, Ricardo Zoratini (who led the attempt on Costa e Silva's life at Recife in 1966), the student leaders Vladimir Palmeira and José Duarte dos Santos, the guerila journalist Flavio Tavares, the organisers of the commando that executed the American captain Charles Chandler at São Paulo (Ivo Marchetti do Monte Lima and ex-Sergeant Onafre Pinto) and a medical student Mario Galharda Zanconato who stated during a press conference held in Mexico that he had organised eight bank hold-ups in Minas Gerais in order to provide money to opponents of the régime.

16 Information given to the press by the Minister of Foreign Affairs.

17 Besides the triumvirate, the following ministers took part in the meeting: Magalhães Pinto (foreign affairs), Gama e Silva (justice), General Portela (Military Household) and General Fontoura (S.N.I.). *Dados* (1971) 191.

18 The Government's decision was announced only eighteen minutes before the end of the terrorists' time limit, which clearly shows how tough the negotiations were.

19 The main passages are the following:

> The seizure of the Ambassador (who represents imperialist interests in our country) is only an act of revolutionary war, which is growing every day and which will launch its rural guerilla phase later this year. By kidnapping Elbrick we wish to demonstrate that it is possible to defeat the dictatorship and exploitation if we arm and organise ourselves.
>
> We shall appear where the enemy least expects us and disappear immediately, thus wearing down the dictatorship, bringing terror and fear to the exploiters and hope and certainty of victory to the exploited ... We warn all those who are torturing, beating and killing our companions that we shall not accept the continuation of this hateful practice.
>
> This is our last warning. Those who go on torturing, beating and killing had better watch out. From now on it is an eye for an eye, a tooth for a tooth. *New York Times* (6 Sep 1969) 2.

20 The State Department expressed its 'deep appreciation' of the co-operation given by the Brazilian Government.

21 All the facts mentioned were reproduced in the daily press between 4 and 15 September and also in the *New York Times* which published every day during this period news from its correspondent Joseph Novitski.

22 It is dated 5 September and must have been signed after the meeting

at which it was decided to accept the terms of Ambassador Elbrick's kidnappers.
23 This act, which was published on 9 September, is also dated the fifth, and its content is quite contrary to Brazilian tradition.
24 This Decree law No. 898 containing 107 articles was published on 27 September. The first three articles are the most characteristic:

Article 1
All persons and corporate bodies are responsible for National Security within the limits laid down by the law.

Article 2
National Security is a guarantee of the fulfilment of the national objectives against the opposing factors both internal and external.

Article 3
National Security covers in essence the means for securing external and internal security including the prevention and repression of adverse psychological warfare and revolutionary or subversive war.

Paragraph 1. Internal security, which forms an integral part of National Security, is directed at adverse threats and pressures whatever their origin, form or nature, which appear or cause effects in the country.

Paragraph 2. Adverse psychological war is the use of propaganda or counter-propaganda and any activity whether political, economic, psycho-social or military undertaken with the object of influencing or inducing opinions, emotions, attitudes and behaviour by groups either foreign, enemy, neutral or friendly, contrary to the fulfilment of the national objectives.

Paragraph 3. Revolutionary war is internal conflict, generally inspired by an ideology, or receiving help from abroad, which aims at seizing power by subversion, by progressively controlling the nation.

25 Ibid., Article 16. Some of the provisions were specially directed at a weekly paper *O Pasquim* (The Lampoon) containing political satire. First published at Rio de Janeiro in June 1969, it was avidly read by the opposition and stung the Military to fury. Censorship of the press was still further strengthened by Instruction 11b of 6 February 1970, especially as regards attacks on 'public morality and good conduct'.
26 List of 12 and 30 September. The senator eliminated from political life was Pedro Ludovico Teixeira, the father of the ex-Governor of Goiás, Mauro Borges.
27 16 September 1969.
28 By Institutional Act No. 15 of 9 September. The exceptions were Goiás and Mato Grosso where municipal elections were still held on 15 November 1969.
29 Supplementary Acts No. 65 and 66 dated 9 and 19 September 1969.

Chapter 37

1 General Jurandir de Bizarria Mamede (President), General Antonio Carlos Muricy, Chief of the Army General Staff, General Emilio Garrastazu Médici, Head of the Third Army.
2 The 1967 Constitution set the period of office at four years but some of the Military thought that this was not long enough. The Constitutional amendment of 17 October 1969 introduced a five-year presidential term of office (Article 75, paragraph 3).

3 In alphabetical order they were: General Albuquerque Lima, José Canavarro Perreira, Orlando Geisel, Bizzaria Mamede, Garrastazu Médici, Antonio Carlos Muricy and Sizeno Sarmento; there was also Colonel Passarinho, Minister of Labour, but he had very little chance of being appointed.
4 The *Jornal do Brasil* of Rio de Janeiro for this period hints at dissensions.
5 The first to be affected by this act was Admiral Ernesto de Mello Batista, formerly Navy Minister under Castello Branco, who was suspended for a year on 17 October.
6 On 7 and 9 October 1969.
7 For example, on 22 October an industrial and commercial exhibition from the U.S.S.R. opened in São Paulo. On 21 November the Russian Vice-Minister for Foreign Trade, Mr Alkimov, arrived in Brazil to negotiate a commercial agreement. On 12 January an industrial exhibition from Yugoslavia was opened. On 2 March an economic mission arrived in Rio from Czechoslovakia led by the Vice-Minister for Foreign Trade, Mr Ivan Peter.
8 Supplementary Act No. 71 also dated 14 October, accorded to Costa e Silva the rights and honours of Head of State until the intended end of his term of office on 15 March 1971, but he died on 17 December 1969.
9 Supplementary Acts No. 72 and 73 dated 15 October.
10 251 deputies and 42 senators of ARENA.
11 62 deputies and 14 senators of the M.D.B.
12 The introduction of this new penal code was finally rejected on 1 January 1974 to enable improvements to be made.
13 Article 182.
14 A survey published by the *Jornal do Brasil* (Rio de Janeiro: 21, 22 December 1969).
15 Parliamentary immunity was raised automatically in cases of endangering national security or 'crimes against honour'.
16 In the November 1970 elections there were 310 deputies against 409 previously. The number of senators was unchanged, as each State was entitled to three seats.
17 Article 87.
18 Born in 1905 at Bagé in Rio Grande do Sul, Emílio Garrastazu Médici came of Basque/Italian parentage. He was Military Attaché in Washington under Castello Branco.
19 See the opinion survey carried out at Rio de Janeiro and published in the *Jornal do Brasil* (Rio de Janeiro: 19, 20 October 1969).
20 Ibid.
21 *New York Times* (10 Nov 1969) 6.

Chapter 38
1 The team consisted of:
Finance: Antonio Delfim Netto (an old hand)
Mines and Energy: Antonio Dias Leite, Jr (an old hand)
Industry and Commerce: Fabio Riodi Yassuda, Director of the Agricultural Co-operative at Cotia, São Paulo
Planning: João Paulo dos Reis Velloso, 38 years old, Head of the Ministry Planning Institute under Roberto Campos and Helio Beltrão
Justice: Alfredo Buzaid, an advocate at São Paulo (Gama e Silva was sent to Lisbon as Ambassador)
Agriculture: Luiz Fernando Cirne Lima, an agronomist (Rio Grande do Sul)

Foreign Affairs: Mário Gibson Barbosa, Ambassador to Washington who had passed through the Superior War College
Health: Dr Francsico de Paula da Rocha Lagoa, who had passed through the Superior War College
Labour and Social Security: Júlio de Carvalho Barata, who had passed through the Superior War College
Communications: Colonel Hygino Caetano Corsetti
Education and Culture: Senator Jarbas Passarinho, formerly Minister of Labour
Transport: Mario Andreazza (an old hand)
Interior: José Costa Cavalcanti (an old hand)
Army: General Orlando Geisel (General Tavares was posted to Paris as Ambassador)
Air: Air Marshal Marcio de Souza e Mello (an old hand)
Navy: Admiral Adalberto de Barros Nunes
Military Household: Brigadier General João Baptista de Oliveira Figueiredo (formerly Médici's Chief Secretary at the S.N.I. and on the staff of the Third Army)
Civil Household: João Leitão de Abreu, an advocate of Porto Alegre (brother-in-law of the ex-Minister of the Army, Lyra Tavares)
National Intelligence Service: Brigadier General Carlos Alberto da Fontoura (an old hand, since March 1969).

2 By the summer of 1972 only two of the team had resigned: the Air Minister, well known for his anti-subversive zeal, whose resignation was handed in at the beginning of December 1971, and that of the Minister of Health, whose fault consisted of permitting administrative delays and showing a lack of dynamism. He was replaced on 15 June 1972 by Mario Machado Lemos, Health Secretary of the State of São Paulo.

3 The decree setting up the organising committee for this exhibition had been signed on 22 February 1969 and José Eugenio de Macedo Soares appointed as its chairman. He resigned on 28 November.

4 *Brazilian Trend* (Editôra Abril, 1972) p. 65.

5 In September 1971, there were sixteen soluble coffee factories in Brazil with an estimated total production equivalent to 2,674,000 bags of green coffee (each bag weighing 60 kg). Six of these factories used the modern procedure of lyophilisation (*Imagem do Brasil*, p. 150).

6 The selling price of ground coffee is controlled by the Brazilian Coffee Institute, I.B.C., which applies a differential rate of exchange that disadvantages exporters of this product. The exchange difference, known as the '*confisco cambial*', is retained by the I.B.C. and used to finance Government policy on coffee. In so far as they regard the *confisco cambial* as being a tax that is not applied to exports of soluble coffee from Brazil whereas it is applied to the coffee berries, foreign producers of soluble coffee consider that this is a discriminatory measure applied against them.

7 *Jornal do Brasil* (Rio de Janeiro: 12 Oct 1968) 4.

8 13 American cents by pound weight (0.45359 kg) of soluble coffee.

9 An editorial in *O Estado de São Paulo* (25 Apr 1969).

10 See the article 'As pressões da General Foods' in *O Estado de São Paulo* (16 Jan 1970) 29. General Foods was said to control about 50 per cent of the soluble coffee market in the United States.

11 Jaime Nogueira Miranda, Vice-President of the Federation of Agriculture of São Paulo, on 5 December replaced Caio de Alcantara Machado, a remarkable promotional specialist, who had been appointed by the previous Government.

12 He himself was replaced by Colonel Miguel Pereira Manso Neto.

13 See *O Estado de São Paulo* (7, 8, 10 May 1970).
14 According to a statement by Senator Edward Kennedy, reproduced by *O Estado de São Paulo* (5 Jan 1971) 46, General Foods was the only American firm that asked for tariff protection.
15 *O Estado de São Paulo* (1 Dec 1970) 52.
16 On 20 August 1970 the press reported a decision of the American Department of Commerce prohibiting the import into the United States of a shipment of cotton textiles produced in Brazil valued at U.S. $2 million. However on 15 September an import quota of 75 million square yards was allocated to Brazil. The problem of the import of American wheat by Brazil was the subject of difficult negotiations during this same period. At last on 21 October an agreement permitting the shipment of U.S. $108 million was signed.
17 The quantity of 'tax free' bags, fixed in relation to average sales of Brazilian soluble coffee in the United States during the period 1968/9, was to vary in line with future exports.
18 In February 1971 the Brazilian system was revamped and a minimum export price standard was set up, expressed in dollars per pound weight (0·45359 kg) for each type of coffee, allied to a 'contribution quota' per bag of coffee exported, which came to the I.B.C. Thenceforward exporters were free to negotiate themselves the exchange rate provided they paid the contribution quota to the I.B.C. This amounted to U.S. $19·20 in February 1971. By December of the same year it had risen to U.S. $21·87 to take account of inflation. *Conjuntura Econômica*, vol. 26, no. 2 (Feb 1972) 47.
19 Based on a contribution quota of U.S. $19·20 (Feb 1971) and 21·87 (Dec 1971) per bag, which was lost to the Fundo de Defesa de Produtos Agropecuarios-Café.
20 *Bulletin de la Banque française et italienne pour l'Amérique du Sud* (Dec 1971).
21 1967: 17·3 million; 1968: 19 million; 1969: 19·5 million; 1970: 17 million; 1971: 18·4 million (60 kg bags). It is worth recalling however that coffee represented a decreasing proportion of the total of Brazilian exports (41·2 per cent by value in 1968; 35·2 per cent in 1969; 34·3 per cent in 1970; in 1971 the percentage fell to around 27 per cent). *Conjuntura Econômica*, vol. 26, no. 2 (Feb 1972) 40, 46.
22 Ibid., p. 47.
23 It may be noted in passing that between 1966 and 1972 American civil and military diplomatic staffs in Brazil were reduced by some 47 per cent in consequence of a political decision which John W. Tuthill, who was Ambassador to Brazil from 1966 to 1969, persuaded Washington to accept. Tuthill, John W., 'Operation Topsy', *Foreign Policy*, vol. 8 (New York, autumn 1972) 62–85.
24 *Notes et Etudes*, no. 3913–14 (28 July 1972) 69.
25 Brazil increased the limit of its territorial waters to 200 miles on 25 March 1970 by Decree Law No. 1098, thus following the example of other Latin American countries. The United States refused in principle to recognise this decision but finally in May 1972 signed an agreement undertaking:
   (a) to limit to 160 the number of boats authorised to fish at any one time in Brazilian waters producing large quantities of crayfish and shrimps;
   (b) to authorise Brazil to board, search and seize any North American shrimp boats that infringed this agreement;
   (c) to pay Brazil U.S. $200,000 per year to help defray the cost of policing this agreement. *Time* (22 May 1972) 16.
26 *Realidade*, no. 52 (July 1970), 26–36.

Chapter 39
1. Ibid.
2. The sample was broken down by age, degree of education, socio-economic group and sex, based on a questionnaire of forty questions.
3. 35 per cent of the total, but 34 per cent well-to-do; 41 per cent average; 29 per cent poor.
4. 22 per cent of the total, but 45 per cent well-to-do; 26 per cent average; 14 per cent poor.
5. 86 per cent of university students gave this answer.
6. 52 per cent would agree to a social security system entirely administered by the State whereas 34 per cent preferred a mixed system.
7. 57 per cent said that they had received proper service the last time they applied to any State agency.
8. A small place: 7.2 per cent; none: 0.8 per cent; don't know: 7 per cent.
9. At the time when this survey was carried out the whole country was in expectancy concerning the world championship that was to take place in Mexico in June. Under the banner of 'king' Pelé, Brazil was to win the title of 'Three times champion' and thus be allowed to keep the Jules Rimet cup. President Médici, who was very fond of football, personally received the victorious team at Brasilia on 23 June before the largest crowd ever to assemble at Three Powers Square. The wave of optimism which swept through the country made the President's task easier by relegating the problems of terrorism to second place
10. 65 per cent of women and 45 per cent of men. It is worth pointing out that a fair amount of miscellaneous highway robbery was taking place among that perpetrated by extremists of the left and right.
11. *Realidade*, no. 52 (July 1970) 27.

Chapter 40
1. Professor Darcy Bessone for example, gave a lecture on 'Openness' at the Superior War College.
2. A statement made on 23 July 1971. *Visão*, 'Quem é Quem no Economia Brasileira', vol. 39, no. 4 (30 Aug 1971) 147 (hereafter cited as *Visão*, 'Quem 1971').
3. Ibid., pp. 147–209.
4. Ibid., p. 173.
5. Ibid.
6. Ibid., p. 174.
7. Ibid.
8. Ibid.
9. Ibid., p. 177.
10. Ibid., p. 203.
11. Ibid., p. 198.
12. Ibid., p. 206.
13. Ibid., p. 148.
14. Ibid., p. 155.
15. Under the Constitution promulgated by Castello Branco in 1967, governors were to be elected by direct suffrage. But for the election that was due to take place in 1970 a temporary arrangement, made by virtue of Institutional Act No. 5 and confirmed by Article 189 of the constitutional modification of October 1969, decided differently.
16. The Governor tried to work with the régime and notwithstanding opposition from the left wing of the M.D.B., he referred to himself in public

on 28 May 1972 as 'an M.D.B. man in the service of the 1964 Revolution'. *Veja*, no. 196 (7 June 1972) 20.
17 The governor's term of office ran from 15 March 1971 to 15 March 1975.
18 *Veja*, no. 169 (1 Dec 1971) 19–23.
19 Ibid., p. 23. On 13 May 1972 the Court of Accounts of Paraná disallowed the accounts of the ex-Governor, a hitherto unheard of event. If the Legislative Assembly to which the case was then sent upheld the verdict Peres could have been sentenced.
20 There were 409 deputies in the old Chamber. The reduction in numbers is explained by subsequent changes in the laws. Henceforward deputies were to be elected by reference to the number of electors and not of the population. Since illiterates did not have the vote, this provision strengthened the weighting of the industrial states in the south over against the rural states in the north.
21 After the civil rights of two senators had been withdrawn, the States of Guanabara and Goiás had to elect three senators instead of two.
22 Oscar Passos and José Ermirio de Moraes.
23 Air Force General José Vicente de Faria Lima, former Mayor of São Paulo, died suddenly on 4 September 1969.
24 Huntington's analysis was studied with interest in Brazil:
> Initially the legitimacy of a modernizing military régime comes from the promises it offers for the future. But eventually this declines as a source of legitimacy. If the régime does not develop a political structure which institutionalizes some principle of legitimacy, the result can only be a military oligarchy in which power is passed among the oligarchs by means of *Coups d'Etat*, and which also stands in danger of a revolutionary overthrow by new social forces which it does not possess the institutional mechanism for assimilating.' Huntington, 'Political Order', p. 242.
25 For example those of Herbert Levy, an influential coffee specialist.
26 Decree No. 69,534 of 11 November 1971.
27 *Visão* (6 Dec 1971) 17. (Pedro Aleixo referred to Article 86 of the Constitution: 'All individuals and corporate bodies are responsible for national security within the limits laid down by the law'.)
28 Ibid.
29 Opinion polls carried out by IBOPE, Instituto Brasileiro de Opinião Publica e Estatistica, gives the Government a popularity index of 82 per cent. *Brazil, The Take-off is Now* (São Paulo: American Chamber of Commerce for Brazil, July 1971) p. 14.
30 But there was no renewal, beyond the fact that the Government was able to have some relatively unknown candidates accepted, as in the case of some of the new governors.
31 Paradoxically, the man who was made responsible for this renewal was himself one of the most seasoned politicians, a former companion of Getúlio Vargas, under whom one of his posts had been that of Chief of Police.
32 The new president who was to take up office on 15 March 1974 had only to be elected by Congress on the preceding 15 January.
33 As for himself he said that he intended to observe the Constitution and refused any extension of his term of office.
34 They were due to take up office in March 1975.
35 Constitução de 1967, Article 13, ch. IX, par. 2.
36 *Veja*, no. 188 (12 Apr 1972) 19.
37 Since October 1965 electors had not gone to the polls except for legislative elections or to appoint the mayors of certain municipalities.

38 The penalty was exclusion from the party and loss of office. See on this subject the leading article in the *Jornal do Brasil* (Rio de Janeiro: 16–17 Apr 1972) 'As Coisas da Política'.
39 Just before Institutional Act No. 5 was promulgated, in December 1968, Victorino Freire had reminded the Chamber about this fable. But he was not listened to, and Parliament was sent into recess.
40 Pedro Parigot de Souza.
41 In principle civil rights could not be withdrawn for more than ten years and therefore it was possible for some of the people who had been so deprived in 1964 to take up political activity again in 1974 if by that time the President had not used the discretionary powers given to him under the Constitution (Article 182).
42 On 31 March, Médici announced that 'at federal level efforts to strengthen the control of inflation would be redoubled' since 'this evil of the century ... complicates economic growth, is a hindrance to progress and stimulates social instability' (speech commemorating the eighth anniversary of the *Revolution*). Therefore the Government must be able to carry on its economic policy without hindrance. Thus he was ordering the governors to see to it that their state budgets were balanced and he forbade them to incur any extra-budgetary expenses on penalty of losing financial support from the State (*Veja*, no. 192 (10 May 1972) 62). The Planning Minister made the same recommendations to his opposite numbers in the states at a meeting held in Brasilia on 15 December 1971 for putting the National Planning System into final form. 'Deficits', he said, 'are to be the privilege of the Federal Republic' (*Visão* (17 Jan 1972) 21, 22).
43 The seminar on 'Development Indicators in Latin America', which was held at the end of May 1972 in Rio de Janeiro under the auspices of UNESCO and the Instituto Universitario de Pesquisas may also be considered as a step in this direction. It was opened by the Minister of Finance, Antonio Delfim Netto, and enabled sociologists, economists and political experts from Brazil and abroad to discuss for five days topical themes such as modernisation, education, political mobilisation, stability of institutions and authoritarianism. Those present included: Christian Anglade, Fernando Henrique Cardoso, Antonio Octavio Cintra, Karl Deutsch, Guillermo O'Donnell, Alex Inkeles, Cândido Mendes de Almeida, Wanderley dos Santos, Glaucio Dilon Soares, Aldo Solari and Gabriel Valdez.
44 Reinato Carneiro Campos, a sociologist; Nilo Perreira, historian and man of letters; Sergio Guerra, economist; Syleno Ribeiro, lawyer.
45 *Veja*, no. 194 (24 May 1972) 16.
46 Ibid.
47 Although Freyre's theses, which were described by the President of ARENA as 'extremely interesting', were officially received with words of praise, they had small chance of being incorporated in the party doctrine. Nevertheless they caused a considerable stir and reopened discussion on 'openness' which was a favourite theme of this sociologist. Typical of this point of view was his statement to the review *Veja*: 'Oppression no longer achieves anything. The time has come to reopen discussion. Institutional Act No. 5 was necessary because the forces that were defeated in 1964 were rallying. But I believe there is no longer any justification for it. However, any possible measure should take into account the international situation, since there are international forces that would like to see Brazil dismembered' (*Veja*, no. 198 (21 June 1972) 40).

Chapter 41

1. See, for example, Revers, Jeanne, 'Le Miracle Brésilien: Mythe ou Réalité?', *Revue de Défense Nationale*, 28th year (Feb 1972) 193–207; and 'Rio de Janeiro', *The Times*, supplement 'Financial Centres of the World, no. 3' (23 May 1972) i–vi.
2. U.S. $41–42 billion in 1971 (approximately Crz. 200 billion). For comparison, the Swiss G.N.P. at current prices was estimated at U.S. $25 billion for 1971. *La Suisse en chiffres 1972*, Union de Banques Suisses (pages unnumbered).
3. Industry: 11·2 per cent; agriculture: 12·2 per cent; transport: 8·4 per cent; trade: 13 per cent.
4. Exports, 1968: + 13·7 per cent; 1969: + 22·9 per cent; 1970: + 18·5 per cent; exports of manufactured goods 1969: + 46·4 per cent; 1970: + 61·4 per cent; 1971: + 68·8 per cent.
5. Inflation was at the rate of 91·9 per cent in 1964.
6. 1971: 19·5 per cent; 1970: 19·3 per cent; 1969: 20·1 per cent. The statistics quoted are taken from *Conjuntura Econômica*, vol. 26 (Feb 1972). They are provisional.
7. In practice money is lent at a certain rate of interest to which is added a monetary correction rate estimated in advance for the period of the loan. Usually these amounts are discounted in advance from the sum lent.
8. Simonsen, *A Estrutura*, p. 41.
9. This summary is based on Simonsen, *A Estrutura*.
10. Médici seems to have had the good judgment to discard this solution and the adaptation of the minimum wage made on 1 May 1972 more than compensated for the increase in the cost of living.
11. Inflation is calculated on the basis of three factors: the cost of living (city of Rio de Janeiro), wholesale prices (internal and world supply), and the cost of construction.
12. *P.N.D.*, p. 41.
13. It is said that dissension arose at this meeting between the ministers and this information was reproduced by Roper, Christopher, 'Blemishes on Brazil's Economy', the *Guardian* (8 May 1972) 3. Questioned on this matter Delfim Netto replied incisively: 'Anybody who knows President Médici knows that he would not tolerate fights within his government' (*Veja*, no. 194 (24 May 1972) 4).
14. Until then the minister concerned used simply to inform the Inter-Ministerial Prices Council of his decision.
15. This is the position taken by the economist Julian Chacel, one of the leading Brazilian experts on this subject: 'For the first time in three years a large production of foodstuffs allied to an efficient marketing system can help to make a significant reduction in the rate of inflation, more than the instruments of monetary and fiscal policy' (*Veja*, no. 191 (3 May 1972) 61).
16. Prices might fall by as much as 23 per cent in certain cases (Ibid., p. 62).
17. Tax exemption, draw-back, financing, etc.
18. The leader of these 'stagnationists', as they were generally called, was Celso Furtado. His main analysis of the latter is to be found in: Furtado, Celso, *Subdesenvolvimento e Estagnação na América Latina* (Rio de Janeiro: Editôra Civilização Brasileira, 1966). In a recent study Furtado had adopted a more flexible position and admitted that under certain conditions the model adopted could be compatible with expansion. Furtado, *Analise*, pp. 56–65.

19 Tavares, Maria de Conceição and Serra, J., *Mas alla del Estancamiento* duplicated (Santiago de Chile: UNO-FLACSO, 1970) pp. 40–1.
20 Ibid., p. 2. This concept could do with some clarification because it applies in fact to consumer durables.
21 Morley, Samuel A. and Smith, Gordon W., *The Effect of Changes in the Distribution of Income on Labor, Foreign Investment and Growth in Brazil*, Program of Development Studies, paper no. 15, duplicated (Houston, Texas: Rice University, 1971) pp. 2–3.
22 This study was made by Professor Carlos Geraldo Langoni of the Institute of Economic Research (I.P.E.). Some of the results were published in *Veja*, no. 196 (7 June 1972) 67–74.
23 The eighth general census in Brazil was taken on 1 September 1970 under the rules of the Inter-American Institute of Statistics (I.A.S.I.). All the respondents replied to ten questions. Out of this total universe a sample (25 per cent of private households, 25 per cent of collective dwellings) replied to twenty-two supplementary questions. This somewhat random method yields results which may contain errors; nevertheless they are the most reliable figures available.

According to the preliminary results, the population of Brazil in 1970 was 94.5 million inhabitants. In September 1971 this figure was lowered to 92.763 million (*Conjuntura Econômica* (Sep 1971) 92). 52.64 per cent of the population was twenty years old or less. The respondents declared monetary incomes to a total of 26.079 million, an increase of 34.4 per cent since 1960 (+ 6.675 million) whereas the total population had increased by only 32.3 per cent.

We have thought it worthwhile to break down the preliminary results of the 1970 census as regards the active population, i.e. persons aged ten years and over in receipt of monetary incomes. This breakdown is shown in the four tables at the end of the book (pp. 285–6) which give the following information:

1. Rural employment had increased by 7 per cent between 1960 and 1970, but its share in the total of employment had fallen from 54 to 44 per cent. In 1970, 90 per cent of agricultural workers were men. Women field workers who represented 30 per cent of wage earners in 1960, represented only 21 per cent in 1970.
2. In contrast, industrial employment increased by 78 per cent between 1960 and 1970, growing from 2.96 million to 5.26 million. Its share in total employment increased from 13 to 18 per cent. In 1970, 88 per cent of wage earners in the industrial sector were males. Compared with 1960 their number had also increased by 88 per cent, notwithstanding the recession, whereas in the preceding decade it had increased by only 26 per cent.
3. The number of jobs in the tertiary sector was almost as large as that for agriculture. It had increased by 49 per cent between 1960 and 1970, but the trend of increase had changed by comparison with the preceding decade in which the increase had amounted to 67 per cent. Nevertheless its share of total employment rose from 33 to 38 per cent. In this sector men accounted for 62 per cent of the jobs in 1970. Nevertheless it is a sector peculiarly suited to female labour, which represented 69 per cent of the total of women employed in 1970. Between 1960 and 1970, their number had increased by 82 per cent whereas during the preceding decade the increase amounted to 71 per cent.
4. In 1970, women represented 21 per cent of the paid work-force. Ten

years earlier they represented only 18 per cent, this shows the quantitative increase in the part played by women in industry.
24 The relative number of declarations below the G.D.P. per capita (i.e. less than Crz. 155 per month) fell. In contrast, there was a 96 per cent increase in ten years of the 5 per cent of declarations forming the top of the pyramid, from 674,000 to 1·323 million.
25 Brazilian statistics designate as 'active population' all individuals aged ten years old and over and thus give a total of 66 million for 1970, 29·5 million of whom were employed (44·8 per cent) of whom 26 million declared a monetary income. If we take a more realistic view and define the active age as starting at fifteen and finishing at fifty-nine years of age we arrive at an active population of 49·4 million of whom about 60 per cent were in employment. As a simplification it could be said that in Brazil in 1970, 50 per cent of the population between fifteen and fifty-nine years of age had no economic activity; 30 per cent of the population had paid employment and 20 per cent was marginalised.
26 Compared with the situation in 1970 when there were 16,300,000 children in primary education, 1,100,000 in secondary education and 430,000 in higher education. The rate of illiteracy which was 26 or 27 per cent, was due to fall to 20 per cent (*P.N.D.*, Table). 23 per cent of the federal budget was spent on education (*Fiches Documentaires*, no. 465, 'Brésil' (Lausanne: OSEC, Dec 1971), 2).
27 The average wage aspect should be emphasised since for reasons of statistical convenience reference is generally made to the statutory minimum wage. But comparatively few workers earned only this, and in practice it has little place in industry with the exception of building. According to the available data, whereas the minimum wage showed a negative trend (falling from index 100 in 1965–6 to 85 in 1967, 84 in 1968, 82 in 1969 and 81 in 1970) the average wage in the State of São Paulo, where most of the leading industries are located, rose from 100 in 1965–6 to 115 in 1967, 99 in 1968, 116 in 1969 and 132 in February 1970. (*Source:* data calculated by the author based on figures published by the review *Visão* (23 May 1970) and repeated by Professor Luiz Carlos Bresser Pereira, also in *Visão*, on 21 November 1970.)
28 These measures included tax advantages granted to companies which merged in order to get a public quotation. By thus compelling businesses to make their shares available to the public, the Government was endeavouring to create a sort of popular capitalism, since tax payers were allowed, under certain conditions, to use a part of their tax payments to buy shares. In 1971, these new share issues attracted about U.S. $500 million worth of investment and in that year by an unprecedented boom, the daily average of transactions on the Rio de Janeiro and São Paulo Stock Exchanges reached 15 million dollars, whereas in 1966 they had amounted to only 300,000 dollars. (Figures quoted by Delfim Netto and reproduced by *Veja*, no. 194 (24 May 1972) 5.
29 See the very complete study carried out under the auspices of E.C.L.A. (Economic Commission for Latin America) and E.P.E.A. (The Economic and Social Planning Bureau of the Brazilian Ministry of Planning) which revealed that in 176 out of the 309 branches examined the four main enterprises accounted for over 50 per cent of total production. Fajnzylber, Fernando, *Sistema Industrial y Exportacion de Manufacturas: Analisis de la Experiencia Brasileira*, duplicated (Santiago, Chile: CEPAL, 1971) pp. 84, 280.
30 Private foreign investment in Brazil at 31 December 1970 was estimated at U.S. $1·546 billion and reinvestments at U.S. $801 million. (Ever

since Article 9 of Law 4390 of August 1964 linked the permission to transfer profits abroad with the registration of the capital at the Central Bank (FIERCE), a register summarising these figures has been kept up to date.) The important part played by the large firms is indicated by the fact that out of 288 subsidiaries of American companies that were analysed, 131 were controlled by enterprises in the 500 largest businesses in the United States. These 131 subsidiaries represented 76·1 per cent of all American investment in Brazil (Fajnzylber, *Sistema Industrial*, p. 20). In 1969 Swiss investment in Brazil was estimated at Swiss Frs 1·3 billion (*Fiches Documentaires*, no. 465, 'Brésil', p. 16c). Professor Charles Iffland of the University of Lausanne has written about Swiss investments in Brazil. The part played by firms such as Nestlé in developing the rural regions is vividly illustrated by a single example, that of Ibia, a small isolated municipality in Minas Gerais. Four years before setting up a factory at Ibia, Nestlé prepared the ground by sending there some of its milk production specialists. These people gave indefatigable technical and financial help to the 1867 cattle owners scattered over an area of 1000 sq. km. Thanks to their help and advice, the average daily production of milk rose from 2 litres per cow to 4 litres and in certain cases reached 8–10 litres. This made it possible to set up in 1965 a powdered milk factory which by 1969 was processing 300,000 litres of milk per day. The income of the municipality rose from Crz. 43,000 in 1964 to Crz. 763,000 in 1969 (approximately U.S. $187,000) of which nearly 40 per cent was directly paid out by Nestlé. The average wage of the 200-odd employees was about double the statutory minimum wage for that district. (*Visão*, vol. 35, no. 5 (29 Aug 1969) 116–22 and personal interview of the chairman of the company, M. Oswaldo Ballarin.)

31 A very interesting study about the integration of Brazilian capitalism into the international financial system was presented at the International Seminar on the Capital Market and Economic Development held in Rio de Janeiro in September 1971. The conclusion reached in this study was that Brazil was on the road to a State capitalism unique in its kind, relying strongly on multinational groups. (Tavares, Maria de Conceição, *Natureza e Contradições do Mercado Financeiro no Brasil*, Cadernos Economicos, duplicated (Rio de Janeiro: FEA-UFRJ, Sep 1971).

32 *Visão* (10 Apr 1972) 22.

33 Based on the balance sheet of the two banks at 31 December 1971 (which had still to be consolidated) the new União de Bancos Bradesco S.A. would have been eighty-second in order of size among international banks. The deposits of the group, which had 861 branches, were said to total approximately U.S. $685 million (*Veja*, no. 184 (15 Mar 1972) 67–70).

34 This merger Banco União Comercial S.A., with Roberto Campos at its head, was the result of a merger of the groups Big–Univest and Comercial Brasul. It was second in size among private commercial banks in Brazil and the largest investment bank. *Veja*, no. 213 (4 Oct 1972) 52–3; press handout.

35 *Visão* (10 Apr 1972) 22.

36 *The First National Development Plan (P.N.D.)* approved by Parliament on 4 November 1971, provided for increased aid to small and medium-sized businesses in Brazil for the period 1972–4:

F.M.R.I.–Fundo de Modernização e Reorganização Industrial, U.S. $153 million approximately.

P.M.R.C.–Programa de Modernização e Reorganização da Comercialização, U.S. $60 million approximately.

FINAME–Agência Especial de Financiamento Industrial, U.S. $805 million approximately.
P.N.D., p. 47 (rate of conversion according to p. 9 of the text: U.S. $1 = Crz. 5.875).
37 *Visão* (10 Apr 1972) 22.
38 Interview published by *Veja*, no. 194 (24 May 1972) p. 4.
39 On average, from 1947 to 1970, Brazil's trading balance showed an annual surplus of U.S. $195 million (*Visão* (13 Mar 1972) 43).
40 On 31 March 1971 short-term debt (operations 289, resolution 63, Law 4131) amounted to U.S. $2.45 billion representing 44.6 per cent of the total debt at that date (U.S. $5.5 billion). *Visão* (13 Mar 1972) 43–6.

Although classed as short-term debt, this sum did not indicate a dangerous situation. For much of the sum represented long-term investment disguised as short-term loans to protect them from the risks inherent in all investment in a developing country. Nevertheless it is a potential threat to the stability of the balance of payments and Brazil is making increasing efforts to obtain long-term loans. This is facilitated by the fact that the country has displayed a remarkable economic vitality.

Results were sufficiently encouraging to enable the Minister of Planning to announce at the annual meeting of the Inter-American Committee of the Alliance for Progress (I.C.A.P.) at the beginning of June 1972 in Washington that from then on Brazil would not accept financial credits having a term of less than five years. If Brazil manages to continue along this path, the problem of short-term debt will be merely of academic interest.

41 The following order of size is planned for investments: education, about U.S. $1.77 billion per year; scientific and technological development, about U.S. $100 million per year; public health, about U.S. $860 million per year; energy, about U.S. $1.14 billion per year; communications, about U.S. $177.7 million per year; housing, about U.S. $990 million per year; national integration (PIN and PROTERRA), about U.S. $600 million per year; social integration, about U.S. $326 million per year. (*Source*: *P.N.D.*, p. 48; rate of exchange U.S. $1 = Crz. 5.875 as p. 9 of the text.)
42 Average for 1969–71: external debt/G.D.P. = 13.6 per cent; external debt/annual volume of exports = 196.8 per cent; international reserves/external debt = 22 per cent. *Visão* (13 Mar 1972) 46.
43 Compared with a rate of growth of G.D.P. of 9 per cent per annum. (Ibid.)
44 Vernay, Alain, 'Brésil: La passion du développement l'emporte sur la défiance envers les investissements étrangers', *Le Figaro* (Paris: 16–17 Sep 1972) 7.
45 Ibid.
46 L'Huillier, Jacques, *Les Organisations internationales de coopération économique et le commerce extérieur des pays en voie de développement*, coll. Etudes et Travaux no. 9 (Geneva: Graduate Institute of International Studies, 1969) p. 103.
47 This group was formed at Geneva in August 1972 and is responsible for more than 95 per cent of world coffee production. The creation of a multinational buffer stock to support prices is envisaged.
48 Whereas between 1960 and 1963 the average value of exports of manufactured products from Brazil was only U.S. $39 million per annum. *Veja*, no. 208 (30 Aug 1972) 68.
49 Ibid., no. 201 (11 July 1972) 72.

50 L'Huillier, *Organisations internationales*, p. 104.
51 The exhibition Brazil Export 1972 held at São Paulo from 5 to 14 September 1972 and the proposed establishment of Trading Companies are tentatives in this direction.
52 The opening of branches of the Bank of Brazil in London and Paris in 1972 and the establishment of Eurobraz, European Brazilian Bank Ltd, are some of the steps that were taken with this object in view.
53 Dependence on outside sources is defined as: 'The measure of the inability to co-ordinate the decisions of the economic agents who control the incorporation of technical progress and the accumulation of capital for the furtherance of our own national objectives, owing to the fact that these agents belong to groups outside the country.' Furtado, *Analise*, p. 71, note 61.
54 Objectives of the *First National Development Plan*, Law No. 5727 dated 4 November 1971, *P.N.D.*, p. 7.
55 The options open to Brazil in foreign policy are examined by Rosenbaum, Jon H., 'Brazil's Foreign Policy: Developmentalism and Beyond', *ORBIS*, vol. xvi, no. 1 (spring 1972) 58–83.
56 Link, Max, *Stand und Zukunftsperspektiven der Industrialisierung Brasiliens*, Lateinamerikanisches Institut an der Hochschule St Gallen für Wirtschafts- und Sozialwissenschaften (Berne, Stuttgart: Verlag Paul Haupt, 1972).

Conclusion
1 Rustow, *World of Nations*, p. 231.
2 Ibid., pp. 129–30.
3 Ibid., p. 204.
4 Supplementary Law No. 7, dated 7 September 1970, detailed rules for the application of which were set out on 25 February 1971 by Resolution No. 174 of the Central Bank published in the *Diario Oficial* on 4 March. The legal foundation for this measure is Article 165, paragraph v of the Constitution concerning social improvement in workers' conditions.
5 Supplementary Law No. 8, of 3 December 1970, 'Programa de Formação de Patrimônio do Servidor Publico'.
6 Each of these two factors had a weighting of 50 per cent in the calculation.
7 For a more complete analysis see *Conjuntura Econômica*, vol. 25, no. 2 (Feb 1971) 127–31. In September 1972, President Médici was able to announce that the average credit per beneficiary would be Crz. 100 (the lowest credit was Crz. 64) for the first year of operation. *Veja*, no. 211 (20 Sep 1972) 71.
8 Decree Law No. 1106 of 16 June 1970 and Decree No. 67,113 of 26 August 1970. The word integration is used in its Brazilian sense, meaning unification of the territory.
9 *Sinopse*, pp. 22, 60 (census of 1 September 1970). Amazonia, defined as the North of Brazil, consisted politically of the States of Amazonas, Pará, Acre and of the territories of Rondônia, Roraima and Amapá. The State of Amazonas alone had an area of 1,558,987 sq. km and its population density was 0·62 inhabitants per sq. km. The population of Roraima is as low as 0·18 inhabitants per sq. km.
10 This euphemism of the Brazilian technocrats means that the project could not yield a financial return commensurate to the invested capital.
   As Professor Gourou says:
   The current mystique of the great motor highways has great geographical effects ... it is pleasing to see here with extreme clarity the creative

effect of a technique on human geography – the case in point being the technique of road haulage – but that does not silence the question of whether this technique was the best possible. Would not the interests of Amazonia and Brazil be best served by developing the areas near the ports and centres of consumption by means of a well-developed system of roads and intensive methods of agriculture? That might bring a better return than intoxication with the wide open spaces.' Gourou, Pierre, *Leçons de Géographie Tropicale*, Ecole Pratique des Hautes Etudes, Sorbonne (The Hague, Paris: Mouton & Co., 1971) pp. 115–16.

11 In this connection Professor Gourou observes:
It would be self-deception to imagine that Amazonia contains inexhaustible resources of petroleum. As for the other 'riches' of Amazonia, they exist only in so far as suitable techniques for exploiting them are developed and applied. It is clear that such techniques are possible; but it is equally clear that as yet they have been neither defined nor applied. Ibid. p. 228.

12 *Metas e Bases para a Ação de Govêrno*, p. 31.
13 The Government gives the colonists free transport, gives each of them 250 acres of land and a primitive little house, gives them technical assistance and grants them loans at favourable or nil rates of interest.
14 RADAM project.
15 *Routes Transamazoniennes*, Ministry of Transport of the Federal Republic of Brazil (Oct 1970).
16 The construction of the Pan-American highway that will link the Atlantic with the Pacific (further south than the Trans-Amazonian route, it crosses Brazil, Paraguay, Bolivia and Peru) was hastened after the United States had made available a credit of U.S. $100 million at the beginning of 1972. *Jornal do Brasil* (Rio de Janeiro: 16, 17 Apr 1972) 20.
17 This city is already linked with Brasilia, São Paulo and Rio de Janeiro.
18 *Veja*, no. 208 (30 Aug 1972) 24.
19 On 29 March 1971 the land for 62 miles on either side of the Trans-Amazonian highway, involving an area of 2,230,000 sq. km, was nationalised by decree. It was planned to locate 10,000 families in this area during 1972, 20,000 in 1973 and 100,000 in the succeeding years. *Notes et Etudes*, no. 3913–14 (28 July 1972) 62.
20 PRORURAL, 'Programa de Assistência ao Trabalhador Rural', Supplementary Law No. 11, of 25 May 1971.
21 The establishment of INCRA, Instituto Nacional de Colonização e Reforma Agrária, which absorbed all the organisations previously dealing with the matter (IBRA, INDA, GERA). Decree Law No. 1110 of 9 July 1970.
22 'Programa de Redistribuição de Terras e de Estimulo à Agroindustria do Norte e do Nordeste', Decreto No. 1179 of 6 July 1971. From 1972 to 1976 PROTERRA will have credits amounting to Crz. 4 billion, approximately U.S. $750 million. *Conjuntura Econômica*, vol. 26 (Feb 1972) 25.
23 This money was lent at the very favourable interest rate of 5 per cent per annum for a period of twelve to twenty years with an initial three-year interest-free period. *Veja*, no. 206 (16 Aug 1972) 84.
24 *Conjuntura Econômica*, vol. 26 (Feb 1972) 7, 17.
25 Owner of an agricultural holding.
26 'Uma distribuição Difícil', *Veja*, no. 206 (16 Aug 1972) 84–6.
27 Chaired by the Minister for the Army, Orlando Geisel, the Army High Command consisted of Generals Isaac Nahon (personnel); Rodrigo

Octavio Jordão Ramos (services); Breno Borges Fortes (general staff); Dyrceu de Araujo Nogueira (engineers); Antônio Jorge Correa (training and research); Vicente de Paulo Dale Coutinho (armaments); Sylvio Couto Ceolha da Frota (First Army); Humberto de Souza Mello (Second Army); Oscar Luis da Silva (Third Army); Walter de Menezes Paes (Fourth Army). (Only Geisel and Nahon were generals in 1964.) *Veja*, no. 204 (2 Aug 1962) 17–19.

28 Spoken at the course beginning 10 March 1970, quoted by *Realidade* (July 1970) 178.

29 *P.N.D.*, p. 15.

30 Without such control, there would be nearly 200 million Brazilians by the year 2000, if present demographic trends continued. Whereas it required four centuries (from 1500 to 1900) for the population of Brazil to reach 27 million, only one century would be required for an increase from 27 to 200 million.

31 It will be recalled that between 1960 and 1970 the number of persons declaring an income above the minimum wage grew by 20 per cent; the salary readjustments granted under the Médici Government outstripped the increase in the cost of living and the indirect incomes of the lower strata of the population were noticeably increased. Nevertheless in 1970, 40 per cent of persons having a declared monetary income shared only 10 per cent of the total of incomes.

32 Delfim Netto, questioned about the political problems which might be caused by the concentration of incomes, replied that this hypothesis would be valid only 'in so far as the Government pursued an inept fiscal policy'. *Veja*, no. 194 (24 May 1972) 4.

President Médici was equally categorical. In the speech he made on Labour Day, 1 May 1970, he said: 'To meet the challenge of development we shall give to industrialists in Brazil the stability and security they require for the growth of their businesses. But we shall take care to put down as far as possible anything that might lead either to an arbitrary increase in profits or abuses of economic power.' *Realidade* (July 1970) 174, 175.

33 Gross capital formation should exceed 18 per cent of gross domestic product whereas on average (bearing in mind the unreliability of Brazilian statistics in this area) it appears to have been only 15·8 to 17·5 per cent between 1964 and 1971. This growth is all the more necessary because part of the expansion that took place in recent years was due to exploitation of unused productive capacity in the existing industrial equipment. But it appears that many branches of industry had reached the limits of productive capacity and that new capital investments and equipment would be required for expansion.

34 The institutional élite drew its strength and prestige from belonging to an institution in contradistinction to the class élite whose role depended on an inherited social situation.

35 It is worth noting that the Médici Government had learnt from the unfortunate experience of Castello Branco and was carrying out a systematic campaign of popular enlightenment with seemingly promising results, through A.E.R.P., Assessoria Especial de Relações Publicas.

36 As regards this liberty, Pierre and Renée Gosset conclude: 'But dare we say it? The good-natured crowds in Rio, São Paulo, Santos, Belo Horizonte or Porto Alegre hardly give the impression of missing their freedom.' *Journal de Genève* (30 Aug 1972) 13. This observation brings to mind what Stefan Zweig wrote in 1942: 'It is not by chance that Brazil

...though living under a dictatorship enjoys more individual liberty and satisfaction than many a country in Europe'. Zweig, *Le Brésil*, p. 27.
37 As Antonio Delfim Netto observed: 'If the economic system works well, the country is prepared for any political system. That's the government's job. And that's the best thing that can be done just now.' *Veja*, no. 194 (24 May 1972) 5.
38 Niedergang, Marcel, 'Brésil, le plus jeune des géants', *Le Monde* (Paris. 9–13 Sep 1972).

TABLE A.1 ACTIVE WAGE-EARNING POPULATION OF BRAZIL, MALE AND FEMALE, AGED 10 YEARS AND OVER*

Sector	1 Sep 1940 Number ('000s)	%	1 July 1950 Number ('000s)	%	1 Sep 1960 Number ('000s)	%	1 Sep 1970 Number ('000s)	%	60/50 % +	70/60 % +
Rural sector	9,726	66	10,254	60	12,163	54	13,071	44	19	7
Industrial sector	1519	10	2347	14	2963	13	5264	18	26	78
Tertiary sector	3514	24	4516	26	7525	33	11,210	38	67	49
Total	14,759	100	17,117	100	22,651	100	29,545	100	—	—

Source: Tables A.1–4 have been compiled by the author on the basis of official figures: *Tabulações Avançadas de Censo Demografico 1970* (Rio de Janeiro: I.B.G.E., 1971) p. xxix.
* These tables relate to note 23, p. 277. See also text p. 195.

TABLE A.2 MALE ACTIVE WAGE-EARNING POPULATION OF BRAZIL, AGED 10 YEARS AND OVER

Sector	1 Sep 1940 Number ('000s)	%	1 July 1950 Number ('000s)	%	1 Sep 1960 Number ('000s)	%	1 Sep 1970 Number ('000s)	%	60/50 % +	70/60 % +
Rural sector	8,415	71	9,496	65	10,942	59	11,792	50	15	7
Industrial sector	1221	10	1955	13	2456	13	4620	20	26	88
Tertiary sector	2323	19	3159	22	5199	28	6978	30	65	34
Total	11,959	100	14,610	100	18,597	100	23,390	100	—	—

TABLE A.3 FEMALE ACTIVE WAGE-EARNING POPULATION OF BRAZIL, AGED 10 YEARS AND OVER

Sector	1 Sep 1940 Number ('000s)	%	1 July 1950 Number ('000s)	%	1 Sep 1960 Number ('000s)	%	1 Sep 1970 Number ('000s)	%	60/50 % +	70/60 % +
Rural sector	1311	47	758	30	1221	30	1279	21	61	5
Industrial sector	298	11	392	16	507	13	644	10	29	19
Tertiary sector	1191	42	1357	54	2326	57	4232	69	71	82
Total	2800	100	2507	100	4054	100	6155	100	—	—

TABLE A.4 ACTIVE WAGE-EARNING POPULATION OF BRAZIL, MALE AND FEMALE, AGED 10 YEARS AND OVER, AS A PERCENTAGE OF THE TOTAL

Sector	Percentage 1960 Men	Women	Percentage 1970 Men	Women
Rural sector	90	10	90	10
Industrial sector	83	17	88	12
Tertiary sector	69	31	62	38
Total	82	18	79	21

Bibliography

UNPUBLISHED SOURCES

Archives of Marshal Castello Branco:

Paulo Castello Branco Collection, Rio de Janeiro and Fortaleza.
ECEME (Escola do Comando e Estado Maior do Exercito) Collection, Rio de Janeiro.
Luiz Vianna Filho Collection, Salvador (Bahia).

PUBLISHED SOURCES

OFFICIAL DOCUMENTS

Brazil
Banco Central da República do Brasil: *Relatório*, 1965.
Consolidação das Leis do Trabalho e Outras Leis Trabalhistas. Rio de Janeiro: Livraria Freitas Bastos S.A., 1950.
A Guide to Investing in Brazil. Documents on Brazil no. 3. Washington, D.C.: Brazilian Embassy, Mar 1969, v.
Inquérito Policial Militar no. 709:
  Vol. 1: *O Comunismo no Brasil*, Rio de Janeiro: Biblioteca do Exército, 1966–7.
Ministério de Planejamento e Coordenação Econômica:
  Programa de Ação Econômica do Governo (1964-1966), 1964.
  O Programa de Ação e as Reformas de Base, Documento EPEA, no. 3, Dec 1965.
  O Debate do Programa de Ação, Conselho Consultivo do Planejamento, Rio de Janeiro, 1965.
  Plano Decenal de Desenvolvimento Econômico e Social (1967–1976), preliminary account, 7 parts, 21 vols., Mar 1967.
Ministério de Planejamento e Coordenação Geral:
  Diretrizes de Govêrno, *Programa Estratégico de Desenvolvimento*, duplicated, July 1967.
  Programa Estratégico de Desenvolvimento (1968–1970), 1968.
  A Experiência Brasileira: Desenvolvimento e Transformação, C.I.A.P., 1971.
  Sinopse Estatística do Brasil 1971, Instituto Brasileiro de Estatística. Rio de Janeiro: Fundação I.B.G.E., 1971.
Ministry of Transport:
  Routes Transamazoniennes. A report submitted to the Sixth World Congress of the International Road Federation, Montreal, Oct 1970.

Presidência da República:
> Plano Trienal de Desenvolvimento Econômico e Social, 1963–1965, Sintese, Dec 1962.
> Metas e Bases para a Ação de Governo, Sep 1970.
> Metas e Bases para a Ação de Governo, Sintese.
> Projeto do Primeiro Plano Nacional de Desenvolvimento Econômico e Social, 1972/74, Sep 1971.
> Projeto do I Plano Nacional de Desenvolvimento – Comentários e Editoriais. Rio de Janeiro, Fundação I.B.G.E., Sep 1971.
> Primeiro Plano Nacional de Desenvolvimento (P.N.D.), 1972/74, I.B.G.E., Dec 1971.

Presidência da República, Secretaria de Imprensa:
Castello Branco, Marshal Humberto de Alencar:
> Discursos 1964. Brasilia: Imprensa Nacional, 1965.
> Discursos 1965. Brasilia: Imprensa Nacional, 1966.
> Discursos 1966. Brasilia: Imprensa Nacional, 1967.

República Federativa do Brasil:
> Constituição da República Federativa do Brasil, Emenda constitucional N° 1 promulgada em 17 de Outubro de 1969 (Div. no. 1116). Departemento de Imprensa Nacional, 1969.
> Diário do Congresso Nacional.
> Diário Oficial da União.

United States

U.S. Congress, Senate, Committee on Foreign Relations, *Hearing Before the Committee on Foreign Relations on the Nomination of Lincoln Gordon to be Assistant Secretary of State for Inter-American Affairs.* 89th Congress, 2nd sess., 7 Feb 1966.

U.S. Department of Commerce, Bureau of International Commerce, 'Brazil in Growth Surge', *International Commerce*, 13 Apr 1970.

NEWSPAPERS AND PERIODICALS REGULARLY CONSULTED FOR THE WHOLE OF THE PERIOD 1964–72

Brazilian newspapers
O Correio da Manhã. Rio de Janeiro, daily.
O Estado de São Paulo. São Paulo, daily.
O Globo. Rio de Janeiro, daily.
Jornal do Brasil. Rio de Janeiro, daily.

Brazilian periodicals
Banas. São Paulo: Editôra Banas S.A., weekly (particularly the annual special numbers 'As mil maiores', which list the thousand largest limited companies in Brazil; and 'Imagem do Brasil', May 1971).

Bulletin de la Banque française et italienne pour l'Amérique du Sud, Sudameris. Paris, Rio de Janeiro, São Paulo, periodical.
Conjuntura Econômica. Fundação Getúlio Vargas, Rio de Janeiro, monthly (especially the annual issue 'A Economia Brasileira').
Dados. Publicacão do Instituto Universitário de Pesquisas do Rio de Janeiro, periodical (especially no. 1, 1966; no. 2/3, 1967; no. 4, 1968; no. 8, 1971).
A Economia Brasileira e suas Perspectivas. Rio de Janeiro: APEC Editôra, annual (especially 1966, Estudos APEC).
Exame. São Paulo: Editôra Abril, monthly (an annual edition in English, *Brazilian Trends*, is also published).
Manchete. Rio de Janeiro: Bloch Editôres S.A., weekly (see also the special annual numbers since 1968: 'Retrato do Brasil' (1968), 'Progresso do Brasil' (1969), 'Brasil 70' (1970) and 'Brazil Export 72', English version of 'Manchete 1000').
Paz e Terra. Rio de Janeiro, periodical.
Realidade. São Paulo: Editôra Abril, monthly.
Revista Brasileira de Economia. Rio de Janeiro, quarterly.
Revista Brasileira de Estudos Políticos. Belo Horizonte, periodical.
Revista Civilização Brasileira. Rio de Janeiro, periodical.
Veja. São Paulo: Editôra Abril, weekly.
Visão. São Paulo: Sociedade Editorial Visão Ltda, fortnightly (especially the annual numbers 'Quem é Quem na Economia Brasileira', and particularly 30 Aug 1968, 29 Aug 1969 and 30 Aug 1971).

Non-Brazilian newspapers
Le Figaro. Paris, daily.
Gazette de Lausanne. Lausanne, daily.
Journal de Genève. Geneva, daily.
Le Monde. Paris, daily.
New York Times. New York, daily.
The Times. London, daily.

Non-Brazilian periodicals
Economic Bulletin for Latin America. New York: United Nations, twice yearly.
Notes et Etudes documentaires, Problèmes d'Amérique Latine. Paris: La Documentation française, Secrétariat général du Gouvernement, Direction de la Documentation. No. 3247, 21 Dec 1965; no. 3300, 17 June, 1966, *PAL* no. 2; no. 3383, 19 Apr 1967, *PAL* no. 5; no. 3423, 29 Sep 1967, *PAL* no. 6; no. 3749–50, 30 Dec 1970, *PAL* no. 18; no. 3913–14, 28 July 1972, *PAL* no. 24.

ACTORS IN AND WITNESSES OF THE PERIOD 1964–72

Brazilian works

Almeida, Rui Gomes de, *Idéias e Atitudes.* Rio de Janeiro: Associação Commercial, 1969.

Arraes, Miguel, *Le Brésil, le pouvoir et le peuple,* coll. Cahiers libres, no. 155. Paris: François Maspero, 1969.

Bonavides, Paulo, *A Crise Politica Brasileira.* Rio de Janeiro: Editôra Forense, 1969.

Borges, Mauro, *O Golpe em Goiás: História de uma grande Traição.* Rio de Janeiro: Editôra Civilização Brasileira, 1965.

Bresser Pereira, Luiz Carlos, *Desenvolvimento e Crise no Brasil,* 2nd ed., rev. São Paulo: Editôra Brasiliense, 1970.

Bulhões, Octavio Gouvêa de, *Dois Conceitos de Lucro.* Rio de Janeiro: APEC Editôra, 1969.

Callado, Antonio, *Tempo de Arraes: Padres e Comunistas na Revolução sem Violência.* Rio de Janeiro: José Alvaro Editor, 1964.

Câmara, Dom Helder:
Revolução dentro de Paz. Rio de Janeiro: Editôra Sabia, 1968.
Le Tiers Monde Trahi, coll. Remise en Cause. Paris: Desclée et Cie, 1968.
Spirale de Violence. Paris: Desclée de Brouwer, 1970.
Pour arriver à Temps. Paris: Desclée de Brouwer, 1970.

Campos, Roberto de Oliveira:
Economia, Planejamento e Nacionalismo. Rio de Janeiro: APEC Editôra, 1963.
A Moeda, O Govêrno e o Tempo. Rio de Janeiro: APEC Editôra, 1964.
Do Outro Lado da Cêrca. Rio de Janeiro: APEC Editôra, 1968.
Ensaios Contra a Maré. Rio de Janeiro: APEC Editôra, 1969.
Reflections on Latin American Development. Austin: University of Texas Press, 1968.

Cardoso, Fernando Henrique, *Política e Desenvolvimento em Sociedades Dependentes. Ideologias do Empresariado Industrial Argentino e Brasileiro,* Biblioteca de Ciências Sociais. Rio de Janeiro: Zahar Editôres, 1971.

Cardoso, Fernando Henrique and Faletto, Enzo, *Dependência e Desenvolvimento na América Latina, Ensaio de Interpretação Sociologica,* Biblioteca de Ciências Sociais. Rio de Janeiro: Zahar Editôres, 1970.

Castro, Josué de, *Une Zone explosive: le Nordeste du Brésil,* coll. Esprit 'Frontière ouverte', new ed., rev. and corrected. Paris: Editions du Seuil, 1970.

Cony, Carlos Heitor, *O Ano e o Fato: Crônicos Politicos.* Rio de Janeiro: Editôra Civilização Brasileira, 1964.

Couto e Silva, General Golbery do, *Geopolítica do Brasil.* Rio de Janeiro: Livraria José Olympio, 1967.
Delfim Netto, Antonio, *Planejamento para o Desenvolvimento Econômico.* São Paulo: Livraria Editôra Pioneira, 1966.
Dias Leite, Antonio, *Caminhos do Desenvolvimento, Contribuição para um Projeto Brasileiro.* Rio de Janeiro: Zahar Editôres, 1966.
Dimas Filho, Nelson, *Costa e Silva: O Homen e o Líder.* Rio de Janeiro: Edições O Cruzeiro, 1966.
A Educação que Nos Convém, Fernando Bastos d'Avila *et al.*, Inst. de Pesquisas e Estudos Sociais. Rio de Janeiro: APEC Editôra, 1969.
Fernandes, Florestan, *Sociedade de Classes e Subdesenvolvimento.* Rio de Janeiro: Zahar Editôres, 1968.
Fernandes, Hélio, *Recordações de um Desterrado em Fernando de Noronha.* Rio de Janeiro: Editôra da Tribuna da Imprensa, 1967.
Ferreira, Oliveiro S.:
As Forças Armadas e o Desafio da Revolução. Rio de Janeiro: Edição GRD, 1964.
O Fim do Poder Civil. São Paulo: Editôra Convívio, 1966.
Ferreira Reis, Arthur C., *A Amazônia e a Cobiça Internacional,* 3rd ed. Rio de Janeiro: Gráfica Record Editôra, 1968.
Figueiredo, M. Poppe de, *A Revolução de 1964 – Um depoimento para a História Patria.* Rio de Janeiro: APEC Editôra, 1970.
Freire, Paulo, *L'Education: pratique de la liberté,* coll. Terre de Feu. Paris: Les Editions du Cerf, 1971.
Furtado, Celso:
Subdesenvolvimento e Estagnação na América Latina. Rio de Janeiro: Editôra Civilização Brasileira, 1966.
Um Projeto para o Brasil. Rio de Janeiro: Editôra Saga, 1968.
Analise do 'Modelo' Brasileira, coll. 'Perspectivas do Homen', no. 92, 2nd ed. Rio de Janeiro: Editôra Civilização Brasileira, 1972.
Diagnosis of the Brazilian Crisis (translation of Dialetica do Desenvolvimento). Berkeley, Los Angeles: University of California Press, 1965.
Les Etats-Unis et le Sous-Développement de l'Amérique Latine, coll. Perspective de l'Economie. Paris: Calmann-Lévy, 1970.
Gasparian, Fernando, *Em Defesa da Economia Nacional.* Rio de Janeiro: Editôra Saga, 1966.
Gudin, Eugenio, *Para um Brasil Melhor.* Rio de Janeiro: APEC Editôra, 1969.
Ianni, Octavio:
Industrialização e Desenvolvimento Social no Brasil. Rio de Janeiro: Editôra Civilização Brasileira, 1963.

Estado e Capitalismo, Estrutura Social e Industrialização no Brasil. Rio de Janeiro: Editôra Civilização Brasileira, 1965.
O Colapso do Populismo no Brasil, coll. Retratos do Brasil no. 70. Rio de Janeiro: Editôra Civilização Brasileira, 1968.
Estado e Planejamento Econômico no Brasil, 1930–1970, coll. Retratos do Brasil no. 83. Rio de Janeiro: Editôra Civilização Brasileira, 1971.
Os Idos de Março e a Queda em Abril. Alberto Dines *et al.* Rio de Janeiro: José Alvaro Editôr, 1964.

Jaguaribe, Hélio:
Problemas do Desenvolvimento Latino Americano: Estudos de Política. Rio de Janeiro: Editôra Civilização Brasileira, 1967.
Desenvolvimento Econômico e Desenvolvimento Político, Uma abordagem téorica e um estudo do caso Brasileiro. Rio de Janeiro: Paz e Terra, 1969 (revised and enlarged reissue of a work published in 1962 under the same title by Fundo da Cultura, Rio de Janeiro).

Julião, Francisco, *Cambão* [The yoke], *la face cachée du Brésil,* coll. Cahiers libres no. 129. Paris: François Maspero, 1968.

Jurema, Abelardo:
Sexta Feira 13: os últimos dias do governo Goulart. Rio de Janeiro: Editôra O Cruzeiro, 1964.
Entre os Andes e a Revolução. Rio de Janeiro: Editôra Leitura, 1965.

Lacerda, Carlos:
Brasil entre a Verdade e a Mentira. Rio de Janeiro: Bloch Editôres, 1965.
Palavras e Ação. Rio de Janeiro: Distribuidora Record, 1965.
Critica e Autocrítica. Rio de Janeiro: Editôra Nova Fronteira, 1966.

Lago, Mario, *Primeiro de Abril: Estórias para a História.* Rio de Janeiro: Editôra Civilização Brasileira, 1964.

Magrassi de SA, Jayme, *Aspectos da Economia Brasileira.* São Paulo: Editôra Alba, 1970.

Marighela, Carlos, *Pour la Libération du Brésil,* new ed. Paris: privately published, 1970.

Martins, Luciano, *Industrialização, Burguesia Nacional e Desenvolvimento. Introdução a crise Brasileira,* Imagem do Brasil, no. 7. Rio de Janeiro: Editôra Saga, 1968.

Mascarenhas, de Moraes, Maréchal João Baptista, *Memorias.* Rio de Janeiro: Livraria José Olympio, 1969.

Medina, Rubem, *Desnacionalização, Crime Contra O Brasil?* Imagem do Brasil, no. 10. Rio de Janeiro: Editôra Saga, 1970.

Meira Penna, J. O. de, *Política Externa, Segurança e Desenvolvimento.* Rio de Janeiro: Livraria Agir Editôra, 1967.

Mendes de Almeida, Cândido A., *Memento dos Vivos, A Esquerda Católica no Brasil.* Rio de Janeiro: Edições Tempo Brasileiro, 1966.
Moniz, Edmundo, *O Golpe de Abril.* Rio de Janeiro: Editôra Civilização Brasileira, 1965.
Moreira Alvès, Márcio:
A Velha Classe. Rio de Janeiro: Editôra Artenova, 1964.
Torturas e Torturados. Rio de Janeiro: Editôra Artenova, 1966.
O Cristo do Povo. Rio de Janeiro: Editôra Sabia, 1968.
Morel, Edmar, *O Golpe Começou em Washington.* Rio de Janeiro: Editôra Civilização Brasileira, 1965.
Nascimento Silva, Luiz Gonzaga do, *Rumos para o Brasil Moderno.* Rio de Janeiro: APEC, 1970.
Nasser, David:
A Revolução que se perdeu a si mesma. Rio de Janeiro: Edições O Cruzeiro, 1965.
João Sem Mêdo. Rio de Janeiro: Edições O Cruzeiro, 1965.
Nobre, José de Freitas:
Lei da Imprensa. São Paulo: Editôra Saraiva, 1965.
Lei da Informação. São Paulo: Editôra Saraiva, 1968.
Pereira, Luiz, *Estudos Sôbre o Brasil Contempôraneo,* Biblioteca Pionera de Ciências Sociais. São Paulo: Livraria Pioneira Editôra, 1971.
Pereira, Osny Duarte:
A Constituição Federal e Suas Modificações Incorporadas ao Texto. Rio de Janeiro: Editôra Civilização Brasileira, 1966.
A Constituição do Brasil. Rio de Janeiro: Editôra Civilização Brasileira, 1967.
Planejamento no Brasil, ed. Betty Mindlin Lafer, coll. Debates. São Paulo: Editôra Perspectiva, 1970.
Poerner, Arthur José, *O Poder Jovem: História da Participação Política dos Estudantes Brasileiros.* Rio de Janeiro: Editôra Civilização Brasileira, 1968.
Reale, Miguel, *Imperativo da Revolução de Março.* São Paulo: Livraria Martins Editôra, 1965.
Rodrigues, José Albertino, *Sindicato e Desenvolvimento no Brasil.* São Paulo: Difusão Europeia do Livro, 1968.
Rodrigues, José Honório:
Aspirações Nacionais: Interpretação Historico-Político. São Paulo: Editôra Fulgor, 1965.
Interesse Nacional e Política Externa. Rio de Janeiro: Editôra Civilização Brasileira, 1966.
Schmidt, Augusto Frederico, *Prelúdio a Revolução.* Rio de Janeiro: Edições do Val, 1964.
Silva Telles, Goffredo Carlos, Jr, *A Democracia e o Brasil, Uma*

doutrina para a Revolução de Março. São Paulo: Editôra Revista dos Tribunais, 1965.

Simonsen, Marío Henrique:
Brasil 2001. Rio de Janeiro: APEC Editôra, 1969.
Inflação: Gradualismo x Tratamento de Choque. Rio de Janeiro: APEC Editôra, 1970.
Ensaios sobre Economia e Política Econômica. Rio de Janeiro: APEC Editôra, 1971.

Sodré, Nelson Werneck:
História Militar do Brasil. Rio de Janeiro: Editôra Civilização Brasileira, 1965.
Memórias de um Soldado. Rio de Janeiro: Editôra Civilização Brasileira, 1967.

Stacchini, José, *Março 1964: Mobilização da Audácia.* São Paulo: Companhia Editôra Nacional, 1965.

Torres, João C. de Oliveira, *Razão e Destino da Revolução.* Petrópolis: Editôra Vôzes, 1964.

Victor, Mário, *6 anos que Abalaram o Brasil: de Jânio Quadros ao Maréchal Castello Branco.* Rio de Janeiro: Editôra Civilização Brasileira, 1965.

Vinhas, M., *Estudos Sôbre o Proletariado Brasileiro*, coll. Retratos do Brasil, no. 75. Rio de Janeiro: Editôra Civilização Brasileira, 1970.

Works by non-Brazilians

Combret, François de, *Les Trois Brésil*, Denoël. Paris: Editions Planète, 1971.

Bergsman, Joel, *Brazil, Industrialization and Trade Policies*, coll. Industry and Trade in Some Developing Countries, OECD. London, New York, Toronto: Oxford University Press, 1970.

Daland, Robert T., *Brazilian Planning, Development, Politics and Administration.* Chapel Hill: University of North Carolina Press, 1967.

The Economy of Brazil, ed. Howard S. Ellis. Berkeley, Los Angeles: University of California Press, 1969.

Einaudi, Luigi R. and Stepan, Alfred C., *Latin American Institutional Development: Changing Military Perspectives in Peru and Brazil.* A report prepared for the Office of External Research, Department of State, Santa Monica, Cal., R-586-DOS, The Rand Corporation, Apr 1971.

Faust, Jean-Jacques, *A Revolução Devora Seus Presidentes.* Rio de Janeiro: Editôra Saga, 1965.

Pau de Arara: La violence militaire au Brésil, coll. Cahiers libres nos 215-16. Paris: François Maspero, 1971.

Schmitter, Philippe C., *Interest Conflict and Political Changes in Brazil.* Stanford University Press, 1971.

Schneider, Ronald M., *The Political System of Brazil, Emergence of a 'Modernizing' Authoritarian Regime. 1964–1970*. New York, London: Columbia University Press for the Institute of Latin American Studies, Columbia University, 1971.
Schuh, G. Edward and Alvès, Eliseu Roberto, *The Agricultural Development of Brazil*, Special Studies in International Economics and Development. New York, Washington, London: Praeger, 1970.
Skidmore, Thomas E., *Politics in Brazil, 1930–1964, An Experiment in Democracy*. London, Oxford, New York: Oxford University Press, 1967 (paperback ed., 1969).
Stepan, Alfred, *The Military in Politics, Changing Patterns in Brazil*. Princeton University Press (for the Rand Corporation), 1971.

Brazilian articles
'*Adesguianos no Govêrno*': *Boletim da ADESG* (Associação dos Diplomados da Escola Superior de Guerra), Rio de Janeiro, no. 103, Mar–Apr 1964.
Alvès, Denysard O. and Sayad, João, 'O Plano Estratégico de Desenvolvimento (1968–1970), *Planejamento no Brasil*, ed. Betty Mindlin Lafer. São Paulo: Editôra Perspectiva, 1970, pp. 91–109.
Araujo, Frei Francisco de, 'O Cristão e a Violência', *Paz e Terra*, Rio de Janeiro, no. 7 (1968) 99–112.
Ayres Filho, Paulo, 'The Brazilian Revolution', *Latin America: Politics, Economics and Hemispheric Security*, ed. Norman A. Bailey, Special Studies in International Politics and Public Affairs. New York, Washington, London: Praeger (for the Center for Strategic Studies), 1965, pp. 239–60.
Belém, José, 'Foreign Investment: Its Contribution to Brazil's Development', *Brazilian Business*, São Paulo, Apr 1967, 11–16.
Bulhões, Octavio Gouvêa de, 'Financial Recuperation for Economic Expansion', *The Economy of Brazil*, ed. Howard S. Ellis. Berkeley, Los Angeles: University of California Press, 1969, pp. 162–76.
Callado, Antonio, 'Les Ligues paysannes du Nord-Est brésilien, *Les Temps Modernes*, Paris, 23rd year, no. 257, Oct 1967, 751–60.
Câmara, Dom Helder:
'Evangelização e Humanização num Mundo em Desenvolvimento', *Paz e Terra*, Rio de Janeiro, no. 1, July 1966, 235–42.
'Imposições da Solidariedade Universal', *Paz e Terra*, Rio de Janeiro, no. 5, Oct 1967, 159–68.
'A Violência – Unica Opção', *Paz e Terra*, Rio de Janeiro, no. 7 (1968) 89–97.
Campos, Roberto de Oliveira:
A Técnica e o Riso. Rio de Janeiro: APEC Editôra, 1967.
'A Função da Empresa Privada', *Jornal do Brasil*, Rio de Janeiro, 22–23 Nov 1970, 6.

'A Retrospect over Brazilian Development Plans', *The Economy of Brazil*, ed. Howard S. Ellis. Berkeley, Los Angeles: University of California Press, 1969, pp. 317–44.

Outlook of the Brazilian Economy. Address delivered at the Union Bank of Switzerland, Zurich, on 4 September 1969; printed in Switzerland, Apr 1970.

Cardoso, Fernando Henrique:
'Aspectos Políticos do Planejamento', *Planejamento no Brasil*, ed. Betty Mindlin Lafer, coll. Debates. São Paulo: Editôra Perspectiva, 1970, pp. 161–84.

'Des élites: les entrepreneurs d'Amérique latine', *Sociologie du Travail*, Paris, 9th year, no. 3, July–Sep 1967, 255–80.

'Hégémonie bourgeoise et indépendance économique', *Les Temps Modernes*, Paris, 23rd year, no. 257, Oct 1967, 650–80.

Carneiro, Glauco, 'A Guerra de Sorbonne', *O Cruzeiro*, Rio de Janeiro, 32nd year, no. 39, 24 June 1967, 16–21.

Chacel, Julian M.:
'Impasse na Reforma Agrária Brasileira', *Correio da Manhã*, Rio de Janeiro, 29 Aug 1968, 'Caderno Econômico', 5.

'The Principal Characteristics of the Agrarian Structure and Agricultural Production in Brazil', *The Economy of Brazil*, ed. Howard S. Ellis. Berkeley, Los Angeles: University of California Press, 1969, pp. 103–29.

Correa da Costa, Sérgio, *Brazil, A Continent In Expansion*. London, Oct 1970 (two lectures given at the University of Edinburgh).

Costa, Rubens Vaz da, *Sharing the Responsibility for Development: Tax Incentives in Brazil*, duplicated. Fortaleza: Banco do Nordeste do Brasil S.A., 1971 (lecture given 26 May 1971).

Dantas, Francisco C. de San Thiago, *Idéias e Rumos para a Revolução Brasileira*. Rio de Janeiro: Livraria José Olympio Editôra, 1963.

Defim Netto, Antonio, 'A Lógica e O Desenvolvimento', *O Estado de São Paulo*, 29 Apr 1970, 25.

Fragoso, Augusto, 'A Escola Superior de Guerra' (Origem–Finalidade–Evolução), *Segurança e Desenvolvimento*, Revista da Associação dos Diplomados da Escola Superior de Guerra, Rio de Janeiro, vol. 18, no. 132, 1969, 7–40.

Furtado, Celso, 'De l'oligarchie à l'Etat Militaire', *Les Temps Modernes*, 23rd year, no. 257, Oct 1967, 578–602.

Gama, José Santos Saldanha da, 'Presidente do Clube Naval fixa sua posição – O militar de hoje existe para ocupar o País', *Ultima Hora*, Rio de Janeiro, 20 Dec 1967, 8.

Goes, Walder de, 'Novas Vias dão Impulso a Integração do Continente', *Jornal do Brasil*, Rio de Janeiro, 16–17 Apr 1972, 20.

Gudin, Eugênio, 'The Chief Characteristics of the Postwar Economic Development of Brazil', *The Economy of Brazil*, ed. Howard S. Ellis. Berkeley, Los Angeles: University of California Press, 1969, pp. 3–25.

Jaguaribe, Hélio:
'The Dynamics of Brazilian Nationalism', *Obstacles to Change in Latin America*, ed. Claudio Veliz. London, New York, Toronto: Oxford University Press, 1965, pp. 162–87.
'Stabilité Sociale par le Colonial-Fascisme', *Les Temps Modernes*, Paris, 23rd year, no. 257, Oct 1967, 603–23.

Lopes, Juarez R. Brandão, 'Some Basic Developments in Brazilian Politics and Society', *New Perspectives of Brazil*, ed. Eric N. Baklanoff. Nashville: Vanderbilt University Press, 1966, pp. 59–77.

Loreto, Silvia, 'Reforma Agrária no Brasil – Implicações Sociologicas', *Revista Brasileira de Estudos Políticos*. Belo Horizonte, no. 27, July 1969, 95–150.

Martins, Luciano, 'Aspectos Políticos de Revolução Brasileira', *Revista Civilização Brasileira*, Rio de Janeiro, no. 2, May 1965, 15–37.

Mendes de Almeida, Cândido A.:
'Sistema Político e Modelos de Poder no Brasil', *Dados*, Rio de Janeiro, no. 1, 1966, 7–41.
'O govêrno Castello Branco: paradigma e prognose', *Dados*, Rio de Janeiro, nos 2–3, 1967, 63–111.
'Prospectiva do comportamento ideológico: o processo da reflexão na crise do desenvolvimento', *Dados*, Rio de Janeiro, no. 4, 1968, 95–132.

Moniz de Aragão, A. C. de Castro, 'Que, Redivivos, os Sacrificados de ontem Empunhem as Espadas e Assumam a Defesa da Pátria', *O Globo*, Rio de Janeiro, 27 Nov 1967, 26.

Pacheco e Silva, Antonio Carlos, 'Guerra Psicológica', *Convivium*, São Paulo, III, no. 2, 1964, 3–31.

Romão, Lucas, 'Perspectives de la lutte démocratique et nationale au Brésil', *La Nouvelle Revue Internationale*, Paris, 8th year, no. 2 (78), Feb 1965, 97–106.

Siegel, Gilbert B., 'The Strategy of Public Administration Reform: The Case of Brazil', *Public Administration Review*, Washington, D.C., 26 Mar 1966, 45–55.

Siegel, Gilbert B. and Tatinge do Nascimento, Kleber, 'Formalism in Brazilian Administrative Reform: The Example of Position Clarification', *International Review of Administrative Sciences*, Brussels, no. 2, 1966, 175–84.

Simonsen, Mario Henrique:
A Estrutura Economica Brasileira, Ensaios Econômicos da Escola de Pos-Graduação em Economia, no. 3, duplicated. Rio de Janeiro: Instituto Brasileiro de Economia da Fundação Getúlio Vargas, 1971.

Desenvolvimento e Distribuição de Rendas, Conselho Interamericano de Comercio e Produção, seção brasileira, Rio de Janeiro, duplicated, n.d.

'Inflation and the Money and Capital Markets of Brazil', *The Economy of Brazil*, ed. Howard S. Ellis. Berkeley, Los Angeles: University of California Press, 1969, pp. 133–61.

Soares, Glaucio Ary Dillon:

'The Political Sociology of Uneven Development in Brazil', *Revolution in Brazil*, ed. Irving Horowitz. New York: Dutton, 1964, pp. 164–95.

'The Economic Development and the Class Structure', *Class Status and Power: Social Stratification in Comparative Perspective*, ed. Reinhard Bendix and Seymour M. Lipset, 2nd ed. New York: The Free Press, 1966, pp. 190–9.

'The New Industrialization and the Brazilian Political System', *Latin America, Reform or Revolution?* ed. James Patras and Maurice Zeitlin. Greenwich: Fawcett, 1968, pp. 186–201.

Weffort, Francisco C.:

'Le Populisme', *Les Temps Modernes*, Paris, 23rd year, no. 257, Oct 1967, 264–649.

'Education et Politique, Réflexions sociologiques sur une pédagogie de la liberté', preface to Freire, Paulo, *L'Education pratique de la Liberté*. Paris: Editions du Cerf, 1971, pp. 7–33.

Articles by non-Brazilians

Antoine, Charles, 'L'Episcopat brésilien Face au Pouvoir, 1962–1969', *Etudes*, Paris, vol. 333, July–Dec 1970, 84–102.

Brésil 69: Torture et Répression: Bulletin de Documentation published by the Association Internationale des Juristes Démocrates, duplicated, Brussels, Nov 1969, pages unnumbered.

Busey, James L., 'The Old and the New in the Politics of Modern Brazil', *The Shaping of Modern Brazil*, ed. Eric W. Baklanoff. Baton Rouge: Louisiana University Press, 1969, pp. 58–85.

Cava, Ralph della, 'Torture in Brazil', *Commonweal*, New York, XCII, no. 6, 24 Apr 1970, 135–41.

Dossier Brésil: 42 témoignages nouveaux sur la torture: Bulletin published by the Association Internationale des Juristes Démocrates, duplicated, Brussels, Apr 1971.

Faravacque, J. C., 'La France veut participer au miracle brésilien', *L'Usine Nouvelle*, Paris, no. 38, 23 Sep 1971, 28–9.

Fesquet, Henri, 'L'Eglise Catholique au Brésil', *Le Monde*, Paris, 8 Sep 1970, 1, 6; 9 Sep 1970, 5.

Gillieron, Henri, 'Brésil: une enquête américaine a fait tiquer les généraux', *Tribune de Genève*, Geneva, 6 June 1972, p. 12.

Gosset, Pierre and Renée, 'Cent millions de Brésiliens', *Journal de*

Genève, Geneva, 29 Aug 1972, 1, 2; 30 Aug 1972, 1, 13; 31 Aug 1972, 1, 5; 1 Sep 1972, 1, 17; 2–3 Sep 1972, 1, 2; 4 Sep 1972, 1, 10.

Kadt, Emmanuel de, 'Religion, the Church and Social Change in Brazil', *The Politics of Conformity in Latin America*, ed. Claudio Veliz, Royal Institute of International Affairs. London, New York, Toronto: Oxford University Press, 1967, pp. 192–220.

Laurentin, René, 'Brésil, un peuple assassiné', *Flashes sur l'Amérique Latine*. Paris: Editions du Seuil, pp. 7–15, followed by 'Lettre de 300 prêtres aux évêques du Brésil' (Aug 1967) pp. 53–73.

'Livre Noir: Terreur et Torture au Brésil', *Croissance des Jeunes Nations*, Paris, no. 94, Dec 1969, 19–34.

Myhr, Robert O., 'The Political Role of University Students in Brazil', *Students and Politics in Developing Nations*, ed. Donald K. Emmerson. New York, Washington, London: Praeger, 1968, pp. 249–85.

Niedergang, Marcel:
'La Guérilla et la Torture au Brésil; l'ampleur du mouvement international de protestation préoccupe les dirigeants', *Le Monde*, Paris, 24–5 May 1970, 5.
'Brésil, le plus jeune des géants', *Le Monde*, Paris, 9 Sep 1972, 1, 6; 10–11 Sep 1972, 4; 12 Sep 1972, 8; 13 Sep 1972, 4.

Rapport concernant la répression policière et les tortures infligées aux opposants et prisonniers politiques au Brésil, Press release, International Commission of Jurists, Geneva, Doc. S. 2827, duplicated, 22 July 1970.

Report on Allegation of Torture in Brazil. London: Amnesty International Publications, duplicated [Sep 1972].

Revers, Jeanne, 'Le Miracle Brésilien: Mythe ou Réalité?', *Revue de Défense Nationale*, Paris, 28th year, Feb 1972, 193–207.

Roper, Christopher, 'Blemishes on Brazil's Booming Economy', *Guardian*, Manchester, 8 May 1972, 3.

Rosenbaum, H. Jon, 'Brazil's Foreign Policy: Developmentalism and Beyond', *Orbis*, Philadelphia, Pa., vol XVI, no. 1, spring 1972, 58–83.

Schmitter, Philippe C., 'The Persecution of Political and Social Scientists in Brazil', *P.S.*, Washington, D.C., III, spring 1970, 123–8.

Sirken, Irving A., 'Fighting Inflation in Brazil: Some Tentative Lesson', *Finance and Development*, Washington, D.C., no. 3, 1968, 36–41.

Tuthill, John W.:
'Economic and Political Aspects of Development in Brazil and US Aid', *Journal of Inter-American Studies*, Miami, XI, Apr 1969, 186–208.

'Operation Topsy', *Foreign Policy*, New York, autumn 1972, 62–85.
Vernay, Alain, 'Brésil: La passion du développement l'emporte sur la défiance envers les investissements étrangers', *Le Figaro*, Paris, 16–17 Sep 1972, 7.

BOOKS

GENERAL SUBJECTS

Works

Almond, Gabriel A., *Political Development: Essays in Heuristic Theory*. Boston: Little, Brown & Co., 1970.

Amin, Samir, *L'Accumulation à l'échelle mondiale, critique de la théorie du sous-développement*, Ifan-Dakar, 2nd ed. with an addendum by the author. Paris: Editions Anthropos, 1971.

Apter, David E.:
  The Politics of Modernization. Chicago, London: University of Chicago Press, 1965 (first published in the United Kingdom 1969).
  Some Conceptual Approaches to the Study of Modernization. Englewood Cliffs, N.J.: Prentice-Hall, 1968.

Black, Cyril E., *The Dynamic of Modernization: A Study in Comparative History*. New York, Evanston, London: Harper & Row, 1967.

Blardone, Gilbert, *Progrès économique dans le Tiers-Monde: L'environnement socio-politique du développement*. Paris: Librairie Sociale et Economique, 1972.

Eisenstadt, Samuel N., *Modernization: Protest and Change*, The Hebrew University, Jerusalem. Englewood Cliffs, N.J.: Prentice-Hall, 1966.

Galbraith, John K., *The New Industrial State*. London: Hamish Hamilton, 1967.

Huntington, Samuel P.:
  The Soldier and the State. The Theory and Politics of Civil Military Relations. Cambridge, Mass.: Belknap Press of Harvard University, 1957.
  Political Order in Changing Societies, Center for International Affairs, Harvard University. New Haven: Yale University Press, 1969.

L'Huillier, Jacques, *Les Organisations internationales de coopération économique et le commerce extérieur des pays en voie de développement*, coll. Etudes et Travaux no. 9. Geneva, Graduate Institute of International Studies, 1969.

Mende, Tibor, *De l'Aide à la Recolonisation, les leçons d'un échec*, coll. L'Histoire Immédiate. Paris: Editions du Seuil, 1972.

Riggs, Fred W., *Administration in Developing Countries: The Theory of Prismatic Society*. Boston: Houghton Mifflin, 1964.

Rostow, Walt W.:
The Stages of Economic Growth, 2nd ed. Cambridge University Press, 1971.
Politics and the Stages of Growth. Cambridge University Press, 1971.

Rustow, Dankwart A., *A World of Nations, Problems of Political Modernization*. Washington, D.C.: Brookings Institution, 1967.

Waterston, Albert, *Development Planning: Lessons of Experience*. Baltimore: Johns Hopkins Press, 1965.

Articles

Almond, Gabriel A., 'Political Development: Analytical and Narrative Perspective', *Comparative Political Studies*. Beverley Hills, Cal., vol. 1, no. 4, Jan 1969, 447–70.

Deutsch, Karl W., 'Social Mobilization and Political Development', *American Political Science Review*, Menasha, Wisc., LV, Sep 1961, 493–514.

Fiechter, Georges-A., 'Critères d'évaluation des effets des investissements privés suisses sur le développement', *Les Investissements privés suisses dans le Tiers Monde*, duplicated, Geneva, Graduate Institute of International Studies, 1971, pp. 98–104.

Rustow, Dankwart A., 'The Organization Triumphs over its Function: Huntington on Modernization', *Journal of International Affairs*, Montpelier, Vt., XXIII, no. 1, 1969, 119–32.

Verba, Sidney, 'Some Dilemmas in Comparative Research', *World Politics*, Princeton, XX, no. 1, Oct 1967, 112–28.

WRITINGS ABOUT LATIN AMERICA AND BRAZIL IN GENERAL

Brazilian works

Barreto, Carlos Eduardo, *Constituições do Brasil*, 6th ed., 2 vols. São Paulo: Edição Saraiva, 1971.

Brayner, Maréchal Floriano de Lima, *A Verdade sobre a FEB: Memórias de um Chefe de Estado Maior na Campanha da Itália*. Rio de Janeiro: Editôra Civilização Brasileira, 1968.

Buescu, Mircea, *História Econômica do Brasil*. Rio de Janeiro: APEC, 1970.

Calogeras, João Pandia, *Formação Histórica do Brasil*, 4th ed., coll. 'Biblioteca Pedagógica Brasileira', no. 42. São Paulo: Companhia Editôra Brasileira, 1945.

Carneiro, Glauco, *História das Revoluções Brasileiras*, 2 vols. Rio de Janeiro: Edições 'O Cruzeiro', 1965.

Carolin, J. S., Pinheiro-Neto, J. M. and Buckeridge, T. G., *Com-*

pany Formation in Brazil, 5th ed. London: Bank of London & South America Ltd., 1964 (rev. 1969).

Ferreira, H. Lopes Rodrigues, *Adhémar de Barros perante a Nação*. São Paulo: Tipografia Piratininga, 1954.

Freyre, Gilberto, *The Masters and the Slaves, A study in the development of Brazilian civilization*, reissue. New York: Alfred A. Knopf, 1956.

Ramos, Arthur:
The Negro in Brazil. Washington, D.C.: Associated Publishers, Inc., 1939.
Le Métissage au Brésil. Paris: Hermann, 1952.
A Reforma Agrária: Problemas—Bases—Solução. Rio de Janeiro: Instituto de Pesquisas e Estudos Sociais, 1964.

Scantimburgo, João de, *Tratado Geral do Brasil*. São Paulo: Companhia Editôria Nacional, Editôra da Universidade de São Paulo, 1971.

Works by non-Brazilians

Baer, Werner, *Industrialization and Economic Development in Brazil*, The Economic Growth Center, Yale University. Homewood, Ill.: Richard D. Irwin, 1965.

Behrman, Jack N., *US International Business and Governments*. New York: McGraw-Hill, 1971.

Elites in Latin America, ed. Seymour M. Lipset and Aldo Solari. New York: Oxford University Press, 1967.

Frank, André Gunder, *Capitalisme et Sous-Développement en Amérique Latine*, coll. 'Textes à l'appui'. Paris: François Maspero, 1968.

Gordon, Lincoln and Grommers, Engelbert L., *United States Manufacturing Investment in Brazil. The Impact of Brazilian Government Policies 1946–1960*, Division of Research, Graduate School of Business Administration, Center for International Affairs. Boston: Harvard University, 1962.

Gourou, Pierre, *Leçons de Géographie tropicale. Leçons données au Collège de France de 1947 à 1970*, Ecole Pratique des Hautes Etudes, Sorbonne, 6th section: Sciences Economiques et Sociales. Coll. le Savoir Géographique no. 1. Paris, La Haye: Mouton, 1971.

Graham, Lawrence S., *Civil Service Reform in Brazil, Principles versus Practice*, Latin American Monographs, no. 13, Institute of Latin American Studies. Austin, London: University of Texas Press, 1968.

Hirsch-Weber, Wolfgang, *Lateinamerika: Abhängigkeit und Selbstbestimmung*, Aktuelle Aussenpolitik; series published by the Forschungsinstitut der Deutschen Gesellschaft für Auswärtige Politik. Opladen: Leske Verlag, 1972.

Lambert, Denis-Clair and Martin, Jean-Marie, *L'Amérique Latine, Economies et Sociétés*, coll. U, Economic science and management ser. Paris: Librairie Armand Colin, 1971.
Lambert, Jacques:
Amérique Latine, structures sociales et institutions politiques, 2nd ed. Paris: Presses Universitaires de France, 1968.
Os Dois Brasis. São Paulo: Companhia Editôra Nacional, 1970 (the French version was published in 1955).
Latin America, Reform or Revolution? A Reader, ed. James Petras and Maurice Zeitlin, Political Perspectives ser. Greenwich, N.Y.: Fawcett, 1968.
Laurentin, René, *L'Amérique Latine à l'Heure de l'Enfantement*. Paris: Editions du Seuil, 1969.
Marini, Ruy Mauro, *Sous-développement et Révolution en Amérique Latine*, coll. Cahiers libres, no. 217–18. Paris: François Maspero, 1972.
Mercier-Vega, Luis, *Technique du Contre-Etat, les guérillas en Amérique du Sud*. Paris: Editions Pierre Belfond, 1968.
Models of Political Changes in Latin America, ed. Paul E. Sigmund. New York, Washington, London: Praeger, 1970.
Moraze, Charles, *Les trois âges du Brésil, essai de politique*, Fondation Nationale des Sciences Politiques, cahiers no. 51. Paris: Armand Colin, 1954.
Niedergang, Marcel, *Les vingts Amériques Latines*, rev. and enlarged ed. Paris: Editions du Seuil, 1969, vol. 1.
The Politics of Conformity in Latin America, ed. Claudio Veliz, Royal Institute of International Affairs. London, New York, Toronto: Oxford University Press, 1967.
Political Systems of Latin America, ed. Martin C. Needler, 2nd ed. New York: Van Nostrand Reinhold, 1970.
Schneider, Ronald M., *An Atlas of Latin American Affairs*. London: Methuen, 1966.
Uri, Pierre, *Une politique monétaire pour l'Amérique Latine* (with the collaboration of Nicholas Kaldor, Richard Ruggles, Robert Triffin), coll. A l'échelle du Monde, Institut Atlantique. Paris: Plon, 1965.
Wirth, J. D., *The Politics of Brazilian Development, 1930–1954.* Stanford University Press, 1970.
Zweig, Stefan, *Le Brésil, Terre d'Avenir*. New York: Editions de la Maison Française, 1942.

Articles by Brazilians
Ribeiro, Darcy, 'Universities and Social Development', *Elites in Latin America*, ed. Lipset and Solari, op. cit., pp. 343–81.
Soares, Glaucio Ary Dillon, 'Intellectual Identity and Political

Ideology among University Students', *Elites in Latin America*, ed. Lipset and Solari, op. cit., pp. 431–53.

Articles by non-Brazilians

Bastide, Roger, 'The Development of Race Relations in Brazil', *Industrialization and Race Relations: a Symposium issued under the auspices of the Institute of Race Relations*, ed. Guy Hunter. London, Oxford, New York: Oxford University Press, 1965, pp. 9–29.

Cameron, Juan, 'Threatening Weather in South America', *Fortune*, Chicago, Oct 1970, 100–1, 206–8.

Gourou, Pierre, 'Sur la géographie humaine et l'économie de l'Amazonie brésilienne', *Recueil d'articles*. Brussels: Société Royale Belge de Géographie, 1970, pp. 317–38.

Klein, Herbert S., 'The Colored Freedmen in Brazilian Slave Society', *Journal of Social History*, Berkeley, Cal., vol. III, no. 1, autumn 1969, 30–52.

Lazar, Arpad von, 'Latin America and the Politics of Post-Authoritarianism: A Model for Decompression', *Comparative Political Studies*, Beverley Hills, Cal., vol. 1, no. 3, Oct 1968, 419–29.

Monk, Abraham, *Black and White Race Relations in Brazil*, Special Studies ser. no. 4. State University of New York at Buffalo, 1972.

Nunn, Frederick M., 'Military Professionalism and Professional Militarism in Brazil, 1870–1970: Historical Perspectives and Political Implications', *Journal of Latin American Studies*, Cambridge, vol. 4, pt 1, May 1972, 29–54.

Rouquié, Alain, 'Révolutions militaires et Indépendance nationale en Amérique Latine (1968–1971)', *Revue française de science politique*, Paris, vol. XXI, nos 5 and 6, Oct, Dec 1971, 1045–69, 1290–316.

Skidmore, Thomas E., 'Toward a Comparative Analysis of Race Relations Since Abolition in Brazil and the United States', *Journal of Latin American Studies*, Cambridge, vol. 4, pt 1, May 1972, 1–28.

WRITINGS ON THE BRAZIL OF 1964–72

Works by Brazilians

Castro, Antonio Barros de, *7 Ensaios sôbre a Economia Brasileira*. Rio de Janeiro: Editôra Forense, vol. I, 1969, vol. II, 1971.

Correia, Oscar Dias, *A Constituição de 1967*. Rio de Janeiro: Forense, 1968.

Costa, Edgard, *Os Grandes Julgamentos do Supremo Tribunal Federal*, 5th vol. 1963–1966. Rio de Janeiro: Editôra Civilização Brasileira, 1967.

Costella, Antonio F., *O Contrôle da Informação no Brasil.* Petrópolis: Editôra Vozes, 1970.
Motta, Paulo Roberto, *Movimentos Partidários no Brasil,* Cadernos de Administração Publica. Rio de Janeiro: Fundação Getúlio Vargas, 1971.
Souza, Levy Xavier de, and Lucca, Domingos de, Jr, *São Paulo Project: A Challenge in the Worldly Race for the Social and Economic Development, Replanning and Reconstruction of a Metropolis.* São Paulo: I.B.R.A.-DOC, Documentos de Nosso Tempo, 1970.

Works by non-Brazilians
Fajnzylber, Fernando, *Sistema Industrial y Exportacion de Manufacturas: Analisis de la Experiencia Brasilera,* duplicated. Santiago de Chile: CEPAL, 1971.
Leff, Nathaniel H., *Economic Policy-Making and Development in Brazil, 1947–1964,* Center for International Affairs and Center for Studies in Education and Development, Harvard University. New York, London, Sydney, Toronto: John Wiley, 1968.
Link, Max., *Stand und Zukunftsperspektiven der Industrialisierung Brasiliens.* Lateinamerikanisches Institut an der Hochschule St Gallen für Wirtschafts- und Sozialwissenschaften. Berne, Stuttgart: Verlag Paul Haupt, 1972.

Articles by Brazilians
Brazil 70 – An answer to many questions. São Paulo: American Chamber of Commerce for Brazil, July 1970.
Brazil – The Take-off is Now. São Paulo: American Chamber of Commerce for Brazil, July 1971.
Gomes, Lucia Maria Gaspar:
  'Cronologia de Govêrno Castello Branco', *Dados,* Rio de Janeiro, no. 2/3, 1967, 112–32.
  'Cronologia do 1° ano do Govêrno Costa e Silva', *Dados,* Rio de Janeiro, no. 4, 1968, 199–220.
Magalhães, Irene M., Alvès Hime, Maria A. and Alessio, Nancy, 'Cronologia – Segundo e Terceiro Ano do Govêrno Costa e Silva', *Dados,* Rio de Janeiro, no. 8, 1971, 152–233.

Articles by non-Brazilians
Abalo, Carlos, 'Comentario sobre el modelo economico brasileno', *Estudios sobre la Economia Argentina,* Buenos-Aires, Oct 1971 (French translation: *Problèmes Economiques, la Documentation Française,* Paris, no. 1265, 29 Mar 1972, 26–32).
Baklanoff, Eric M., 'Foreign Private Investment and Industrialization in Brazil', *New Perspectives of Brazil,* ed. Eric N. Baklanoff. Nashville: Vanderbilt University Press, 1966, pp. 101–36.

MacKenzie, Eileen, 'Training Managers For Brazil's Boom', *International Management*, New York, July 1971, 20-4.

Morley, Samuel A. and Smith, Gordon W., *The Effect of Changes in the Distribution of Income on Labor, Foreign Investment and Growth in Brazil*, duplicated, Program of Development Studies, paper no. 15. Houston, Texas: Rice University, 1971.

Moser, Rudolf, *Die Unkündbarkeit (Estabilidade) im Brazilianischen Arbeitsrecht*, Lateinamerikanisches Institut an der Hochschule St Gallen für Wirtschafts- und Sozialwissenschaften; Lateinamerikanische Studien ser., no. 2. Zurich: Orell Füssli Verlag, 1968.

Nagy, Laszlo, 'Après le "Putsch" de la Droite au Brésil, Un Triomphe dangereux', *Gazette de Lausanne*, 6 Apr 1964.

Nun, José:
'A Latin American Phenomenon: The Middle Class Military Coup', *Latin America Reform or Revolution?* ed. James Patras and Maurice Zeitlin. Greenwich: Fawcett, 1968, pp. 145-85.
'The Middle Class Military Coup', *The Politics of Conformity in Latin America*, ed. Claudio Veliz, Royal Institute of International Affairs. London, New York, Toronto: Oxford University Press, 1967, pp. 66-118.

Tavares, Maria da Conceição, *Natureza e Contradições do Mercado Financeiro no Brasil*, duplicated. Cadernos Econômicos; Seminario Internacional Sôbre Mercado de Capitais e Desenvolvimento Econômico. Rio de Janeiro: Universidade Federal do Rio de Janeiro, 1971.

Tavares, Maria da Conceição and Serra, J., *Mas alla del Estancamiento*, duplicated. Santiago de Chile, UNO-FLACSO (Facultad Latino-Americana de Ciencias Sociales) 1970.

Zoppo, Ciro Elliot, 'Brazil', *Technology, Politics, and Proliferation*, Arms Control Special Studies Program, ACDA/WEC-126, vol. x, duplicated; Security Studies Project, University of California, Los Angeles, prepared for the U.S. Arms Control and Disarmament Agency, Washington, D.C., 30 June 1968, 14-21.

Index

Abraão, João, 108, 111
Academia Militar das Agulhas Negras (A.M.A.N.), 30, 32
Ação Democrática Parlamentar, 64
Ação Popular, 102, 139
Action for National Liberation, 144
Albuquerque Lima, Affonso A. de, 80, 87, 134, 159, 165, 166, 175
Aleixo, Pedro, 80, 108, 125, 170, 187
Alkimin, José Maria, 38
Almeida, Hélio de, 78
Alvès, Hermano, 160, 163
Alvès Bastos, Justino, 91
AMFORP (American and Foreign Power Utility Company), 61–3
Andreazza, Mario, 174
APEC, 106
Araripe Macedo, Admiral Z. Campos de, 87
ARENA (National Renewal Alliance), 88, 91, 110, 111, 112, 133, 157–61 *passim*, 169, 186–187, 188–92
Arraes, Miguel, 44, 75, 76

Barcelos, W. Peracchi, 87, 93, 94
Barros, Adhémar de, 6, 7, 41, 90, 92, 95, 125
Barros Câmara, Cardinal Jaime de, 153, 154
Batalha, Wander, 180
Bevilacqua, Pery C., 91, 163
Bilac Pinto, Octavio, 68
B.N.H., *see* National Housing Bank
Borges Texeira, Mauro, 47–8, 64, 79, 95
Braga, Ney, 87, 94
Brazilian Communist Party (P.C.B.), 7, 102, 136, 143
Brazilian Democratic Movement, *see* M.D.B.
Bresser Pereira, Luiz Carlos, 14, 15, 20, 185
Brizola, Leonel, 44, 62, 70

Bulhões, Octavio Gouvêa de, 51, 54, 167
Burnier, João-Paulo, 149

Calheiros, Dom Valdir, 150, 152
Câmara, Dom Helder, ix, 149, 150–153, 184
Câmara Ferreira, Joaquim, 147
Campos, Milton, 81
Campos, Roberto Oliveira de, 50, 54, 58, 63, 93, 96, 103, 121, 185–6
  and the P.A.E.G., 20, 51–2, 54, 56, 60, 61, 72, 73
  and the Ten-Year Plan, 118–20
Capivara, 146
Cardoso, Fernando Henrique, 122
Carvalho, Ribeiro, 149
Castello Branco, Humberto de Alencar
  as President, 38, 44–9, 58, 62, 63, 64, 68–9, 112, 113, 118, 131
  death of, 130
  and the E.S.G., 29, 39–43
  policies of, 75–95 *passim*, 104, 117, 120–2
Castello Branco, Paulo, 90
Catholic Action, 139, 155
Catholic Church, 149–55
Cavalcanti, J. Costa, 166
Cavalcanti, Francisco Boaventura, Jr, 126, 169, 172
CHISAM, 157
Cirne Lima, Rui, 93
Civilian–Military Patriotic Front, 42
C.N.B.B. (National Conference of Brazilian Bishops), 150–4
C.N.E., *see* National Economic Council
Coffee, 18–19, 58, 179–81, 202
Comando Geral dos Trabalhadores (C.G.T.), 102, 137
Communism, 25, 44, 75, 102–3, 109, 136, 171, 184

Communist Party of Brazil (P.C.D.B.), 7, 143
Companhia Vale do Rio Doce, 67
CONSPLAN (Conselho Consultivo do Planejamento), 69–70, 95, 119
Constant, Benjamin, 4
Constitutional Amendments, 40, 64, 99, 100, 190
Constitutions
 1824, 4
 1937, 118
 1946, xii, xviii, 3, 6, 8, 12, 35, 37, 38, 48, 64, 71, 82, 85, 115
 1967, 112–18, 157, 173
Cordeiro de Farias, Oswaldo, 63, 89, 91
Costa, Ribeiro da, 75, 81, 82
Costa e Silva, Arthur da, 45, 80, 81
 as President, 123–6, 127, 133–5, 142, 155–62, 165–7, 169–70
 bid for presidency, 89–91, 108–9
 illness, 163, 170

Daland, Robert, 121
Dantas, F.C. de San Thiago, 7, 50, 62
'Death Squad', 144, 147, 148
Delfim Netto, Antonio, 127, 166, 178, 179, 180, 202
Dias Leite, Antonio, 70, 71, 74, 166, 178
Dominican Republic, 50, 76

Economic Action Plan of the Government, see P.A.E.G.
Egídio Martins, Paulo, 73, 88
Elbrick, Charles Burke, 172
Electrobrás, 64
Escritório de Pesquisa Econômica Aplicada, 118
E.S.G. (Superior War College), 28, 39–40, 50, 91, 171

Fagundes Gomes, Severo, 94
Farhat, Saïd, 168
Faria Lima, José V. de, 68, 69
Fernandes, Florestan, 185
Fernandes, Hélio, 125, 130

Ferreira, Oliveiro S., 9
Figueiredo, Edson de, 76
Figueiredo, Mario Poppe de, 159
Fleury, Sérgio F. P., 148
Flexa Ribeiro, Carlos, 78
Fragoso, Dom Antonio, 152
Frente Parlamentar Nacionalista, 7, 137
Frey, Eduardo, 159
Freyre, Gilberto, 191
Furtado, Celso, 7, 12, 18, 44, 52

Garrastazu Médici, Emilio, 148, 149, 154, 175, 176, 177–82, 186, 188, 189–90, 193, 211
Gasparian, Fernando, 71–2
Geisel, Orlando, 91, 131, 175
General Commission of Inquiry (C.G.I.), 44, 164
Gomes, Eduardo, 49
Goulart, João, 6, 9, 25, 35, 44, 47, 61, 94, 132, 137
Guimarães de Brito, Juarez, 146
Gutko, Pawel, 47

Herculino, João, 108
Huntington, Samuel P., xii, 82

Inqueritos Policial Militar (I.P.M.), 44, 47, 48, 75, 76, 79, 92
Institutional Acts, 91, 112, 114
 No. 1, 34, 35, 37–9, 41, 45, 46, 90
 No. 2, xiii, 82, 85, 131, 191
 No. 3, 88
 No. 4, 113
 No. 5, xiii, 161, 176, 188, 191
 No. 9, 166
 No. 12, 170
 No. 13, 173
 No. 14, 174
 No. 16, 176
 No. 17, 175
Instituto Brasiliero de Reforma Agraria (I.B.R.A.), 65, 66, 157, 166
Instituto Nacional do Desenvolvimento Agraria (I.N.D.A.), 65, 66, 166

Index

Inter-American Commission for Human Rights, 148
Inter-American Peace Force, 50, 76
Interministerial Instruction No. 71, 73-4

Jaguaribe, Hélio, 9, 123
Johnson, Lyndon, 49, 50
Jordão Ramos, R. O., 184

Kruel, Amaury, 92
Kruel, Riograndino, 47
Kubitscheck, Juscelino, 6, 21, 41, 45, 46, 48, 79, 94, 108, 125

Lacerda, Carlos, ix, 7, 41, 46, 62-3, 72, 78, 81, 90, 94, 95, 113, 131-3, 160, 163
Lamarca, Carlos, 146
L'Huillier, Jacques, 202
LIDER (Radical Democratic League), 76, 80, 87
Link, Max, 203
Lott, H. B. D. Texeira, 78
Ludovico Borges Texeira, Pedro, 47
Lyra Tavares, Aurelio de, 169, 173

Magalhães, Juracy, 81, 82, 87
Magalhães, Paulo Reis de, 168
Magalhães Pinto, José de, 41, 79, 95
Mamede, J. de Bizarria, 87
Marighela, Carlos, ix, 143, 144-6
Martinelli, Osnelli, 76, 80
Mazzili, Ranieri, 35, 68
M.D.B. (Brazilian Democratic Movement), 88, 90, 91, 92, 94, 108, 110, 111, 133, 158, 164, 169, 176, 186-7, 189-90
Medeiros da Silva, Carlos, 94
Médici, President, see Garrastazu Médici, Emilio
Meira Mattos, Carlos de, 48, 109, 140
Mem de Sá, Senator, 87, 93, 112
Mena Barreto, Dalisio, 92
Mendes de Almeida, Cândido A., 111, 123

Mindlin, José, 185
MOBRAL, 157
Moniz de Aragão, A. C. de Castro, 131, 136, 139, 169, 172
Moreira Alvès, Marcio, 160, 163
Moura Andrade, Auro de, 35
Mourão Filho, Olympio, 91
Muricy, A. C. da Silva, 175

Nascimento e Silva, Luiz G. do, 94, 184
Natel, Laudo, 93
National Economic Council (C.N.E.), 45, 58, 70, 71, 72, 95
National Housing Bank (B.N.H.), 60, 104, 105, 106
National Integration Scheme, 208-209
National Intelligence Service (S.N.I.), 117-18, 177
National Parliamentary Front, see Frente Parliamentar Nacionalista
National Renewal Alliance, see ARENA
National Security Council (C.S.N.), 117, 141, 159, 177
Negrão de Lima, Francisco, 79, 94
Nixon, Richard, 181
Nobre, José Freitas, 114
Novitski, Joseph, 175

Obrigações Reajustaveis do Tesouro Nacional, 59

P.A.E.G. (Economic Action Plan of the Government), 20, 52-61, 70-5, 95
Paes de Almeida, Sebastião, 79, 109
PARA-SAR, 149
Partido Democrático Cristão (P.D.C.), 7, 77
Partido Social Democrático (P.S.D.), 6, 47, 48, 64, 68, 77, 79
Partido Social Progressista (P.S.P.), 7, 77, 92
Partido Trabalhista Brasileiro (P.T.B.), 6, 48, 68, 77, 78, 79

Index

Passarinho, Jarbas G., 142, 148, 159, 178-9
Passos, Oscar, 135, 160
P.E.D. (Strategic Development Programme), 127-30
Pedroso d'Horta, Oscar, 184-5
Peres, Haroldo Leon, 186, 191
Pina, Gerson de, 76
Pinheiro, Israël, 79, 94
Pope Paul VI, 154
Portela de Melo, Jaime, 135
Portugal, 1, 3, 14
Prado, Eduardo, 168
Pratini de Morães, M. V., 179, 180
Prestes, Luiz Carlos, 7, 143
PROTERRA, 209-10

Quadros, Jânio, 6, 38, 44, 47, 69, 94, 162
Queiroz, Adhémar de, 94

Rademacker Grünewald, A. H., 173, 175, 176
Radical Democratic League, see LIDER
Raposo, Amerino, 126
Resende, Roberto, 79
Rezende, E. Taurino de, 44, 45
Ribas, Emílio R., Jr, 48
Rocha, Itamar, 149
Rockefeller, Nelson, 177
Rossi, Dom Agnelo, 150, 151, 153, 154
Rossi, Luis R., 168
Rural Workers Aid Programme, 209
Rustow, Dankwart A., xii, 25, 82, 83, 207

Saldanha da Gama, José S., 135
Salles, Dom Eugenio, 149
Schmitter, Philippe C., 9
Service Time Guarantee Fund, 104, 105, 106
Simonsen, M. H., 21

Social Integration Programme, 208
Social Research and Studies Institute (I.P.E.S.), 28
Sodré, Roberto de Abreu, 93, 101
Souza e Mello, Marcio de, 149, 173, 175
Statute of the Land, 64-6
Stepan, Alfred, 30, 40
Strategic Development Programme, see P.E.D.
SUDAM, 134, 165, 210
SUDANAM, 167
SUDECO, 134
SUDENE, 134, 165, 210
SUMOC Instruction 289, 95-7
Superior War College, see E.S.G.
Suplicy de Lacerda, Flavio, 88
Supplementary Acts, 88, 93, 109, 161, 166, 174
Sussekind, Arnaldo L., 87

Tribuna da Imprensa, 63, 125, 131, 160

União Democrática Nacional (U.D.N.), 7, 47, 48, 62, 64, 77, 78, 79, 88
União Nacional dos Estudantes, 102, 136-7, 139, 141
United States of America, 49-51, 119, 171-3, 179-81

Vargas, Getúlio, xii, 5-6, 11, 27, 37, 67, 102, 118, 121, 128, 136
Veja, 186
Vernay, Alain, 200
Vianna Filho, Luiz, 94, 135, 185
Vinhas, M., 12-14
Visão, 167, 168, 184

Waterston, Albert, 122
World Bank, 50, 51

Yassuda, Fabio Riodi, 179, 180